AOL|UK
HANDBOOK

Version
6.0

The Official

AOL|UK
HANDBOOK

So easy to use, no wonder we're the World's No. 1!

Version
6.0

CAPSTONE

Nigel Whitfield

The right of AOL UK to be identified as the author of this work has been asserted in accordance with
the Copyright, Designs and Patents Act 1988

First published 2001 by
Capstone Publishing Limited
8 Newtec Place
Magdalen Road
Oxford OX4 1RE
United Kingdom
http://www.capstone.co.uk

CIP catalogue records for this book are available from the British Library and the US Library of Congress

ISBN 1-84112-162-2

Typeset in 9/12 pt Frutiger by
Sparks Computer Solutions Ltd, Oxford, UK
http://www.sparks.co.uk
Printed and bound by
Biddles Ltd, Guildford, Surrey

This book is printed on acid-free paper

Substantial discounts on bulk quantities of Capstone books are available to corporations,
professional associations and other organizations. To order, phone Capstone Publishing on
(+44-1865-798623) or fax (+44-1865-240941).

Contents

Foreword

We started AOL UK in 1996 with a hearty band of beta testers, a small but dedicated staff, and an excellent product. Now, some four years later, AOL is one of the UK's leading Internet online services in the UK. Why's that? I was hoping you would ask.

One reason is that when you join AOL, you're not alone out there in the World Wide Web. Sure you can surf the net to your heart's content, and this book will show you how to get started, but AOL is much much more than the Internet. As an AOL member, you're part of a community of a million members here in the UK and over 24 million members around the world.

What are the benefits of being a member of this community? For just about every interest – including technology, sport, learning, shopping, news and weather, finance, travel, games and even romance – we offer Chat rooms, Message boards, feature articles and other resources. We do all the work to bring you the very best and most current information, all just a mouse click away.

Email is one of the most popular features on AOL. You can exchange email with anyone in the world who has an email address. Your AOL account includes seven email addresses – you can use them to separate your work and personal correspondence, for example, or assign one name to each member of the family.

Family and friends are an important part of AOL, just as they are in any community. With your AOL buddy list you can invite friends to a Chat room or to join a group, start up an Instant Message conversation, set up an event using My Calendar or locate your friends online. Parents will want to take advantage of our Parental Controls, which let members manage their child's online experience.

Because we are a community, AOL and your fellow members are here to help. If you've got a question this book doesn't answer we have fast, friendly and free phone support. We've also got an interactive Tech Chat room, extensive online and offline Help files, and a dedicated team of volunteer Guides and Hosts to help you along.

AOL is such an extensive service, even I'm constantly discovering new features and content. If you're an AOL subscriber, this book will help you make the most of your AOL experience and have you navigating the service in no time. Even AOL veterans will probably pick up a few new tips and tricks from the chapters that follow. If you are not already one of our members, I hope this book will persuade you to join us!

Dominic Wells
Editorial Director

About the Author

Nigel Whitfield is a freelance computer journalist who writes regularly for the UK's top selling PC magazine, *Computeractive!* He also writes a regular column on Internet issues for *Personal Computer World* and makes regular appearances on the TV show *Chips With Everything*. His work has also featured in other UK computer magazines such as *What PC?* and *Mac User*, and from time to time in national newspapers.

When he's not writing, he helps community and voluntary groups to make the most of their computers and the Internet, and has helped create Web sites for both community and commercial organisations.

Acknowledgements

AOL would like to thank the author, Nigel Whitfield, for his dedication and commitment to writing the *AOL Handbook 6.0*, and Susi Pink for project managing its development and production. AOL would also like to thank the following people for their highly valuable contribution in editing this handbook. Their unparalleled knowledge of the service means that AOL members can now benefit from the most comprehensive and informative guide to AOL UK ever published.

Graham Anderson, Jason Boswell, Elise Bradbury, Mary Branscombe, Caroline Chappel, Sasha Chisholm, Joss Cole, Graham Coleman, Chris Condron, Jane Crinnion, David Cushing, Andrew Flower, Alan Griffin, Kate Hall, James Harrison, Clare Hatfield, Magnus Hjert, Nichola Lashmar, Ben Le Foe, Sam Lewis, James Mahon, Tom Morgan, Dan O'Mally, Dale Price, Danielle Simon, Tara Stockford, Mario Vella, Dominic Wells and Alasdair Wright.

CHAPTER

1

Introduction

WELCOME

INITIAL SIGN-ON

Welcome to the Official AOL UK Handbook 6.0. This guide has been written to help you make the most of AOL, and in particular the latest version of the AOL software, AOL 6.0.

Don't worry if you don't have the latest version – perhaps we'll show you so many great new features that you will want to upgrade. And even if you don't, this book will still be packed with tips and information that you'll find useful whichever version of AOL you're using.

We've divided it into easy sections, and whether you're a complete newcomer or a seasoned user, you should be able to easily find the information that you need to make the most of AOL.

For new members, *Chapter 1, Introduction,* tells you a little about what AOL is and how to create an account with the service, while *Chapter 2, First Steps on AOL*, explains how to start exploring the service and exchange email with other users.

Chapter 3, The AOL Experience, is all about the things you can do with AOL. You can find out how to chat, shop, look up information and find any extra help that you need.

AOL's Channels are the key to finding the information you want, without any extra clutter getting in the way, and we've dedicated the whole of *Chapter 4* to explaining the key points of each one.

Whether you're a seasoned user who wants to know how to customise AOL, or a parent who wants to make sure your children have the best experience when they go online, *Chapter 5, AOL and You*, will tell you everything you need to know to make AOL's service work the way you want it to.

In *Chapter 6, The Internet*, you can find out how to use AOL to access some of the amazing resources on the Internet, while *Chapter 7, Advanced AOL*, contains tips, tricks and information for people who want to make sure they're getting the best from the service.

Lastly, *Chapter 8, AOL Anywhere*, explains some of the exciting services AOL provides to help make sure that you never need to be out of touch and can always access your email, messages and other important information.

So, whether you're a first-timer or an old hand, read on. We hope you find plenty of useful information inside.

1.1 Welcome

A few years ago, relatively few people had heard of the Internet, let alone the many companies that can get you online. Now, however, it's a very different story. The Internet is such big news, and plays such an important part in our lives that when AOL announced it was to join forces with Time Warner, it wasn't just something to read about on the business pages, but real news on the front pages.

Why's that? And what makes AOL so special?

Simply, AOL is the most popular way for people to get online. Around the world, more people get online using AOL than any other single company.

That's because AOL isn't just a way of connecting to the Internet. AOL is a complete information service in itself. That means that within AOL, you can find information on just about any topic you want. There are shops, reference areas, places for discussing politics, or catching up on the latest news. You can chat to people live online – including with celebrities – or leave messages for other people to read later. There are classified ads, to sell your old stereo, or look for love, and there's help on everything from personal finance to using AOL itself.

And you can do all this using just the one AOL service.

So what? Well, you might think that's pretty obvious, but when it comes to the Internet, things aren't always the way you'd expect. Lots of Internet companies expect you to use one program for this, one for that, and they might not even work in the same way.

With AOL, however, there's no need to learn how different bits of software work, or switch from one to another. AOL gives you one service, with everything designed to work together so you can move effortlessly from one task to the next – and there's always help close at hand if you need it.

On top of all that, there's also all the information that you can access via the Internet too. AOL gives you access to all the pages on the World Wide Web, and if you're worried that some of that might not be suitable for your children, we've taken care of that too!

AOL is designed to be simple for anyone to use, whatever their age. Your AOL account lets your whole family use the service for a single fee, and parental controls let you choose which areas of AOL everyone can access. So as well as knowing that you're using a service that's simple and straightforward, you can have the confidence that your family will be protected from things you'd rather they don't see.

The big picture

You might be a bit bewildered by the Internet, but it's really not so different from things that you're already used to. Teletext, for instance, provides you with access to lots of selected information, like news, television listings, and holiday deals, all at the press of a few buttons on your TV remote control.

AOL's own information is a bit like that, except that you access it via the AOL service on your home computer, and there's much, much more to look at. It's also easier to find what you want. You don't need to remember that TV is on one page, and sport on another. Just click on one of the buttons on your computer screen to go straight to the information you want.

You can search, too, so if you want to find areas to do with cars, just tell AOL that's what you want, and you'll see a list in a few seconds, showing you a summary of all the information about cars that you can access. Make your choice, and you're there!

What's more, AOL doesn't just grab the pages of information it can find on the Internet and serve them up to you, like some other Internet companies. Of course you can access all that – but AOL has a dedicated team of editors who work to bring you the very best of what is available. That includes producing information especially for AOL, with news, views, features and comments that you won't find anywhere else. You'll have heard people complain that when they look for information online, there's just too much; think of AOL as a bit like your personal research team, sifting out what's useful and what's not, so that you don't have to.

AOL is interactive, too. While you just read a newspaper or the headlines on Teletext, with AOL you can join in discussions about topics raised in the news, sharing your views, or challenging those of others. Sometimes you can end up having a heated debate, while at others you might be surprised by how many people share your viewpoint.

In a newspaper, one of the ways you can have your say is by writing to the letters page, and on AOL you can post your message in a discussion forum for other people to see. You can also send a letter electronically, using AOL's email service.

Email is fast and cheap. You just type your message into the computer, as if you were using a word processor, give the address, and in a few moments it'll be delivered – halfway round the world, if necessary.

Email isn't just about words, though. You can email anything that's stored on a computer, so if you have a picture of yourself, or perhaps your new baby, a few clicks of the mouse is all it takes to send the picture to anyone else. AOL's email service is, like the rest of AOL, connected to the Internet, so you can send your messages to anyone, anywhere in the world – and it doesn't cost anything more than the cost of your connection to AOL.

So, AOL can do everything you'll want from going online, and it makes it easy to boot. Can it really be that simple? Well, yes. Here's an example of what you can do in just a short time online.

Going online

When you've installed the AOL software on your computer, connecting is a breeze – and we'll show you shortly how to install AOL and set it up for the first time.

Connecting to AOL is a simple matter of clicking the icon on my computer's desktop. When the AOL program starts, I have a choice of who I want to connect as – an AOL account lets me have seven different email addresses, so I can have one for work, and one for home, or some for other family members.

I can also choose where I'm connecting from. If I'm not at home, I can still use AOL. In fact, I can connect to AOL from almost every country in the world.

Click the **Connect** button, and after a few moments the computer says 'Welcome to AOL'. The Welcome screen appears, with the latest news headlines, and buttons telling me about some of the other parts of the AOL service.

There's another announcement too – 'You have email', which tells me that someone's sent me an email.

Clicking the **Read** button takes me to my inbox, where I can see there's an email from my sister, in Seattle. Opening the email, I can see it's a picture of my nephew. I've never met him, but I have seen plenty of pictures via AOL. She also tells me that she's planning a trip to the UK, and asks when would be convenient for me.

Fortunately, I can use My Calendar to keep track of all my appointments, so I know right away that the last two weeks in May are fairly free. And a quick glance at my Buddy List shows that I'm in luck – my sister has actually dialled into AOL at the same time as me.

Now I don't need to send her an email. Instead I can use an Instant Message, which will pop up on her screen whatever she's doing, and tell her the dates that are suitable for me. We can chat like this, exchanging typed messages, at no extra cost. And while Susan's telling me about her new job, I can look at the British Airways site on the World Wide Web, and find out flight numbers and times for direct trips between London and Seattle.

When Susan's signed off, I decide to check the discussion boards in the news settings, where I've been talking to people about my views on the European Union. There are a few replies, which I can read through before adding another comment of my own, in the hope that people will be so bowled over by my wit that they'll have to agree with me.

Before I leave, I need to check the weather for my trip to visit a client tomorrow. The AOL weather map can be clicked to zoom in on different areas, but both home in London and my destination near Southampton are covered by ominous bouncing clouds. The forecast for the next five days doesn't look much better, so there's no point postponing the trip. I'll just have to wrap up warm and take a raincoat.

Finally, there's just one last thing to do – more email. A click on the **Write** button brings up a blank message, and I just type in my accountant's address, and a short note asking her if I really have to pay tax on the fee for writing this book. Click **Send**, and I can sign off AOL, checking later to see if she's replied to me. 'Goodbye' says the computer, and my phone line disconnects. And that's all there is to it.

Experts? Not needed!
Everything sounds that simple when an expert does it, you're probably thinking. Ordinary people will spend ages fiddling with settings, losing their email messages, and shouting at the screen in frustration, won't they?

Not at all! If you can work your computer – you have a basic understanding of how to write and save a letter in your word processor, for example, then you're well on the way to using AOL. Even if you can't do that much, don't worry. Just point the mouse at the **AOL** icon, and click twice in rapid succession. When AOL starts, just type, or click buttons once with the mouse.

Most of the time you're using AOL, that's about all you'll need to do. Everything is clearly labelled, and you'll find it easy to get to grips with. As we work through the book, we'll show you tips and tricks to make it easier and faster to go where you like and do what you want, but for now, all you need to do is point and click – AOL really is that easy.

Most of this book is written for users of PCs with Microsoft Windows. AOL also runs on the Apple Macintosh, and we'll cover the main differences between the two versions later on, but the bulk of what you'll read is equally applicable to both systems.

AOL is also available in other ways. AOL Anywhere is the name for AOL services that you can access when you're not logged onto your PC at home but when you are out and about. For example, AOL Mail on personal organisers, and WAP-enabled devices. There's a whole chapter on these too, including details of how you can access your AOL email from any computer in the world with an Internet connection.

How to get connected
So, if you want to connect to AOL, just what do you need? Well, you'll need a computer and a modem – that's the device that links your computer to the telephone line. Most modern computers have one built in, and if you don't have one, they're pretty cheap.

In the future, AOL will be available using some of the new technologies you might have heard about, like ADSL. That's a sort of super-fast phone line that makes it possible for you to receive TV-quality pictures and access information much more quickly. For most people, though, that's firmly in the future.

For now, you'll be accessing AOL with an ordinary computer and a modem. You can find out the exact requirements, to check that your system is up to the job – don't worry, almost every system made in the last few years will be – just check the back of this book (*Appendix 4, Hardware Requirements*).

Who are these people anyway?
So you've got your computer, and a modem, and you're ready to connect. But you're probably thinking 'Just what is AOL, anyway?'

With AOL, what you're connecting to is a UK service that has lots of information especially for UK users, but also provides access to all the information that's on AOL services around the world.

You can just access the UK information if you like, or you can take a peek in the chat rooms for users around the world – as long as you speak the right languages. Whether you're reading the UK news, or chatting with people in a room for Seattle locals, you're still paying the same price.

Most importantly, don't forget that AOL is more than just the people who run the service and the information that it provides. It's a real community, with millions of members, all over the world.

You can talk to people, make friendships online, and ask for advice. With millions of people, there's bound to be someone who knows the answers to your questions – and some of them could be a lot closer to home than you think.

That's one of the joys of going online, in fact. Of course you can chat to people around the world, finding out about how they live and what they do. But you can also find people who might be literally around the corner – new friends in your own community that you might never have come across if it weren't for AOL.

Like any community, you'll find AOL has a lot to offer – and one of the best ways to find that out is to contribute. If you see someone asking a question you can answer, don't be shy – speak up! With AOL everyone can make a difference.

1.2 Signing on for the first time

Before we go any further

If you have your computer and modem connected, you're almost ready to connect to AOL for the first time and create your new account.

Before you do, let's check you have everything you need. It's a good idea to have a pen and paper to note down any important information that's displayed on the screen during the sign-up process.

Normally, everything goes smoothly – but, of course, sometimes people do run into problems. Don't worry if things seem to go wrong. There are people at AOL Member Services who will be able to talk you through problems 24 hours a day. All you have to do is call 0800 376 5432.

If your computer came with AOL software installed on it, you'll need to find the sign-up program, which should be in the Online Services folder. You'll see that on the computer's desktop – it's usually on the left-hand side.

Often, you'll be signing up from an AOL CD instead, in which case, you just need to pop the CD into your computer's CD-ROM drive and follow the instructions on the screen. As well as the CD, you'll need a 'registration number' which is usually printed on a label in the CD case, along with a password. You need to enter these when you register.

You'll also need a credit card so that you can sign up to AOL – but don't worry, you can safely use the free trial confident that nothing will be charged to your card until after your trial period is over.

Connect the modem to your phone line, and if you have a service like Call Waiting, turn it off. On a BT line, you dial #43#, while on Cable phone lines, the code may be #7 instead. You need to turn call waiting off, since the beeps that it makes will confuse your modem and make it disconnect from AOL.

Installing AOL and creating your account

The first stage in signing on to AOL is to install the software on your computer. If AOL came with your computer, double-click on the **Setup** program. If you have an AOL CD, just pop it in the computer's CD-ROM drive, and after a moment you should see the AOL Setup program start automatically. If it doesn't, double-click the **My Computer** icon, then the icon for your CD-ROM drive. Next, you'll see a folder for the version of Windows that you're using, so double-click the appropriate one, and then on the **AOL Installer**.

Walkthrough

Now, let's go through the process step by step. If you've already got AOL installed on your computer, you can skip this section and turn to the next chapter, *First Steps on AOL*. Otherwise, stick with us, and you'll soon be up and running.

Fig. 1.1
Old or new screen

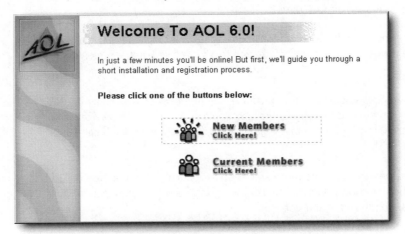

The first thing the installer needs to know is whether you have an AOL account or you want to create a new one. Here we're going to show you how to set up a new account. If you have one already, you'll simply need the Screen Name and password. Click **New Members** to continue.

Now AOL will check to see what software needs to be installed, and whether there's any AOL software to update already on your computer.

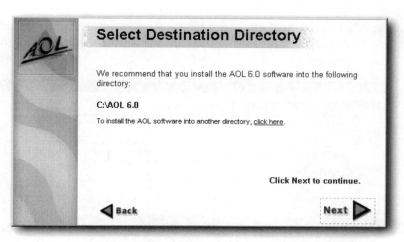

Fig. 1.2
Directory

When that's been done, you'll see the screen above, asking where you want to install AOL. Unless you have a good reason not to, you should accept the suggested location, and then click the **Next** button.

You'll see a screen asking you to wait while AOL does some more checks on your computer and then the progress bar will appear.

As the progress bar moves along, you'll also see information about AOL appearing on your screen, so sit back and read it while you wait. It all takes just a few minutes. You may see a few other boxes appear on the screen while files are being copied and updated. You may be asked if you want to restart Windows. Click **Yes** to continue if this screen appears.

Fig. 1.3
Windows restart query

The AOL installation will continue automatically when your computer has restarted, and you'll see the AOL splash screen as some more updates are made. After that, the main AOL software will start up, and a box will appear with this message:

Fig. 1.4
**Connecting to
AOL**

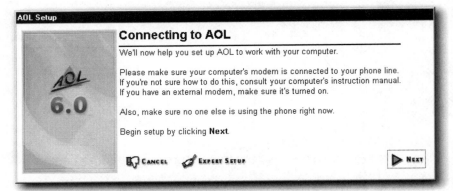

Now we're ready to connect. Make sure no one else is using the phone line, and click the **Next** button.

AOL is now looking to see what modem you have, which may take a few minutes. When it's examined your system, you'll see a screen like the one overleaf – don't worry if you only have one option, instead of the two we've got here. Most computers will only have the one modem listed.

Fig. 1.5
**Select
connection**

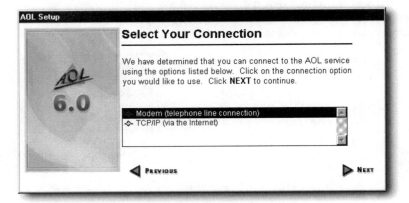

Click on **Modem** and then click the **Next** button. Now you need to tell AOL which country you're connecting from.

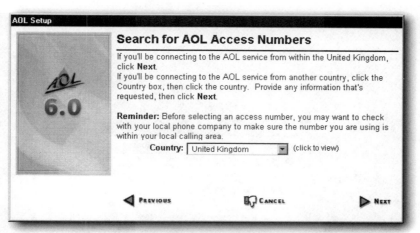

Fig. 1.6
Search for access numbers

On this screen, make sure it's set to United Kingdom (unless of course you're somewhere else!), then click the **Next** button.

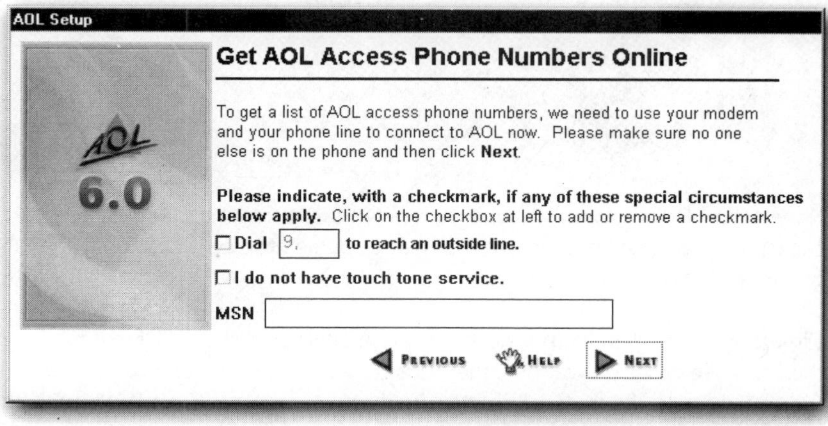

Fig. 1.7
Get numbers online

If you need any special codes, like dialling a 9 for an outside line if your computer is in an office, add them on this screen.

You'll need to click the check box to the left of the word Dial, then put the code for an outside line into the box to the right, if it's not 9. Once again, click **Next** when you're ready to continue. Most users won't need to make any changes on this screen.

Fig. 1.8
Select numbers

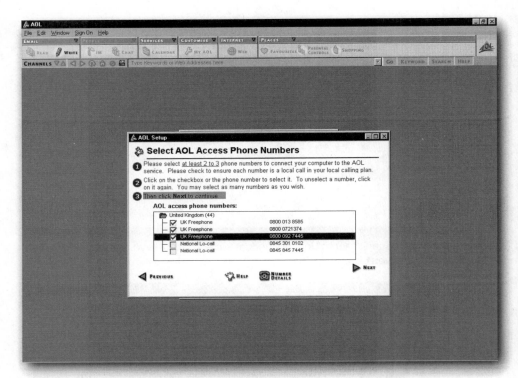

Now, AOL will dial a special number to find out the current list of phone numbers that can be used to access the service. You'll see a couple of screens flash past, then this one will appear.

Click to put a check in the box next to the numbers you'd like to call to reach AOL, and then click **Next**. As you can see, there are quite a few different numbers, and some of them may attract different call charges, so if you're not sure, it's a good idea to check with Member Services at this stage before clicking to put a check mark in the box next to each number you want to call.

Remember, the more numbers you choose, the greater the chance of AOL not having any problems when you try to connect – each number will be tried in turn.

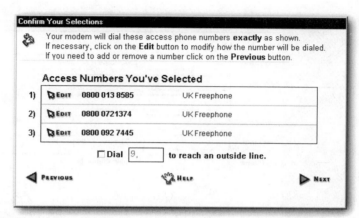

Fig. 1.9
**Confirm
numbers**

This screen asks you to confirm the numbers you want to use. Check they're OK, and then click the **Next** button.

We're almost there! In just a moment AOL will connect again, and it'll be almost time to create a Screen Name – that's the name people will know you by online. As your modem dials, you'll see a series of messages showing you the progress of the connection and then, once your computer is connected to the AOL network, this screen will appear.

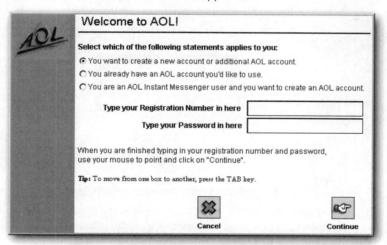

Fig. 1.10
**Create new
account screen**

If you're a new member, then you need to make sure the first option on this screen is selected, to create a new account. In the two boxes, you'll need to enter the details that are printed on your CD case. The number goes in the first box, and the password in the second. When you've filled in the information, click the **Continue** button.

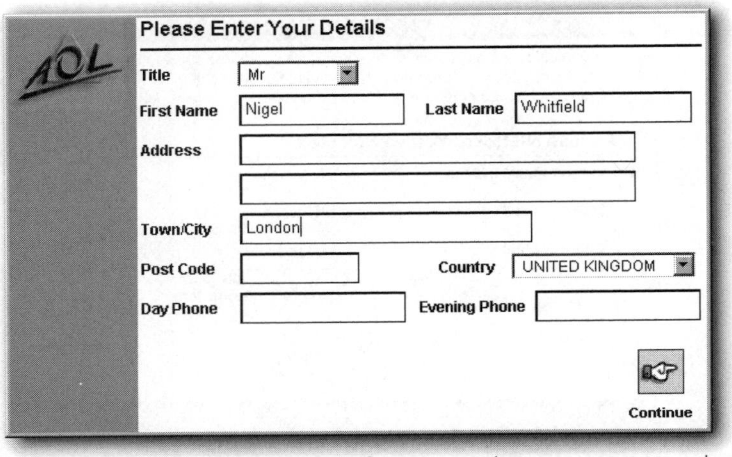

Fig. 1.11
Personal details screen

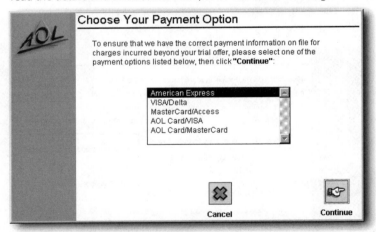

AOL needs to know who you are before you can have an account, and you should fill in the details on this screen. Click the **Continue** button when you're done. On the next screen, you'll see details of how your AOL account works, and the terms of any trial period. Make sure you read the details and understand them, then click **Continue** again to reach this screen.

Fig. 1.12
Payment type

Even though you may have a free trial period, AOL still needs to know your payment options, so that you can carry on using the service afterwards. Choose a type of card that you want to pay with, then click **Continue**. The following screen will ask for the card details themselves, such as name and expiry date.

After giving your card details, you'll be presented with AOL's Conditions of Service, or COS.

You must read the Conditions of Service carefully. They are an agreement between you and AOL.

After reading the COS, make sure that **I Agree** is selected at the bottom of the screen, and then click the **Continue** button again. On the next screen you can type in the name that you'd like to use online. Just enter it in the box and click **Continue**.

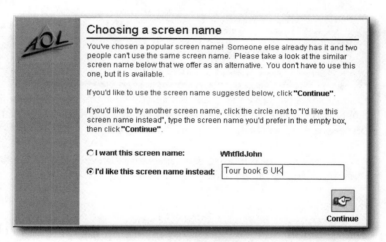

Fig. 1.13
Name taken

Now you need to choose a screen name. This is the name that people will know you by online and will also be known as your email address.

Unless you chose a really unusual name, you'll probably see a screen like this, telling you that the name you want has been taken – there are millions of AOL members around the world, and so you'll probably have to try again.

Why not put 'UK' or the name of your town on the end of a name, to try making it unique?

To try another screen name, just enter it into the box. AOL will suggest a name for you too, which you can choose if you prefer. Click **Continue** to move on to the next screen.

Fig. 1.14
Name OK

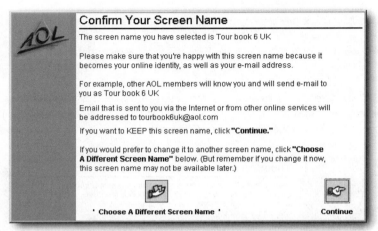

If the screen name you entered is available, you'll see this screen appear. This is the last chance you have to change your screen name, so if you're not happy with it, click **Choose A Different Screen Name**. Otherwise, click on **OK**.

You can create up to six more screen names to use on your AOL account as well. We'll explain about those later on in the book.

The next screen is where you type a password.

Fig. 1.19
Password screen

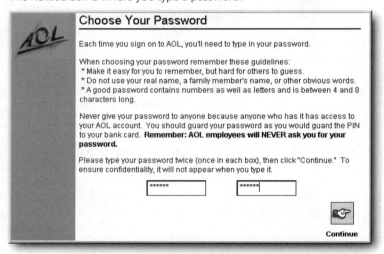

You need to type the password in twice, to make sure you got it right. As you type, you'll just see a row of stars appear, so even if someone's looking over your shoulder, they won't know what your password is.

Choose a password that's easy to remember, but not for someone else to guess. Don't use your partner's name, for example – other people could find it out easily. Remember that you should never tell anyone else your password. AOL staff will *never* ask you for your password.

When you click **Continue**, you'll see a Congratulations screen. You're now the newest member of AOL! Click **Continue** a final time, and the Welcome screen will appear.

Now you're ready to take your first steps on AOL.

2

First Steps on AOL

FIRST STEPS

FINDING YOUR WAY

NAVIGATION

EMAIL

MEMBER SERVICES

Now you've set up your AOL account, you'll want to start exploring the service and find out what it has to offer you.

In this chapter we'll show you how to start sending and receiving email, how to call for help when you need it, and how to find your way around AOL.

If you're an experienced user, then why not check out the information in *Chapters 4 and 5* to find out how to make AOL work better for you, and the latest changes to AOL's Channels.

2.1 Taking your first steps on AOL

Now you've signed on for the first time, you'll want to take a look around. There's a lot of stuff on AOL, but to begin with, we'll take a whistle-stop tour of the basic things, and show you how to move from one place to another.

The Welcome screen and the Channel Menu give you access to all the main features of AOL. Channels on AOL are a bit like digital television – you'll find one for travel, for kids, computing and so on. They're an easy way to get to the information you want without being distracted by other things.

Fig. 2.1
Welcome screen

Of course, AOL isn't just the service – it's the members too. With millions of people connected to AOL across the world, there's almost certain to be someone out there who shares the same interests as yourself. When you start using discussion areas, or chat rooms, you'll quickly learn that AOL can feel a little like your favourite club or pub, with people that you look out for and chat with.

Good manners

Despite what you may think, the online world isn't really so different from the offline one. Just like meeting people in real life, there are conventions and rules. Mostly, they're common sense, but it's as well to be aware of them to make sure that you don't make mistakes, or upset other people.

Perhaps the most important thing to bear in mind is that, no matter how disembodied, the people you're in touch with via AOL are just that – people. What you see may be an email with sad words written a few hours ago, or an Instant Message that raises your hackles. But it's not a message from AOL – it's from another person, sitting in front of their own computer.

In short, no matter how strongly you feel about something that you see on your screen, remember that on the other side of it there's a real person. Never say something to someone electronically that you wouldn't say to them face to face.

While that's the most important rule, there are some other 'rules of the road' that it's worth remembering. Collectively they're often referred to as 'netiquette'. These are some of the most important points to bear in mind:

Before joining an online discussion, whether it's in a chat room, or on a message board, sit and watch for a while. That way you'll get a feeling for how things work, and what sort of comments are welcome.

Many online areas may have something called an FAQ. It stands for Frequently Asked Questions, and it might well contain the information you need. If you can find a FAQ, read it before you ask other people your question.

Words in capital letters are the electronic equivalent of shouting. So, DON'T MAKE ALL YOUR CHAT ROOM COMMENTS LIKE THIS. It's not very easy to read, either, is it?

You don't need to be as formal online as on paper – people don't usually use Dear Sir in email, for example – but you should still be polite, and write proper sentences.

Punctuation and spelling do make a difference to how people interpret what you say online. However, it's considered impolite to pick holes in someone's grammar or spelling, especially if you have nothing else to say about their message.

When you respond to a message, it's common to include quotes from the one you're replying to. Try to make sure you only quote what's absolutely necessary. To include a whole message, and just add a comment like 'I agree' is a waste of time.

Remember that other people will probably have to pay to read messages that you send them. Don't assume that they'll be delighted to receive a huge file from you, or information from a complete stranger telling them about a get-rich-quick scheme.

Sending unsolicited email to multiple recipients may be a breach of AOL's Conditions of Service.

Conventions
Just like ordinary etiquette, netiquette has its own conventions – though it's less about which way to pass the port than making sure that people understand the sense of what you're saying, as well as the meaning. What do we mean? Well, when you're talking to someone face to face, or listening to them on the phone, you can usually tell from their voice or body language if they're serious, or telling a joke.

When all you can do is read letters on a computer screen, it's not so easy, so over the years, various conventions have developed, to add extra clues to your email and other online messages. Often it's in the form of abbreviations, which save typing a few words, and you'll also see Smileys.

You might have heard of those – the idea is that by typing a few bits of punctuation, then turning your head to one side, you'll see something that looks a little like a face. The name Smiley is a bit of a misnomer – there are frowns, sad faces and winks too.

So, here, to help you make sense of anything strange you see in your messages, is a quick list of some of the most common abbreviations and Smileys.

<G>   Grin

<VBG> Very Big Grin

lol   Lots of laughs / Laugh out loud

IMHO   In My Humble Opinion

ROFL   Rolls On Floor Laughing

YMMV   Your Mileage May Vary

:-)   Smiling face, humour

:-(Sad face

;-)   Winking face

:-| Frowning face

You'll see other Smileys – including some that are probably completely impossible to fathom – and plenty of different abbreviations. However, it's best to stick to the most common ones, rather than risk being misunderstood.

> *Remember that even though you might use Smileys or other shorthand to try and convey the meaning of your words, people may still take them at face value. If you're criticising someone, for example, putting <G> or a Smiley at the end of your message won't necessarily make sure that they take your comments the way you intended.*

Hopefully, we've put your mind at rest. This netiquette business isn't so complicated, after all, is it? It's really just about being considerate for other people, and understanding a few simple conventions – not so different from life when you're away from your computer.

A cautionary word
Like any bar or club, there are also sometimes people that you'd rather not come across. While AOL tries very hard to make sure people don't do anti-social things, sometimes you might come across people who are rude, or devious. Some of them will, just like playground bullies, try to find newcomers and take advantage.

Before you go any further, we'll explain a few rules of the road, and how to deal with any problems – but don't worry, you really are in good hands. Think of this more like the safety demonstration on an airline flight. You probably won't need to use the information, but it's best to know, just in case.

One of the most common problems online is that sometimes people pretend to be AOL staff, and trick you into giving them your credit card information or password.

> *AOL will never, ever ask you to confirm your account details in an email or Instant Message. No matter how authentic someone sounds, even if they say your account will be terminated, never tell them your password or billing information.*

AOL provides ways to ignore people you don't want to speak with, and to report anyone who is breaking the Conditions of Service. The Trouble area of AOL is designed to make it easy to report any problems you run into. At the top of the screen, just below the row of buttons, you'll see a space that says 'Type keyword or Web Address here.' If you click in this space and type the word **Trouble**, then press the **Enter** key. The Trouble screen will appear, and you can click on one of the buttons on the screen, according to the type of problem you want to report. There's a helpful explanation to the right to help you choose the right button, depending on what sort of problem you're having.

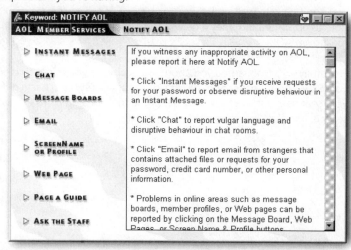

Fig. 2.2
The Trouble screen

And what are those Conditions of Service? Well, you agreed to them when you signed up to AOL. Any time you want to, you can refresh your memory by clicking the little arrow on the **People** button and choosing **Conditions of Service** from the menu that appears.

Usually, AOL's staff will deal with someone who's causing trouble – but while they will often acknowledge your report, they can't tell you exactly what action they've taken.

Sometimes, you might want a more personal touch, and that's where AOL's Guides come in handy.

Your friendly Guide
Guides are special AOL members that you can recognise by their names online, which all begin with GuideUK. Guides are there to answer your questions, or point you to places where you can find the solution if they can't solve it themselves. You'll find Guides roaming around AOL, visiting chat rooms and making sure everything's running smoothly.

If you're in a chat room and someone's being disruptive – making offensive comments, for example, you can use the **Trouble** page to summon a Guide. They'll come along and try to calm the situation down, or warn people who are causing problems.

There's another type of special member, called a Host. They have names beginning with UKHost, and rather than roaming around the whole of AOL, they specialise in a single area. That means that if it's detailed information you want, they're often the best people to ask.

You'll find Guides and Hosts online all the time – there's always one not far away – and you don't have to wait until there's a problem to call on them. If you're just a bit lost about how to do something, they'll be willing to help out and make sure that you're getting the most from AOL.

Hopefully we've reassured you about any problems you might find online, rather than worried you. So without further ado, it's time to put the safety card back in the seat pocket, fasten your seat belt, and wait for takeoff – in the form of a guide to the basics of AOL's email service.

2.2 Finding your way around

When you first sign on to AOL, a page will pop up that says 'Welcome,' next to your screen name. For example, if your name is BookWriter6UK, it will be headed Welcome BookWriter6UK.

Welcome screen

The Welcome screen is a handy place to start exploring some of AOL's features. Different parts of AOL are featured on it from time to time, so it won't always look exactly the same. If, for example, a new service is launched on AOL, you'll probably see it appearing here.

Fig. 2.3
Welcome screen

As you move your mouse around the screen, you'll see that the pointer changes shape, from an arrowhead to a hand. That means that it's on top of a link – an area of the screen that you can click on to reach something else. You'll also see that sometimes the thing you're pointing at will change. Perhaps the colour will alter, or a little arrow will appear. When this happens, it's just another way for AOL to tell you that if you click, you'll see more information.

For example, when you're looking at one of AOL's Channels (don't worry – we'll come to those later) you'll see that moving the mouse over some things on the screen will make a small arrow appear. Click with the mouse, and a menu pops up, letting you choose where to go.

So, watching to see what changes on the screen as you move the pointer around is a good way to work out what you can click on – just try it and see what happens. For example, on the Welcome screen, you'll see a Latest News heading. Just move the mouse over it, and when the pointer changes, click to go to this area.

> *When you're looking at information on AOL, following a link will usually open a new window, so your screen can quickly become quite full. You can close windows you don't want to read by clicking on the **X** at the top right of the window. Some of the windows, like the Welcome screen, won't actually close – they'll be minimised at the bottom of the screen, so you can reach them later easily.*

At the top of the Welcome screen, you'll see a **Mailroom** button for your email. When there's new mail waiting, the button will show an envelope with a letter sticking out. **Read** will be in red type. Click it, and you'll be taken to your mailbox, so you can read the messages that have been sent to you; if you've just set up your AOL account, you'll find a welcome message waiting for you.

If you click the mail button when it's showing a closed envelope and **Read** is in black type, you'll be taken to the Mailbox Room.

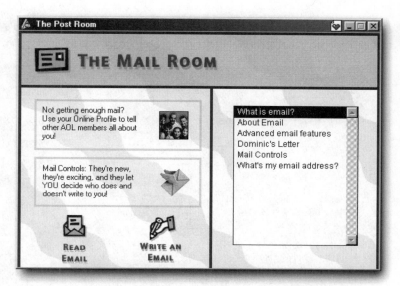

Fig. 2.4
The Mail Room

The **Read Email** and **Write an Email** buttons in the Mail Room work just like the Read and Write icons on the Email button at the top of your screen. In *Chapter 5, AOL and You*, you can read about Profiles and Mail Controls. For now, don't worry about them – you don't need them to get started. A little later on in this chapter, we'll show you how you can start to send and receive email messages.

Beneath the **Mail** button on the Welcome screen is another one labelled **Weather**. When you click on it, you'll see a weather summary for the UK and Ireland.

Fig. 2.5
**The weather
map**

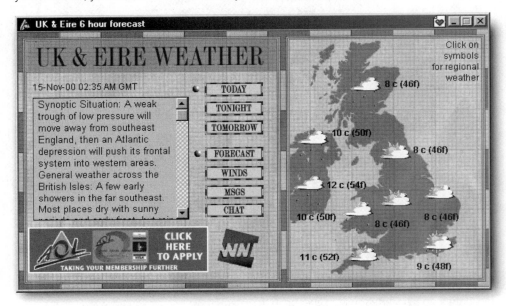

You can click on areas of the map to see a more detailed forecast for a particular area, or just take a quick look at the map to see roughly what's going to happen in your area.

Weather, of course, often has an impact on what we're planning to do, and AOL also provides a way you can keep on top of all your dates and appointments. All you need to do is click the button underneath Weather, labelled **My Calendar**.

My Calendar is a complete online calendar – you can add appointments, look up meetings, and even add dates to it from a list of special events, like rock concerts, that AOL keeps up to date for you. Best of all, you can even access your calendar from anywhere in the world, as long as you can get access to the Internet.

Just click the **My Calendar** button to get started, or take a look at the detailed instructions in *Chapter 5, AOL and you (see section 5.3)*.

Below the Calendar button you'll see a section labelled **Daily Essentials**. This is where you'll see links to some of the highlights of AOL – keep an eye on it, and you'll plenty of great stuff there. For example, there might be a deal of the day on something you can buy online, or hints and tips on dealing with your finances.

Along the bottom of the Welcome screen is a section labelled **Today's Chats**, where you'll see different AOL chat sessions highlighted. Sometimes you'll see links to areas like the news discussions, while other times you might see information about a live chat with a celebrity, or a politician. Just click on one of the links, and you can go straight to one of AOL's chat rooms (*see section 3.1, Chatting on AOL*).

In the centre of the Welcome screen, near the top, you'll see a **Latest News** heading, which you can click to go straight to the headlines. Below that, you'll see other links on the screen, highlighting different areas of the AOL service. If a new area is added, you'll almost certainly see it appear here, and old favourites will be featured from time to time too, helping to make sure you don't miss out on anything.

So, those are the main things you'll find on the Welcome screen. If you'd like to get a feel for some of the different areas on AOL, just click on the featured areas, and see where you're taken. Alternatively, take a look at the next chapter, where we'll guide you through some of the key things that make up the AOL experience, like chatting to people online, shopping and searching for useful information.

2.3 Navigation

Before you can start to get to grips with AOL, we need to take a look at the ways you can move around the service to reach the information that you want.

Fig. 2.6
The AOL main screen

The AOL software has lots of features, but it's surprisingly easy to get to where you want to go. When you start it, you'll see something similar to the picture above. You'll probably find it easiest to maximise the window – double-click on the title bar at the top, and it'll expand to fill up the whole of your computer's screen. Each area of AOL that you go to will open a new window within the AOL screen – a little like the way that a word processor can open a new window for each document that you're working with.

The best way to get around AOL is to use the main tool bar under the menus. From left to right you'll see big buttons labelled **Email**, **People**, **Services**, **Customise**, **Internet** and **Places**, with the AOL logo at the right. This is what's called the toolbar, and the buttons help group the different services and functions of AOL into logical areas. For example, under

Customise you'll find everything you need to make AOL behave the way you want, while the **People** button is all about interacting with other AOL users.

When you're connected to AOL the logo will animate while your computer is working or waiting for AOL to send it information.

Each of the buttons can be used in a number of ways. The top part of the button, where the label is, will produce a menu when you click on it. The bottom of each button will take you directly to a particular part of the whole area – for example the left of the Email button takes you to your inbox, while the right lets you compose a new message.

Below the buttons is the **AOL Channels** menu, some other navigation buttons, and a space where you can type a keyword. To the right of the Keyword box are buttons for **Go**, **Keyword**, **Search** and **Help**.

What's in a keyword?

Keywords are one of the fastest ways to move around AOL. Often, when you go to a section, you'll see a note at the top of the window saying what its keyword is. If you make a note of the word, you can type it in the Keyword box – where the message 'Type keyword or Web address here' appears – then press the Enter key or click **Go** to reach the information you want.

There's a list of keywords at the back of this book, but you can also try exploring by typing in words and seeing where they lead you – you might be surprised at just how much information there is on AOL.

We'll tell you what the keywords are for important parts of AOL as we go on, so if you have trouble finding your way to an area via the menus, you can type in the keyword to go straight to the screens we're showing you in the book.

When there's a keyword that we want to tell you about in the text, we'll show it in a special typeface. For example the **Help** keyword. If we're talking about a section of AOL that can be reached via a specific word, then you'll see a mark like this:

Help

You can also click the button that says **Keyword**, near the top of the screen, to bring up a box where you can type a keyword, like this one:

Fig. 2.7
Keyword input box

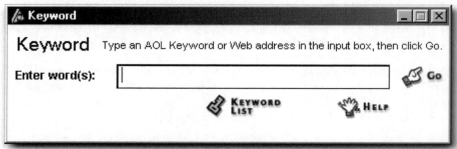

Instead of clicking the button, you can also hold down the Ctrl key on your keyboard and press K. And if you can't think what keyword might take you to a particular place, just click with the mouse on the button labelled **Keyword List**.

Fig. 2.8
Keyword list screen

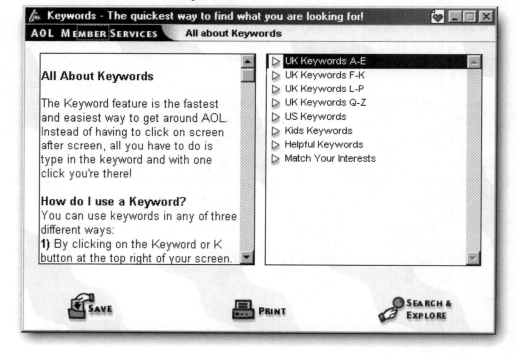

Here, you can look at all the keywords for AOL UK, and a special section for kids. Just click on the list that you'd like to see in the right hand half of the screen.

Favourites

As well as keywords, there's also another quick way to move around AOL, called Favourites. As you look at information on AOL, you'll notice that at the top of a window, to the right of the titles, there's a small heart. That's the **Favourites** icon, and if you double-click on it, you'll see a screen like this appear.

Fig. 2.9
Add favourite screen

For now, just remember that if you click the first button, **Add to Favourites**, AOL will remember the place you've visited, and you can get there using the **Favourites** button at the top of the screen. It's a little like putting bookmarks in your encyclopedia, so you can find the entries you want easily. You can do other things with Favourites, but we'll explain those later, in *Chapter 5, AOL and You (5.4, Customising AOL)*.

Now, back to those buttons. What's underneath each one?

Email
The **Email** button gives you access to everything you'll need for sending, receiving and managing your emails. You can use the icons on the button to read and write messages, as we've already seen, and the **Email** menu lets you access features such as the **Address Book** and email controls, and the **Automatic AOL** facility.

People
This is the button to use when you want to talk with other people on AOL, making new friends or catching up with old ones. The **IM** icon lets you send an Instant Message to another user, while the **Chat** button takes you to the Chat Channel where you can experience your first online chat. From the **People** menu you can search the AOL Member Directory, or look at the Profile – a short description – that another user may have created about themselves. You can also check to see if a member is signed on to AOL at the same time as you.

Services
Services is the way you reach a wide range of the things that AOL has to offer. Click on the icon to access **My Calendar**, where you can keep track of your appointments. On the menu you'll find things like Horoscopes, Stock quotes, Homework help, TV listings and Travel Reservations.

Customise
Although AOL has tried hard to make sure everything works in a most convenient way, there are times when you might want to change some things. The **Customise** button lets you change lots of settings. For example, via this menu you can change **Parental Controls**, which can restrict what your children see online. Other options include **Screen Names**, where you can create additional screen names on your AOL account. The **My AOL** icon takes you to an area where you can customise AOL.

Internet
As well as all its own information, AOL also gives you access to the whole of the Internet, and the **Internet** button is the quickest way to get started. The **Web** icon will take you to AOL's home page on the Internet, and on the menu you can find tools to search the Internet, download files, or access the Internet's discussion areas and make your own Web page.

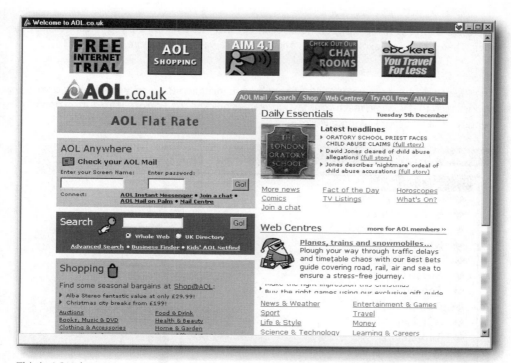

Fig. 2.10
AOL UK home page

This is AOL's home page on the Internet. Move your mouse pointer over the page, and you'll see that, just like when you're looking at information on AOL, sometimes it changes from an arrow into a small hand.

Just click the mouse button 'follow' the link. When you're looking at Internet pages, they'll usually – but not always – appear in the same window. If you want to move back to the last Web page you looked at, use the little left pointing arrow on the toolbar.

Of course, not all Web pages look quite as good as the information you see on AOL, and some of them may contain information that you'd rather not see.

You can use AOL's Parental Controls if you don't want to see some types of information from the Internet. *Chapter 5* explains how you can set them up, and we recommend that you read it before letting your children use AOL unsupervised.

Regardless of what's on an Internet page, as you can see, they're almost as easy to move around as AOL itself. So wherever you want to find information, it's simple. And you can explore the same way too – if your mouse pointer turns into a hand, and you're curious, just click. There's plenty to explore on AOL, and it's a great way to learn more.

Places
The **Places** menu has more of AOL's Channels on it, including the facility to add your own shortcuts so that you can reach your favourite areas quickly. The **Favourites** button opens a window that lists your Favourite Places.

Fig. 2.11
Favourite places

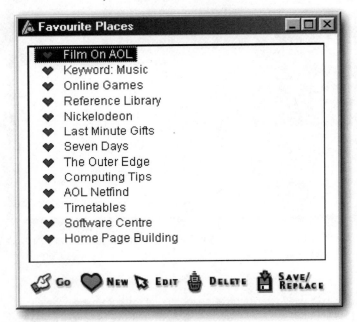

To start with, there will be some entries that AOL has added for you, as well as any others that you've added yourself by clicking on the heart icon in a window's title bar. You can go directly to any of your Favourite Places by double-clicking on its name in the list.

To the right of the Favourites, you'll see three more icons: **Parental Controls**, **Shopping** and **Help**.

Parental Controls let you decide what each of the people who use your AOL account can access when they're connected – you can use them to stop your children seeing unsuitable material, for example, or control who they can send email messages to. You can find out all about them later on in the book (*5.1, Screen names and controls*). For now let's concentrate on finding your own way around AOL.

The **Shopping** button takes you to Shop@AOL, AOL's online shopping area, where you can buy CDs, books, clothes, gifts and all sorts of other things – in complete safety. If you want to start shopping right away, take a look at *Chapter 3*, where you can find out exactly how it's done (*3.2, Shopping on AOL*).

The **Help** button takes you to AOL's Member Services section.

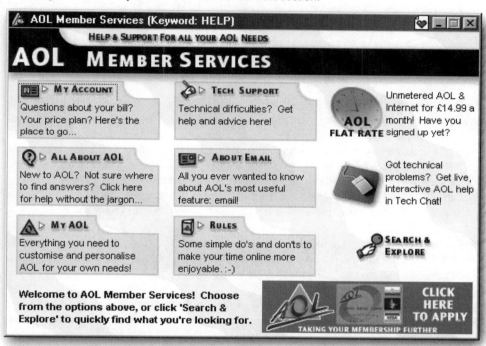

Fig. 2.12
Member services screen

You can also reach this screen at any time by typing the word **Help** into the keyword box underneath the AOL buttons. This screen is the place to find answers to lots of your questions, including billing options, technical support for when things go wrong, rules and customising AOL to work the way you like it.

In fact, it's such a useful section of AOL that we'll be taking a closer look at it later on in this chapter (*2.5, Member services*).

Finally, you'll probably wonder why there's all that empty space to the right of the **Help** button. If there are parts of AOL that you want to be able to reach really quickly and easily, you can add them to the toolbar yourself, so that they're just a single click away. You can also remove the items that are on there, like the **Shopping** button, for example.

All the information you'll need to find out how to adjust the toolbar is in *Chapter 5, AOL and You (5.4, Customising AOL)*.

Web and channel icons
Below all the buttons, to the left of the Keyword box, you'll see a few smaller icons. Next to the word **Channels** are two small arrowheads. Click on the down arrow, and **AOL's Channel List** will appear, so you can go quickly to one of the areas featured on it. Click the up arrow, and the list disappears.

The next two icons, the left and right arrows, are used to help you move through both AOL and Web sites, going back to the last page you looked at, and forward again. These are especially useful on the Web – as we mentioned earlier, with Web pages, when you follow a link, the new page often replaces the old one on your screen. If you want to refer back to the last page, use the left arrow to recall it, and instead of clicking on the link again, you can use the right arrow to follow your path forwards. You can backtrack more than one step through the Web pages like this to help find what you're looking for. The buttons work in a similar way when you're moving through AOL, stepping through the windows that are open on your computer screen.

Next is the **Reload** button, which tells AOL to get another copy of the Web page that you're looking at. You can use this if a page doesn't appear properly or to see, for example, if a sports result page has had a new score added.

The **House** icon takes you to the home page of AOL on the Internet, and next to it is the **Stop** icon, which you can use to tell AOL to stop downloading a long page if you've decided that you don't want to see it all.

Finally, immediately to the left of the Keyword box is the **Print** button, which you can use to print the AOL window that you're currently looking at – that will be the one with the title bar blue, rather than shaded grey.

At the right of the Keyword box, you'll see another downward-pointing arrow. Click this and you'll see a list of the areas you've visited since signing on to AOL, so if you want to go back somewhere but can't remember how you got there, try looking through the list. Just click on an item to go there again.

The **Keyword** button brings up the screen we showed you earlier, where you can type in a keyword, instead of typing it on the toolbar.

To search AOL for a particular piece of information, use the **Search** button, and if you can't figure out how you do something, click **Help**.

We'll look at searching in more detail later. For now, have a look round the menus and see what sort of information you can find. In a moment, we'll see how to join chat rooms, and leave comments on message boards.

Before then, one more useful trick – signing off. You can disconnect from AOL by choosing **Exit** from the **File** menu right at the top of the screen, or by going to the **Sign Off** menu and choosing **Sign Off**.

The **Sign Off** menu also lets you switch to another screen name, so you can check for email there without having to disconnect the phone call. If you choose **Exit** from the **File** menu, you'll see a screen like this:

Fig. 2.13
Sign off screen

You can change your mind and stay on, disconnect but leave the AOL software running – so you could write some emails to send later, or catch up on ones you've downloaded – or exit the AOL software completely.

2.4 Email

For many people, email is one of the most useful tools around. Sure, the World Wide Web is glamorous, and you can find out all sorts of things about celebrities, or book plane tickets. And you can chat to people live online. But email, despite being less glamorous, is one of the most useful tools on the Internet.

Email is just text that's sent from one person to another via the Internet. Because the Internet is so fast, and so big, email can be virtually instantaneous – though like any motorway, sometimes there are hold ups.

Nevertheless, it's an amazing tool. With a quick call to AOL, you can send a message that will be delivered to any Internet address in the world, usually within seconds or minutes. And distance is no object – it all costs the same.

So, there are none of the delays of using airmail, and waiting weeks for a letter to wing its way back from Australia. And unlike sending a fax, you don't have to pay expensive international phone charges to get a message to someone in India.

Hold on! Isn't email text though? So doesn't that mean that fax has the edge when you want to send things like pictures, or plans of a building? Well, if you've ever used a fax machine to send a picture, you'll know it can look pretty fuzzy at the other end.

Email doesn't have to be just text. AOL's email service is sophisticated, and you can send messages with different coloured text, bold and italic letters, and even a background picture – like using special notepaper.

When you're sending messages to other AOL Members, you can add all sorts of special features. And you can send pictures or other computer files to people around the world too, by 'attaching' them to your message. When the message is received, the attachment can be saved and looked at. You could attach a sales report, or a picture of your new home, and send the message over the Internet.

The person you're writing to will have a perfect copy of the file, or the picture that you've sent – no more smudged faxes, or creased airmail notes. It's quick and cheap – even if you're sending a big file down the street, you'll still find it costs less to send via AOL than giving a floppy disk to a bike courier.

Your email address

Email addresses are the key to contacting people. Even if you've never used one before, you'll probably be familiar with them. An address is an email name, followed by an @ symbol and then the name of the computer where the email has to be delivered.

Your email address is just your AOL Screen Name followed by @aol.com. So, for example, my Screen Name of Bookwriter6uk has an email address bookwriter6uk@aol.com.

Some addresses are longer. For example, the BBC's education department can be reached via education.online@bbc.co.uk. At first, email addresses might look confusing, but the part to the right of the @ isn't really that different from a postal address. Just imagine the words between each full stop being written on a different line, like this:

Education.online

BBC

CO

UK

The last line is often the country, then there's usually something to say what type of address it is – a company, here – and the name of the firm.

You can tell all your friends your new email address on AOL easily. When you're giving out your address, it doesn't matter whether you put letters in capitals or not – but do remove any spaces that you have in the AOL Screen Name. For example if your name is John Q Smith, then tell people to email you using the address JohnQSmith@aol.com.

Writing your first email

Sending a simple email is very easy. At the top left of the screen, you'll see a button labelled **Email**. Click on the right-hand side, where there's a pencil shown. You'll see a screen like this appearing, which is where you write your message.

Fig. 2.14
Write email

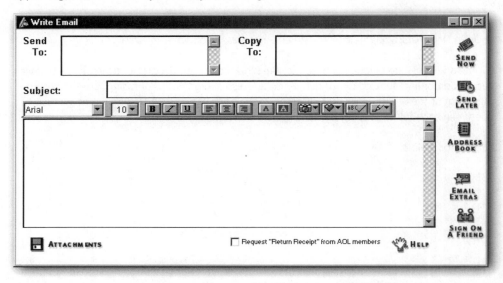

Click with the mouse in the top left box, where it says **Send To**, and type in the email address of the person that you want to send your message to.

You can save time when you're writing to another AOL member by missing out the @aol.com from the address. If there's no @ symbol, AOL will assume you're sending your message to another member, and you don't need to worry about spaces in the name, either.

You can move between the boxes on the Email screen by pressing the Tab key on your keyboard, or just click with the mouse in the area you want to change. The top right box, Copy to, lets you send the same email to other people. You can actually put as many addresses as you like in each box, but remember that people who receive the message will see all the addresses.

If you want to keep an address private, type it in the Copy to box, but put brackets round it, like this: (bookwriter6uk). That way, the address will be what's called a Blind Carbon Copy – no one else will know that a copy of the message was sent there.

When you've added the addresses that you want, type a short subject for your message, like 'When can we meet?' Try to make sure it's something that's going to help the recipient work out whether it's important to read the message right away or not.

Now, go to the big blank area at the bottom, and type the text of your message. People are usually much more informal when they use email than in letters, so there's no need for a Dear Sir.

Just above the area where you type your text, you'll see a row of buttons. The first few of these are just like you'll see in a word processor, and let you change the style of your text, or centre lines, and so on. If you hold the mouse pointer over the buttons, you'll see a short description of them.

For now, though, just type a message without using any fancy features. We'll explain about the enhanced features of email later on in the book. If you do want to use things like coloured text, remember not to go too wild – your message is supposed to be readable, after all. Also, while AOL members will see your message in all its glory, people you write to on the Internet will just see plain text anyway.

When you've typed your message, click on the **Send Now** button, and it'll be delivered almost immediately. If you mistyped the name of an AOL member, you'll be told right away, so you can correct the mistake. If you make a mistake with other email addresses, you may instead receive a warning message later, from a computer elsewhere on the Internet.

Reading your messages

When you sign up with AOL, you'll be sent a couple of welcome emails, so let's use those to show you how to read messages that you've been sent.

As soon as you sign on, you'll hear your computer tell you if you have post waiting for you, and there'll be an icon on the main Welcome screen that you can click to read the messages. You can also look at your email box by clicking the **Read** icon – it looks like an envelope – which is at the left-hand end of the **Email** button at the top of your screen. This is the screen you'll see when you have new messages:

Fig. 2.15
New mail

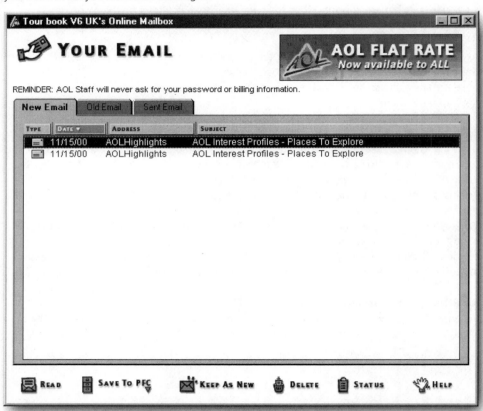

You can open a message by double-clicking on it with the mouse, or click once to choose a message, and then click the **Read** button to open it. The message will pop up in a new window of its own, and you can read it just like you would a document in your word processor.

In the screen listing your mail – called your Online Mailbox – you'll see a row of tabs across the top. You can select these to look at old mail – that's messages you've read already – or sent mail, which are the ones you wrote to other people. Just click with the mouse on one of the tabs, and you'll see the list update.

When you read a message, and then close the window that it's in, it automatically moves to the Old Mail section of your mailbox, so you'll find it there.

Perhaps you've realised that you need to think about a message and reply to it later. You can remind yourself easily by finding the message in your list of Old Mail, and clicking once to select it, then click the **Keep As New** button at the bottom of the mailbox. The message will be moved back to New Mail, and the next time you sign on to AOL, you'll be reminded again that you have messages to read.

Keeping on top of your email

There are a couple of other handy features that the AOL Mail system provides which are worth looking at here.

What do you do if you've sent a message, but there's been no reply? Are you agonising over whether or not you're being ignored? Or perhaps the other person just hasn't read it yet. No problem!

Choose the **Sent mail** tab in your mailbox, and find the message you want to know about. Click once with the mouse to highlight the message, and then click the **Status** button at the bottom of the screen.

The box that appears will tell you if your message has been read, which will either stop you worrying, or make things worse, but at least you'll know!

What about, horror of horrors, if you send the wrong message to someone? You've accidentally posted your job application email to your current boss, and the sales reports to your aunt. Can you fix the problem?

If the email was sent to another AOL user, and they've not read it, yes you can! All you need to do is find the message in your list of sent mail, and click on the **Unsend** button. All trace of the message will be removed, so you're safe – no one except you will ever know that you made a mistake.

Remember that you can't unsend messages to people elsewhere on the Internet – once the message leaves AOL there's nothing you can do. So if you've posted something embarrassing to the Internet, or to an AOL user who's read the message before you realise your mistake, sorry, but the best thing you can do is smile and get ready to apologise.

The final button that we'll deal with here is the **Delete** button. If you send and receive a lot of emails, the lists in your mailbox will soon grow, and it'll take AOL longer to show you what's there. You can delete messages to keep the lists manageable. If you delete a message that you've sent, all that's deleted is your copy – the recipient will still see the message.

How long does mail last?

Obviously, the number of emails you receive could be quite large, so there are some limits on how long messages are kept in your mailbox for. You can keep messages for ever if you transfer them to your Personal Filing Cabinet, which is stored on your computer's hard disk, rather than on AOL.

Messages that you've sent will be kept in your AOL mailbox for about a week, and the same is true of messages that you've read – the ones in the Old Mail list. You can change how long old messages are kept for using the email Preferences, which are described in *Chapter 3, The AOL Experience* (*3.4, Advanced email*).

New messages, the ones that you haven't read, are kept for longer, around four weeks. After that, they're deleted, and you won't be able to get them back. Unless you take very long breaks from using your AOL account, you shouldn't have any problems, but if you're planning a world cruise, it might be best to let people know that there's no point sending you email while you're away.

Replying to messages

By now you should know how to read messages and send them. What about sending a response to someone?

That's easy! When you read a message, you'll see buttons to the right of the text for **Reply**, **Forward**, and **Reply All**.

To send a response back to the person who wrote to you, just click the **Reply** button, and you'll see the same screen as you would for writing a new email, but with the address already filled in for you in the **Send To** box. The subject may have been changed too, with the word 'Re:' put in front, so that your correspondent knows this is a response to their message.

All you have to do is type your message, and click the **Send** button.

Sometimes, the message you read may have been sent to more than one person – it might be about the arrangements for a party, perhaps, or a Neighbourhood Watch committee meeting – and everyone needs to see your response. When you click the **Reply All** button, AOL will automatically add all the original recipients of the message to your reply, so once again, all you need to do is type your response, click **Send**, and you can be sure that everyone who needs to know will be in the picture.

The last button is the **Forward** button. You use this when you receive an email and instead of replying to the sender, you want to show it to someone else. For instance, you can't believe the request for a pay cut that your boss has just emailed to you, so you decide to share it with a colleague.

Click the **Forward** button, and a new message will appear. Although the new message looks blank, when the other person receives it, they'll see your comments at the top of it, with the original message underneath. Just as with writing a new message, click the **Send To** box and type in the address of the person you want to forward it to.

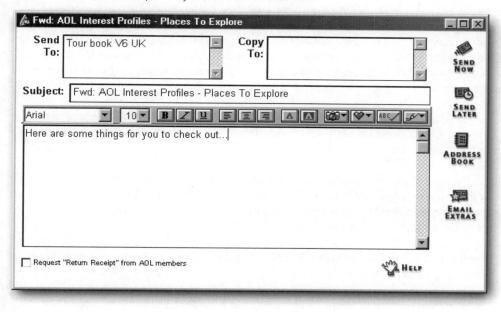

Fig. 2.16
Message forward

Some quirks of Internet email

Most of the things we've talked about so far will work for both email on AOL and to people elsewhere on the Internet. You should know how to send and receive messages, and in the section on advanced email, we'll look at more ways to manage your messages and make them look more attractive.

There are a couple of things that might seem a little confusing if you exchange mail with Internet users, however.

Firstly, when you receive a message from someone on the Internet, you'll see a section at the bottom of their text labelled 'Headers'. You can usually ignore this. The headers are information that shows how a message reached you over the Internet. If you can ignore them, why are they there? Well, if you receive a message that you want to complain about, the headers will help AOL find out where it came from, so that comments can be passed on to the appropriate people.

Secondly, as we hinted at before, you don't always know when you send a message to the Internet if the address you used was correct, since AOL can't check all the millions of possible addresses there are.

So, if you do make a mistake, your message will probably be returned to you, sometimes within a few minutes, sometimes not for a day or more. Typically you'll receive a message from someone called Mailer Daemon or Postmaster, with a subject like 'Undeliverable mail,' or 'Returned Mail: User Unknown'.

If you read the message, among all the technical gobbledegook, you'll see a description of what the problem was, or at the very least the address you were trying to reach.

Sometimes, you'll receive one of these messages as a warning, just to let you know that a computer somewhere out there is still trying to deliver your message to its recipient, but hasn't had any luck so far. It's usually clear from the subject of the first few lines if the message is just a warning.

Advanced email

If you want to know more about email right away, then turn to *Chapter 3,* where you can find out how to send files with your messages, use the Address Book and transfer mail to your own computer to read when you've disconnected from AOL (*3.6, Advanced email*).

In *Chapter 5*, you can read more about how to block email from people you don't know, and other privacy features on AOL (*Chapter 5, AOL and You*).

For now, you should know enough to get started, so we'll go on and look at some of the other important parts of AOL.

2.5 Member Services – AOL Help

We hope that what we've told you so far is enough to get you started, and show you how to move around AOL, and start to find the things that you want. If you still want to know more, however, don't worry – help is at hand.

We've mentioned it briefly earlier on, but now we're going to take a closer look at AOL's Member Services, which is where you can find help whenever you need it. Incidentally, depending on when you read this book, you might find that the name has changed to AOL Help. Don't worry – you'll still find all the same useful information there, even though some of the screens might look slightly different to the ones we've shown in the book. Just remember that where we talk about Member Services, you might see the name AOL Help on screen instead.

Fig. 2.17
Member services screen

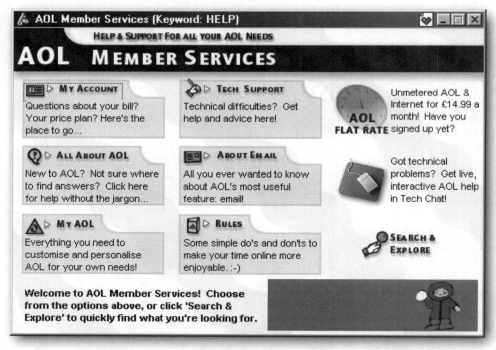

Help

This is the Member Services screen. As we mentioned before, you can reach it by clicking **Help** from the Main screen. You can also use the keyword **Help** – remember that all you need to do is type the word into the box that says Enter keyword or Web addresses here. And finally, you can click at the right-hand end of the tool bar, just to the left of the AOL logo, where it says **Help**.

There are six main buttons on the screen, though we'll skip two of them, **My Account** and **My AOL,** for now, since you won't need them just yet. **My Account** is where you can change your billing options, and **My AOL** lets you customise some other aspects of AOL. If you want, you can find out more about these options in *Chapter 5, AOL and You (5.4, Customising AOL).*

The other buttons on this screen will help you to find out the answers to most of your questions, and solve any problems you might experience when you're using AOL.

Remember that if you have problems, you can also call AOL's Member Services, which is a freephone call. Call 0800 376 5432 from the United Kingdom, or 1800 60 50 40 in the Republic of Ireland. If you're calling from another country, you need to dial +353 1 806 9000 – change the + to the international dialling code, which is 00 in most of Europe, or 011 in the US.

Let's start off our tour round Member Services by looking at the **All About AOL** button. This is where you can find tips and tricks, a letter from AOL's editor, a quick tour of AOL and a glossary.

All about AOL

Fig. 2.18
**All About AOL
screen**

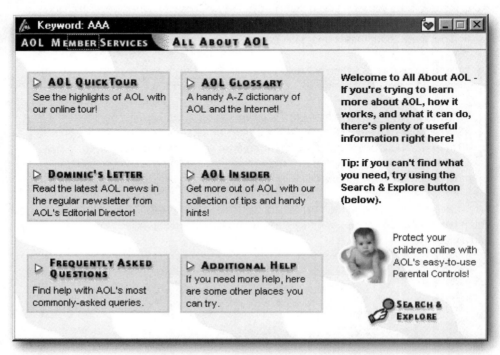

AAA

You can also reach this screen via the keyword **AAA**. As you can see, there are six large buttons, each of which will give you a little more information about AOL – though you'll find that some of the information is in this book too.

If you click the **Online tour** button on this screen, you'll be taken to a screen where AOL's Connie – you might have seen her in the television adverts – will explain different aspects of the service, like chatting to people, sending email, and using the Internet. When you don't have this book handy, but want to know about using AOL, this is a great place to look. On Connie's screen, you'll also find a button that lets you chat directly with a member of AOL staff who's there specially to help new members. All you'll have to do is type your questions and press the **Enter** key on your keyboard.

Dominic's Letter is where you can read a regular message from the man in charge of what's on AOL in the UK. You'll find news about changes to AOL, and some hints and tips too.

All about AOL also includes a link to **Frequently Asked Questions**, a **Glossary**, and **AOL Insider**. You can use these to find out what the solution is to a common query, to look behind the jargon, or to get regular tips and tricks about the service. Frequently Asked Questions is one of the most useful areas, so we'll take a closer look at that in a moment. For now, let's carry on with our tour of the Member Services screen.

Technical support

Technical support is one of the most useful things that you can find via the Member Services screen. You can also reach this screen directly using the keyword **Tech**, and it should probably be your first port of call if you have any problems using AOL.

Tech

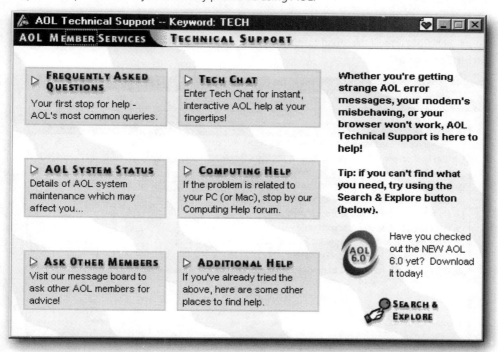

Fig. 2.19
Tech support screen

As with the other screens in this section, you'll see six main buttons. We'll start from the bottom right and work backwards through them.

Additional Help is the button to use when you can't find a solution to your problem anywhere else on this screen. Clicking it will bring up a screen of instructions telling you about other ways you can find help, including the phone numbers for AOL's technical support team.

The **Computing Help** button will let you sort out problems with your computer that aren't really connected with AOL. If, for example, you don't know why your mouse isn't working, or you're having problems installing a program on your computer, this is the place to look. You'll find plenty of information to help you make the most of your PC.

Tech Chat is where you can speak directly with one of AOL's technical support team, by typing messages into your computer. Why would you want to do that? Well, lots of people only have the one phone line to connect them to the Internet, so if you use Tech Chat, you can stay connected to AOL while you talk with a support representative. That way, if they suggest a way to do something, you can try it instantly, and tell them if it didn't work out.

When you click the **Tech Chat** button you'll see a screen of information telling you what hours Tech Chat is available; read through it and then click the button below, which says **Enter Tech Chat**.

Fig. 2.20
Tech Chat topics

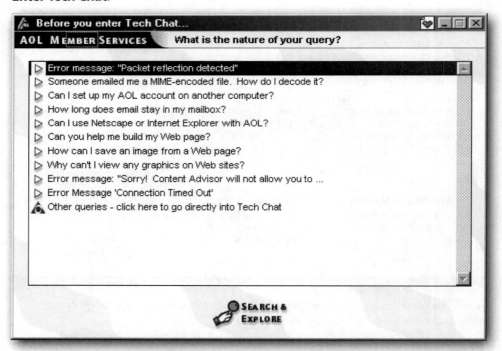

On this screen, read through the common questions, and if one of them describes your problem, click it. If not, don't worry – just click the last entry instead. If your question is listed, clicking on it will display the answer, and offer you the chance to enter Tech Chat if the suggestions don't solve your problem.

When you enter Tech Chat, you'll see a screen like this one:

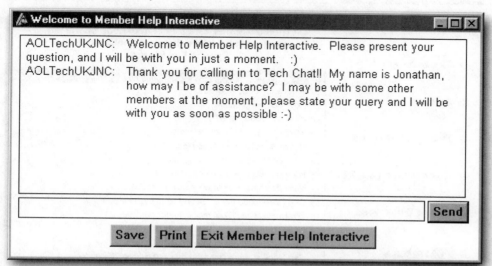

Fig. 2.21
Tech Chat screen

All you have to do is wait for an AOL representative to join you, and then you can type your question, and press the Enter key. The words you type will appear on the screen. Use the **Exit** button when you're finished.

The AOL **System Status** button tells you when and if parts of AOL are being worked on, or if there's a known problem with a particular area. Click this button and you'll know right away if there's something happening – it could save you a lot of time working out why you can't do something.

The last button on the screen, **Frequently Asked Questions**, is probably one of the most useful, so we're going to look at it in more detail.

Frequently Asked Questions

Fig. 2.22
FAQ screen

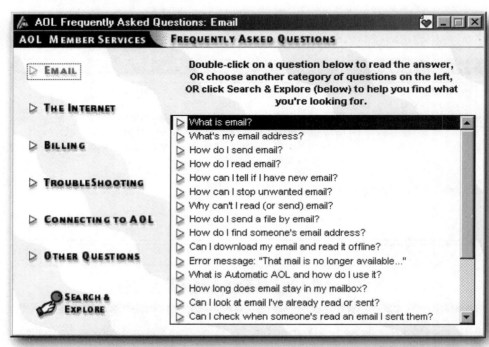

FAQ

This is the screen that you see when you choose **Frequently Asked Questions** from the technical support screen in **Member Services**. You can also reach it directly using the keyword **FAQ** from anywhere on AOL.

What's a FAQ?
You'll often see the term FAQ used when you're on AOL. It's just the abbreviation for Frequently Asked Questions, and people tend to say it as if it's spelt f-a-c-k. It's one of those slightly confusing words, since it can mean slightly different things – a FAQ could be a single question, like 'Why are you asking that? It's a FAQ.' It can also be the list of questions and answers, for example 'You'll find the solution in the FAQ.'

So, what does AOL's FAQ section have in it? As you can see from the screen, there's a large box, and a set of buttons down the left-hand side. The buttons are your quick way into the questions – they let you choose a category and then see all the questions within it. There are categories for **Email**, the **Internet**, **Billing**, **TroubleShooting**, **Connecting to AOL** and **Other Questions**.

Click on one of the categories and you'll see a list of all the questions on that topic. To see the answer to a question, just double-click on it, and you'll see the answer appear on a screen like this one:

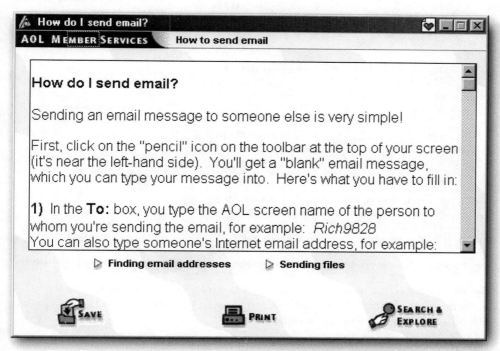

Fig. 2.23
FAQ answer screen

You can read through the answer, and on some of them you'll see a button labelled **Try it now**. Just click the button, and you'll be taken to the part of AOL that the answer is talking about.

Now you know what's on the Technical Support screen, let's get back to the main Member Services screen, and take a look at its **About Email** button.

About Email

Fig. 2.24
**About Email
screen**

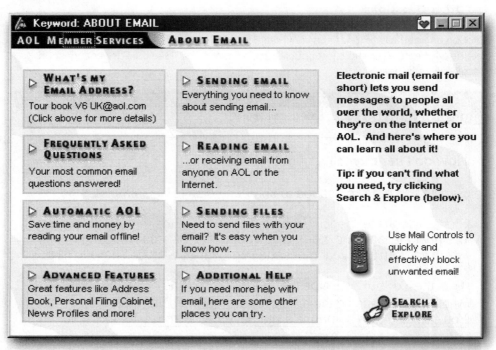

About email

The **About Email** button on the Member Services screen is there to help you answer most of the questions you might have about AOL's email service – but don't forget that you can find out most of what you need to know in this book too!

As well as using the **About Email** button on the Member Services screen, you can also type 'About email' into the Keyword box at the top of the AOL screen, and press the Enter key on your keyboard.

The buttons on this screen let you find out about sending and receiving email, using the Address Book, and even Automatic AOL.

We won't look at them in any more detail here, because everything on this screen is explained in the book too, but if you manage to mislay it, remember that you can use the About email screen to find the answers to any of your email questions.

Rules

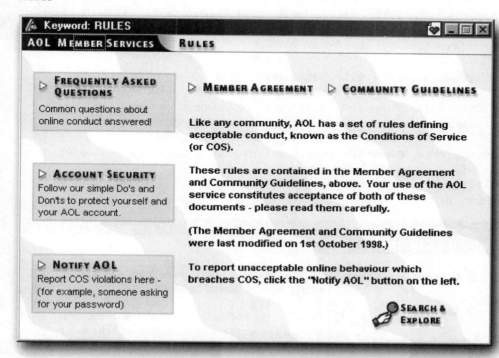

Fig. 2.25
Rules screen

The **Rules** button on the Member Services screen is where you can check on the rules that you're expected to abide by when you're using AOL. You can also reach this information using the keywords **COS** or **Rules**. As part of signing up with AOL, you had to agree with the Conditions of Service. Those conditions are made up of the Member agreement, which covers things like billing and prices, and the Community Guidelines, which are to do with what people can say on AOL, and how they should behave. You can read both by clicking on the appropriate button.

COS

The online versions of the Conditions of Service will usually be the most up to date. However, you can find a copy at the back of this book, in Appendix 3, Conditions of Service. While you may find it useful as a reference, remember that changes may have been made since the book was printed (A.3, Conditions of Service).

The **Frequently Asked Questions** button on the Rules screen answers some of the questions that you might have about the Conditions of Service.

To find out about how to protect the security of your AOL account, use the **Account Security** button. You can read about all the different types of security, including how to protect yourself against computer viruses, keeping your credit card information secure, and controlling what your children can access online.

We recommend that you familiarise yourself with the information on the Account security screen to make sure that you have a safe and trouble-free experience online. While AOL makes every effort to provide the best online environment, you should also take steps yourself, including using a virus-checking program on your computer.

The final button, **Notify AOL**, takes you to a screen where you can report problems that you've encountered while you're using AOL.

Notify AOL

Fig. 2.26
Notify AOL screen

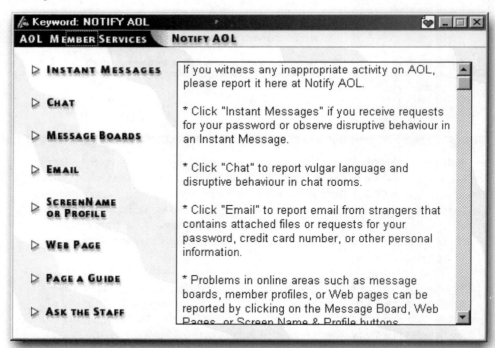

Trouble

We've briefly mentioned this screen before – you can reach it from anywhere on AOL by using the keywords **Trouble** or **Notify AOL**. Just type the keyword into the box at the top of the screen where it says 'Enter Keywords or Web addresses here', and then press **Enter**.

AOL Handbook 6.0

This is the screen to use if you come across someone else on AOL behaving in a way that you think is inappropriate and breaches the Conditions of Service.

You'll see that there's a button for reporting different types of problem, like problems in a chat room, or on a message board, or in Instant Messages. Just click on the appropriate option, and you'll see a form to fill in.

On most of the forms, you'll have to copy and paste information, for example from an Instant Message. Don't worry if you're not too sure how to do that – it's easy. Click with your mouse at the beginning of the text you want to report to AOL and while you hold the mouse button down, drag the pointer to the end of the text.

Now, hold down the Ctrl key and press C, then click with the mouse in the box on the trouble reporting form, and press Ctrl and V to paste the highlighted text.

And that's all there is to it!

Whether it's finding out the answers to common questions, checking what you can and can't do, or taking Connie's quick tour of AOL, the Member Services section is there to help you make the most of AOL. And remember, it's always just a click away, via the Help button on your AOL toolbar.

By now, we hope you should be feeling a little more confident about how to move around AOL and how to get help if you need it, so let's move on and take a look at some of the things that make up the AOL experience.

3

The AOL Experience

Using AOL is about much more than just sending and receiving email. There's a wealth of information available, as well as people to meet and things to buy.

In this chapter, you can find out all about the different ways that AOL provides for you to chat and swap messages with other people online.

You'll also find out how to shop, look for the information that you want with just a few mouse clicks, and track down additional help from AOL's Member Services team if you need it.

There's even information on how you can use AOL to play all the latest music and video clips that you download from the Net – including the much talked about MP3.

We've also included more information on AOL's email service, so you can learn how to send and receive messages that are much more than just a few lines of text, with pictures, sounds and more.

If you're already used to using AOL, you might not need to spend too much time on this chapter – but take a look anyway. You never know – you might pick up some handy new tips.

3.1 An introduction to chat

An online service like AOL isn't just about looking up useful information. You've almost certainly heard the Internet described as like a massive library, but that's not quite right. In a library, no one speaks. In the online world, everyone can have a voice – and it's often pretty noisy.

All the facts and information you want can be right at your fingertips – but most people would probably prefer a good chinwag over a pint of beer or a cup of tea to an evening in the reference section.

Chat is a huge part of what people do on the Internet. You've already looked at email, so what's the difference? And isn't it all just something that only people with no friends do?

Let's get that misconception out of the way right away. Chatting to people on the Internet is for everyone, from kids to grandparents. You can chat to people who might help you professionally, or get advice on dealing with a particular illness, or swap jokes with people around the world, discuss politics or the death penalty, or simply just chat for the hell of it.

So what is chat, then?

OK, if you're convinced by that, you'll want to know what it's all about, and how it is different from email.

Well, with email, you send a message, usually just to a single person, and wait for them to reply, and then send a reply to that, and so on. Of course it's much quicker than using the post, but it's still not that quick.

Chatting online can be much more immediate. In AOL's chat rooms, you can type a comment, press the Enter key, and it'll appear on the screens of everyone else in the chat room immediately. Other people can read your comment and maybe they'll pay no attention, or maybe they'll write something themselves. Perhaps what they write strikes you as funny, so you say so. Before you know it, you're having a conversation – the only difference is that instead of talking, you're typing, with as many as twenty-two other people at the same time – or even more in larger chat rooms.

There's another type of chat, too, called Instant Messaging. While a chat room is shared with lots of people, and everyone can see what you're typing, an Instant Message, or IM as people call them, is private. The only people who can see what's in it are the sender and the receiver.

You might, for example, see a comment from someone in a chat room that makes you think they work in the same business as you. Instead of having to ask in public, where everyone can see you, you can send them an IM, and wait for a reply. Sometimes you might find that there appears to be nothing much happening in a chat room, but in fact, lots of the people may be chatting to each other privately. Don't worry though – they're probably not talking about you!

AOL's going to add another new way of chatting soon, called Voice IM, where you can send a spoken message to another user too – so if you have friends and relatives a long way away, you can hear their voices at the same time as you're typing messages to them.

Finally, there's one way of exchanging comments with people that's not quite so immediate. Message boards are areas where you can post a message, just by typing it into your computer, and then other people can come along and read what you've said. They can post a response, or start a discussion about something else.

For now, we're going to concentrate on chat rooms and Instant Messages, which are the best way to get started with meeting new people on AOL. You can read about Message boards later on in this chapter (*3.7, Message boards*).

Let's get chatting

Now you know what it's all about, how do you get into it? One place to start is in the News Chat room – even if you can't think of how to start a conversation, you'll be sure to see someone talking about something you've seen on the news, or read in the newspaper. There are plenty of other chat areas on AOL, but they all work in the same way – so if you don't fancy joining in the cut and thrust of current affairs, take a look at the keyword **Quick Chat**, and see what other chat rooms in the list take your fancy.

Fig. 3.1
Quick Chat screen

If you want to go to any of the chats listed here, all you need to do is double click on the name. If, on the other hand, you want to join us in the News Chat area, then simply hold the Ctrl key, press K and then type the keyword News Chat into the box that appears. Whichever room you decide to go to, they all look very much the same.

Fig. 3.2
News chat room

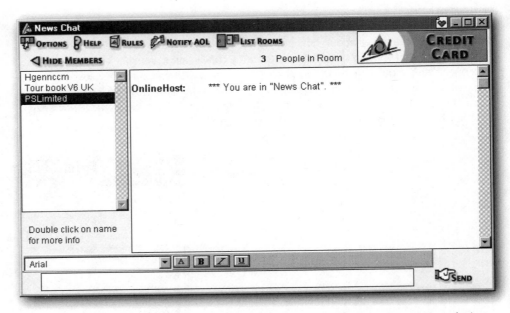

At the top of the screen is the name of the chat room. It will usually give you an idea of what sort of things you can expect to be discussed in a chat room. Before we start chatting, though, let's look around and explain what you'll see on the screen.

There are three main areas in any AOL chat room – they all look very similar. The main part of the page is taken up by the chat itself. You'll see the words that people have written appear at the bottom of the area, and move up as more people make comments. As well as comments you might also see some messages from the AOL chat system, telling you when people have joined or left the chat room.

To the left of the screen is a list of names, which shows you who's in the room at the moment. You can scroll up and down the list to see who's there. After you've been using AOL for a while, you'll probably start to recognise people who you chat to regularly, so you might want to look at the list of people in a room to see if any of your online friends are there.

Remember the special names we told you about earlier on? When you see someone in the list of users with a name beginning GuideUK or UKHost, they're someone on the AOL team, of volunteers, whom you can ask for help and assistance. They won't mind you asking them a question, either in the chat room or by sending them an Instant Message.

Right at the bottom of the chat screen is a blank area where you can type your comments. Just write what you want to say, and then press the enter key. You can type around two lines at a time – 128 letters, to be exact – and then AOL will beep to let you know you've written too much.

Of course, you can type something, press enter, then type some more, and so on, sending lots of lines to the chat room. But before you do that, remember that other people are in the room too, and your lines will be appearing in the middle of their conversations, so try not to flood the chat room with your own comments. No one likes someone who doesn't let anyone get a word in, after all!

Just like when you're writing an email, you can use different sized letters or colours in a chat room too. The controls for that are right above the area where you type your comments, and they work in exactly the same way. So, if you can use bold or coloured type in your word processor, you know how to do it in a chat room.

Now you know enough about the chat room to start talking to people, but what about the other buttons on the screen?

First, above the list of members, you'll see an arrow and the words **Hide Members**. Click on the arrow and the list of members will disappear, so there's more space to read the comments in the chat room. If you've hidden the list, the arrow will change direction and the label will read Show Members – click again to see the list.

Chat room options
Across the top of the chat page are five more buttons, **Options, Help, Rules, Notify AOL** and **List Rooms**.

When you click on the Options button, you'll see a menu appear with lots of options, which can let you go directly to many of the different chat-related parts of AOL. For now though, we're just interested in the Chat Preferences. Select that and a screen like this will pop up.

Fig. 3.3
Chat Preferences

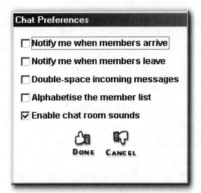

Each of the options here lets you control parts of the chat room. Just click to put a check in the box next to an option to turn it on, or clear the box to turn it off.

The first two options control the lines in the chat room that appear to be from someone called OnlineHost. That's really just the AOL computer, and it tells you when someone has joined the room or left it, along with the name of that person.

Next, you can choose to double-space Incoming Messages. That means that AOL will add extra blank lines between each line in the chat room, which some people find makes them easier to read.

You can also choose to alphabetise the list of members. Yep, it's a horrible word – there wasn't enough space to say 'List members in alphabetical order' but that's what it means, and if you're looking out for a particular person, it's probably easier to select it.

Finally, you can enable sounds in the chat room. That means that people will be able to make your computer play sounds by typing in the chat room. It can be pretty noisy sometimes, not to mention confusing, so you might want to turn this option off.

If your computer tells you you've got post, and there's none there, it's likely you're in a chat room. Look at what's been typed recently, and you'll probably see someone's typed a strange looking incantation, like {S gotmail.wav, which tells AOL to play the You've Got Post sound.

That's the chat preferences done. Now, let's take a quick look at the other buttons. The **Help** button displays a short piece of information about chat rooms and how they work, while the **Rules** button will take you to AOL's Member Services page, where you can read about the Conditions of Service and find answers to common questions about what you can and can't do.

If someone's being disruptive in a chat room, perhaps by making rude comments, or flooding the chat room with nonsense so that it's hard to read real messages, then you can use the **Notify AOL** button. In fact, the screen that this button brings up is the same one that you see if you visit the **trouble** keyword, which we explained in *Chapter 2 (2.1, First steps)*.

The last button, **List Rooms**, is the way that you can move to other chat rooms on AOL. When you click on it, you'll see a list of other chat rooms – though the list looks different depending on where on AOL you're chatting.

You could see a screen showing categories of rooms on the left, and the names of rooms on the right. Sometimes, especially if you're chatting in one of AOL's channels, you'll see a list of rooms in the same area. Clicking the **More** button will take you to a similar screen.

Both types of screen let you click once on a room and then use a button – labelled **Who's Chatting** or **Who's Here**, to see a list of the people in the room. You can click **Chat Now** or **Go** to move into a room that you've highlighted, or you can just double click on the name of a room.

There are some other things you can do with chat rooms too, like creating one of your own, but we'll look at those later, when we cover more advanced chat. Now, let's move on and take a look at Instant Messages, which are one of AOL's most popular features (*3.8, Advanced chat*).

The best way to get started with Instant Messages is to double click on someone in the list of users for a chat room – either when you're in the chat room, or when you've asked AOL for a list of the people in a room.

Fig. 3.4
User double clicked

If you don't want to speak to someone right away, AOL gives you the opportunity of checking their profile. Click the button and if they've created one, you'll be shown their user profile. That's usually just a short piece of information about themselves, but it might make you think they're worth speaking with.

You can also click the box at the bottom of the page here if you want to ignore someone.

Profiles are one of the ways people find friends to talk with on AOL. You can find out how to create your own profile in Chapter 5. It's a good idea to make one when you feel more comfortable about using AOL – some people won't respond to Instant Messages if you don't have a profile, since they don't know whom they'll be speaking with (5.2, Finding people on AOL).

To speak with someone, all you need to do is click on the **Send IM** button, and a page will pop up for you to type your comment. A simple Hello is probably the best way to get started.

Instant Messages

Instant messages are quick and simple. If you know the name of someone, you don't have to find them in a chat room to speak with them. You can just click the **IM** icon in the **People** button at the top of the AOL screen and a page like this will appear.

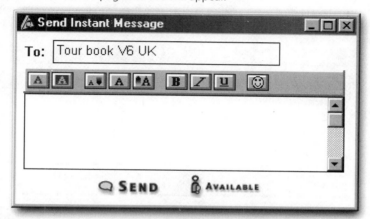

Fig. 3.5
Send IM screen

To send a message to someone when this screen appears, all you need to do is type their screen name in the box labelled To, then click in the main area and type your message.

If you chose to send a message to someone from a chat room list, then their name will already have been filled in for you, and you'll just have to type your message. You can use effects like different sized letters, or coloured text, by using the small buttons just above where you're typing – just the same as when you're composing an email.

At the bottom of the page, there are two buttons. When you've typed your message you can click on the **Send** button and AOL will deliver it to the person whose screen name you entered. Of course, they might not be connected to AOL, or they might have turned off Instant Messages, so if you're going to send a long message, it's a good idea to use the second button. That's labelled **Available**, and you can click on it to see if the other person is able to receive your IM at the moment.

Fig. 3.6
Available for IM screen

You'll see a short message telling you if you will be able to send them a message; just click on **OK** and carry on.

What happens when you receive a message? Firstly, your computer will make a special noise so that you know you've received one. And then the message will appear on your screen, looking a little like this:

Fig. 3.7
Incoming IM

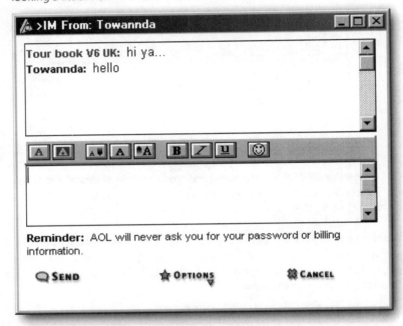

Below the text from the other person, you can just type your own response, and click on **Send**. Hey presto! You're having a conversation with someone else. If you don't want to respond, click on the **Cancel** button and the page will disappear.

Right at the bottom of the page are two extra options. If you click on the one marked **Options**, this will display three more options. AOL will display any information that the user has filled in about themselves, so you can get an idea of who you're chatting with.

Below that is another button labelled **Notify AOL**. You should use this message if someone sends you an offensive IM or tries to ask for your password.

AOL staff will never ask you to confirm your password or billing information via an Instant Message or an email. If anyone attempts to get this information, even if they say your account will be terminated if you don't respond, ignore them. Use the Notify AOL button to let AOL staff know that someone is trying to obtain confidential information.

When you click on the button, this screen will appear. You can add extra information in the space provided – you don't need to copy the message itself.

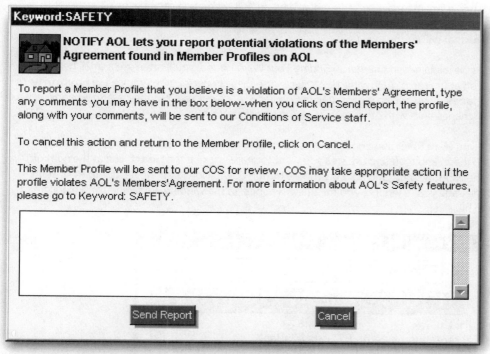

Fig. 3.8
Notify AOL/IM screen

You might, for example, want to include comments about what chat room you were in, if you think that the message you received was a response to comments you made in the chat room.

While you're chatting
Instant Messages are mostly, well, instant. Within a couple of seconds of typing your message, it will appear on your friend's screen. You'll see your messages and theirs in the top half of the Instant Message window, with the screen name at the start of each line, so you can see who said what.

Sometimes, however, the AOL system does get busy, and it may take a little while longer for your message to appear on the screen. When this happens, your mouse pointer will change, to let you know that the system is busy. Don't worry – your message will still appear.

One last word on Instant Messages – you don't have to restrict yourself to sending words. If you've found something on AOL or on the Internet that you like, you can tell someone about it in an IM – and even include a link, so that they can click on the highlighted text, and they'll be taken right to the area that you've been raving about. You might, perhaps, be telling your sister in Atlanta that you've found an area on AOL where she can buy the plane ticket to visit you cheaply, and rather than explain how to find it on AOL's menus, you can send a link that will do the job for you.

As we explained in *Chapter 2, Finding Your Way Around,* you'll often see a small heart icon at the top of AOL windows. You can use these to personalise AOL via the **Favourite Places** menu, which is explained in *Chapter 5, AOL and You*, but they're also a handy way to exchange links with other users (*5.4, Customising AOL*).

If you want to tell someone about something in an Instant Message, just type a message to them, and then find the area you want to share, click on the **Heart** icon at the right of the window's title, and hold the mouse button down. Now drag the heart into the Instant Message you're writing, and the title will appear in the window, underlined and highlighted in blue.

Fig. 3.9
IM with link

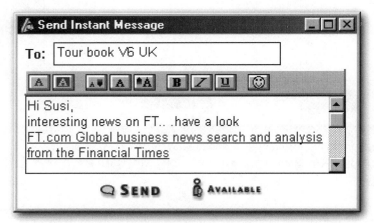

When someone receives your message, they'll see the same highlighted text, and they can click on it to go directly to the same area you were looking at.

Instant Messages and the Internet

With AOL, you're not restricted to exchanging Instant Messages with people who are signed on to AOL. Thanks to a program called AIM – AOL Instant Messenger – people who don't have an AOL account can swap IMs, both with AOL users and with other AIM users (*8.3, AIM*).

You can find out more about using AIM in *Chapter 8*, but for now we'll mention it because there's one way in which it differs from talking with other AOL users. You can send a message to an AIM user just like you would to an AOL user. You just need to know their AIM screen name.

When you receive a message from an Internet user, however, it won't appear on your screen immediately. Instead you'll receive a 'Knock knock' message.

If you click on the **Yes** button, then the message will appear in the usual way, and you can carry on chatting. When you don't know who the message is from – or the name suggests that it might not be too pleasant – you can click on the **No** button, and AOL will automatically ignore any more messages from that user.

Remember that AOL's Parental Controls can also block Instant Messages. If you've created screen names for your children, you should review carefully the options that allow you to control who can send them IMs.

Now you know all there is to know about chatting with Instant Messages and in chat rooms, let's move on to look at some of the other things you can do on AOL.

3.2 Shopping on AOL

When you're not working, or chatting with friends, what are you most likely to be doing? Perhaps it's sleep – but that's about the only area where AOL can't help you. However, if you're not sleeping, there's a pretty good chance you might be shopping.

AOL can help you to make the most of your shopping, whether it's saving time on the weekly slog, or making sure you get the best deals when you're looking for those little luxuries. And if you have opted for **AOL Flat Rate** you don't have to worry about how long it takes.

Flat Rate

A few clicks of the mouse, and you'll have flowers delivered to take for the hostess, a bottle of wine to accompany dinner, and a CD for the birthday guest.

A word about security
But what about security? Isn't all this rather dangerous? Firstly, let's dispel that myth. The technology that is used on the Internet can make your card details very safe. The biggest problem is more likely to be whether or not you trust the people you're doing business with – and that's where AOL comes in.

By providing a special shopping area, you can be confident that all the shops featured in it have satisfied AOL that they'll treat your information properly and securely, and meet the right standards of customer service.

What's more, before you fret about security on the Internet, remember that it takes a lot of work to sniff out a single piece of information that's sent, amongst the many millions – and then to turn that into a credit card number. Compared to other types of shopping, shopping on the net is pretty safe. In short, shopping on AOL is safe, and secure – and probably a lot more secure than many other things you'll do with your credit card.

What's in store?
Later on in this book, we'll be looking in more detail at the **Shop@AOL** channel, but let's explain a little more here about what sort of things you can expect when you decide to visit the online store.

Shopping

You'll find the AOL shopping area at the keyword **Shopping**, and unlike a mall where you may have to wander round for ages to find the shop that you're interested in, you'll find that everything's organised into clear simple categories. There's no more traipsing past dozens of fashion shops to find the gadget that you want.

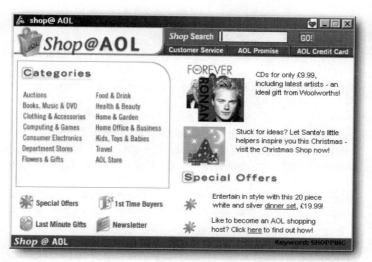

Fig. 3.10
Shop@AOL main screen

There are categories in Shop@AOL for Food and Drink; Clothing and Accessories; Books, Music and DVDs; Consumer Electronics; Online Auctions; Computing; Toys and Games; Travel; Department Stores; Office and Business; Flowers and Gifts; Home and Garden and Health and Beauty. Within those categories, you'll find specially selected stores, and most of the things that you might want to buy.

What's more, AOL is the world's leading Internet service provider and works closely with Shop@AOL partners to provide online shoppers with a high-quality service, security and peace of mind when shopping online.

And if you're unhappy with the way a shop has behaved, all the details of how to contact them to resolve the problem are just a click away. Even better, if you still can't sort things out, AOL has a special email address and a freephone number that you can use. We'll do everything we can to help you with your order. Just try doing that at your local shopping centre!

Who's there?
Of course, one of the important things about shopping online is who's there to sell you things. If you wandered into a shopping centre and didn't recognise the names on any of the stores, you might feel a little disorientated.

The same's true when you're shopping online, and of course if you've never heard of someone, why should you be expected to give them your credit card details? That's why AOL has worked with lots of the names that you know, to make sure that you can buy from people you trust, and with complete confidence.

Ok, so who is there to shop with? There are lots of stores, and more are being added to Shop@AOL all the time. But how about Comet for your electrical goods? Or Woolworths? If you want gifts, there are flowers from Interflora and chocolates from Thorntons.

You can get a mobile from Carphone Warehouse, and clothes from Kays and Lands End, or stock up on stationery from Viking.

As well as established names like those, you'll find AOL has some of the most well know names in online shopping too, like Lastminute.com, Perfuma.com and Ebay. These are just a small selection of the great shops you will find featured on Shop@AOL.

When you buy online then, you're not just dealing with a small store you've never heard of. Shop@AOL really is bringing you the best stores and the best service.

There's more!
Shop@AOL isn't just about making sure you can get to the shops any time you like, 24 hours a day. It's also about making sure you never forget anything, and you always know where the best bargains are.

For example, with the shopping newsletter, you can have the latest updates and news of special offers delivered to your mailbox regularly – so even if you don't actually shop online all the time, you'll still know where to go when it comes to finding that essential gift.

Fig. 3.11
Gift Reminder Service

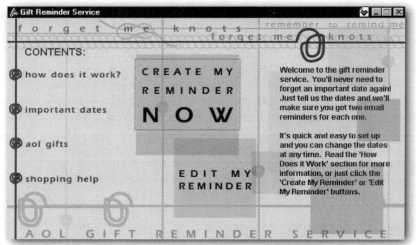

Gifts are one of the most popular things that people buy when they shop online – and with AOL you'll never have to suffer the embarrassment of a missed birthday or anniversary again. The

Gift Reminder Service will remember all those important dates for you, and make sure it alerts you in plenty of time, so you can order the perfect present (*4.12, Gift Reminder Service*).

There are guides, too, so if you're not sure about how everything works, or you just want tips on the best way to shop, all the information you need is at your fingertips.

That even includes helping you out when you forgot to use the Gift Reminder Service and you need something in a hurry. AOL provides a handy last minute area, and you can see at a glance how long each shop takes to deliver.

What more could you want? Even if you're sceptical, try it – you could be surprised at how simple and straightforward shopping online really can be.

Buying online with AOL

There are two ways you can buy things on AOL. The simplest is by using a pop-up. That's a special window that appears on your screen, with details of a special offer from AOL. The other is by using an online shop. Let's start by guiding you through using a pop up to take advantage of one of AOL's special offers.

Fig. 3.12
Example popup

When you see a screen like this appear, you can simply click **No Thanks** if you don't want to take advantage of the offer. But if you do, it's really simple! With a pop-up offer, you don't need to enter any credit card details at all. Since the offers are from AOL, they can be billed to your AOL account, just like your monthly subscription.

To find out more, click on the **Tell Me More** or **Yes Please** button, and you'll see another screen appear, giving you a little more information, like this.

Fig. 3.13
Popup order screen

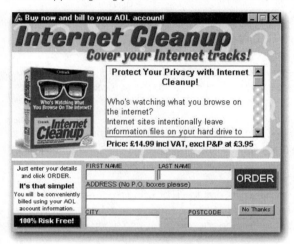

You can read details of the offer here, and if you decide that you're not interested after all, click the **No Thanks** button, and you won't have spent anything.

If, on the other hand, you do want to order, all you need to do is fill in the details at the bottom of the screen, to say where you want to have things delivered. Then, just click the **Order** button, and the amount will be added to your next AOL bill. That's all there is to it!

Of course, not everything you want to buy is going to be available through a pop-up offer, so you'll have to visit the online shops to find out the full range of what's available.

Making your first purchase from the AOL Store

Later on in this book we'll tell you more about the different stores that you'll find on AOL, and how to use the Shopping features like the Gift Reminder Service to make sure that you never forget an important date again.

First, though, we'll show you how to make your first purchase from the AOL Store. Once you've bought something the first time, you'll see how simple it can be, and then there's nothing stopping you – except of course how much money you have!

The AOL Store is the part of Shop@AOL where you can buy AOL merchandise, like T shirts and mouse mats, as well as selected books or software for your computer. The other shops that you can access on AOL work in a very similar way, though some of them will have small differences – but don't worry! Once you've bought from one shop online, you'll have no trouble finding your way around another one.

To get started, choose Shop@AOL from the Services menu – just click on the small triangle next to the word Services at the top of your screen, and select **Shopping** from the menu. You can also click the **Shopping** button on the toolbar, towards the top right corner of the screen.

Here's the main screen. You'll see there's a deal of the day, and some other highlighted special offers. For now, we're interested in AOL's own shop, so click on **AOL Store**.

Fig. 3.14
AOL Store main screen

This is the front page of AOL's own shop. As you can see, there's a **Deal of the Day**, which you can click to add to your shopping basket right away, and featured products. If you click on them, you'll see more details of each one, then you can decide if you want to buy them. There's also a search facility, and an A to Z list of all the products, as well as some of the recommended ones.

And, to make it easier to find things that you like, you can browse the store via Departments, like Gifts, PC Maintenance or Digital Imaging. Click on the Gifts department for example, and you'll see a screen like this one.

Fig. 3.15
Product details

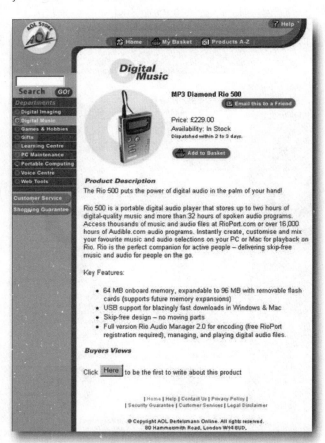

In each department, you'll see a screen like this, showing the goods on offer. If you know exactly what you want, you can click to add it straight to your shopping basked, or you can click for more details if you're still not sure. So, scroll through the list to find something you want to buy, and click to view the details.

Pretty nice, isn't it? We like it so much we're going to order one. For some products, like computer programs, remember to read the details carefully – you don't want to order something that's not compatible with your computer, for example. The product page has a button near the bottom so that you can add your comments about each product, and there's one near the top that lets you tell friends about something you've found – perhaps you could use that to drop hints around birthday time!

If you'd like to go back to the list of products, just click on the name of one of the departments at the side of the screen, or use the Product A-Z button at the top.

You'll also see a button labelled **Add to Basket** next to the product, which is what you need to click to order it.

A shopping basket is what you use when you're shopping online, just like you'd use a shopping trolley in a supermarket. You can add things to it, or take them out if you change your mind. When you've chosen everything you want, you go to the checkout to pay.

Shopping online is really very similar to using a supermarket – the only difference is that the trolley doesn't exist in real life. It's a set of details of what you want to order, stored on AOL's computers. Oh, it also always goes in the direction you want, which is a definite plus over supermarket trolleys!

The different stores within AOL's shopping area each use shopping baskets of their own. You have to do your shopping in one area, pay for your goods, and do the same in another one. Think of it as like a shopping centre, where you can't leave a store with things you haven't bought.

So, you want to buy the product you're looking at? Click on the button that says **Add to Basket**. In some stores, it might say **Order** instead, but don't worry – although some stores look slightly different, they all work in a very similar way. Here's what the AOL Store's shopping basket looks like.

Fig. 3.16
Shopping basket

OK, how many do you want? On this screen, you can click in the box next to each product to select how many you'd like. As well as the product you just chose, anything you've already chosen from the AOL store will be shown in your basket too.

If you just want to remind yourself of what you've bought, you can also reach this screen directly by clicking on the **My Basket** button at the top of the AOL Store screens.

If you decide that you don't want to buy something after all, click the word Delete next to it. When you've made changes, click **Update Basket** to recalculate the total price.

If you want to go back to the shops, just click on **Continue Shopping**, or pick another department to visit.

After you've chosen all the things that you want, and checked you have the right things in your shopping basket, it's time to go to the checkout, just like in a real shop. So, click on the **Continue to Checkout** button.

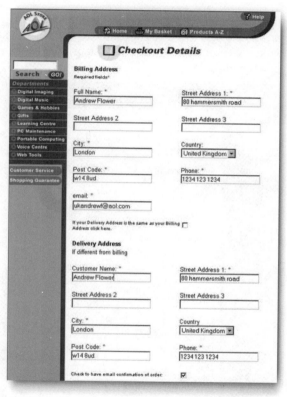

Fig. 3.17
Billing and delivery screen

On this screen, you need to enter the address for the credit card that you're using.

Remember that unless you give the same address as the credit card bills are delivered to, your order can't be processed.

You'll notice that some of the blank spaces on the screen have a red star next to them – you have to fill those in for your Billing Address. When you've entered all the details, you can choose whether you want the goods delivered to the same address, or to somewhere else.

If you click the box to use the same address for both, then you don't need to fill the delivery details; otherwise, enter them in the appropriate boxes.

Next, click to put a tick in the box if you'd like to receive an email confirmation of your order, and scroll down to the bottom of the screen, where you'll see a **Continue to Checkout** button. Click it to go on to the next stage of ordering, where you need to fill in your payment details.

Fig. 3.18
Credit card details screen

This screen is where your card information is entered. You need to fill in all the details, exactly as they appear on the card. You'll also see a summary of the billing and delivery details you entered on the last screen, and the total amount that will be billed to your card.

To change the address details you gave, click on the text that says **Click here to change Customer Details**. If you change your mind and want to carry on shopping, or change the details of anything in your basket, use the next link, labelled **Click here to view ordered products**.

If everything is in order, fill in the details of your card – and make sure you don't forget any of the extra details required by some cards, like the issue number, or start date.

> When you click the **Checkout** button on this screen, your order will be confirmed and sent to AOL. You will not be able to cancel it after clicking on **Checkout**.

After completing your order, you'll see a screen like this one.

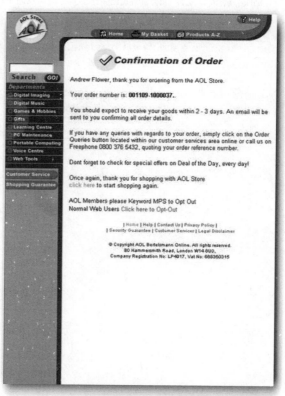

Fig. 3.19
Order confirmation screen

Your order number appears on this screen, which you'll need if you have any queries, and you can also see the phone number for AOL's Customer Service team.

If you didn't choose to have an email confirmation sent to you, it's a good idea to print out this screen, so that you have a handy note of all the information for your order.

Congratulations! You've just bought something online for the first time. It wasn't too hard, was it?

As we said earlier, some of the stores featured on AOL may work in a slightly different way, but if you've managed to follow our example here, you won't be in for any big surprises, whether shopping on AOL or the Internet.

Remember that AOL has its own shopping promise to ensure you have a safe and secure shopping experience. when you shop online using the stores featured on AOL's shopping channel, which have all been chosen to provide you with good service, fair prices and the best security.

You can read more about the stores featured on AOL, and find out how to use the Gift Reminder Service in *Chapter 4, AOL Channels* (*4.12, Shopping*).

Now, though, let's move on and look at some more of the useful tools of AOL, with an explanation of how to find the information that you're looking for.

3.3 Information on AOL

Chat and shopping are important parts of the AOL experience, but there's a lot more that you can do online.

AOL is packed full of useful information, including reference material, travel details, maps and literature. Whatever you want, it's there somewhere. In this section, we'll show you how to get started with finding the information that you want, whatever it is.

We'll also show you how to manage files that you can download from AOL. There are lots ready for you to look at, including programs to enhance your computer, and even music and video clips – which you can play using the AOL software.

An encyclopedia on your desktop

We'll begin with one of the main AOL areas for looking up information, the online reference section.

Reference

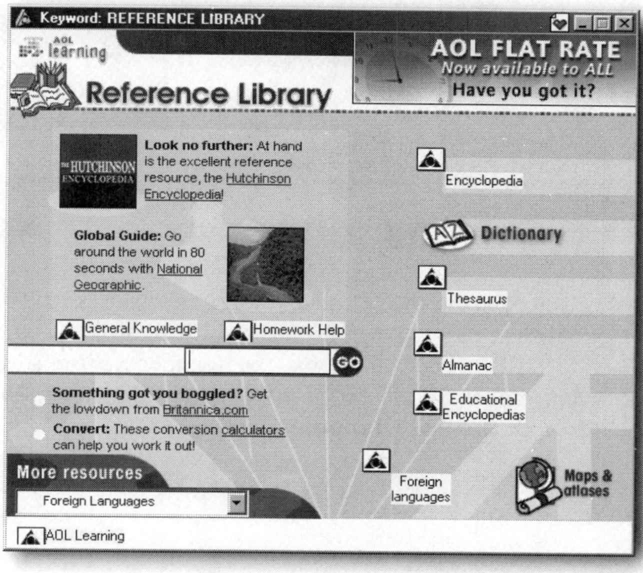

Fig. 3.20
Reference screen

You can reach this screen by choosing **Reference Library** from the **Places** menu on AOL. If you want to find out the sort of facts that you'd normally look up in an encyclopedia, this is the place to go. From this page you can go directly to some of the main reference tools on AOL, like the *Hutchinson Multimedia Encyclopedia*, or the *New Oxford Dictionary*.

It's a little like your own bookshelf, and all you have to do to open one of the books is click its name with the mouse. Each of the sections will look slightly different, but they all work in a similar way.

Let's delve into the *Hutchinson Encyclopedia*, and see what it has to say about hovercraft.

Fig. 3.21
**Hutchinson
opening screen**

When you open the encyclopedia, you'll see a screen like this one, with highlighted information at the bottom of the page. You can use this page as a starting point if you just want to browse through the entries, but for now, we're interested in hovercraft, so just type the word into the box labelled Search for Entries, and then click with the mouse where it says **Search the Encyclopedia**.

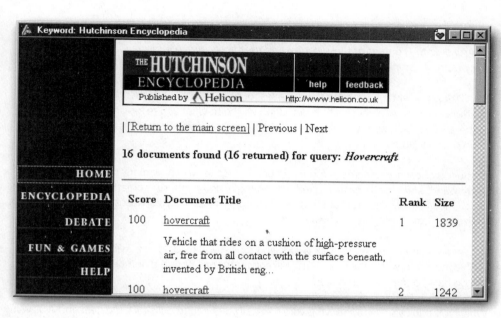

Fig. 3.22
Search results

AOL Search

Searching AOL is easy. If you've already used the toolbar to enter a keyword, then you're halfway to using AOL Search. When you want to look for something, for example Classic Cars, just click the button marked **Search**, which you will find to the right of the box. Next type a few words into the box that says 'Enter keywords or Web addresses here', and the click **Go**.

If you're looking for a particular phrase, you should put quotation marks around it. Typing 'Classic Cars' will make sure that items containing that phrase appear higher up the list than ones that may contain only one of the words.

There's one important difference between this and typing in a keyword – when you want to search, don't press the Enter key after typing the words you're looking for. Instead, click with the mouse on the button marked **Search**, which you'll find to the right of the box.

After a short pause, a screen will appear with the results of your search.

Remember that although AOL Search finds pages on the Internet for you, AOL has no control over the content of those pages, and they may contain information that you feel is inappropriate, or inaccurate.

You'll see a percentage to the left of the titles for each result. The higher the percentage, the more relevant AOL thinks the information will be to what you're looking for. The title of the article is highlighted in blue, and clicking it will take you there, whether it's an article on AOL or a Web page.

At the top of each list, there are more numbers. These tell you how many matching items have been found, and which ones are listed. For example, you might see something like (1–5 of 79) which means that AOL has found a total of 79 items matching your words, and numbers one to five are shown in the list at the moment.

To see more entries in the list, click **Next**, and the list you're looking at will be updated. When you've moved forward, the word Back will appear to the left of the numbers, so that you can go back to the previous screen.

When you think you've found what you want, all you need to do is click the item and AOL will take you there. What could be simpler?

More tricks with AOL Search

AOL search can do a lot more than just find information on AOL and the Internet for you. It has its own main screen, which you can reach by clicking the **Search** button on the toolbar without typing anything into the Keyword box.

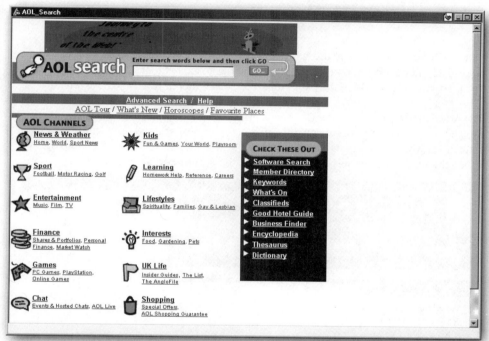

Fig. 3.23
AOL Search main screen

As you can see, there's a section on this page for each of AOL's Channels, with a few of the highlights of that channel listed underneath it. You can click any of the words in blue to go directly to that part of AOL, which makes this screen a good place to start exploring if you want to take a wander round by yourself.

Down the right-hand side of the screen, you'll also see some other highlighted areas, including Software Search, Member Directory, Good Hotel Guide, Business Finder, Thesaurus and Dictionary.

To access any of these areas, all you need to do is click them and you'll be taken right there. Although each of these areas will work slightly differently, they all provide their own help and advice on using them – and if you managed to look up information in the Hutchinson Encyclopedia earlier on in this chapter, then you should have no problems with them.

One of the areas that's most useful, especially if you want to make sure you're getting the most from your computer, is the Software Search. Using this, you can access literally thousands of files that you can download to your computer, including programs to look at different types of picture, new typefaces for your word processor and even games. We'll cover that in more detail a little later on in this section.

Advanced searching on AOL
While AOL Search is simple to use, simple isn't always best, of course. Sometimes you'll type in a word, click **Search** and end up with a list of things to look at that's as long as your arm. By the time you've looked at all the pages that AOL Search found, you could have retired!

The Advanced Search facility in AOL Search lets you give more details about what you're looking for, so that you can cut down the number of results returned. To start using it, just click the **Search** button on the toolbar without typing any words into the Keyword box. When the AOL Search home page appears, click the **Advanced Search** button.

Fig. 3.24
AOL Advanced search

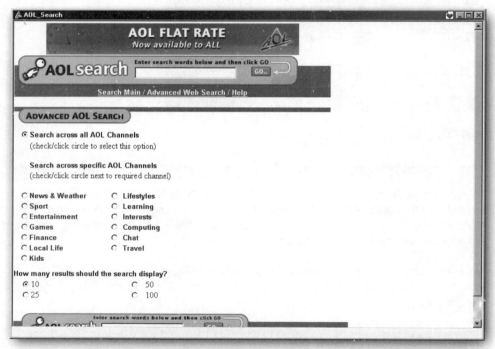

On this screen, you can choose to search the whole of AOL, or just information on a particular channel.

If you'd like to search a single channel, just click the small circle next to its name, or click next to **Search across all AOL Channels** if you want to search all the information on AOL.

Underneath the list of channels, you can say how many results you want to see at a time. You can select 10, 25, 50 or 100 results. AOL Search will still find the same amount of results, but this just says how many you want to see on a page before you have to click **Next** to see more.

When you've chosen how many results you want to see in one go, type the word or phrase you're looking for into the box labelled AOL Search (you can use either the one at the top of the page or the one at the bottom) and click the **Go** button.

You can also use a special advanced AOL Search to find information on the Internet, but for now we'll concentrate on information that's on AOL, which has all been specially selected by the AOL team of editors.

If you'd like to find out more about searching the Internet using the advanced functions in AOL Search, take a look at *Chapter 6, The Internet (6.2, Searching the Internet).*

Downloading files

As we've mentioned already, on AOL you can find thousands of files to download to your computer. There are games, programs that will let you listen to the MP3 music files that you can access on the Internet, typefaces to spice up your letters, and utilities to make your computer work better, or fix problems that have cropped up.

SWC

You'll find files that can be downloaded in lots of areas on AOL, including things like pictures of users in some of the chat rooms, but one of the most useful places is the Software Centre. You can reach it by clicking **Software Search** from the AOL Search main screen, or using the keyword **SWC**.

Wherever you find files on AOL, you download them in the same way, so we'll use the Software Centre to see how it's done.

Downloading files from the Internet works in a slightly different way, and you can read about it in Chapter 6, The Internet.

On the main screen of the Software Centre, you'll see buttons for different types of software, like Games, Macintosh Software and Windows Software. There's also a large button that you can use to search for software.

Let's start by looking at software for computers running Windows. Click **Windows** and you'll see a screen like this one, with more categories listed on the left and some highlighted categories or programs on the right.

Fig. 3.25
**Windows
software
download**

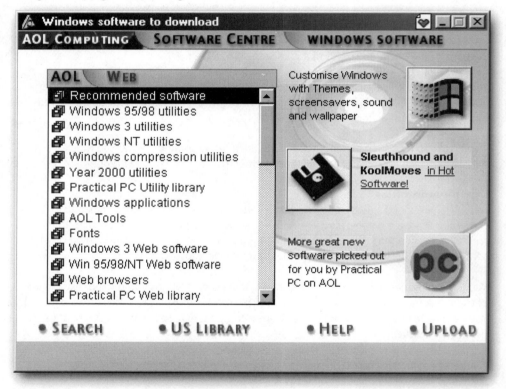

We'll start by taking a look at the Recommended Software category. Here you'll find some of the files that AOL's editors think are the must-haves for your computer. Just double-click any category to see the list of files that it contains.

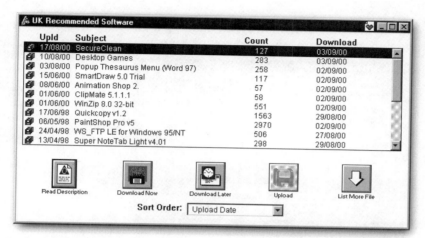

Fig. 3.26
**Windows files
list**

The list here shows the files in the category that you've selected. You can see the date the file was 'uploaded' which is when it was made available on AOL, a short description in the Subject column, and the number of people who've downloaded it so far.

Along the bottom of the screen are five buttons. To find out more about a particular file, you can double-click it, or click once and then click the **Read Description** button.

This is the description for a typical file. You'll see that there's a bit of information about it, including where it came from, how big it is, and how long it will take to download. The **Download Now** and **Download Later** buttons at the bottom of this screen do the same as the ones on the main file list screen. You can click **Related Files** to see other files that might be related to the one you're reading about.

Back on the file list, the **Download Now** button is the one to use if you decide that you'd like to transfer a copy of this file to your computer.

Remember that files you download could contain inappropriate comment, or may be infected with a virus. AOL makes every effort to check all the files on its computers for viruses, but you should always check files that you download, before opening them. You should use anti-virus software on your computer, and make sure that it's regularly updated.

When you click the **Download Now** button, you'll see a screen appearing asking where you want to save the file on your computer.

Fig. 3.27
Download save file box

Usually, all you'll need to do is click the **Save** button, but you can change the name of the file if you like, or the folder where it's going to be stored on your computer.

As the file is transferred to your computer, you'll see a progress box so you know roughly how much longer it will take. If you want to walk away and leave the computer, without worrying about running up your phone bill, click to put a check in the box labelled **Sign off after transfer**, and AOL will automatically disconnect when the file is safely on your computer. You can also click **Cancel** to stop the file transfer completely, or click **Finish Later** if you want to stop and carry on the file download another time.

When you click **Finish Later**, or if you use the **Download Later** button, the file will be listed in your Download Manager, which you can read about later on in this section.

The **Upload** button in the list of files only works in some areas of AOL. You can use it to make your own contribution to a file area, for example by submitting a picture of yourself to a members' gallery in one of AOL's Lifestyle areas.

The **List More** button displays more entries in the list of files to download – when you first look at a file list, AOL will list only the first 21 entries.

Finally on the **File List** screen, right at the bottom you'll see **Sort Order** followed by a menu with an arrow at the right. Click the arrow, and you can choose how you'd like the list of files to be sorted. You can choose **Upload Date**, **Subject**, **Download Date** and **Download Count**.

Searching for files

As well as browsing through the different categories of files in the Software Centre, you can search. You might be after a particular program, for instance, and want to access it, but you're not sure which area of AOL it's stored in.

You can search by clicking **Search for Software** from the main Software Centre Screen, or using the keyword **FileSearch**.

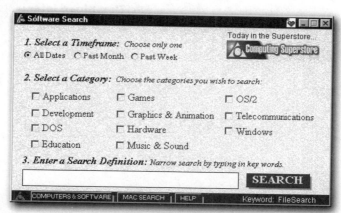

Fig. 3.28
**File search
screen**

The first step in finding the files you want is deciding how new you want it to be. You can click the circles at the top of the screen to choose from all files, files uploaded in the last month, or files uploaded in the last week.

Next you can choose what category of file you're looking for. Click to put a check mark in the box next to any of the categories that apply. You can choose more than one, for example **Applications and Graphics**.

Finally, type a few words that describe what you're looking for into the box at the bottom of the screen, and click the **Search** button. You might, for example, type the name of a program that you're looking for, or a word like fax for programs to help you use your computer as a fax machine.

When the search has finished, you'll see a list of files, just like the ones that appear when you browse through a section of the file library – but this time you'll know that they've been selected to fulfil your criteria.

Now you know how to download files from AOL's Software Centre – and the files you find in other places on AOL can be downloaded in just the same way.

What happens if you have lots of files that you want to download, though? Won't it be a bit tedious clicking the **Save** button to say where you want each one stored, and then watching while it's being downloaded?

Well, yes, it can be. And that's where the **Download later** button comes in – together with the **Download Manager**, which we'll look at in a moment.

First, though, let's look at one of the other great facilities in AOL – the Media Player.

3.4 The AOL Media Player

Media Player? What's that? Well, it's not anything to do with computers. Media here means electronic files that you've downloaded, in a range of formats, which can be played back to let you hear sounds or watch video clips.

AOL's built-in Media Player means that you don't have to mess around downloading a program just to play a file. If you've downloaded it from AOL or the Internet, then you'll be able to play it using the AOL Media Player.

To get technical for a moment, the AOL Media Player will play back Real System, QuickTime, MP3, Wav and most of the other major formats. Just try opening a file, and if it can't understand it, Media Player will tell you.

In fact, the AOL Media Player doesn't just let you listen to files that you've downloaded, it lets you create a playlist too. That's a list of the files you want to listen to, and the order you want to listen to them in. You can even have the same file in more than one list. Making a playlist is a bit like putting together a tape of your favourite songs, except you don't have to record them all again. You just tell AOL which ones you want to hear, and it fetches them for you.

So, let's take a look at how you play a song with the AOL Media Player – say you've just downloaded one of the hot MP3 sound samples of an up-and-coming band.

Fig. 3.29
File open

All you need to do is go to the **File** menu in AOL, and click **Open**. When this box appears, just find the file that you want on your hard disk. If you know what format the file is, you can make the list of available files shorter by choosing the appropriate type from the list at the bottom of the box – just click the arrow and select a type, like MP3 music files. Click the **Open** button when you've selected the file you want.

Fig. 3.30
**Media player
playing MP3**

This is what you'll see on your screen. As you can see, it's pretty straightforward, isn't it? The buttons use the same labels that you'll be familiar with from a tape recorder – just click the big play button and you'll start to hear the file that you've downloaded.

From left to right, the buttons are: **Beginning**, to take you to the start of a file; **Rewind**, to skip backwards; **Stop**; **Play**; **Pause**; **Fast forward**; and **End**, which takes you to the end. Simple, isn't it?

Playing a video clip is just as easy too. Once again, just choose **Open** from the File menu, and then select the file you'd like to view.

When you click **Play**, the video window will appear, and you'll see similar buttons at the bottom – though without the **Start** and **End** buttons. Of course, you won't see TV-quality pictures just yet, but as links to AOL and the Internet get faster, the pictures you can watch will be even better quality, and they won't take so long to download.

Playlists

Earlier we mentioned playlists. They're a great way to choose all the music that you'd like to listen to in one go – you can just make a list, and then leave AOL to play all the sounds for you. Once you've collected a few music files, you'll find playlists really invaluable.

To start creating one, open any sound clip in the Media Player, and then click the **My Playlist** link, which you'll see near the top of the Media Player.

Fig. 3.31
Playlist window

The playlist automatically includes the file that you opened. You'll see its name, and the time it will take to play. To add another file, just click the **Add Item** button and select another file, as if you were playing it.

Fig. 3.32
Playlist window, multiple files

As you add files, you'll see the list grow. If you'd like to change the order that the files will be played in, just click to highlight a file, and then use the up and down arrows to move it around in the list. Fed up with a track? Just delete it from the playlist by clicking it with the mouse and choosing the **Remove** button.

When you remove a file from your playlist, remember that you're not deleting it from your computer's disk. The file is still there – it just won't be included in the collection of songs that you're working with.

At the top of the window, the **Create a new Playlist** and **Load one of my Playlists** buttons let you manage playlists. Click the **Save** button and you can give your playlist a name, so that you can use it later.

Click **Create a new Playlist** and the list of files will be emptied, so you can start creating another one. You can use **Load one of my Playlists** to read a playlist file that you created earlier, if you'd like to change it.

And how about playing your list? It's simple. When you choose **Open** from the **File** menu, just click the name of the playlist file that you want to listen to. AOL Media Player will work through it from start to finish, and you'll hear each of the tracks in turn.

Now you know how to listen to all the great media files you can download, there's just one problem. Online music and video can be pretty good quality, especially the music, but the files are quite large.

Fortunately, AOL provides a handy way to keep track of what you've downloaded, and make it as easy as possible to let your computer get on with fetching the files you want, without you hanging around waiting. So, let's carry on with a look at the Download Manager.

3.5 The Download Manager

The Download Manager is the part of AOL that lets you organise all the files you've chosen to transfer from AOL to your computer. Instead of sitting and twiddling your thumbs each time you see a file that might be useful, like a new font for your computer, or a report that's been emailed to you, you can use the **Download Later** button and let AOL take care of it for you.

Clicking **Download Later** puts a file into a sort of 'to-do' list for the Download Manager, leaving you to carry on with your AOL session. When you want to collect the files, Download manager will fetch them all in one go for you, even if they're on different parts of AOL. You can even tell it to sign off when it's finished, which means you just start it up, and walk away. There's no need to sit and watch the PC downloading file after file and then hang up the phone yourself.

So, where do you find it? Simple. Just go to the **File** menu at the top left of the screen, and click **Download Manager**.

Before we get stuck into the explanation of how you use Download Manager, a word of warning: Remember that files you download could contain computer viruses or material you don't think is appropriate. AOL tries to ensure that none of the files in its library areas are infected with computer viruses, but you may still receive one via email or from the Internet. You should always make sure that your computer has an up-to-date anti-virus program installed on it, and check files for viruses before opening them.

Fig. 3.33
**Download
Manager
waiting**

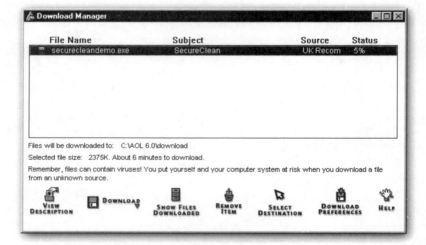

Downloading files with Download manager

This screen is really just an easier way of looking at the Files to be downloaded tab in your filing cabinet. You can find out more about using your Personal Filing Cabinet in *Chapter 5, AOL and You*, but here we'll tell you everything you need to know to download files efficiently from AOL (*5.5, Personal filing cabinet*).

On the main part of the screen, you'll see a list of the files waiting to be downloaded, and along the bottom is a row of buttons.

The first, **View Description**, will show you information about the file, if you found it on AOL, or open the email that it's attached to. By using this button, you'll be able to check what a file is if you've forgotten, before deciding that you really do want it.

Next, the **Download** button tells AOL that you want to start downloading files right now. Click it, and you'll see a bar displaying the progress as all the files are transferred to your computer.

What happens if you suddenly realise you need to make an important phone call while a load of files are downloading? No problem. Click the **Finish Later** button, and AOL will stop the download, but let you carry on whenever you want. Just sign off, and use your phone.

While files are being downloaded, you can also click **Cancel** to stop the download completely, but the file will remain in your download list.

And how about when you don't want to hang around for AOL to finish? All you need to do is click to put a tick in the box marked **Sign off after transfer**. Once the last file has been saved on your computer, AOL will automatically disconnect. So you could go to bed, for instance, and just leave the computer to it. All your files will be waiting for you in the morning when you get up.

View Description and **Download** are probably the two buttons you'll use most in the Download Manager, but there are a few more to tell you about.

Next to **Download**, the **Show Files Downloaded** button will take you to another screen which lists the files already transferred to your computer. We'll come back to that one in a moment after looking at the other options.

Click the **Remove Item** button when you've decided that you don't want to download a file after all – you need to select a file from the list with the mouse, and then AOL will delete it from the list of files for you to download.

The **Select Destination** button lets you choose where on your computer's disk you want a file to be saved when it's downloaded. Just click to select the file first, and then click here.

The box you see should look fairly familiar – it's the same type that you'll see when you choose to save a file in your word processor or spreadsheet program, for example. Just find your way to the folder where you want the file to be stored, and click the **Save** button.

If you don't select a location for a specific file, it will be stored in the default download directory. You can see where that is using the next option along, **Download Preferences**.

Fig. 3.34
**Download
Preferences**

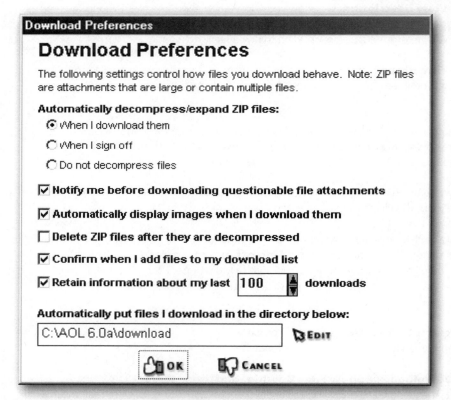

We'll explain more about the different options on this screen in *Chapter 5, AOL and you*. If you're not sure exactly what the options mean, don't worry. AOL will have chosen the most sensible ones for you when it was installed. The location where files are saved on your computer is the last entry on the screen (*5.4, Customising AOL*).

Files you've downloaded

When you click the **Show Files Downloaded** button on the Download Manager screen, you'll see a screen like this:

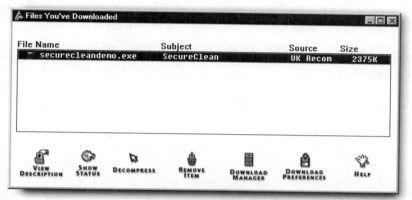

Fig. 3.35
Download Manager transferred

As you can see, the main part of the screen is the list of files, with a subject listed for each one, a location and the size. The subject shown for a file will either be the title it was given in one of AOL's file libraries, or the subject of the email address the file was attached to.

Just as with the main Download Manager screen, the **View Description** button will take you to the email message that accompanied the file, or to its description on AOL.

Click the **Show Status** button after you've selected a file, and a small message will pop up to tell you where the file was stored on your computer's disk.

Fig. 3.36
Status display

If you want help finding the file on your computer's hard disk, click the **Locate** button, and the folder containing the file will be opened for you.

Next along the screen is the **Decompress** button. Some of the files that you may download or be sent by email are compressed, to save space and allow a single file to contain many others. If the file that you downloaded is a compressed file – usually these have names ending in .ZIP – then click the file and then on the **Decompress** button to expand the file and turn it back into its constituent parts.

> *Unless you turned off the option in your preferences, AOL will automatically decompress files that you download. Using this button again will replace the files you decompressed with new copies from the compressed original.*

Remove Item will delete the downloaded file from the list in your download manager. It doesn't delete the file itself, just the list. You could use this option if you don't want other people with access to your computer to see what files you have downloaded.

Click **Download Manager** to go back to the Download Manager main screen, and **Download Preferences** to see the Preferences screen.

Finally, if you want to download a file a second time, just double-click it to be taken to the location where you found it originally, whether that's an email message or a file area on AOL. Once again, you'll be able to choose to download the file immediately, or click **Download Later** to put it into the Download Manager.

There you have it! With the Download Manager, it's easy to keep on top of the files that you want to fetch from AOL, and you don't even have to hang around waiting while they're transferred to your computer.

You can find out more about downloading files, including how to arrange to have them all collected at a particular time, in *Chapter 5, AOL and You* (*5.6, Automatic AOL*).

Now you know how to find information on AOL, whether it's an entry in an online encyclopedia, an article about a particular topic on one of AOL's Channels, or a file that might help improve the performance of your computer.

If you've been working through the book, you'll also have found out how to join in online chats and send Instant Messages too. That means that you know pretty much all the basics of AOL already!

With that in mind, let's carry on by taking a more detailed look at email.

3.6 Advanced email

We've already seen how you can send a simple email, read messages and reply to them, but AOL's email offers you much more than that, and you can have a lot of control over exactly who can email you, and sort all your messages according to who sent them, when they were sent, or what they're about.

In this chapter we'll show you how to manage your email more effectively, how you can make it look more professional, and how to keep track of email addresses.

All the features of AOL that we're going to cover in this section can be found on the **Email** menu, by clicking the arrow at the top of the **Email** button.

The Email screen

Let's go back to the main Email screen and start looking at some of the features we didn't cover last time. If you've come here straight away, then you should really skip back to *Chapter 2, Email basics*, and make sure you're familiar with the information covered there first.

You can reach this screen by clicking the icon marked **Read** at the left side of the **Email** button. As we explained, the tabs across the top let you see new messages, messages you've already read, and messages that you've sent to other people.

Fig. 3.37
Email screen

If you send and receive a lot of email, it can be tricky to find the message you want in the lists that are shown here. You can find things much quicker by telling AOL to sort the list.

The headings for each of the columns are actually buttons. When you first open the screen, the **Date** column will be white, with a little arrow next to it. That means that the messages are sorted by date at the moment. Click **Date** again, and the little arrow will turn upside down, sorting in the opposite direction – showing oldest messages first, rather than newer ones, or the other way round.

You can sort by email address instead, or by the subject of a message, or its type. Just click the appropriate column, and if you want to sort in the opposite order, just click the same column again.

The email address and subject are obvious, but what's the type? Well, the icons that AOL uses let you know right away what sort of message someone's sent you – whether it's just text, or if it has pictures embedded in it, or if there are files attached to it.

The screen shows the different icons. There's an ordinary envelope for messages that don't have any special things like pictures or attachments. If there are files attached to the message, you'll see an envelope with a floppy disk behind it, and for messages with pictures embedded in them there's an envelope with a little round disk. Old messages that you've already read will have a tick through them.

Types of messages

Before going on, let's take a closer look at the types of messages that you can send and receive with AOL.

Ordinary email messages just consist of text. When you're sending them to other AOL members, you can use the tools at the top of the **Write Email** screen to use different typefaces, put words in bold, or centre them. You can even change the colour of the letters or the background, like using coloured notepaper.

When you send a message to someone who's not using AOL, remember that they won't see any of these features – even if you tell AOL to use letters an inch high and bright green, they'll just receive the words that you write.

Similarly, although you can embed a picture into your message, or use it as a background, pictures that you use this way won't appear when your message leaves the AOL system, so Internet users will just see the text that you wrote.

Messages that have attachments, however, can be exchanged with Internet users as well as with other AOL members. So, if you want to send a picture to someone on the Internet, you should make sure you attach it to your email, instead of embedding it in there. What's the difference? Well, it's a bit like the difference between sticking a picture to a sheet of paper and writing your message round it, or attaching it to the back with a paperclip.

Some earlier versions of the AOL program don't understand embedded pictures either. Although most people have upgraded, you may still come across people using AOL 3.0 who can't see pictures that you've embedded in your message. If that happens, you'll have to send them a message with an attachment instead.

So, as a simple rule of thumb, if you're sending to AOL members, you can send any type of message that you like. If you're writing to someone on the Internet, remember to attach pictures to messages instead of embedding them, and don't forget that effects like bold, italic and different colours won't be seen by the person you're writing to.

Using pictures and effects in your messages
Writing a message using AOL's effects is simple. Just start the normal way by clicking the **Write** icon on the **Email** button.

You can access all the effects for email from the buttons at the top of the area where you write your message. They work just like the ones in your word processor. From left to right you'll see controls for typeface, size, bold, italic and underline.

Next are buttons to align text to the left, centre it, or right align it, and then buttons that let you choose the text colour and the background colour. Click either of these and a small window will pop up with the different colours available.

Next to the button that lets you choose the background colour of your text you'll see a button with a picture of a camera on it. This is the button that lets you include pictures in your messages.

Click the camera and you'll see a small menu with three choices – **Insert a picture**, **Background picture** and **Insert text file**. Choose any of these, and you'll see the standard file open box, which should be familiar from other programs on your computer.

Just browse your computer's hard disk, and choose the file that you want to use. You'll only be able to see the types of file that AOL will let you insert – pictures, or text, depending on which of the options you chose.

When you choose a picture to insert, you'll see a screen appearing asking if you want to resize the picture – that makes sure that when someone's reading the message they can see it easily. If the picture you chose is very large, then it's a good idea to choose **Yes**.

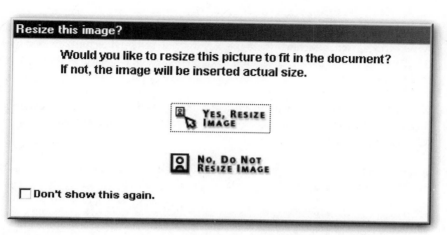

Fig. 3.38
Resize picture box

If you like, you can check the box at the bottom of the screen and AOL won't ask you the same question again. Instead, it'll remember the answer you gave this time. The picture will be inserted after the last thing you typed in your message. If you'd like to insert it anywhere else, just click with the mouse, and the picture will be inserted there.

You can insert as many pictures as you like in a single message, or one background image. A background picture appears behind the words you write – so make sure that you can still read the message itself! You might need to change the colour of the text, or make it bigger.

The **Insert text file** option adds text to your message just as if you'd typed it yourself, so like ordinary typing, anything you insert using this option can be read by people on the Internet as well as other AOL members.

The next button along is the **Favourite Places** button. If you find an area on AOL that you think is so great you want to tell someone else, just add it to your **Favourite Places**, and then you can use this button to include a link to it in an email message. When an AOL member receives the message, they can click the link to go directly to the same place. Internet users will receive the link, but they won't be able to do anything with it unless they have AOL installed on their computer (5.4, Customising AOL).

The last two buttons let you check the spelling of your message, or add a signature to it. We'll come back to those options later. For now, let's carry on looking at sending files as attachments to your email.

Email attachments

As we've explained, attachments are the way that you can send pictures to people who aren't on AOL. They're also useful for sending any type of file that you have on your computer to other AOL members.

You could, for example, send a spreadsheet with your budget back to your boss after working on it at home, or email a digital recording of your own band to a friend who's going to add the drum track to it.

When you receive an email that has files attached to it, you can simply save the files onto your hard disk, and then open them in whichever program you like.

Sending attachments
Sending an attachment is easy!

At the bottom left corner of the **Write Email** page, you'll see a button that says **Attachments**, with an icon of a floppy disk. Click the disk and you'll see a screen like this:

Fig. 3.39
Attachments screen

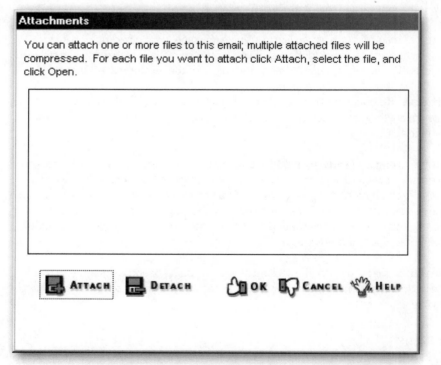

To add a file, click the **Attach** button, then find the file on your hard disk and click OK.

If you decide that you don't want to attach a particular file, then you can click it once with the mouse, then click **Detach** to remove it from the list.

When you've added all the files that you want to attach, click the **OK** button at the bottom of the list of files, or click **Cancel** if you've changed your mind and don't want to attach any files to your message.

When you click the **Send** button, you'll see a progress bar displayed on the screen and, if there was more than one file, a message will ask you to wait while the files are compressed. Compressing files helps make sure that you have to spend as little time connected as possible.

Don't worry if it takes a little longer than usual to send messages. After all, AOL has to send the files as well as whatever text you attached to them.

Since it may take some time to send the files, AOL will show a screen like this one:

Fig. 3.40
Sign off/upload screen

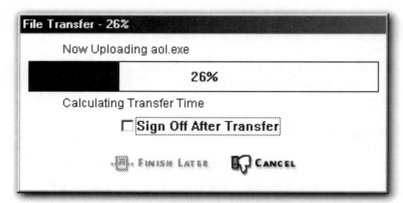

Fig. 3.40
**Sign off/upload
screen**

If you want, you can just click to check the box marked **Sign Off After Transfer**, and then AOL will automatically hang up the phone when your message has been sent, so you don't have to worry – you can run for your train if you like, and leave AOL to finish up for you.

If you decide that you don't want to upload the files at the moment, just click the **Cancel** button. You may have to wait for AOL to clear up before it acknowledges your request.

After the attachments have been sent, the message 'File transfer complete' will appear. Just click **OK**.

Receiving attachments
When you read a message that has files attached to it, it'll look just like an ordinary email message. You'll know that there are attachments because the icon for the message will show a floppy disk behind the envelope.

When you open a message with attachments, you'll see a button at the bottom left labelled **Download**. When you click it, you'll be given a choice of **Download Now** or **Download Later**.

For now, choose **Download Now**. You'll see a warning like this one:

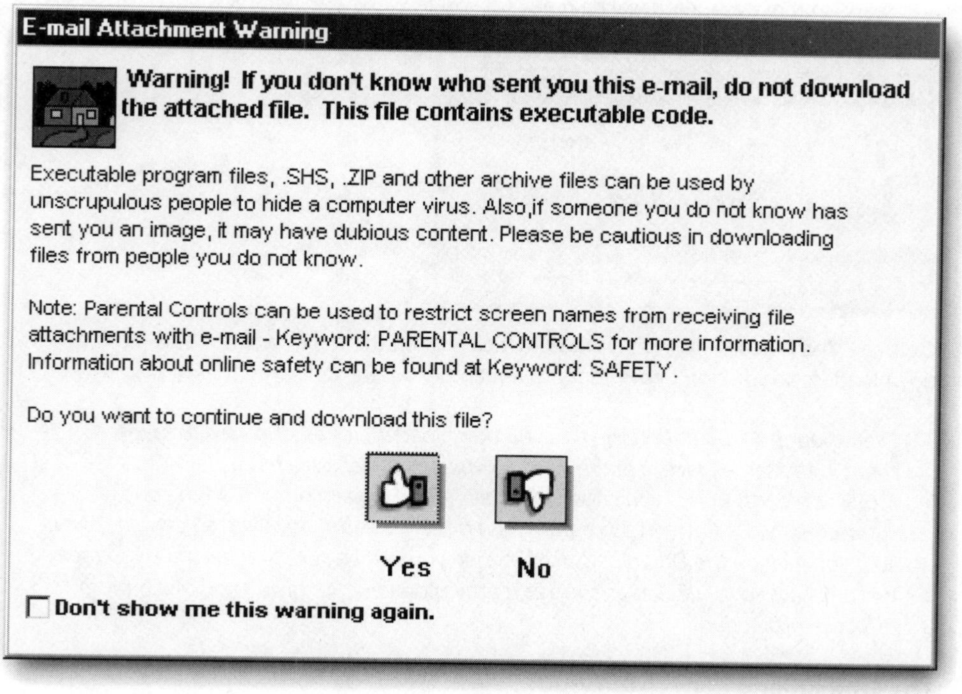

E-mail Attachment Warning

Warning! If you don't know who sent you this e-mail, do not download the attached file. This file contains executable code.

Executable program files, .SHS, .ZIP and other archive files can be used by unscrupulous people to hide a computer virus. Also,if someone you do not know has sent you an image, it may have dubious content. Please be cautious in downloading files from people you do not know.

Note: Parental Controls can be used to restrict screen names from receiving file attachments with e-mail - Keyword: PARENTAL CONTROLS for more information. Information about online safety can be found at Keyword: SAFETY.

Do you want to continue and download this file?

Yes   No

☐ **Don't show me this warning again.**

Fig. 3.41
**Download
warning screen**

If you're not sure who the message is from click to say **No**, and you can delete the message instead. If you do want to see the message, click **Yes**. If you're confident about dealing with files you receive via email, you can check the box so that AOL won't warn you in future about mail containing files and pictures.

Remember that files you receive via email could contain material you find offensive, or viruses that may damage your computer. Always be careful with files that you receive, and do not open them until you have checked them with anti-virus software.

After you click **Yes**, you'll see a standard screen asking where you want to save the files. Find the appropriate place on your computer's hard disk and click the **Save** button. AOL will display a progress bar, and you can click the option **Sign Off After Transfer** if you want the phone to be disconnected as soon as the files have be transferred to your PC.

When AOL has transferred the file to your computer, it will automatically uncompress it if necessary, so that everything will be ready for you to work with whatever you've just been sent. You'll see a message like this one appear on your screen:

Fig. 3.42
Find file screen

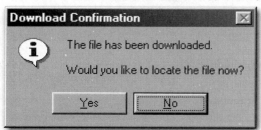

Click the **Yes** button and AOL will automatically open the folder where it's stored the files you downloaded, so you don't have to try to remember where you saved them.

Even though AOL can find the files you downloaded, it's a good idea to save them in the same place, like the AOL Downloads folder, which is usually C:\AOL 6.0\Downloads, unless you chose to install AOL in a place other than the one it suggested. Most Anti-Virus programs can be set to automatically scan certain folders, so if you include the Downloads folder, then you can be sure that each file you receive will be checked for viruses as soon as it arrives on your PC, giving you much more effective protection.

The Email menu
Now you can send and receive messages with pictures and file attachments, you can do most of the things that you'll need to with email, but there are still plenty of other things that AOL's email service offers.

We'll go through them in the order they appear on the **Email** menu – but remember that you can also reach some of them by other buttons on some of the Email screens – we'll tell you how as we go along.

We've already covered the first four things on the Email menu – **Read**, **Write**, **Old** and **Sent mail**. These options take you to your online mailbox or, in the case of **Write email**, call up a blank message for you to fill in.

Recently deleted email

When you delete an email on AOL, it's not completely removed right away. So, if you accidentally click the **Delete** button on that important message from your boss, you can get it back. Just choose this option from the Email menu and you'll see a list of messages that you deleted in the last 24 hours.

Fig. 3.43
Recently deleted mail

You can click once on a message to highlight it, and then choose from the options at the bottom. To check what a message said, click the **Read** button. If you want to move the message back into your New mail box, click **Keep As New**, and if you want to completely delete it, click **Permanently Delete**.

*When you click the **Permanently Delete** button, you won't be able to retrieve the message again.*

Communications Centre
The Communications Centre is a screen that provides you with quick access to some of AOL's email-related features.

Fig. 3.44
**Communications
centre**

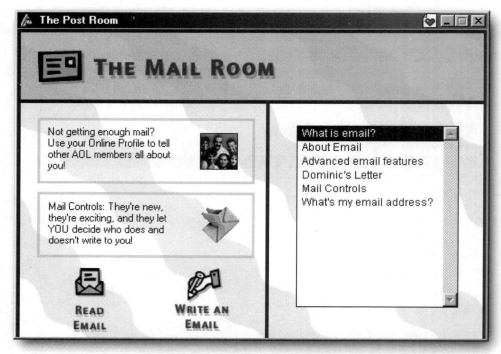

You can use the buttons at the bottom left to read or send email messages. At the top, you'll see a link to create your online Profile. A Profile is a short description of yourself, and other members can search through them to find people with similar interests.

You can read more about creating a profile in *Chapter 5*.

Below the **Profile** button is another that gives you quick access to the Mail Controls, which are part of the Parental Controls on AOL. You can use these to determine who can send messages to you (*5.1, Screen names and controls*).

Finally, at the right of the screen is a list of things you can read, including more information about AOL's email service and how to use some of the features. You'll also see an item labelled Dominic's Letter, which is a regular update from the head of AOL UK. It usually contains topical tips to help you make the most of AOL, as well as news about new features, so it's well worth a look.

Address Book

The Address Book is one of the tools that AOL provides to help you keep track of the people that you exchange email with – but it does a lot more than that. The AOL Address Book lets you record people's work and home addresses, phone numbers and other information, so you can use it to hold all the information about people you know. And when you want to contact them, a click of the mouse will automatically address an email to them.

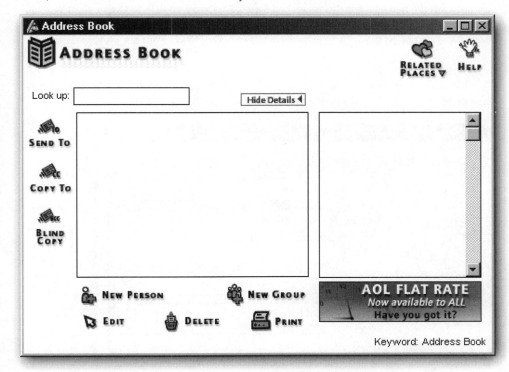

Fig. 3.45
Address Book

This is the screen you'll see when you select the **Address Book** from the **Email** menu. You may see a brief message telling you that the **Address Book** is being 'Synchronised'. That means that AOL is just checking that your information is up to date with a copy stored on the AOL computer. That way, you can access your **Address Book**, even when you use AOL on another system.

The first time you open the **Address Book**, of course there won't be any entries in it. We'll explain in a moment how to make entries, but first let's look at what's on the **Address Book** screen.

Across the top is a box where you can type a name that you want to look up, and a row of buttons underneath labelled **New Contact**, **New Group**, **Edit**, **Delete** and **Print**.

On the left, you'll see a list of the names in your **Address Book,** and on the right is the information for the name that you've currently selected.

Underneath the names are buttons labelled **Send To**, **Copy To**, **Blind Copy** and **IM**. Finally, in the bottom right are two symbols – plus and minus. You can click these to hide or show the right-hand section of the address list, where the details of the current address are shown.

Adding an entry to your Address Book
To add someone to your Address Book, click the **New Person** button and a blank screen will appear, ready for you to fill in their name and email address.

Fig. 3.46
**Contact Details
screen**

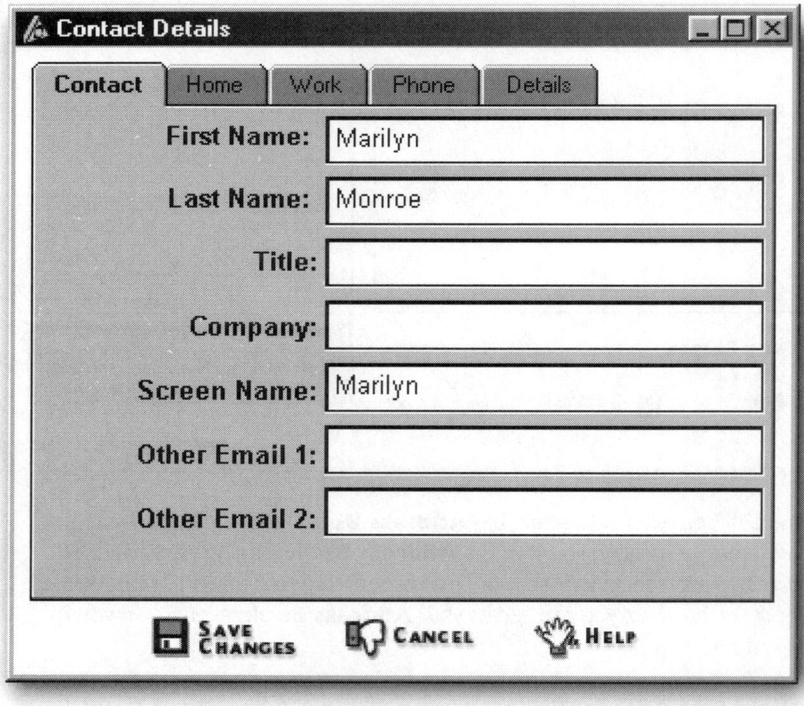

Just fill in each of the blank spaces – you can leave any of them blank if you don't know the information, or don't want to use it in the Address Book. You'll see there are spaces at the bottom for Screen Name, Email 1 and Email 2.

If you want to use the Address Book to send email messages to other people, you need to enter their email address in either **Email 1** or **Email 2**. For an AOL member, you can just enter their screen name, as long as you put it in one or the other of those spaces.

The space labelled **Screen Name** is used when you want to send an Instant Message to someone that you've looked up in the Address Book.

Some people have more than one email address, and you can store two in the Address Book. Normally AOL will use the one you enter as Email 1 when you want to send a message using the Address Book. At the bottom of the page you'll see Primary Email address, and a choice between Email 1 and Email 2. You can click here to select which of the two addresses you want AOL to use when you write a message using the Address Book.

*If you've received a message from someone, whether on AOL or from the Internet, you can click the **Add Address** button that appears on the right of the email message, and AOL will make a new entry in your Address Book for you, filling in as much of the information on this screen as possible.*

The other tabs across the top of the Address Book panel let you add other information about people, such as their home and work addresses, phone numbers, and even their birthday and anniversary dates. Just click one of the tabs to enter the information that you want.

Fig. 3.47
Address home details screen

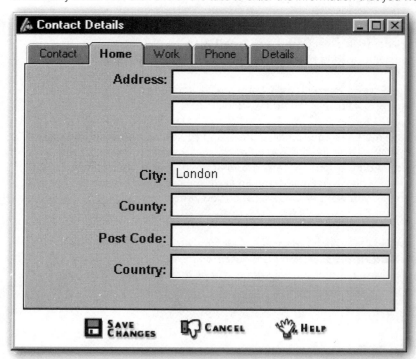

At the bottom of the **Home** details page, you'll see another choice you can make, between **Home** and **Work**, labelled **Primary Mailing Address**. The address you choose here is the one that will be shown in the right-hand panel of the main Address Book page when you click an entry once, so you should set it to the address you're most likely to need, if you have both a home and a work address for someone.

When you've entered all the details you need, click the **Save** button to update them.

Sending messages from your Address Book

Now you have at least one entry in your Address Book, we can look at how to use it. First, just click the person that you'd like to contact. If you've entered lots of names, you might have to scroll through the list to find them.

You can also click in the box at the top of the Address Book, marked **Look up**. Start typing a surname, and the Address Book will go directly to the first entry that matches what you typed, so you can press just a letter like W to go to the start of those entries, or type Whit to get a little closer to the entries for White, Whitfield and so on.

Either way, when you've found the name that you want to contact, you can use the buttons at the bottom of the Address Book.

Click **Send To** and AOL will open a blank email for you with the address already entered in the **Sent To** box. And, you've guessed it, click the **Copy To** or **Blind Copy** buttons and the same happens, except the email address is put in the appropriate box on the blank message.

If you're already writing a message, the buttons will add the next address that you click to the message you're writing. So, you can click the **Send To** button to start a new message, then if you realise you need to send a copy of the message to someone else, go back to the Address Book, find the name you want and click **Copy To** to add it to the same message.

If you entered an AOL screen name for someone in your Address Book, you can also send them an Instant Message. Just find their name in the Address Book, and click the **IM** button.

Groups in your Address Book

Next to the **New Contact** button, you'll see a **New Group** button. What's a Group? It's just a collection of names that you might want to use together. For example, there might be people you want to invite each time you have a party, or other people who work in the same business as you, or family members.

Creating a Group in your Address Book means that you can send a message to all the members of the Group with just a couple of clicks. For example, if you had a Group called 'Party Animals' then just click it, choose **Send To**, and all the addresses in the Group will be added to a blank message for you.

Fig. 3.48
New Group button

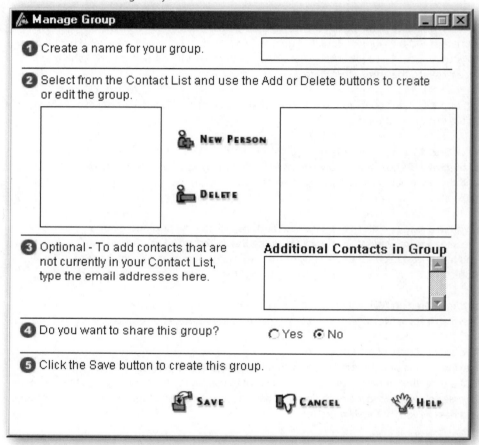

To make a Group, click the **New Group** button and this screen will appear. The first thing you need to do is choose a name. Make it something descriptive, so you know what it's for when you see it later in your Address Book. The name will appear in bold type in the Address Book, so you can tell Groups apart from people.

When you've chosen a name, you can choose members for the Group. You do that using the two lists of names either side of the **Add** and **Remove** buttons. The list on the left shows people who are in your Address Book but not in this Group, while the list on the right shows people who are in the Group.

To add a name, find it in the list on the left, click it once, and then click the **Add** button. The name will move from the left to the right. If you wanted to remove someone from a Group, click the name in the right hand column, then click **Remove**.

You might also want to add email addresses that you haven't put in your Address Book. You can do that in the next box. Just click in the box, and type in email addresses, one on each line.

The next question asks if you want to share the Group with other people. For now, make sure that **No** is selected (*5-7 Groups @ AOL*).

Shared Groups are an exciting new way of sharing email, pictures and even appointments between a group of people. You can find out more about them in *Chapter 5-7*.

You can share your Group later if you like. For now, we'll just make it an ordinary Group in your Address Book.

When you've added all the names you want to your Group, just click the **Save** button at the bottom of the screen.

If you'd like to make changes to a Group, click the button next to **New Group**, and the same screen will appear, so you can add or remove names.

*Remember that when you use a Group to send a message, all the email addresses of the members of the Group will be listed in the **Send To** or **Copy To** box of your message. That means that other members of the Group will be able to see the addresses of everyone in it. Some people may consider that you've breached their privacy, exposing their email address in this way.*

*If you don't want that to happen, then you should use the **Blind Copy** button instead, and put your own address in the **Send To** box of the message. That way, people will only see your address and their own one.*

There are two final options in the Address Book – **Delete** and **Print**.

Delete allows you to remove an entry, or a Group, from your Address Book. Find the entry that you want to remove, and click the **Delete** button.

If you'd like a printed copy of your addresses, perhaps to keep in the back of your diary, click the **Print** button.

Email Preferences
The Preferences screen gives you fine control over how AOL's email works. You can change the settings here to find the options that suit you best. They're divided into sections for **Reading Email**, **Sending Email** and **Writing Email**.

Fig. 3.49
**Email
preferences
screen**

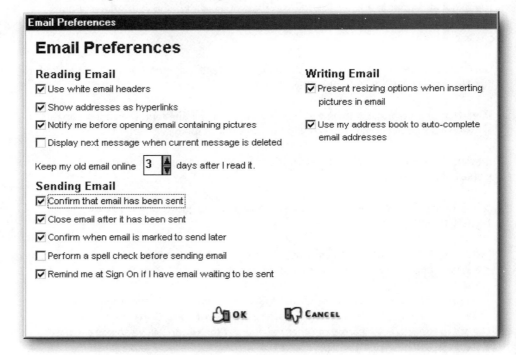

Reading Mail
This section of the preferences controls what happens when you read a message you've been sent by someone else.

Use white mail headers tells AOL that you want the headers – that's the information telling you who sent a message, the subject and date – displayed in a white box at the top of the message. If you turn this option off, the information will be displayed in a grey box instead.

Show addresses as hyperlinks lets you choose to have addresses in email messages turning into clickable links. If you select this option, you'll see that the mouse pointer changes when you move it over any of the addresses in a message, whether in the message itself, or in the **Sent To** and **Copy To** boxes. You can write a new message to any of the addresses just by clicking them.

Notify me before opening mail containing pictures. Choose this option if you want AOL to pop up a warning screen when you try to open an email that has pictures in it. If you've turned the warning off when it appeared, you can turn it back on by clicking to put a check in the box.

Display next message when current message is deleted can help you to move through your mailbox quickly. If you choose this option, then when you click the **Delete** button, AOL will automatically go to the next new message in your inbox.

Keep my old mail online. This option lets you tell AOL how long you want your messages to be kept in the Old Mail list. You can increase it to seven days if you like. You could do that, for example, if you'll be accessing AOL from somewhere else on a business trip and want to be sure you can read recent messages even if they're not saved on the computer you're using.

Sending mail
The Preferences in this section control what happens when you're sending a message, by clicking the **Send** button.

Confirm that mail has been sent. If you click the check box next to this option, then AOL will pop up a message to tell you an email has been sent. You need to click to make the message go away, but you'll have the reassurance of knowing that it's been delivered ok. If there is a problem, though, AOL will tell you whether or not this option is selected.

Close mail after it has been sent. When this option is selected, as soon as your mail has been sent, it will disappear from the screen. You'll still be able to see it in your Sent Mail list, but you'll have fewer things cluttering up your screen. If you turn the option off, you'll need to close the email window after it's been sent.

Confirm when mail is marked to send later. Next to the **Send** button is one marked **Send Later**. Click to place a check in the box next to this option, and AOL will ask you if you're sure when you click the **Send Later** button, in case you chose it by mistake.

Perform a spell check before sending mail. If you're not that good at spelling, or you simply want to make sure a silly mistake doesn't reflect badly on you, you can click to put a check mark in this box, and AOL will check the spelling of your messages automatically. You can check the spelling of each message individually instead, by using the spell check button when you're writing the email.

Remind me at sign-on if I have mail waiting to be sent is a helpful option to select if you've been using the **Send Later** facility. It will make AOL remind you that you wrote messages while you were disconnected, so that you can send them as soon as you sign on. If you don't select this option, it's up to you to remember to send any waiting emails.

Writing mail
The options here control what happens when you're creating your message.

Present resizing options when inserting pictures in email. If you select this option, AOL will always ask you if you want to change the size of a picture so that it fits into the message. If you like, you can turn this option off after making your choice for a picture, and AOL will remember whether you chose to resize a picture or not for all your future emails.

Use my Address Book to auto-complete email addresses. If you click to put a check in the box next to this option, then you won't have to type the whole of an email address, if it's already in your Address Book. Instead, when you start typing, AOL will fill in the rest of a matching address, if it can find one in your Address Book. If the address AOL chooses is correct, you can stop typing. Otherwise, just carry on typing the correct address.

Email controls
AOL's Email controls are part of the *Parental Controls*, and they give you complete control over who can send you email. You can find out more about how to use them in *Chapter 5, AOL and You (5–1 Parental Controls)*.

Email signatures
Signatures are a useful part of AOL's Email service. A signature is a short piece of text that you can add to the bottom of your email message. It might include your name and address for a business user, or a witty quote for personal messages.

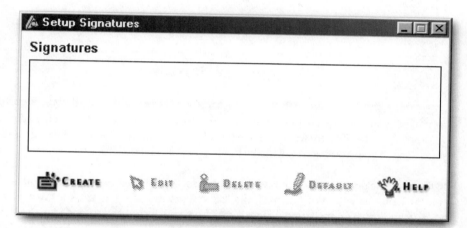

Fig. 3.50
Signatures screen

Choose **Signatures** from the **Email** menu and this screen will appear. At first, there won't be any signatures listed. Click the **Create** button and you'll see what appears to be a miniature version of the Write Email window.

Fig. 3.51
**Create/edit
signature screen**

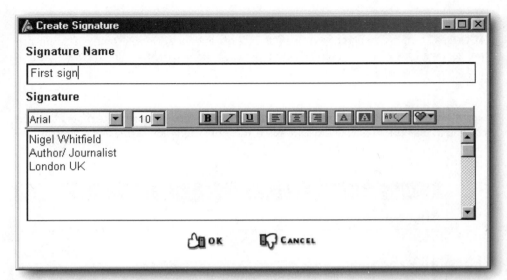

At the top, you can give a name to the signature. This won't be added to your message, but will appear on the **Signature** menu when you're writing messages, so make sure it means something to you. You might call the first one 'Work' or 'General' for example.

In the space below, type the words you want to use. Don't forget that although you can use some of the features of AOL mail here, like colours and different text, they won't be seen when people on the Internet receive mail from you. It could be a good idea to create a separate signature for using when you send mail to Internet users.

Generally, people consider signatures longer than four lines to be over the top – you should keep the information in a signature short and relevant, not include your life story or a complete advert for your company.

On the Internet, many people expect a signature to be separated from the rest of your message by a line that has just two minus signs followed by a space. If you create a special Internet signature, it's a good idea to make it start like that.

When you've typed your signature, click the **Save** button. The **Edit** button on the Signature page will let you make any changes to a signature. Just click one, then click the **Edit** button. You can delete a signature in the same way, using the **Delete** button.

AOL will let you choose a default signature, which will be added to all your messages automatically. To pick a default signature, click the name of the one you want to use, then click the **Default on/off** button. If you want to use a different one as the default, highlight that instead, and click the button.

A red tick will appear next to a signature that's being used as your default. If you don't want one added automatically, select the signature with the tick next to it, then click **Default on/off** again and the tick will disappear.

When you've finished making your changes, just close the Signatures window .

Using signatures in your messages

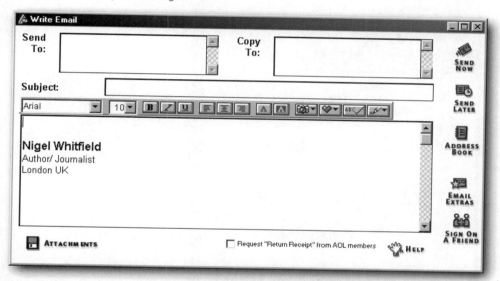

Fig. 3.52
Message window with sig menu

Selecting a signature when you're writing an email is easy. If you chose a default signature, it will appear at the bottom of each new message. Perhaps you don't want that signature on this particular message? No problem. Just highlight it with the mouse, and delete it, like you would any other text.

To add a different signature, just click the **Signature** button, which is at the right of the area where you type your message. Highlight a signature and it'll be added to your message. If you choose **Setup signatures**, you'll be taken to the Signatures screen.

Email extras

The **Email extras** option on the **Email** menu displays a page that gives you options for adding a little extra pizzazz to your messages. Some of the options are just explanations of things that we've looked at already, with step-by-step instructions.

Fig. 3.53
Email extras screen

You can also call up this page by clicking the **Email Xtras** button at the right-hand side of the page when you're writing a new email.

If you want help adding a picture to your email, click the **Photos** button. As well as instructions, you'll also find some links that you can click to other areas of AOL where you can find photos that you might want to use in your own messages.

Smileys are combinations of punctuation that lots of people on the Internet use to represent emotions. For example, :-) is often used to show that you're joking. If you don't understand why, turn your head on it's side, and imagine a smiling face.

The **Smileys** button shows you a long list of different smileys that you can use in your messages – but don't assume that everyone will understand all of them.

The **Colours & Styles** button tells you more about the other tools in the **Write email** box, while the **Hyperlinks** button is there to give you help about adding links to your email, and includes buttons to help you add parts of AOL to your **Favourite Places**. You can also search the Internet for sites that you might want to add to your email messages as links.

Automatic AOL
The next two options on the Email menu are for Automatic AOL, which is a feature you can use to tell AOL to do lots of things for you, while you go and make a cup of tea.

With Automatic AOL you can tell AOL to collect your new messages, send ones that you've written, collect postings from message boards, and download files you've asked for.

Automatic AOL can be very useful, and it can save you a lot of time. But to make the most of it, you'll need to spend some time setting it up, so we'll look at it in detail in *Chapter 5* (*5.6, Automatic AOL*).

Read offline email
Emails that you read or send don't just disappear into thin air after a few days. AOL automatically keeps copies of them all on your computer's hard disk, though you can turn the option off in your Preferences, if you like. Once you've read a new message, or sent one to someone, then there'll be a copy made.

What's the point of that? Well, it means that if you need to check, for example, the time of that meeting, or see what cinema you told your friend you'd meet them at, you don't need to connect to AOL itself. You can just start the AOL program, and find the message, which will be much quicker.

From the Email menu, choose **Read offline email**, and a small menu will pop out to the right, so you can look at **Incoming/saved mail** or **Copies of mail you have sent**. When you choose either of these options, you'll see a screen something like this one:

Fig. 3.54
Incoming mail

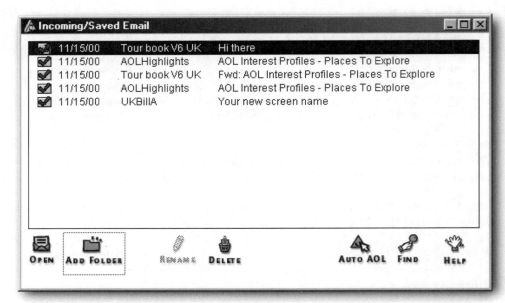

Incoming/saved mail is where you'll find copies of all the messages that you've read while you were signed on to AOL. And you'll also see copies of messages if, instead of reading them, you clicked the Save to PFC button.

You can read any of the messages in the list simply by double-clicking them, or clicking once and then clicking the **Open** button at the bottom of the page. If you decide that you don't want to keep a copy of the message, select it with the mouse, and then click **Delete**.

The **Add Folder** button is there to help you organise your messages. When you've been using AOL for a while, you'll find that you have lots of messages, and it can be hard to find the ones that you want. Adding a folder gives you an area where you can put all the messages that you want to keep together, like all the messages from a certain person, or to do with a particular event.

Fig. 3.55
Add folder window

When you click the **Add Folder** button you'll be asked for the name of the folder you want to create. Type the name, then press the **Enter** key. You'll see the name of the folder appear in the list of messages.

The folder name will also appear on the **PFC** button at the bottom of each email message you read. When you click the button and choose either **Incoming mail** or **Mail you have sent**, the folder will be listed too. Just choose it with the mouse, and the message that you're reading will be added to the folder.

You can change the name of a folder by clicking it and using the **Rename** button. Double-clicking the folder icon will open it, so you can see what messages are in there. Double-click again to close it.

The folders that you can create here are part of your Personal Filing Cabinet. You can read more about that in *Chapter 5, AOL and You* (5-5 PFC).

The **Auto AOL** button will let you set up Automatic AOL. For more details, see *Chapter 5*. Next to it is the **Find** button.

Finding email

The **Find** button will let you go quickly to a message, even if you can't remember which folder you saved it in, or who sent it. You can look for a particular word, so if you remember someone sent you directions to their office in Harlow, you could search for that. Or you might remember someone sent you a message with the word URGENT in the subject, and you want to go straight to it.

Fig. 3.56
**Find email
screen**

When you click the **Find** button, this is what you'll see. Type the word or phrase that you're looking for into the box at the top. Underneath is a box labelled **Match case**. If you click to put a check in the box, then only words that have capital letters exactly where you typed them will be found. For example, if you typed 'URGENT' in the search box, and chose **Match case**, then only messages with the word 'URGENT' would be found – even if someone typed 'Urgent', their message wouldn't match.

If you want to find messages regardless of which letters are in capitals, don't select the **Match case** option.

Next you can choose where you want to search – either just the folders you have open on your screen, or all the folders. If you have lots of messages, and you're pretty sure you know where you saved the one you want, then choose the second option, **Open folders only**, as it will be quicker than searching through all your email.

Finally, do you want to look for a word that appears in a message, or just in the subject of the message? If you can't remember, choose **Full text**. If you know the word you want is in the subject of a message, click **Titles only**.

When you've made your changes, click the **Find Now** button. AOL will highlight the first message that it can find, or display a message saying that nothing could be found.

If the first message AOL finds is not the right one, you'll notice that the **Find Now** button has changed to **Find Next**. Click it to search again, and carry on until you find what you're looking for. Click the **Cancel** button to stop searching.

Email waiting to be sent
This is the last option on the **Email** menu, and it's where you'll find any messages that you wrote but didn't send. That means that instead of clicking the **Send** button, you clicked **Send Later**.

Fig. 3.57
Email waiting to be sent

Just like when you were looking at saved or sent mail, you'll see a list of messages here. You can choose a message and then click the **Edit** button if you want to read it or make changes.

When you're making changes to a message, you'll see that it looks just like when you were writing the email originally – you can click either **Send** or **Send Later**. If you click **Send**, the message will be sent right away, and will disappear from the list of email waiting to be sent. Click **Send Later** to save any changes to the message and leave it in the list.

If you decide you don't want to send a message – perhaps it's asking a question you've already found out the answer to – then you can highlight it with the mouse and click the **Delete** button.

To send a message right away, choose it and click the **Send** button. Remember that you'll have to be connected to AOL to send it.

Finally, if you want to send all the waiting email messages, just click the **Send All** button and they'll all be sent, one at a time.

And there you are! That's your tour of the AOL Email menu done. You should be able to send and receive email to your heart's content now. Once you're confident you know how to do everything you want, you might want to learn about how Automatic AOL and your Personal Filing Cabinet can make it even easier and save you lots of time (*5.5, PFC*).

3.7 Message boards

So far, the type of chat that we've looked at on AOL happens in real time – when you type a comment, it appears on the screen right away, and someone else can read and respond to it immediately. If someone's not connected to AOL, then they miss out on what you said – just like a conversation in a pub, your words disappear the minute you said them. If someone's not there at the time, they don't hear you.

Message boards are different. They're a way of taking part in a discussion with people who might not be around at the same time as you. Think of them as a little like letters to the editor of a newspaper – but where every letter is published. You can make your contributions, and then other people can come along and read it. If they feel strongly enough about what you've written, or they have the answer to your question, they'll respond.

Message boards can be one of the most vigorous areas of discussion that you'll find on AOL. Since they're not as instantaneous as chat or Instant Messages, people often take the time to think about what they want to say, and put forward a good argument.

Let's start by taking a look at one of the lighter Message boards, in the AOL Live area. AOL Live is a part of AOL that features topical interviews. For example, the author of the Harry Potter books joined AOL Live to talk about the fourth book when it was launched. We'll look some more at AOL Live later on, but for now we're interested in the message boards.

From the AOL main screen, click the arrow next to the word **People**, and you'll see a menu appear. Choose **AOL Live** and you'll see this screen:

Fig. 3.58
AOL Live

At the left-hand side, you'll see the word Messages. Click it, and you'll be taken to the AOL Live message board. The first thing that will appear is the list of current topics. All the Message boards on AOL work in the same way, so once you've got the hang of this one, you'll be able to use any of AOL's Message boards without any difficulty.

Topics and subjects

The message board main screen lists topics and subjects, and below those, there's a row of buttons that you can use to help you move around, and keep track of which messages have been posted since you last visited.

The board is divided into topics and subjects, which helps make it easier for you to find messages that you're interested in. Topics are created by AOL, and divide messages into broad categories. For example, in the AOL Live Message board, you'll see topics including Best TV Programmes, Favourite Bands and Sporting Heroes. Next to the name of each topic there's a number, which is the number of subjects under that topic.

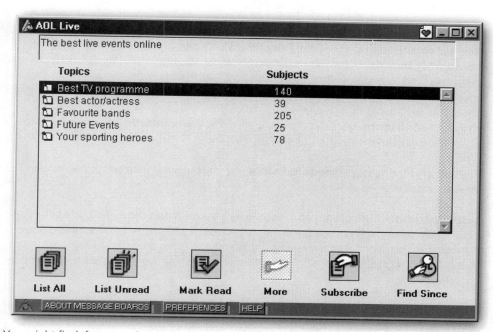

Fig. 3.59
**AOL Live
Message board
main folder**

You might find, for example, messages with a subject of Casualty or Teletubbies in the Best TV Programmes category, or Alan Shearer and Viv Richards in the Sporting Heroes topic.

Before we move on to reading the messages themselves, let's look at the buttons along the bottom of the Message board screen.

The first three buttons let you choose which messages you see when you look at the topics in the message board. Just highlight the topic you're interested in, and then click one of the buttons.

If you click the **List All** button, you'll see all the messages that have been posted in the last 30 days, including ones that you've read already. The **List Unread** button will just show you a list of messages that haven't been read, while the **Mark Read** button tells AOL that you've read all the messages in the topic you selected. That way, you can skip a lot of messages, and come back later to just read the newest ones. Of course, if you've read all the messages and ask to see unread ones, there's nothing to see. Instead, AOL pop up a screen telling you, and asking if you want to list all messages, create a new subject, or change your Preferences.

The button marked **More** is used when there are lots of topics on a message board. AOL will list the first section of the topic list, and then you can click **More** to see the rest.

The **Subscribe** button works a little like AOL's Favourite Places, but instead of adding the message board directly to your list of Favourites, it adds it to an area that you'll find at the keyword **My Boards**. That way, you can access all the Message boards that you want to take part in with just a couple of clicks. You can also tell AOL that you want to transfer messages to your computer to read when you've disconnected, which will save you time online. For more about this, see *Chapter 5, AOL and You*. If you've already subscribed to a Message board, clicking the **Subscribe** button again will remove it from **My Boards**. You can read more about My Boards later on in this chapter (*5.5, PFC*).

The button at the right is labelled **Find since** and you can use it to select messages that have appeared in a certain time.

When you click the button, you can choose to see new messages, messages posted in a certain number of days or, if you prefer, messages that people posted between two dates. For example, you might want to see what the reactions were in the first two days after a particular TV programme, rather than after the second episode had been shown. Just enter the dates and click the **OK** button.

Remember that you have to enter the dates either as a month followed by a day, or a month, day and then year. For example, you could enter the 20 July 1999 as either 7/20 or 7/20/99. You can't use the more common 20/7/99 format for dates.

Right at the bottom of the screen, below the large buttons, you'll see three more things you can click. There's a button labelled **About Message Boards**, which will tell you a little more about how AOL's Message boards work and what they are. Next is the **Preferences** button, which we'll explain shortly, and finally there's a **Help** button.

Whether you've used the **Find** button, **List All** or **List Unread**, you'll end up with a list of subjects appearing on your screen.

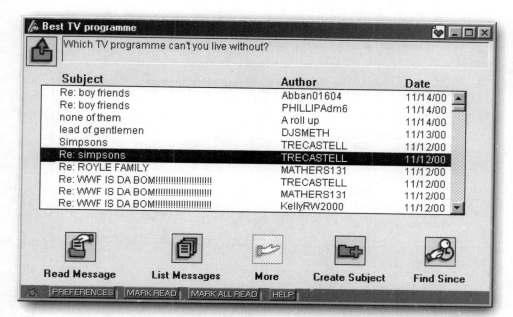

Fig. 3.60
**Subject listing
screen – non
threaded**

Although this looks very similar to the main **Message Board** screen, it's slightly different.
The list shows all the subjects in the current topic. Depending on how the Message board is
organised, you might see a list of subjects, with each followed by the Screen Name of the
author, and a date, or something more like the second screen, with a list of subjects and
the number of messages.

Fig. 3.61
**Subject listing
screen –
threaded**

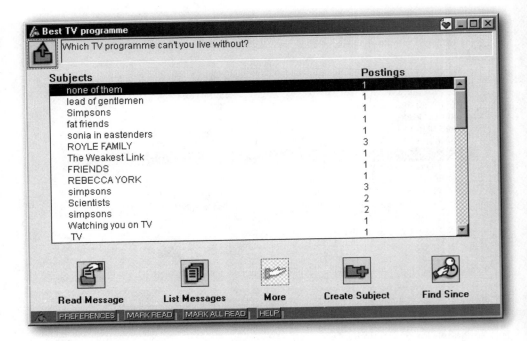

What's a thread?

The difference is that some messages are in threads. A thread is just a chain of messages, where AOL has remembered that someone made a particular comment in response to someone else's, and so on. It's often easier to follow a discussion when it's a thread, since you'll see messages with the comments that people made to them. The alternative is to read messages in the date that they were written, usually starting with the newest messages.

Reading messages

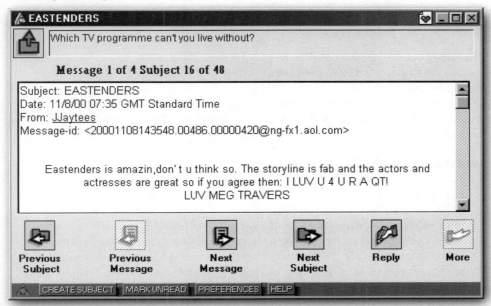

Fig. 3.62
**Read message
screen**

Just look through the list of subjects that you've called up, and double-click one that you think looks interesting. A message will appear in a screen like the one above. As you can see, it doesn't look that different from reading an email, does it?

The difference is in the buttons along the bottom of the message, so let's take a closer look at those.

The first four buttons are all to do with moving around the message board. Once you've opened the first message, you can use these buttons to read all the messages in the topic without having to go back to the list of subjects.

If you're reading messages that are not threaded then you'll see that the buttons for **Next Message** and **Previous Message** are dimmed and don't work. That's because each message is treated as a subject on its own. You can use the **Next Subject** button to move on to the next unread message, and the **Previous Subject** button will move you in the opposite direction.

If you think you'd like to come back to a message later, perhaps to read it more in depth, or when you've thought about it a little, you can click **Mark Unread** right at the bottom of the page.

The **Reply** button lets you post a comment to the message board in reply to the one you're reading, and if you click **Create Subject**, you can start a new subject all of your own.

The last button, labelled **More**, is for long messages. AOL will display the first part of the message, and if you want to see the rest, just click **More** and the next section will appear in the message window.

We'll cover creating messages in a while, but first a cautionary word.

Like many communities online, different Message boards each have their own character. There may be contributors that people know and respect, or others that regulars know are usually joking. Since you can't be expected to know who's who right away, it's usually a good idea to read a Message board for a little while before making your own contributions. That way you'll get a feel for who uses it and what sort of tone the messages have. It's a little like listening to a group of people in a pub before sitting down at their table and joining in their conversation.

Message Board Preferences
Before going on to look at how you can post messages, let's take a quick look at the Preferences for message boards. You can use these to decide how many messages you see when you join a board, and so on.

From main message board screen, or the list of subjects, click the **Preferences** button and you'll see a screen list this one.

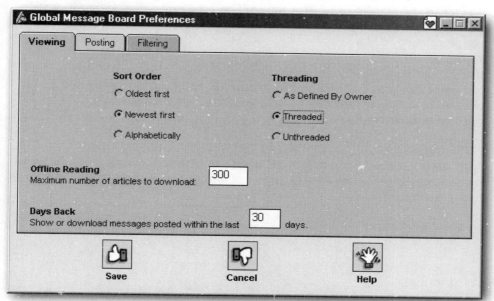

Fig. 3.63
Message Board Preferences – viewing

The three tabs along the top let you change preferences for viewing messages, posting your own ones and filtering. Click the tab for the **Preferences** that you want to change.

Viewing preferences
Sort order lets you decide how the subjects in a topic are listed. You can choose **Oldest first**, **Newest first**, or **Alphabetically**.

Threading is where you can decide whether or not you want to view messages by thread, or just in the order that you've selected with the **Sort Order** option. As well as **Threaded** or **Unthreaded**, you can also select a third option, **As Defined By Owner**. When you choose this option, you'll see messages in threads if the owner of the forum thinks they're best viewed that way.

Offline Reading. If you want to read messages when you've disconnected from AOL, this option lets you say how many messages should be transferred to your own computer. By setting the maximum number here, you can make sure that you don't end up with thousands of messages to read, clogging up your hard disk. You can find out more about reading your messages offline in *Chapter 5, AOL and you (5.5, PFC)*.

Days Back is the option that says how many days worth of messages you'll see when you use the **List all** option. It's normally set to 30, but if you visit very busy message boards, it's a good idea to set this to a smaller number.

Posting preferences
Here you can fill in a signature, which is a short piece of text that will be added to the end of each message you post on the Message boards. You might put, for example, your job title, or a witty quote. You can enter up to 254 letters, and as with email you can use colours and differently sized text.

Filtering preferences
Filters let you cut down the number of messages that you see in a Message board. On busy message boards, you can use these to ensure that you only see messages that you're likely to be interested in.

You can filter messages based on the author, a particular subject, or a word in the subject. You could, perhaps, have a filter that ensures you see all the messages that have the name of your favourite TV programme, like Buffy, in the subject, and another that shows all the messages created by your partner.

When you've set your Preferences, click the **Save** button, and carry on with reading the messages. Once you're confident about moving around the Message boards, it's time to think about making your own contribution.

Posting to message boards

There are two ways of posting a message to a Message board. You can create a new subject of your own, or you can respond to a message that someone else has created. Let's start by looking at creating your own message. To do that, you click the **Create Subject** button.

You'll find that button in one of three different places. If you're reading someone's message, it's at the bottom, underneath the large buttons. When you're looking at the list of messages in a topic, there's a large button below the list, and if you try to list unread messages in a topic that you've read, the box that appears on your screen will also have a **Create Subject** button on it.

However you reach the screen, it always looks the same.

Fig. 3.64
Create subject screen

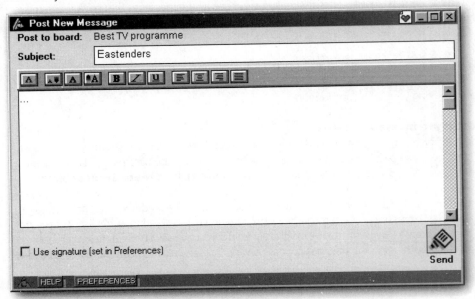

At the top, you'll see the message board and subject that your message will be posted to. Check that it's correct and if not, close the window. Below is a space labelled Subject, where you can type a short description of your message.

Try to find a good compromise between length and information. If the subject is meaningless, then people may not bother looking at your message. If it's too detailed, you might make some people think they don't need to read the message itself.

When you've chosen a subject, you can type your message in the space below, just as if you were composing an email message. Along the top of the message area you'll see the same buttons for typefaces, sizes and so on.

Below the message area is a check box labelled **Use signature**. If you created a signature in the Preferences, you just need to check this box and it'll be automatically added to your message, so you can save time by not having to type your name on the end of each message, for example.

When you're done, just click the **Send** button and your message will be added to the message board.

Replying to messages
Sooner or later, you'll want to respond to a comment from someone else. All you have to do is click the **Reply** button at the bottom of the message you're reading.

As you can see from the screen, replying to a message is a little more complicated than creating a subject of your own.

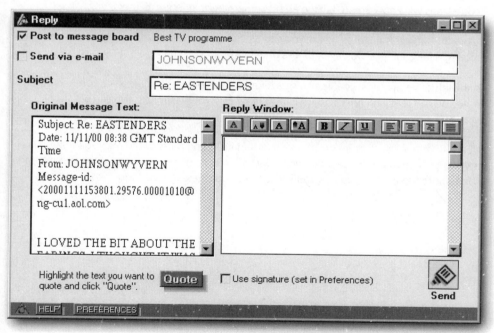

Fig. 3.65
Reply to message

Right at the top of the page, you'll see two check boxes, one labelled **Post to message board** and one **Send via email**. Normally, the first one will be checked, and the name of the board where you read the message will be to the right of it.

To the right of the **Send via email** check box is a box where the author of the message you've just read will be displayed. If you check the **Send via email box**, then your response will be sent to them as an email – or to anyone else. You can change the email address if you like.

If you see someone asking for personal advice on a message board, you might decide to share your own experiences, for example, but you'd rather not do so in public. In that case, just check the **Send via email** box, and click to uncheck the **Post to message board** box. When you click **Send**, your message will just be delivered as a private email.

Underneath the name of the author is another space for the subject of your message. It's usually a good idea to leave it the same as the original, unless you really are talking about something completely different. Perhaps you've started off with a discussion about Buffy the Vampire Slayer and now you're mentioning Scooby Doo. In that case, change the subject, so Scooby fans will know you're talking about something that interests them.

Below the subject is the area where you can type your own message, just like when you were creating a new subject. However, there's one important difference.

To the left of your words, you'll see a smaller area that contains the message you're replying to, so you can read and refer to it while you're writing your response. You can also quote parts of the message.

What's that then? Well, quoting is a good way of including parts of the message that you're replying to, so that people can follow the discussion even if they've not read the first message. Don't quote too much, though – you'll just make your message too long.

For example, the message you're reading might say something like:

I never understood why Thelma and Fred didn't get together. They seemed made for each other in my opinion.

If you want to copy the first sentence into your message, find it in the left-hand window, and select it with the mouse, by holding down the button as you drag the pointer over the text. Next, click the **Quote** button and the text will appear in your new message looking like this:

> I never understood why Thelma and Fred didn't get together

The > lets people know that the comment is a quote from another message. You can alter the way AOL shows quotes in the email **Preferences**, which we looked at in the Advanced email section of this chapter (*3.4, Quoting preferences*).

Next to the **Quote** button is another check box, which you can use to say whether or not you want your signature added to the message when it's sent. You can set the signature using the message board Preferences.

When you've finished, click the **Send** button, and your message will be delivered, via email, to the message board or both, depending on the options you selected at the top of the page.

And that's all there is to it! Now you can exchange messages with other AOL members via chat, Instant Messages and Message boards. You're well on the way to becoming part of the world's biggest online community.

My Boards

If you start to use AOL's Message boards a lot, you might find that you just don't want to have to browse through all the screens necessary to reach each of the boards that you want to visit.

My Boards

Of course, you can always add each one to your **Favourite Places** so that you can go there quickly, but wouldn't it be great to have them all together in one place? That's what **My Boards** is for. You can reach it by typing **My Boards** into the Keyword box at the top of the AOL screen.

Fig. 3.66
My Boards main screen

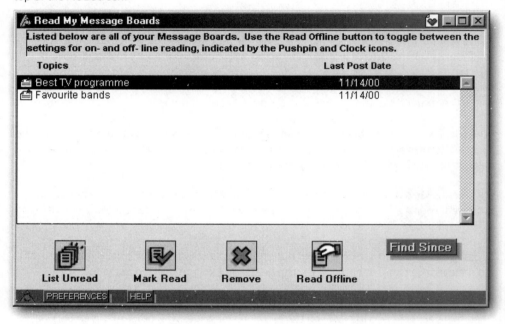

As you can see, the **My Boards** screen looks a little like the list of topics that you'll see when you go into an individual message board. It lists all the message boards that you chose to subscribe to when you were reading them.

You can use the same **Find Since** and **List Unread** buttons as you would when you were looking at a particular Message board in the area of AOL where you found it. All you need to do is click the Message board, and then choose one of the buttons at the bottom of the screen.

Double-clicking one of the message boards is the same as asking for a list of unread topics, and if there are no new messages since you last visited, you'll see a screen telling you – it really is just the same as the normal way of reading messages.

However, there's one important difference – the **Read Offline** button. Next to each of the Message boards in your **My Boards** listing, you'll see an icon, immediately to the left of the Message board's name.

Normally, it looks like a piece of paper with a red pin through it, as if it's being stuck to a notice-board on the wall. When this icon is showing the Message board is set so that you can read it when you're connected to AOL.

If you'd like to have AOL collect all the messages for you in one go, so that you can read them when you've disconnected, highlight one of the message boards and then click the button marked **Read Offline**.

The icon will change to one with a small clock on top of a message. When you run Automatic AOL, messages for any message board marked with this icon will be collected. You can find out more about Automatic AOL in *Chapter 5, AOL and You (5.6, Automatic AOL)*.

To change a Message board back, so that new postings aren't automatically collected, just highlight it and click the **Read Offline** button again, and the icon will change back.

Even when you've marked a Message board to read offline, you can still read messages while you're connected to AOL in the normal way. Any messages that you read won't be new any more, so they won't be collected by Automatic AOL, but other new postings in the message board will.

3.8 More about chat rooms

We've already looked at the basics of chat rooms, but there are some other things that you can do with them.

All the chat rooms we've come across so far are ones created by AOL, but that's not the only type of room there is. You can create a private chat room, that people can only join if they know the exact name. You might, for example, arrange with other members of your family at 8pm GMT, you'll be in a chat room called JonesChat99.

When they sign on, they can join that chat room, and you can have an online family reunion, no matter where in the world everyone is.

Private chat rooms

The simplest way to create a chat room is to make a private one. All you need to do is go to any AOL chat room, and click the **Options** button at the top left.

Fig. 3.67
Chat menu

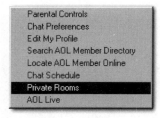

You'll see this menu appear, and you need to choose **Private Rooms**, which lets you create a new room, or join one if it's already been created.

Fig. 3.68
Private rooms screen

All you need to do is type the name of the room in the box, and press **Enter**, or click **Chat Now**. The title of the chat room on your screen will change to the name that you just entered, and you're in your own room.

Remember that people might not be able to find you easily, so if you see someone you'd like to join the room, why not send them an Instant Message. They'll be able to use the Locate button on the bottom of the IM screen to see where you are, and can join you easily, without having to type the name of the room.

AOL logs

Message boards, of course, are designed so that you don't have to be there at the time someone makes a comment to see what they said. With chat and Instant Messages, if you miss something, then it's gone for good, isn't it?

Fig. 3.69
Log manager main screen

As you can see, there are two types of log file that you can create – chat logs and sessions logs.

Chat logs

A chat log is the log of all the things that happen in a particular chat room. Everything that appears in the main chat window will be saved to the log file, so that you can read it later. Everything that appears after you've started logging will be saved, but not messages that are already on your computer screen.

The first item in this section will show you the name of the room that's being logged – check that it's the right one, and then click either **Open Log** or **Append Log** to start recording what's said.

When you choose **Open Log**, a new log file will be created. Perhaps you're creating a log of all the chats you've watched with celebrities though, and you want everything in one place. In that case, choose **Append Log**, and then find the log file you want to add information to. Double-click it, and AOL will add new information on to the end of the file.

To stop recording what's happening in the chat room, come back to the **Log Manager**, and click **Close Log**.

Session logs

A session log records all the information that you read on AOL, including areas like news stories and other articles. You could use a session log, for example, to make sure you have a record of all the financial news you looked at online, to read later.

The **Open Log** and **Append Log** buttons work in exactly the same way for session logs as for chat logs, so you can carry on adding information to an existing file, or create a new one.

Session logs also allow you to record the Instant Messages that people send you, too. If you'd like to keep a record of what people have said to you via Instant Messages, click to put a check in the box marked **Log Instant Message conversations**. You can only click this box when a Session Log has already been started.

Reading your logs

Once you've saved information in a log file, you'll probably want to read it – after all, there wouldn't be much point otherwise, would there?

Fortunately, it's easy. From the **File** menu, all you have to do is choose **Open**, then pick the log file that you want to view, and double-click it.

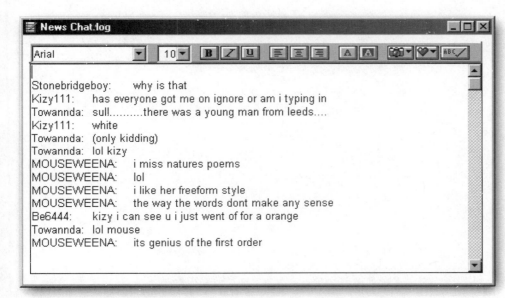

Fig. 3.70
Open log file in AOL

You can also open the log files in any other program that can read a text file, like your word processor, though you may need to set the file type to All Files to be able to see the log file when you choose Open in other programs.

AOL can only read log files that are less than 32k long. If you have saved a lot of information to a single log file, AOL may tell you that it can't open the file. Don't worry – you'll still be able to open the log, but you'll have to do it using your word-processing program.

That's all there is to it – now you know how to keep on top of Chat and Instant Messages, no matter how busy you are. And if you'd like to find out more about reading your message boards when you've signed off, don't forget that you can find out how in *Chapter 5, AOL and You (5.6, Automatic AOL)*.

Before you look at that, though, it's about time we explored AOL's Channels and gave you a flavour of the incredible amount of information that's on offer.

4

Channels

4.1 Navigating AOL's Channels

AOL's Channels are the heart of its information. On the Channels you'll find useful articles, files you can download, chat rooms and just about all the information you'll ever need, from reviews of the latest gadgets to the pros and cons of different types of pension scheme.

With so much information on each Channel, you could be forgiven for thinking that they must be pretty confusing, but you'll actually find that each one has been designed to make it as simple as possible to find the information that you want.

What's more, all the Channels work in the same way – they may have different information, and they might use unique graphics, but you'll find that once you know how to move around one Channel, you'll have no problems moving around the others.

4.2 The Chat Channel

AOL's Chat Channel is where you can find new friends to chat with, or hang out with people you've already met on AOL. You can explore chat rooms in other areas of AOL, and even connect to the chat rooms of AOL services in other countries, so you can talk with people in Germany, France, the USA and elsewhere.

Chat

What's on the Chat Channel?

Perhaps a better question to ask is 'Who's on the Chat Channel?' AOL Chat, after all, is where you'll find people just like yourself – the members who make the AOL community such fun to be a part of.

The Chat Channel is there to help you find chat rooms and message boards wherever they are on AOL, so you'll find that some of the buttons and links will take you to rooms in other Channels.

If you're not sure about how to use the chat facilities, you'll find all the information you need in the help area – and don't forget that you can read all about using Chat rooms and Message boards in *Chapter 3, The AOL Experience.* (*3.1, Chatting on AOL*; *3.5, Advanced chat*).

Perhaps you fancy a talk about nothing in particular, rather than delving into the intricacies of car engines, or whatever other specialised chat room you normally visit. Why not try the New Members Lobby? You'll find it on the **Quick Chat** list, and the will be other people who, like you, are just starting to explore AOL. Drop in and see what hints and tips you can pick up.

And if you're in one of those moods where you just want to talk about strange things, like why the moon can't possibly be *that* colour, or just about anything else that's a little out of the ordinary, you can join like-minded souls in Diadem chat, where the most important rule is that nothing should be ordinary.

While some rooms might ramble a little – and that's probably an understatement – they're not all like that. The Chat Channel is also home to AOL's Hosted Chats. Those are chats on a specific topic, where there's an AOL Host to make sure that if the chat is about the Olympic Games, it doesn't suddenly veer off into a discussion about the Great Barrier Reef.

As the saying goes, it's good to talk, and whether you want a serious discussion or a light-hearted diversion, AOL's Chat Channel is the place to start.

A guide to the Chat Channel's main screen

Fig. 4.1
**Chat Channel
main screen**

If you just want to chat, but you're not sure what about, the Chat Channel's main screen is a great place to seek inspiration. You'll see featured chats here, whatever AOL Channel they're on, so it's a great place to see what's happening.

You'll also see handy links to help you find out more about chatting on AOL, and checking up on the Conditions of Service.

Another of the links will guide you through creating a Private Chat Room, so you can talk with family or colleagues, away from the crowds in some of the more public areas.

Some highlights of the Chat Channel

The real highlight of the Chat Channel is the people that you'll find using the different rooms and Message boards, but there are some areas that are well worth looking at in a little more detail. If neither of the things we've mentioned here takes your fancy, why not just browse through the Channel. Whatever your interests, you're sure to find a place where you can make new friends and talk with like-minded people.

Diadem

Diadem is AOL's area for the weird, the wacky and the off-the-wall. You'll find message boards and chat rooms, with people talking about all sorts of topics, the stranger the better.

Diadem

There are also links to some of the best humour sites on the Internet, celebrity caricatures, and much more. You can even win prizes, in the form of a Diadem badge. All you have to do is make a witty or wacky contribution to the message boards or chat rooms, and you'll be in with a chance!

Quick Chat

If you're a chat addict, or you just can't remember exactly how you got to that chat room you enjoyed so much last night, Quick Chat is the solution. It will take you directly to any of the main chat areas on AOL UK. You can access it via the Chat Channel's main screen, or via it's own keyword, which you can shorten to just **QC** – so you're closer to your favourite chat rooms than ever.

Quick chat

As you can see, Quick Chat couldn't be easier to use. You'll see a list of all the AOL chat areas for the UK. Just scroll through the list, and double-click the room you want to visit.

Message boards and chat on the Chat Channel

The Chat Channel isn't just about Chat rooms, of course. There are plenty of Message boards, and you'll find them all at this keyword, including boards for the AOL Pub and Diadem Chat areas.

Chat message boards

There are also Message boards for twenty-somethings, and a place where you can discuss issues with AOL's Editor.

Keywords for the Chat Channel

You can find everything you need to know about chatting on AOL's Chat Channel, and these keywords will help you reach the right place as quickly as possible.

| Chat Rooms |

- **Chat Rooms** – Search for chat rooms by name, or by interest – and if you want an international feel, at this keyword you can link up with people chatting on AOL around the world.

| ChatMessageBoards |

- **ChatMessageBoards** – Quick access to all the message boards in the Chat Channel.

| Chatterbox |

- **Chatterbox** – Find out what's new on AOL's Chat Channel, including news about new rooms and Hosted Chats.

| Diadem |

- **Diadem** – For the weird and wonderful, use your wit to win a stylish badge in Diadem.

| Private Rooms |

- **Private Rooms** – Create your own private chat area for friends or family, far from the madding crowd.

| QuickChat |

- **QuickChat** – Can't remember where you found that great chat room the other day? Quick Chat is the fastest way to get to your favourite rooms.

4.3 The Entertainment Channel

Entertainment covers a wide range of things – TV, radio, books, films and music – and you'll find all those on AOL's Entertainment Channel, together with information on new entertainment technologies.

Entertainment

What's on the Entertainment Channel?
If television is the way you like to be entertained, you'll find TV reviews, recommended viewing and plenty of places to talk about what's on. There are chat rooms for popular programmes and even a whole area from Inside Soap magazine, so you can find out about the stars and characters of your favourite programmes.

Perhaps the big screen is more your thing? You'll find information about every film that's on release at the moment, so you can decide what you really want to see, and read what AOL's film critic John Marriott thought of it.

When you want to step out in style, how about a trip to the theatre? With a guide to the West End shows, and special ticket offers, the Entertainment Channel can help you plan a special night out.

For the musically minded, you'll find gig guides, news and information about the latest releases, whatever type of music you like – whether it's dance, rap, pop, classical or jazz. You can even keep up to date on pop news with a ticker service from WorldPop.

Bookworms are catered for as well, with extracts from forthcoming titles – and of course you can shop for the books online with AOL too. If you want suggestions for things to read, why not join the AOL Book Club, where author Melanie McGrath talks about books?

Traditional arts are covered too, with information on exhibitions and galleries, so if you want the low-down on the Tate Modern, the Entertainment Channel is the place to look.

And as if all that's not enough, the latest digital entertainment technologies are covered, with help and information to make sure you have no problems at all watching live concerts online, or downloading the latest music clips.

A guide to the Entertainment Channel's main screen

Fig. 4.2
**Entertainment
Channel main
screen**

The main screen of the Entertainment Channel has a menu for each of the main types of entertainment that you might want to find out about. You'll see options along the top, for example, for **music**, **film**, **TV**, and **books**. Just click them, and you can reach the information you're interested in really quickly.

As usual, there's also a search box, so you can find information on the Channel really easily, and you'll see some of the most interesting news and events – of all types – highlighted on the Channel's main screen.

Watch out too for links to special chat sessions at AOL Live – the Entertainment Channel will bring you exclusive live chats with the stars of some of the most popular films and TV programmes.

Some highlights of the Entertainment Channel
The Entertainment Channel is home to masses of information. There are so many different things on the Channel that it's hard to pick out just one or two, but here are some of the ones you may like to look at.

Book Club

Some people like their entertainment brash and noisy on the big screen, while others simply love books and reading. If your idea of bliss is wandering round a bookshop deciding what to buy, then AOL's Book Club is a place you'll be dying to visit.

Hosted by author Melanie McGrath, the Book Club chooses a book each month for members to read. You can join other AOL members talking about the book and what it meant to them, and make your own suggestions for titles that other people might want to read.

There are links to help you order the featured books of the month, and you can check to see what books have been featured recently.

Whether you're spoilt for choice in a bookshop, or wondering if you've been missing out on the latest hot titles, take a look at AOL's Book Club for inspiration and advice.

Book club

Message boards and chat on the Entertainment Channel

You'll find plenty of places to chat and take part in discussions on the Entertainment Channel, including Message boards where you can discuss the latest film and record releases, sharing your opinions with other members.

Keywords for the Entertainment Channel

Whatever your interest, you'll find a keyword on AOL that will take you right to the part of the Entertainment Channel that caters specially for you. Take a look through this list, and you're sure to find some that will match your interests.

- **Arts** – Find out about the latest exhibitions, galleries and other news from the arts world.

- **Classical** – News and latest releases from the world of classical music.

- **Film** – Reviews and listings of all the films that are currently on release.

- **Sound and Vision** – Everything you need to know about entertainment in the digital age – how to play MP3, load Webcasts and more.

- **TV** – Find out what's on TV and what's happening in the world of soap.

Arts
Classical
Film
Sound and Vision
TV

4.4 The Finance Channel

Finance

AOL's Finance Channel is where you'll find everything to do with financial matters. That includes banking, credit cards, savings accounts, pensions and mortgages. In short, if it's to do with money, then you'll probably find it on the Finance Channel.

What's on the Finance Channel?
The Finance Channel is absolutely packed with information. You'll find share prices, and business news from respected services like Bloomberg, and even links to online share-dealing, so you can buy and sell shares without having to get a broker involved.

There are news reports covering different markets, so you can read about what's happening around the world, or investigate the latest dot com entrepreneurs trying to make their millions.

Perhaps you'd like to try your own hand at running a business? The Finance Channel will help with that too. You can read about how to make a business plan, or the ins and outs of the tax system – and you might be able to find someone on the Message boards who can recommend a good local accountant for you to use.

Finance isn't just about stocks, shares and running your own business, of course. For many of us, it's about where we live, how we're going to pay for a new car, and what will happen to us when we retire.

You'll find information about all that too. For example, there's a special section dedicated to pensions, and it even includes information about the thorny topic of long-term care for the elderly.

Worried about how to make ends meet? The Finance Channel can help you to understand the ins and outs of borrowing and saving, so you'll be able to make better decisions about what to do with your hard-earned cash. You might even be able to understand the difference between an ISA and a PEP, thanks to the online experts!

Homeowners can find out information about their mortgage, or how to deal with the landlord if you live in a leasehold flat. And if you want to know what the tax implications of taking in a lodger might be, you can check that out too.

From a savings account for your grandchildren to cutting your tax bill with canny investments, from choosing a pension to choosing the right time to sell your Building Society shares, you'll find it on the Finance Channel.

A guide to the Finance Channel's main screen

Fig. 4.3
Finance Channel main screen

The main screen of the Finance Channel is where you'll find quick links to take you to some of the most popular areas. From left to right, you'll see links for **News**, **Market Watch**, **Company Focus**, **Shares & Portfolios**, **Investing**, **Personal Finance** and **Small Business**.

You'll also see the latest figures from the stock markets, including the FTSE, Nasdaq and Dow Jones indices, so you can see right away how things are going in the financial world.

The **News** section is where you'll find a wide range of financial news, including information like announcements of job losses, or inflation figures.

Market Watch is for people who want to know what's happening in the different markets around the world. You can click the button to go to the main Market Watch Screen, or use the menu to select more detailed screens for UK, Europe, World, Emerging and High tech markets.

Want to know how a particular company is performing, and look up its most recent results? **Company Focus** is the place to look, and you'll also find tips from top brokers, and tools to help you find out more about the firms you're interested in.

Click **Shares and Portfolios** to find the latest information on your own stocks and shares, and to look up the very latest prices – you too can have up-to-date information just like brokers. This is also where you'll find **My Portfolios**, where you can easily keep track of all your stock market investments – tell AOL once, and it will remember what you've invested in for the next time you visit.

The **Investing Area** is where you can find the low-down on ISAs, trusts, bonds and other types of investment. It includes the Trading Pit, where you'll find up-to-date prices, and all the other information you'll need to pick the right time to buy or sell those windfall shares.

Personal Finance is where you'll find those essential things that we all need to think about – banking, saving, property, pensions, tax and so on. You can visit the Personal Finance page, or use the menu to go directly to one of the special sections within it. There are plenty of guides to help you make the right decisions, like a pension calculator, and the latest information on how to plan for care in your future.

Finally, if you run your own business, or you're thinking of starting one, the **Small Business** section is the place to look for help and advice, including tax and accounting.

Some highlights of the Finance Channel
There really is a huge amount of information on the Finance Channel – far too much to describe it all here. But we'll take a look at some of the things that you might find most useful. If you want to see if there's an area on the Channel for something that you're particularly interested in, don't forget that at the end of this section there's a complete list of all the keywords for different areas in the Channel. And, of course, you can always browse through the Finance Channel, or type a word into the Search box on the main screen and see what happens.

My Portfolio

If you invest in shares, My Portfolio could be one of the most useful things you've come across. Are you fed up with scanning the small print on the financial pages to see how much your investments are worth, and if you should sell anything before it's too late? My Portfolio could be the answer to your prayers.

My Portfolio

With My Portfolio, you can tell AOL what investments you have, and then each time you sign on, it will take only moments to find out if you have extra money for your holiday, or it's time to sell up and move on.

When you first visit My Portfolio, there won't be any shares in it. If you don't know what the symbol – the short name used by dealers – is for your shares, you can use the **Lookup** button to find out. For example, click **Lookup** and this screen appears.

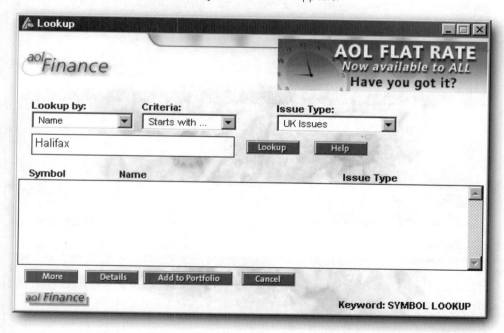

Fig. 4.4
Share lookup screen

Type 'Halifax' into the box at the top, click to choose **Lookup**. Make sure the option in the next box is set to London – that's the market on which the shares are traded – and then click the **Search** button. All the latest information about the shares will be retrieved, and the symbol is the first thing on the top line – in this case, HFX.

To add a share to your portfolio when you know it's symbol, you just need to click the **Add** button on the My Portfolio screen.

You need to fill in the symbol, and the market on which it's traded – as you'll see from the list, you can find out about shares that are traded on lots of different markets around the world. You also need to say how many shares you own.

If you'd like to know how much you've lost or gained, you can fill in extra information, like the price you paid originally, and the date you bought the shares – but it's not essential.

To see how much your shares are worth, just double-click **Portfolio 1**, and you'll see a screen like this one:

Fig. 4.5
Portfolio display

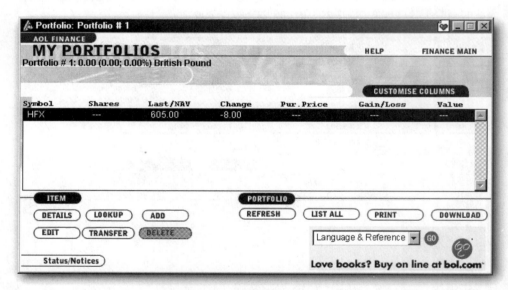

The buttons at the left-hand side, below the list of your portfolio items, let you alter details of one of the shares, while those at the right can be used to print out your current information, or download it to your computer. By downloading the information, you could read it into a database or spreadsheet program on your own computer. Experienced traders might, for example, do this to see if they can spot any trends.

You don't have to group all your shares together. AOL's My Portfolio actually lets you create up to 20 different portfolios, each of which can have 100 different shares in it – that's a total of 2000 different shares.

On the main My Portfolio screen, the buttons under the Portfolio heading will let you add a new portfolio, delete one, or change its name. Those under the Item heading let you add new shares to the currently selected portfolio. Just click once on the portfolio that you want to work with.

Pensions
These days, everyone should be thinking about their pension – you can't rely on having enough to live on when you've finished work unless you start to put something aside in plenty of time.

Pensions

The Pensions area is where you can find out all the information you need to know to make what could be one of the most important financial decisions you'll ever make.

On the main screen you'll see the latest annuity rates from some of the top pension providers, and there's a link where you can calculate how much your pension is likely to be worth when you finally stop working. Even if you think you have everything in hand, it's worth checking – you might get a surprise when you realise what you'll have to live on.

There's also an impartial guide to pension planning, and you'll find lots of other articles to help you make sure your retirement is a time to enjoy, rather than worry about money.

Message boards and chat on the Finance Channel
As you'd expect, there are plenty of Message boards on the Finance Channel. You can use them to ask people for advice, or to swap tips about which companies you think are going to do well in future. You might be able to find someone who can recommend an accountant to help with your small business, or another person who's dealt with the hassles of a landlord overcharging for repairs to a flat.

Have your say

Whatever it is you want to talk about, you should find a place on one of the Finance Channel Message boards. You can go directly to them at the keyword **Have your say**, and you'll see a button to take you there on many of the screens within the Channel.

The Have your say screen also lets you access the chat areas on the Finance Channel, and you'll see a poll that you can take part in to express your views on a current topic.

Here's a list of all the Message boards you'll find on the Channel:

- Stock Market News and Tips

- Company News

- Investment Boards

- Retirement

- Property and Mortgages

- Savings and Banking

- Tax

- Debts and Borrowing

- Insurance

- Working at home & Small Business

- Dun & Bradstreet

- Economist Intelligence Unit

- Interactive Investor

- Small Business Library

Keywords for the Finance Channel

The Finance Channel is packed with information. To help you find your way around it, and reach the information you want quickly, here's a list of the keywords that you can use to go directly to a particular area.

- **Have your say** – Use this keyword to go directly to the message boards for the Finance Channel.

Have your say

- **Investing** – The Investing keyword in where you'll find guides to all sorts of investment, from buying property abroad to stocks and shares.

Investing

- **Pensions** – This is the place to look for information on every aspect of pensions. You can find out how much you'll need to save for your retirement, or read about some of the problems affecting those who no longer work.

Pensions

- **Shares** – Shows you how to get real-time share prices, and build your own portfolio.

Shares

- **Market Watch** – All the most up-to-date companies and markets news as well as features and analysis.

Market Watch

- **Mortgage** – No matter whether you're a first-time buyer or looking to remortgage your home, you'll get help here.

Mortgage

4.5 The Games Channel

Games

Computers aren't just for serious, worthy work, of course. They're a great way to play games, shooting at imaginary enemies, or pitting your wits against the logic of the machine. AOL's Games Channel is for anyone who enjoys playing games on their PC or on the latest consoles.

What's on the Games Channel?

The Games Channel is home to a wealth of information, whatever the type of games that you're interested in, and however old you are – games aren't just for kids, after all.

If you're frustrated with the game you're playing, and you just can't get past the current level, why not give into temptation and ask other gamers on the Channel's message boards? You could find that there's a tip or cheat that will take you to the next level and one step closer to reaching your ultimate goal.

Perhaps, you're a parent who wants to buy a great game as a surprise present for your child. No problem! On the Games Channel, you can find out all about the latest releases and guides to the greatest games around.

You can check out reviews of hundreds of games, past and present, so you'll be able to see whether or not it's worth buying that classic you saw for a knock-down price, or if you'd be better off saving up for something else.

Gamers on a budget will appreciate the download areas of the Channel, where you can find demos and even some completely free games. And, of course, you can find patches, extra levels and lots of other files to help improve the games you already have.

At AOL, they know that gaming isn't just about playing on your PC, so there are also special areas for the main consoles like the PlayStation, PS2, Dreamcast and N64. You'll be able to swap hints and tips with other users, and also discuss the latest releases.

Whatever type of game you're interested in, visit the Games Channel and you'll find a wealth of information to help you pass your time.

A guide to the Games Channel's main screen

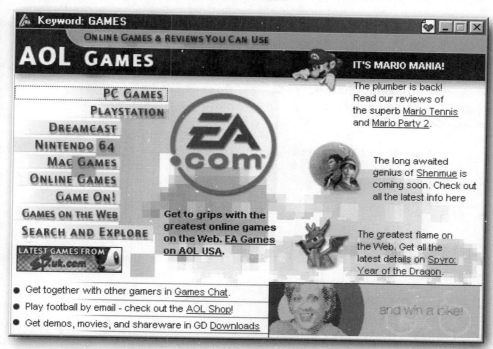

Fig. 4.6
**Games Channel
main screen**

The Games Channel's main screen is where you should be able to find everything you need, whatever sort of games you like.

As you can see, there are buttons on the screen for each of the main games systems, so whether it's Dreamcast or a PC that you're interested in, just click the button and you'll go right there.

The screen also has links to some of the latest news stories from the gaming world, so you can find out what's the latest news on the XBox, or which are the hot games to look out for, and when they'll be available on your console.

You can also click to buy the latest games – so there's no need to search through the online shops – and there are even demos highlighted for you to try out. You really could help the games companies make their products even more fun to play.

Message boards and chat on the Games Channel

If you're serious about gaming, chatting to other players is a great way to find out how to progress in your favourite games, or swap opinions on the latest releases, or even chew the fat about whether Microsoft's new XBox will beat the established players of the PS2 and Dreamcast. The Games Channel provides plenty of places to talk and discuss all the hot issues for gamers.

Games Chat

At the keyword **Games Chat** you'll find rooms for a general chatter, online games, Pokemon and Sim City. You can also jump straight to the Message boards or look up cheats for the popular gaming platforms.

You'll find Message boards for these areas on the Games Channel:

- PC Games

- PlayStation

- Nintendo 64

- Dreamcast

- Online Games

Keywords for the Games Channel

You'll find keywords on the Games Channel to help you go straight to the section you want, whether you're playing with your PC, or on the latest consoles.

Dreamcast

- **Dreamcast** – The latest news and chat about Sega's super console.

N64

- **N64** – Nintendo games start here! Everything a N64 and Gameboy owner will ever need.

Online Games

- **Online Games** – Blast for Britain – pit your wits against other gamers online, playing live via AOL.

PC Games

- **PC Games** – Everything a PC gamer will need.

PlayStation

- **PlayStation** – All the games news and reviews for your Sony PlayStation and PlayStation2.

4.6 The Health Channel

The Health Channel is home to a wide range of information covering everything you're ever likely to need to know about the health of you and your family, including alternative therapies, fitness and nutrition.

Health

What's on the Health Channel?

When you think of health, you might just imagine a trip to the doctor's with flu, or maybe even the dentist. But AOL's Health Channel is about much more than that. Of course, you'll find information to help you if you're feeling ill, but there's plenty to help make sure that you stay well, too.

If you're trying to keep in shape, why not check in with the fitness section, where you'll be able to find help in planning a workout regime that will keep you in shape, without wearing you out.

Or perhaps you're a pregnant mother, wondering about whether or not you're eating properly. Don't worry – you can join other new families online and share experiences in chat rooms, and like everyone else, you can use AOL to look up information on your diet, to help make sure you don't miss out on anything important.

The young, and the young at heart, might be keen to make a good impression when going out on the town, and with beauty tips, the Health Channel can help there too, whether it's making you look your best for an interview, or slowing down the march of time.

Maybe you're keen to keep your family free of the clinical approaches of modern medicine. The Health Channel caters for you too, with information on alternative therapies, so you can make sure you understand what your options for treatment really are, whatever type of medicine you decide to opt for.

There's news too, so you can find out the low-down on the latest medical developments, and if you're confused about them – or perhaps just too shy to ask your own doctor about personal matters – you'll find healthcare professionals online and ready to answer your questions.

A guide to the Health Channel's main screen

Fig. 4.7
**Health Channel
main screen**

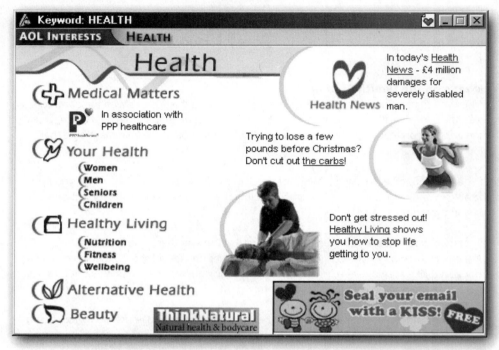

On the Health Channel's main screen, you'll find quick links to plenty of useful information, whether it's news, or a quick answer to a medical question that's worrying you.

From left to right, you'll see links at the top for the main areas, **Medical Matters**, **Family Health**, **Fitness**, **Nutrition**, **Alternative Health** and **Beauty**.

Medical Matters is where you'll find information about specific medical conditions, like what to do after a heart attack, plus fact sheets on a range of issues, and the opportunity to send questions to medical experts, or read the replies they've given to other people.

In the **Family Health** section you'll find tips and information about the health of all your family, including how to deal with allergies, or specific illnesses that affect children.

Fitness is where you can find hints and tips to help you stay in shape – and it's not just for those who want to spend hours each day at the gym. There's information for everyone, whatever age they are. You'll also find a weekly column on fitness issues.

Want to be sure you're eating properly? The **Nutrition** area will help you out, whether it's just making sure you eat the right foods when you're pregnant, or tricks to make sure the children really do eat a little of what's good for them.

If you're interested in acupuncture, or you want to know what osteopathy is all about, you can find the answers in the **Alternative Health** section, along with plenty of other information on all aspects of healthcare that lie outside the mainstream.

Finally, the **Beauty** area is where you can find tips on make-up, makeovers and grooming. If you want to look your best, as well as feel your best, this is the place to turn. You'll also see links to the latest health news, and regular features on different aspects of health, fitness, nutrition and beauty.

Some highlights of the Health Channel

Check out the Health Channel's Cool Tools, which you'll see on the main screen, for handy online question-and-answer sessions, designed to help you find out just what sort of shape you're in. You can choose to take a beauty quiz, or find out just how fit you really are, or check your diet to make sure you're eating properly.

Message boards and chat on the Health Channel

You'll find plenty of places to chat on the Health Channel, so don't be shy – remember that on AOL, no one can see your blushes. There are message boards for Men's Health, Women's Health and plenty of other topics too. No matter what's on your mind, you can get it off your chest, and perhaps find someone who's experienced the same health issues.

As well as message boards, the Health Channel is also home to regular chats, including a twice-weekly Family Health chat, where you can talk about keeping your kids healthy, dealing with sickness, or just share experiences with other people and their families.

Keywords for the Health Channel

As you can see, the Health Channel covers a wide range of information. Of course you can reach it all from the main screen, but to help reach some areas quicker, here are some more keywords that you might find helpful.

- **Alternative Health**

- **Family Health**

- **Mind and Body**

- **Nutrition**

- **Wellbeing**

| Alternative Health |
| Family Health |
| Mind and Body |
| Nutrition |
| Wellbeing |

4.7 The Interests Channel

Interests

AOL's Interests Channel is quite possibly the most wide-ranging Channel you'll find anywhere, covering everything from cars to monarchy and gardening to charities. If it's a hobby, pastime or interest that you want to find out about, then it'll be on AOL's Interests Channel.

What's on the Interests Channel?

Whatever your hobbies and interests, you'll find the things you're looking for on AOL's Interests Channel. If you're a pet owner, for instance, why not look at the Pets area, where you can share information about your animals with other members, or maybe find someone on a message board who can recommend a good kennel for when you're on holiday. If you're lucky, perhaps you can have your entry chosen as the Pet of the Week for everyone else to read about.

Those whose interests are more mechanical will find all the information they need in the Drive area, whether it's tips on repairing your own car, or opinions on the latest models from the top manufacturers. And if you're a collector, why not take a look at the Classic Cars area, where you can read about – and contribute to – members' experiences with their own cars.

Perhaps you want to find out about helping other people? Why not try the Charities area, where you can read about what different charities are doing, and find out from the Message boards how you can get involved in their work, from Human Rights to working with the Blind.

Families are welcome on the Interests Channel, and as well as offering plenty of places to talk about their interests, there's also the opportunity to find out more about your own one. Visit the Genealogy area for ideas and information on tracing your own family tree.

One family that doesn't need much work done tracing it is the royal family, and the Interests Channel even has a monarchy area. You can read about what's going on in the royal world, and join others talking about the Queen Mother, or the future of the royal family.

You'll find plenty more here too, including gardening, cycling, experts to ask for advice, and plenty of people to meet in the chat rooms and message areas. So, whatever you're interested in, you'll find this Channel is a great place to meet like-minded souls.

A guide to the Interests Channel's main screen

As you can see from the main screen, there are plenty of areas to visit on this Channel, and different ones will be highlighted on the main screen from time to time.

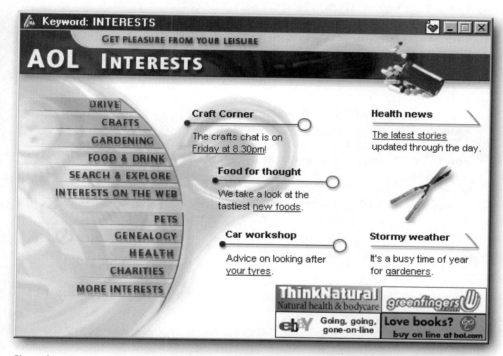

Fig. 4.8
Interests Channel main screen

Since there's so much information on this Channel, on such a wide range of topics, remember that you can use the Search & Explore box on the main screen to find exactly what it is you're looking for.

All you need to do is type a couple of words into the box, and click the **Go** button, then AOL will look for information within the Interests Channel. You can read more about searching a Channel earlier on in this chapter (*4.1, Searching a channel*).

Of course, as well as searching, you can find the information you want very easily using the menus along the top of the main screen. As you can see, from left to right, there are buttons for Drive, Crafts, Gardening, Food & Drink, etc.

You'll find all the things that we've talked about already on these menus – remember that you can click the title, or use the menu to go straight to an area.

Keywords for the Interests Channel

With such a wide range of topics on the Interests Channel, you'll probably want to go straight to the area that interests you most. As well as using the menus on the main screen, why not try some of these keywords to get you where you want to go?

Cars

- **Cars** – Old or new, you'll find all you want to know about cars in this section of the Channel.

Drink

- **Drink** – Wine-tasting tips and recommendations, plus everything else for people who like their drink.

Fashion

- **Fashion** – News, shows and the latest clothes from the world of fashion.

Food

- **Food** – From gourmet recommendations to favourite recipes for a quick supper, you'll find it all here.

Gardening

- **Gardening** – Watch out for those green fingers – you don't want to stain the keyboard!

4.8 The Kids Channel

At AOL, kids are important, and there's a whole Channel specially for them, catering for their interests in a friendly way. Remember that by using AOL's Parental Controls, you can limit your children to the Kids Only areas on AOL so that they'll only see things that are suitable for them.

Kids

You can find out more about Parental Controls in *Chapter 5, AOL and You* (*5.1, Parental controls*).

What's on the Kids Channel?
The Kids Channel is home to plenty of information for your children, whatever age they are from 0 up to 15.

Younger children might want to play with some of the pre-school sections of the Channel, like the Green Ted storybook, and whatever the age, they're sure to love the bright colourful feel of the Channel. When they're a bit older, they can use the StoryMaker section to make their own stories online.

Pokémon collectors will find a special area on the Channel just for them, so they can read about their favourite characters, or perhaps chat with other children who share their interest.

Pokemon

If the Hogwarts School of Wizardry and Witchcraft is where your child dreams of going, then let them check out the Harry Potter section of the Channel, with info, trivia and plenty more about the young wizard and his friends.

Harry Potter

Kids wouldn't be kids if they didn't listen to pop music, and you'll find plenty of that on the Channel too, with the Mega! Pop Calendar. There are details of the new releases, shows and the birthdays of popular stars.

For children who prefer to be outside, why not check out the section on caring for your pony? And there's plenty more too, with news stories specially for children, TV information, an online agony aunt and a Web search that's guaranteed only to show you kid-friendly sites to visit. Give your children a screen name of their own with AOL's Parental Controls and the Kids Channel, you can be sure they'll be safe online (*5.1, Screen names and parental controls*).

A guide to the Kids Channel's main screen

Fig. 4.9
**Kids Channel
main screen**

AOL's Kids Channel is special. Because it's designed to be a fun, safe place for your children, it doesn't look quite like the rest of the Channels.

Instead of the menus that you see on normal AOL Channels, the Kids Channel has plenty of big icons to take you to different parts of the Channel.

When you move the mouse over one of the pictures, you'll see it change to reveal what sort of information is hidden under it. Just click the picture to go to that area.

So, what's on this screen? The best way to find your way around the Kids Channel is to click the buttons and explore. You'll find there are sections for **Your World**, **Sporty Stuff**, **Pop Music**, **TV and Films**, **Chit Chat**, **Know Your Stuff**, **Fun and Games** and the **Playroom**.

Some highlights of the Kids Channel

There really is something for children of every age on the Kids Channel, and you can be sure that when you use AOL's Parental Controls, you'll be keeping your kids safe, and still giving them access to a wide range of really useful information. Here are a couple of the things we think are best about the Kids Channel.

Dear Joanie

Kids have problems too, and AOL's agony aunt Joanie is here to help. Each week, Joanie features a problem and offering no-nonsense advice for the kids.

| Dear Joanie |

As well as reading the answer to this week's issue, kids can click **Problems** to read the previous issues that have been tackled, and if there's something that's bothering them that hasn't been asked before, they can click **Ask Joanie** to send in their own question.

There are regular online chats with Joanie too, so kids can share their comments and experiences in a chat room, and if they've got a problem, they'll find the phone numbers for lots of useful services like ChildLine too.

Kids Contents

There's so much for kids on AOL that there's even a special keyword they can use to find all the information just for them.

| AOL Kids Contents |

Kids Contents has a great list of areas that you can reach just by scrolling through the list and double-clicking the highlighted words. And, of course, you can make a note of the keywords you're interested in and go directly to them later.

At the bottom of the screen, there's a special search box too, so kids can type in a word or phrase and click the **Go** button to see a list of special kids content. Click the **Web Sites** button and you'll see a list of specially selected sites on the Internet, all guaranteed to be suitable for your kids, so you can let them play without any worries.

And for those days when the kids just can't decide what they want to look at, click **Surprise Me!**, at the bottom of the Kids Contents page, and AOL will pick one of the kids areas for you! How's that for a way to solve arguments on a rainy day?

Chit Chat

Message boards and chat on the Kids Channel

Chit Chat is where kids can make friends and swap messages with other people in their age group – and to give parents peace of mind, the Chat rooms and Message boards are all supervised by AOL, to make sure that there's nothing inappropriate. You really can let your children use the Kids Channel without worrying.

Keywords for the Kids Channel

As we said earlier, there are lots of keywords just for kids, and you can find a complete list at the **Kids Contents** keyword. To save you time, here are some of the most popular ones that you might want to look at.

Green Ted

- **Green Ted** – Pre-school storybook and colouring book.

Harry Potter

- **Harry Potter** – Info, trivia and fun with the popular J.K. Rowling books.

Mega

- **Mega** – Mega! Pop Calendar, details of record releases, shows and star birthdays.

The Buzz

- **The Buzz** – Weekly AOL Kids Channel newsletter.

Storymaker

- **Storymaker** – Create a personalised story.

4.9 The Learning Channel

Learning isn't just something you do at school – you can do it however old you are, and AOL's Learning Channel is there to help you, with all the resources and information you'll need.

Learning

What's on the Learning Channel?
The Learning Channel is home to lots of great resources that can help you wherever you are in life. You've probably heard ministers and other people talk about Lifelong learning – well, the AOL Learning Channel is where that talk can really turn into action.

If you're feeling stuck in a rut, why not take a look at the Careers section, where you'll find guidance and advice, with trained professionals to help you. Who knows, you might realise that there's a job out there you're perfectly suited to. You'll even be able to find help with tracking the jobs down when you've selected your career, with online job searches. Whether you're a school leaver, graduate or looking to change direction later in life, it's all here.

Careers

What about people still at school? Of course, there's plenty for them, with a special area for revision to help if you're coming up for important tests. It includes resources for people studying at A level, GCSE and plenty of other key stages in the school career, from some of the most well-known names in the business.

Even when you're not doing exams, you might still want some guidance with your school work, and the Homework Help section could be the answer. It won't write your essays for you, but you will be able to call on experts to give you hints when you're stuck, or chat with other people who are tackling the same topics as you.

It's not just exams and homework, of course. When you're coming up to the end of your time in school, you need to make some pretty tough decisions about what to do next – university, college, or training courses. AOL can help with those too, right down to telling you which is the best bar at the university you're thinking about.

Parents and teachers both play an important part in learning, and you'll find lots of information whichever category you fall into. There are full details of the National Curriculum, and regular online chats where you can talk to other parents about how they make the kids do homework.

And finally, don't forget all the reference information you'll find on the Learning Channel, with encyclopedias, dictionaries, almanacs and atlases.

Whether you want to learn something new, brush up your Shakespeare, or simply find reassurance about your child's progress at school, the Learning Channel is the place to look.

A guide to the Learning Channel's main screen

Fig. 4.10
Learning Channel main screen

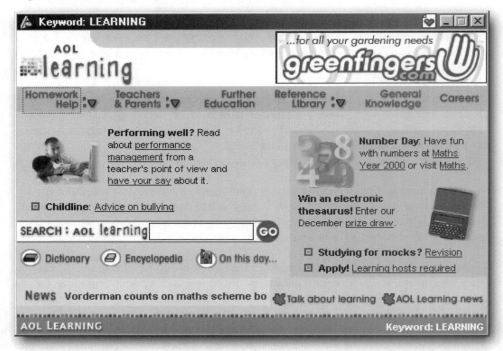

As you can see from the screen, the Learning Channel is divided into clear sections on the main screen. **Homework Help** is the place to look if you're having problems with an assignment from school, while the **Teachers & Parents** menu is where you'll be able to find answers to all your questions about schools and the National Curriculum.

If you want to find out about options for life after school, why not click **Further Education**? You'll be able to find out all about universities and colleges, how to pick the right one to apply to, and there are even special chat areas for students to talk with each other – or with those thinking of studying at the same place.

The **Reference Library** is your gateway to AOL's online encyclopedia, thesaurus, dictionary, almanac and educational encyclopedia. You can go directly to one of them by clicking the arrow next to Reference Library, or just visit the reference section's main screen by clicking the words. If it's more general information you want, why not click **General Knowledge** instead?

And if you want to find out about jobs, training and other related issues, use the **Careers** button.

At the bottom of the screen, you'll also see handy buttons to access AOL's online dictionary and encyclopedia, so the most important tools are only just a click away. And, the **On this day** button will give you useful facts and figures about what's happened in history.

To access the Chat rooms and Message boards, all you need to do is click **Talk about Learning**, so whether you're learning, looking for a new direction in life, or trying to help your kids with their homework, you'll find everything you need just a click away on the Learning Channel's screen.

Some highlights of the Learning Channel

There are so many resources on the Learning Channel that it's hard to pick just one or two. You'll find more keywords at the end of this section, so you can see some more of the great stuff that's available, but here we've picked two of the most useful things you'll find on AOL.

Careers

Not sure what path your life is going to take? The Careers section is here to help, with plenty of advice, whether you're a teenager just wondering about what to do after GCSEs, a graduate or someone older looking for a change.

You'll find hints and tips on how to sell yourself with a well-written CV, and discussion areas for different professions, so you can ask questions and swap advice with other people.

To help you make up your mind, you'll find profiles of different careers, and a special section for school leavers too. There's even special information for people who want to do voluntary work.

At the bottom of the screen, you'll see a menu of different types of job. Just click the arrow to see the whole list, pick an option, and AOL will search for job vacancies in that category. What could be simpler?

Careers

Homework Help

Homework Help

If you have children at school, you've probably been asked to help with their homework more than once – and isn't it awful when you don't know the answer? Well, with AOL, that need never be a problem again.

Homework Help is a special area where your children can find hints and advice on the problems they have with their homework, with teachers ready to give assistance on whatever subject you like.

You'll find plenty of useful resources too, like links to study guides based on the National Curriculum and revision tips to help you in the run up to those all-important exams.

Message boards and chat on the Learning Channel

There's plenty to talk about when you're learning, whatever the level. AOL's Learning Channel has plenty of resources to help you keep in touch and seek advice.

There are regular homework chats during school terms, so you can talk with other people studying the same subject, and every week there's a parents' night, where you can chat with other parents and teachers to discuss your child's progress.

Keywords for the Learning Channel

Careers

- **Careers** – Find out the best path from AOL's online careers advisor, and search for top jobs online.

General Knowledge

- **General Knowledge** – If you've a passion for learning, this is the place to find the facts you want on a range of subjects.

Post-18 Education

- **Post-18 Education** – All you need to know for higher education, lifelong learning and information about universities.

Reference Library

- **Reference Library** – A comprehensive selection of reference books and resources, including maps, almanacs and encyclopedias.

Revision

- **Revision** – Tests and study resources whether you're studying for GCSE or A level.

Teachers & Parents

- **Teachers & Parents** – Education news, and resources for teachers and parents, including details of the national curriculum.

4.10 The Lifestyles Channel

There are lots of different things that unite groups of people – it could be their religion, their nationality, the colour of their skin, or their age. AOL's Lifestyles Channel is home to thousands of members, coming together because of common feelings, thoughts or ways of life.

Lifestyles

What's on the Lifestyles Channel?

Lifestyles is crammed to the seams with information for just about every group of people imaginable, not to mention chat rooms, message boards and even picture galleries, so you can see who you're talking with.

If you fancy a makeover, take a look at Sugar magazine, exclusively online with AOL, where you can find advice for teenagers on fashion, make-up, and hair. Perhaps you have other things on your mind though, like problems at school, or worries about family life? Don't worry – AOL's Agony Uncle Matt Whyman is ready to help out with teenage problems, whatever they are.

Britain's black community will find lots of information on the Lifestyles Channel too, where the Black Britain section has won awards for its coverage of community news and issues. And, of course, other cultures are catered for on the Lifestyles Channel too.

Some people might say that religion and computers don't belong together, but that's certainly not the case on AOL. Whether it's Christianity, Judaism, Islam or another religion, you'll find that the spiritual is amply catered for, with Chat rooms, Message boards and links to some of the best Web sites selected for you.

Mystic Gardens is for the more exotic topics, and you'll find information on astrology, with daily horoscopes. There are Message boards on topics from ancient Egypt to paganism, and plenty of places to chat too.

Perhaps you're thinking of starting a family. If so, there's information for you on the Lifestyles Channel too, covering everything from fun days out for parents and kids to adoption and fostering.

And, of course, Lifestyles is where you can look for love and romance. You can flirt in the Love Shack, place a personals ad, and there's even a special section for AOL's lesbian, gay and bisexual members.

However you live your life, the Lifestyles Channel will be there for you.

A guide to the Lifestyles Channel's main screen

Fig. 4.11
Lifestyles Channel main screen

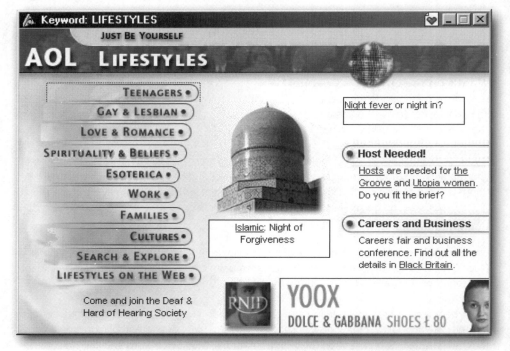

This is the main screen of the Lifestyles Channel. As you can see, there are handy links to each of the main areas of the Channel, such as **Spirituality**, **Love and Romance**, **Work** and **Families**.

You'll also see special areas highlighted from time to time – there are so many different areas on the Lifestyles Channel, that you might not have realised there are some that would be perfect for you.

Some highlights of the Lifestyles Channel
The Lifestyles Channel is a great place to come when you want to meet people, whether it's to share interests and experiences, or if you're looking for love and romance. You can also find advice and support too – there really is something for everyone.

Love Shack
If you're looking for love, you don't need to use the small ads in the newspapers any more. Why not try AOL's very own Love Shack, where you can chat to other single people, or place a personals ad for other people to look at?

Love Shack is where you can chat with people, flirt on the Message boards, or place an advert in the online classifieds section.

Click the **Place an Advert** button to start filling in your advert. On the next screen, you need to say what you're looking for – man seeking woman, and so on. Click the appropriate option and the Personals screen will appear.

When you've filled in all the information you want to give, you'll find a button at the bottom of the screen to click and place your advert. It's as simple as that. If you want to look at other people's ads, just use the **Browse** or **Search** buttons on the left hand side of the screen.

Stressed Out
Exams, love affairs, parents who don't understand. The list of things that can worry a teenager is pretty long. That's why AOL has an Agony Uncle specially for teenagers.

In the **Stressed Out** area, Matt Whyman tackles the topics on the minds of teenagers, with frank advice on a wide range of topics. You'll find plenty of information on topics like sex, school, friends and money, and there's the opportunity to send your questions direct to Matt if you can't find the advice you're looking for.

Stressed Out is also the place to look for useful help line numbers, or just to chat and share experiences with other teenagers in the chat rooms and message boards.

Message boards and chat on the Lifestyles Channel
You'll find lots of different places to chat on the Lifestyles Channel, with special areas for all of the main groups, like Black Britain, Lesbian and Gay, Teens, and Love.

Love Shack

Stressed Out

Keywords for the Lifestyles Channel

Want to find a quick way to meet people who live the same sort of life as you? Use one of these keywords to reach them.

Cultures	• **Cultures** – Where people from every culture can come together.
Families	• **Families** – Every aspect of family life is here.
Gay	• **Gay** – AOL welcomes everyone, and if you're lesbian, bisexual or gay, you'll find a thriving community here, called Utopia. There are message boards, chat rooms and picture galleries.
Teens	• **Teens** – Chat rooms, message boards and other information specially for teenagers.
Work	• **Work** – Want to meet other people in your line of business? There's a space here for everyone, from factory floor to boardroom.

4.11 **The News and Weather Channel**

Keeping up to date with what's happening in the world is one of the best reasons for going online. Without being tied to regular schedules like TV or radio, the online world can bring you the news as it's really happening, and provide you with all the background that there's never enough room for in the newspaper. AOL's News and Weather Channel is like your own daily paper, updated 24 hours a day.

News

What's on the News and Weather Channel?

You probably read a newspaper every day to keep you up to date with what's happening in the world, but AOL's News and Weather Channel can bring you the latest information – including video clips and interviews – far faster than any paper.

If it's home news you're interested in, you'll find over 150 stories every day, with sections for law, the media, politics, society and royalty. Maybe something you've read has got your goat, so why not join in the discussions in the News Chat rooms and Message boards?

The internationally minded will find stories from around the world too, and the Out There team brings a unique perspective by looking behind some of the biggest stories.

You'll find news to suit you if you're in business too, with city pages keeping you up to date on the movers and shakers.

As well as having your say on all the news stories in the chat rooms and on the message boards, how about taking part in the regular news polls? The polls will let you see at a glance how people feel about the issues in the headlines – and there are other ways to get involved too. There's also a caption competition, where you can review the pictures of the week and see if you can make up the best headline for them.

News is important, of course, but don't forget the weather! AOL's News and Weather Channel includes detailed weather too, with forecasts for the next days ahead, so you can plan your weekend, or decide whether to wrap up warm.

Whatever's happening, the News and Weather Channel will keep you up to date.

Fig. 4.12
**News and
Weather
Channel main
screen**

A guide to the News and Weather Channel's main screen

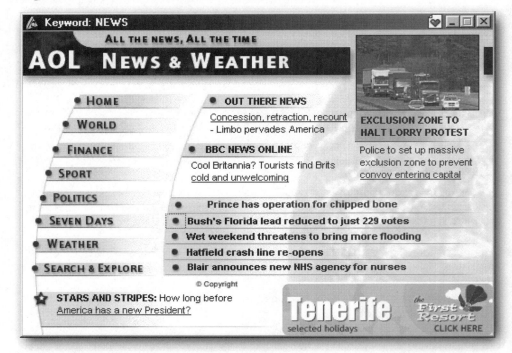

News and Weather is where you'll find out about current affairs around the world. On the screen, you'll see buttons that will take you to the latest news for categories such as Finance, Home News, World News and so on.

The latest headlines appear on the screen too, in the form of a ticker tape, which scrolls past showing you all the latest news. If you want to read a story, just click it as it passes under the mouse, and AOL will take you right there.

And, of course, the biggest stories will appear on the Channel's main screen, so you can quickly see the most important things at a glance.

You can use the **News on the Web** button for a different perspective, a little like picking up another daily paper. Don't forget the weather too – click the button, and you can find detailed forecasts for every area of the UK.

Some highlights of the News and Weather Channel

Want to keep an eye on what's going on in the world? Or find out a little more of the detail behind some of the big stories? Perhaps you just want to know if the weather will be good enough for a barbecue at the weekend. Here are some highlights of the News and Weather Channel to help you out.

News Profiles

AOL's News Channel keeps you up to date with all the news, but sometimes you might want to know about the stories that don't make it through to the main news pages.

News Profiles

With AOL News Profiles, you can tell AOL to search for the stories that you're interested in, and they'll be automatically delivered to you via email. It's like having your own personal newspaper, with information from Reuters and the Press Association.

You can find out all about how to create a News Profile in *Chapter 5, AOL and You (5.4, News profiles)*.

Out There news

All too often, the news is filtered through the editorial eyes of a newspaper, TV station, or online editor – and you don't find out the background behind the stories.

OutThere

Out There news aims to be different. Rather than giving you a little of everything, Out There, which is created by ex-Reuters journalists, concentrates in detail on a key report, with information from people on the ground.

You'll find in-depth coverage of different issues every day, and you can look behind the news to find out how people are affected by what's happening. You can also look back through the old reports, to see how stories around the world have developed.

Weather

Like it or not, the weather all too often plays a major part in what we can do, so it's important to be able to find out what's going to happen. At the keyword **Weather**: you can see at a glance what's happening across the whole country.

Weather

AOL's weather reporting doesn't just stop there, though. If you'd like to find out more, just click one of the icons on the map, whether it's a bouncing fluffy cloud, the sun or a thunderbolt. You'll see a more detailed map for your region.

You can even plan ahead using AOL's weather service. Key towns in each region are featured, with their own weather symbol, and all you need to do is click the one nearest you for a detailed five-day weather forecast.

As you can see, there's even more than just the weather outlook. AOL will tell you what time the sun rises and sets, as well as the high and low temperatures to expect. What more could you want?

Message boards and chat on the News and Weather Channel

Everyone likes to talk about what's happening in the world, and AOL's News and Weather Channel is no exception. You'll find plenty of chat areas and Message boards, covering both Home News and World News.

AOL creates Message boards for special events and big news stories, where you'll find members expressing their opinions, shock, elation and countless other emotions.

If you want to get a feel for how other people are reacting, whether it's a disaster like the Concorde crash, or the Queen Mum's 100th birthday, come along to AOL's News Channel and you'll soon find out.

Keywords for the News and Weather Channel

You can find plenty of information on the News Channel, or have your say, by using these keywords:

Letters

OutThere

Pictures

Politics

- **Letters** – Have your say about the news and how it's been reported on AOL.

- **OutThere** – Independent news from journalists around the world.

- **Pictures** – The week's news in pictures.

- **Politics** – Complete coverage of what's happening in Westminster and the rest of the political world.

4.12 The Shopping Channel – Shop@AOL

Shopping with AOL is fun and easy, and Shop@AOL is like a self-contained shopping centre – but without the long walk from the car park, the noisy crowds and the traffic jams at closing time.

Shopping

If you're not sure how online shopping works, why not turn back a few pages to *Chapter 3, The AOL Experience (3.2, Shopping on AOL)*, where you can find out exactly how you buy things online, and put your mind at rest about any security worries.

What's on Shop@AOL?

The Shopping Channel is where you'll find all the stores that make up AOL's shopping service, together with customer service, and extras like the Gift Reminder Service.

Buying online is about much more than buying things to do with computers – though of course if you visit the Computer Shop area, you'll find plenty of accessories for your system.

If you're planning a special dinner party, why not use AOL to order some delicacies, like smoked salmon and fine wines, to help the evening go well. You could lay on some soothing background music too, with a new CD ordered from the Music and Video area.

Perhaps you're a bargain hunter, the sort of person who visits car boot sales, or house clearances? Why not try your hand at online auctions, where you can bid for the things you're interested in simply by saying how much you're prepared to pay – no more trying to catch the auctioneer's eye.

If you've got an interview coming up, or a special occasion like a graduation, you'll want to look your best, so why not buy a new outfit from the Clothes shop on AOL? You could spruce yourself up even more with some new make-up, or get in shape with equipment from the Health and Beauty shop.

Then there are toys for the children, consumer electronics – or is that toys for adults? – and everything you need for the home and garden, from washing machines to shrubs.

In short, just like the best malls, if you need to buy something, you'll find it in one of the stores on Shop@AOL .

A guide to the Shopping Channel's main screen

Fig. 4.13
**Shopping
Channel main
screen**

The shopping Channel is packed with information, and there are lots of categories to choose from.

As you can see, it doesn't look quite like some of the other Channels, because there's simply so much to choose from. On the left, you'll see a list of categories, and you can click one to visit the stores in that area.

To the right, there are special offers and featured highlights. If one of the shops is having a sale, for example, that's where you'll find it.

If you need help with shopping, you'll find the buttons for customer services at the top, as well as details of how to apply for AOL's own credit card.

The Features area is where you can find more useful things, like the Gift Reminder Service, a newsletter and a complete list of contents for the Channel.

Just like any store, you can go directly to the place you want, or if you're just looking, please feel free to browse.

Some highlights of Shop@AOL

As you can see, AOL's shopping Channel has an awful lot of things on it – you really could do some serious damage to your credit card bill. And while you might not be able to buy absolutely everything you need, there's certainly plenty to keep your mouse clicking and the delivery man coming.

Earlier on we mentioned that one of the most useful things that you can use online shopping for is gifts, but there's still that thorny old problem of remembering the important dates, isn't there?

Not with AOL! Shop@AOL includes a built in reminder service, so you can make sure you never forget an important present again.

Gift Reminder Service

There's nothing more embarrassing than forgetting an important date, like an anniversary or birthday, but with AOL's Gift Reminder Service, you don't have to worry. Just type the keyword **Reminder** into the box at the top of the screen, and you'll be taken right here.

Reminder

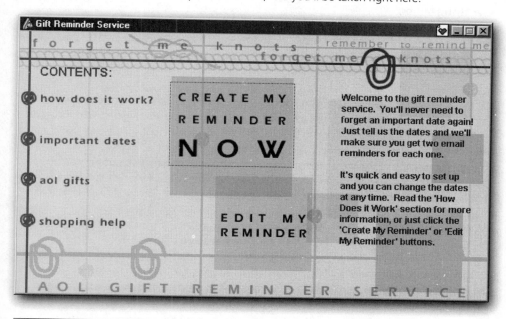

Fig. 4.14
Reminder main screen

What's this all about? Well, the Gift Reminder Service lets you type in those important dates just once, and then AOL will send you an email two weeks beforehand, so that you know it's time to start looking for a present.

Just to make sure that you don't forget – after all, two weeks can seem like a long time – you'll be sent another message four days before. Setting up the reminders is simple, too. Just click **Create my reminder now**.

The first step in creating your reminder is filling in this screen. Fill in your name, and whether you're male or female.

Next you can choose whether or not you'd like the second reminder message four days before your dates – if you're the sort of person who forgets things, it's probably wise to select **Yes**.

The check boxes at the bottom allow you to select special dates that you want automatic reminders for, like Mother's Day or Easter. When you choose these options, you don't even have to know what date they fall on – AOL will keep track of it for you.

After you've clicked to put a check next to the dates you want reminders for, click the **Continue** button.

Now, you'll see a list of reminders, which will show the dates that you selected on the previous screen. The next step is to create your own personal reminders, so click the **Add Personal Reminder** button. at the bottom.

On this screen, you need to fill in who you have to buy a gift for, and then give some information about the type of event it is. Enter the date in the boxes provided, and then choose whether or not it's something that happens every year.

The bottom section of the screen lets you give AOL a little information about the person you'll be buying a gift for. You don't have to fill it in, but if you do, it helps the Gift Reminder Service make suggestions to save you even more time and trouble.

After filling in the form, click the **Save** button. You can change any of your reminders using the **Edit** button, or remove it completely using the **Remove** button.

To add an event like Valentine's Day, Halloween, Christmas, Mother's Day or Father's Day, click the **Holiday reminder** box. Instead of having to fill in the date, all you need to do is say which holiday the reminder is for. What could be easier?

Message boards and chat on Shop@AOL

It's probably no surprise to know that most of the people who visit Shop@AOL aren't there to chat, but that doesn't mean that it's not a place where people talk.

There's a chat room, where you can swap tips with other shoppers who are online, and there are also message boards. The most popular Message board is 'where can I find' and it's the place to ask for help from other shoppers when you're trying to track down those hard-to-find things. So, don't give up and get in the car – Shop@AOL's Message boards may be able to help you find what you want online.

There are some other Message boards too. Here's the list:

- Beanie Babies

- Where can I buy music?

- Where to buy DVD and video

- Setting up an online shop

Keywords for Shop@AOL

If your preferred way of shopping is to work out what you want, go straight to the shops you need, then back to the car, perhaps you'll want these keywords, so you can do the same thing on AOL.

| AOL Credit Card |

- **AOL Credit Card** – AOL's own credit card gives you points when you shop online, which you can use as credit against your subscription.

| Auctions |

- **Auctions** – Pay what you think something is worth with online auctions. Be quick before everything's going … going … gone.

| Gifts |

- **Gifts** – Flowers, chocolates and other things to smooth the path of love, or say sorry.

| Guarantee |

- **Guarantee** – Shopping on AOL comes with a cast-iron guarantee of security and good service. You can find out what that means to you at this keyword.

| Special Offers |

- **Special Offers** – From time to time, you'll find exclusive offers for AOL shoppers at this keyword.

| Travel Shop |

- **Travel Shop** – Tickets and other essentials for the traveller.

4.13 The Sport Channel

To some people, sport is life – and on AOL's Sport Channel you'll find plenty of people who agree with that view. Whether it's ice hockey, horse racing, athletics or golf, there's plenty for every sports fan.

Sport

What's on the Sport Channel?

Perhaps it might be quicker to say what isn't on this Channel! Sport on AOL covers everything you can think of, with information, news, facts and figures all at your fingertips.

There are other football clubs too, of course, and you'll be able to find out all the facts on them with AOL's Club Corner. There are detailed results from all the different leagues – including many of the popular European ones as well.

How about something horsey? You'll find plenty for equestrians too, with tips and form, results and news about the horses and trainers.

Whether it's golf, cricket, rugby or just about anything else, you'll find the latest news and results courtesy of AOL's sports reporting team. You can even talk about how your favourite team or player is doing in one of the many sports message boards. There's live chat too, with experts in different sports hosting in AOL chat rooms.

Sport is news too, especially when there's a big event like Euro 2000, Wimbledon or the Olympics. You can rest assured that there'll be special areas on the Sport Channel for every major event, keeping you up to date with the results every time you're online.

So when you come back from the changing room, don't just flop in a chair and relax – use AOL's Sport Channel to find out what other enthusiasts are thinking, or catch up on how your team has done.

A guide to the Sport Channel's main screen

Fig. 4.15
**Sport Channel
main screen**

On the main screen of the Sport Channel, you'll find a quick way to reach whatever sport you're interested in.

The buttons on the screen take you to some of the most popular sports directly, so you can look up the results you're interested in, or follow the progress of your favourite stars.

And if you want to discuss their performance with other fans, or talk about putting together a team of your own, you'll find the chat rooms and message boards just a couple of clicks away.

Whenever there's a major tournament – like the Olympics, or the World Cup – you can rest assured you'll see the latest news and results highlights on the main screen, each time you visit the Channel.

Message boards and chat on the Sport Channel

Whatever your sport, you'll find plenty to talk about at the keyword **Sport Chat**.

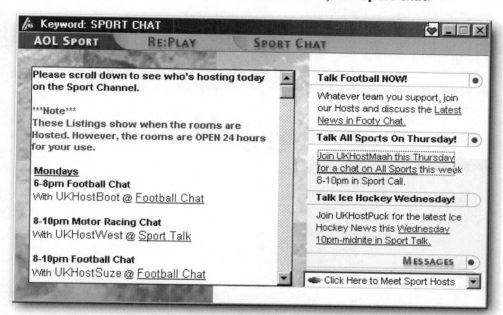

Fig. 4.16
**Sport Chat
screen**

As you can see, there are lots of regular chats, with AOL's Hosts there to help out and guide the discussion if you need. You'll find that all the Hosts in the Sport chat section know the ins and outs of their respective sports, and you can follow the links from the Sport chat screen to find out more about them.

You'll also find plenty of message boards on the Sport Channel, including ones dedicated to cricket, football, golf, ice hockey, horse racing, rugby, motor racing and tennis.

Keywords for the Sport Channel

Want to know how to find the sport you're most interested in? Here are the keywords to take you right to the heart of the Channel.

Clubs Corner

- **Clubs Corner** – Up-to-date statistics, news and contact information for all the top football teams.

Football

- **Football** – Coverage of the UK and European football scenes, with news from all the major continental leagues.

Motorsport

- **Motorsport** – News and results from the world of rallies and racers.

Tennis

- **Tennis**

Cricket

- **Cricket**

4.14 The Technology Channel

Technology is all around us, whether in the computer that you use to connect to AOL, your mobile phone, or high tech gadgets to play with in your living room. Keep up to date with the latest developments on AOL's Technology Channel.

Technology

What's on the Technology Channel?

If you're interested in computers, the Technology Channel is the place to come. You'll find lots of software to download, and some of the top magazines offering you news, reviews and other information.

How about some help with building your Web page? You'll find that on the Technology Channel, along with more general help for your computer.

And don't worry if you're not that good with technical things! There's a whole section specially for newcomers to computing, with tips and information to help you make the most of your system. On top of that, you'll find award-winning magazines like Computer Active, with articles specially written in plain English so that anyone can understand what's going on.

Perhaps you're more interested in pure science, though? You'll find plenty to keep you occupied, with the New Scientist online, and a whole section on the Natural World, where you can read about meteorology, cloning and all sorts of other developments that will affect the way that we live. There's even a dedicated section for space, so you can keep up to date with shuttle flights or the new International Space Station.

There's much more to technology than computing and science, of course, and you'll find a whole section full of gadgets too, so you can find out what MP3 really is, and read about the latest players. There are other hot new technologies to read about too, such as DVD.

If you fancy a read, AOL's Technology Channel is packed with online magazines too, covering a wide range of areas, with plenty of different viewpoints.

There are competitions as well, quizzes and plenty of Chat rooms and Message boards for advice and inspiration. Whether you're a computer addict, someone looking for a new system, or just a lover of the latest gadgets and gizmos, you'll find it here.

A guide to the Technology Channel's main screen
The Technology Channel is divided into several sections, covering a huge range of subjects, as you can see.

Fig. 4.17
Technology Channel main screen

From the menus along the top of the Channel's main screen, you can choose News, Downloads, Science & Technology, Computing, Objects of Desire, Buying Advice and Web page building.

If you want to keep up to date with what's happening in the science and technology world, take a look at the **News** section, where you'll find a technology diary, what the papers say, and information about the latest magazines.

The **Downloads** area is where you can find the hottest software, demos, games and search through the thousands of files on AOL.

The **Science and Technology** area is where you can find links to topics such as Space, The Natural World, How things work, and a special section dedicated just to the weird and strange.

Computing, as you'd expect, is the biggest area of the Technology Channel, and you'll find information about everything under the sun here – there are sections for Mac users, as well as PC fans. There's help and advice when things go wrong, tips and tricks to make sure they don't, and information for everyone from beginners to experts.

Fans of gadgets and gizmos will want to check out the **Objects of desire**, where you can read about things like DVD players, camcorders, photography, hi-fi and mobile phones. If it's shiny and has lots of lights, it's probably in here!

Buying advice is where you can turn to make sure that your forays into the high street don't fall foul of any problems, and there's even a PC Finder to help you make the right choice.

Finally, the **Web Builder** section will tell you all you need to know to make your own home on the Web.

As well as all those sections, you'll see links on the main screen to technology magazines, chat, and the top Web sites that will help you keep abreast with whatever is your favourite subject.

Some highlights of the Technology Channel

Technology is great, but sometimes it needs a little taming, and with AOL's Technology Channel, it's easy to find out how to do it. Here are two parts of the Channel that should really help to put your mind at rest.

Computing Beginners

If you're new to computing, as well as AOL, this is a great place to start exploring.

Computing Beginners

There are plenty of options in this section, designed to answer common questions you might have about using your computer, or carrying out simple tasks. Just click one of the items, and you'll find there's plenty of information to help you out. There are even regular monthly sections, so you can learn a stage at a time, as you start to feel more comfortable with your computer. You can post your own problems too, and see what the experts on AOL have to say to help you.

Virus

We've mentioned several times in this book how important it is to have anti-virus software on your computer, and here's a part of AOL where you can read more about it.

Virus

In fact, you can do much more than just find out about viruses here. As well as all the information explaining viruses, you'll find links to some of the most popular anti-virus programs, so you can download them and try them out on your computer.

You'll also find information on the latest viruses, and hoaxes too. Don't forget to pay special attention to information about protecting yourself. All this might sound scary, but it's not really – there are just some simple rules that you should follow to protect yourself online, and the **Virus** keyword is a great place to start.

Keywords for the Technology Channel

There are lots of keywords to help you find the right part of the Technology Channel, and even if you don't think you'll need them, some, like **Virus**, are essential, whichever part of AOL you decide to make your home.

- **Buying** – Advice and information on buying a computer.

- **Computing magazines** – Your starting point for the online editions of the best computer mags.

- **Gadgets** – Toys for the technologically minded.

- **Hot software** – Top downloads for you to try on your own computer.

- **Space** – Explore the final frontier. Go boldly to this keyword.

- **OOD** – Objects of desire.

| Buying |
| Computing magazines |
| Gadgets |
| Hot software |
| Space |
| OOD |

4.15 The Travel Channel

Travel

Travel broadens the mind, they say, but it can take a lot of planning to make sure you get a good deal, and know what to do when you arrive. AOL's Travel Channel is here to share the experience with you.

What's on the Travel Channel?
If you want to get away, for a short break or a long vacation then the Travel Channel is the place to be. It's not a destination in itself – except for your mouse – but it is packed with useful information.

Do you want to know what it's really going to be like visiting Thailand? Come along to the Travel Channel and you can read all about it in our free online travel guidebooks, or see pictures that other members took in the Travellers Tales section.

To make sure that you don't forget anything important, you'll find plenty of help at hand in the Expert Advice section, and if you can't find the solution to your problems in a chat room or a message board, just ask the editor, and see if they can come up with the right solution for you.

Planning is an important part of any successful trip, and that's why you'll find all the things you need, like online timetables for planes and ferries, and when you've found the right flight, of course you can book it on AOL with complete confidence, knowing your credit card details are safe.

What about if you're not even sure what you want to do? You just have time off work, and you're feeling at a loose end. How about taking a look at the UK Guide to see what's on around the country, then jumping in the car and driving. You could use the Good Hotel Guide to find a place to stay when you arrive, rather than taking pot luck in a strange town.

Maybe an exotic holiday or a week in a health spa is something you dream of being able to afford, so why not enter one of AOL's regular travel competitions, and your dreams might come true!

The Travel Channel even caters for the armchair traveller, too. If you don't want to leave home, why not just sit back and relax while you read our travel magazine?

A guide to the Travel Channel's main screen

The main screen is the first thing you'll see when you select Travel from AOL's list of Channels, or if you call up the keyword **Travel**.

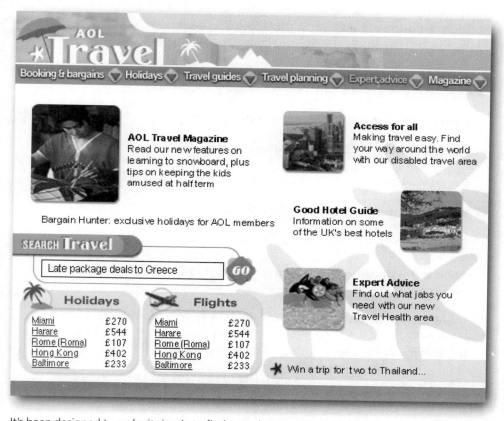

Fig. 4.18
Travel Channel main screen

It's been designed to make it simple to find out what you need, whether you're planning or ready to book all your tickets.

In the **Booking Centre** you can find information on flights to book online, including some of the best last-minute deals around.

Choose Holiday for information on complete deals and destinations, while the Travel Guides will give you the inside information on places that you're thinking of visiting, with highlights such as the Lonely Planet guides.

Travel Planning is where you can find all the information you need to know before you start making bookings, while Expert Advice is where you'll be able to check those tricky issues, like whether or not you need a malaria jab for a particular country.

Finally, the **Magazine** is where you'll find AOL's own online travel magazine, so start clicking, and explore the virtual world of travel before you step outside and begin your real journey.

Keywords for the Travel Channel
Take a journey through AOL's Travel Channel using these keywords.

Travel magazine	• **Travel Magazine** – AOL's own online travel magazine.
Ask the editor	• **Ask the editor** – Personal assistance with your travel queries.
Expert Advice	• **Expert Advice** – Specialist travel advice for AOL members.
Bargain Hunter	• **Bargain Hunter** – Exclusive offers for AOL members.
Flights	• **Flights** – Find the ideal flight for you, and book it online.
Good Hotel Guide	• **Good Hotel Guide** – Don't end up in a flea-pit. Use AOL's guide to make sure you have a comfortable stay.
Travel competition	• **Travel Competition** – Why pay for a holiday, when you can win one free with AOL?
UK Guide	• **UK Guide** – Things to see and places to go within the UK.
World Guide	• **World Guide** – Information from the world-famous *Lonely Planet* guidebooks.

4.16 The UK Life Channel

Just because AOL is part of a global service, that doesn't mean that there's nothing on it that isn't close to home. On UK Life, you can find out information right down to street level.

UK Life

What's on the UK Life Channel?

UK Life is where you'll find people who care about where they live, whether it's England, Northern Ireland, Scotland or Wales. You'll find a dedicated area specially for you, with chat and features on major places around the UK.

Want to know what's happening near you? You can type in your postcode, and AOL will look up all the places that you could visit, or events you might want to take part in.

There's a lot more to UK Life than events, however. You can also find out about politics, including looking up the name of your local MP. Or how would you like to know whether your council is really doing as well as it says, compared to the rest of the UK? There's even a house-price comparison, which could make the crucial difference to whether or not that job in a new city is practical.

Planning a holiday? Why not check out the region you are going to visit before you leave?

Why not look up the list of museums and galleries, where you'll be able to find out what's going to be worth seeing in the areas you're visiting? And there are even special guides to help you plan days out around the country written by those who know those places the best: the insiders.

It's not just regions that merit a section of their own on UK Life. Are you visiting a different county within the UK? You'll find features like AngloFile for England, or North of the Border for Scotland.

So whether you're a visitor looking for the best places to see and the most exciting things to do, or a local who wants to see what's a little off the beaten track in your home town, pop along to the UK Life Channel, and see what you can find.

A guide to the UK Life Channel's main screen
The UK Life Channel has been designed to make it really easy to get right to the information that you need, whatever part of the UK you're interested in.

Fig. 4.19
UK Life Channel main screen

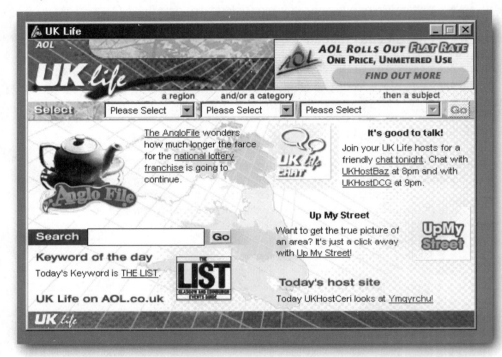

On most Channels, the menus across the top of the screen are independent of each other, but on UK Life you can use them to go straight to information for a particular region. All you need to do is select a region from the first menu, a category from the second, and a subject from the last one. So you could select Scotland, then News and Media, and then finally the weather, for example. What could be simpler?

As well as things like News, you'll find the Services section for details of facilities, a Leisure section with ideas for great days out, Community and Features – and by choosing an area from the menus you can find out about either your own part of the country, or somewhere that you're planning to visit.

You'll find the usual Search box on the front page too, so you can find information if you're not sure which category it might be in, and links to take you to the UK Life chat areas, together with details of when the hosts will be there to help out.

To top it off, there's a button for **Up My Street**, so you can find out about your own street, and a link to a top UK Web site selected by the Channel's Hosts. And there'll be links to the latest features, like AngloFile, AOL's weekly UK column.

Some highlights of the UK Life Channel
If you don't believe just how local the information you can find on AOL could be, try this great part of the UK Life Channel.

Up My Street
Have you ever wondered how your street compares to the national average? Now, thanks to AOL and Up My Street, you can find out.

UMS

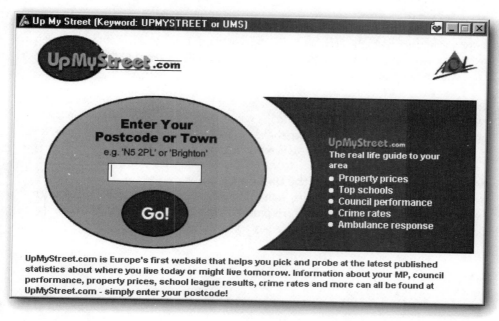

Fig. 4.20
**UMS main
screen**

At the **UMS** keyword, you'll see this screen, and all you need to do is type your postcode – or anyone else's for that matter – into the box in the middle of the screen, and then click the **Go** button.

In just a few moments, you'll see a graph showing how your street compares to the national average for the price of a terraced home. You don't live in a terraced home? No problem! All you need to do is click the arrow next to Terraced Price, and choose a different type of home from the list, then click **Compare now**. The dotted line shows the national average, and the other line shows the information for your postcode – which is right down to the street that you live on.

You can even choose up to three more things to show on the graph, including Council Tax charges, exam pass rates and plenty more information.

It doesn't stop there, either!

If you scroll down the page, you'll see lots of other information, comparing how your local authority matches up to the average, how long ambulances take to arrive, and you'll even see the name of your MP. You can follow the link to read all the speeches they've made in the Commons recently too!

There's just one more trick with Up My Street. Back at the top of the page, you'll see that you can not only compare where you live with the national average, but you can type in another postcode instead, and see how the two shape up. So, before you move house, sign on to AOL and check to see what life's really like where you're moving.

Message boards and chat on the UK Life Channel
You'll find plenty of chatter on UK Life, with a distinctly social aspect to it. If you want to meet people who are really close at hand, this is probably the place to look. You'll find message boards too, for all the different featured areas.

Keywords for the UK Life Channel

- **AngloFile** – All the things that make England so special.

- **Border** – Go north of the border with this section dedicated to things Scottish.

- **Days Out** – Great ideas for things to do in the UK.

- **Insider Guides** – A collection of features and guides written by the people who know.

- **Museums** – A guide to museums and galleries all around the country.

- **Underground** – Comments and observations on life in London.

- **Virtual Wales** – All points west of Bristol and Chester.

AngloFile
Border
Days Out
Insider Guides
Museums
Underground
Virtual Wales

4.17 The International Channel

International

As we've mentioned already in this book, AOL isn't just a UK service. Although most of what you've seen so far is specially for members in the UK and Ireland, the AOL service spans the globe.

What's on the International Channel?
The International Channel is your gateway to AOL around the world. Using the Channel, you can find your way to the international AOL services, no matter which country they're in.

And it's not just more AOL that you'll find. If you're travelling, wouldn't it be a good idea to look up some information about the places you're visiting, before you leave home? With its comprehensive guides to every country under the sun, the International Channel can put you in touch with people all over the world, and make sure that when you get there you'll know how to phone home and what currency to use.

Do you have relatives around the world? Why not join them in a chat room where they can speak their own language? AOL's International Channel is home to dozens of chat rooms, where you can speak in whatever language you want, even if you just want to practise before your holiday, so that you don't order the wrong food for dinner.

There's news too, so if you'd like a more global perspective on what's happening in the world, this is the place to come. At the Global Newsstand, you can read the pick of the international newspapers and magazines, so why not find out what people over there think about us over here?

You'll also find other helpful tools on the International Channel, like a currency converter and the latest global news headlines, and of course the information you need to connect your laptop to AOL wherever you are.

So, while we can't quite promise that AOL's International Channel will catapult you into the jet-set with the likes of Sophia Loren, at least you'll be much wiser when you pack your passport and set off globetrotting.

A guide to the International Channel's main screen

The International Channel's main screen is your gateway to AOL around the world.

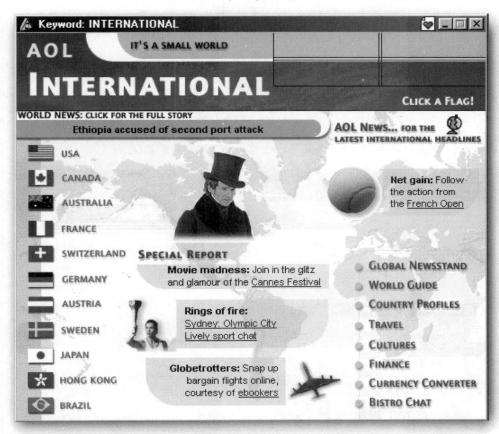

Fig. 4.21
International Channel main screen

On this screen, you'll see links to major countries around the world, where you can chat with other AOL members, or look up information that might be helpful if you're going on holiday.

The featured items on the Channel's screen will take you to information about some of the most important or popular events happening around the world – things like the Cannes Film Festival, or the Olympic Games.

And you can quickly access information like exchange rates, international news on the **Global Newsstand**, and AOL's **Country Profiles**, which are packed with essential information for every country under the sun.

Some highlights of the International Channel

When the world is your oyster, it's hard to single out just one pearl as special, but there are some things on the International Channel that you'll find useful wherever you go in the world.

Country Profiles

Country Profiles

You don't have to be a member of the jet-set to travel to faraway places these days, but one thing that is essential is knowing what to expect before you leave home.

AOL's Country Profiles service can fill you in on all the facts that you're likely to need before you leave home. Just click a region and then pick the country you want to know about, and you'll be amazed at what detail there is – even for the smallest of places.

Fig. 4.22
**Country Profiles
– Estonia**

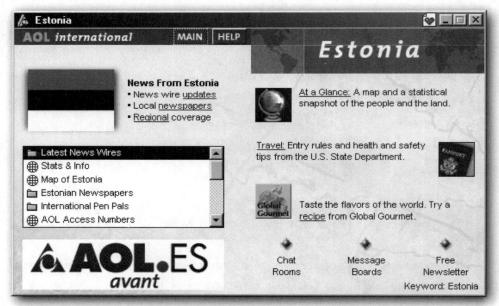

How about Estonia? It might not be your first choice destination, but that doesn't mean no detail has been spared. Take a look at any country, and just like this you'll find message boards, chat rooms, and that all-important information, like which jabs you'll need, whether there are any visa requirements and, of course, the access numbers to connect you to AOL.

You can find out more about connecting to AOL when you're abroad in *Chapter 7, Advanced AOL (7.2, Travelling with your computer)*.

Message boards and chat on the International Channel
The AOL Bistro is where you can chat with people around the world.

Bistro offers a main chat room where every language is welcome – this really is where the online world becomes a melting-pot of nationalities.

As well as the main chat room, you'll also see buttons down the left of the Channel for a range of different languages. If you're fluent – or even just practising – in a foreign language, why not click it and you'll find a chat room where you can speak in the language of your choice.

There are Message boards too, so you can take a more leisurely approach to things, with time to consult your dictionary if you like!

Keywords for the International Channel
Every AOL service around the world has its own keywords, but here are some of the ones that will take you to useful sections of the International Channel.

- **Country Profiles** – Essential information for travellers, and links to local AOL services.

- **Global Access** – Find out how to connect to AOL, wherever you are in the world.

- **Global Newsstand** – Catch up on news from around the world, with information from the leading international newspapers and magazines.

Bistro

Country Profiles

Global Access

Global Newsstand

5

AOL and You

This chapter is all about you – and how AOL can work even better for you and your family than it does already.

You'll find out how to create extra Screen Names on AOL so your family can use the service too, and how to make sure that your kids are safe with AOL's unique Parental Controls.

There's also information on creating a Profile so that people can find out about you, keeping track of your online friends, and having a private chat with them.

We'll show you how to make your own home page on the Web, and how to customise AOL to work how you want it, with your Favourite Places just a couple of clicks away.

You can also learn how to automate your AOL sessions to cut down on the time you spend connected, and there's information on two great new features – My Calendar and Groups@AOL, which help you plan your time and keep in touch with friends both on AOL and elsewhere on the Net.

5.1 Screen names and controls

When you signed up for AOL, you had to choose a name for yourself, known as your Screen Name. If you have more than one family member, they'll probably want to use AOL too – especially when they realise how simple it is.

One of the most useful features of AOL's service is that you can have more than one Screen Name. In fact, you can have up to seven with a single AOL account. So you can create one for each of your children, one for your partner and perhaps another for your home business.

So, what's the point of all these names? Well, firstly, they mean that each person who uses your AOL account can do what they want. You can be sure that the kids won't be able to accidentally read the email you sent to their aunt planning her surprise visit, and you won't be bothered with homework problems from their friends in your own mailbox.

That's only a part of what AOL offers, though. Screen Names can have different privileges, so you can, for example, tell the AOL program that some of the names on your account belong to your children, and set options so that they can only send email to people you know, or can't access the Internet – and, of course, they can't access the parts of AOL that would let them change the options back, because it's password protected.

By letting you do this, AOL makes it much easier for you to let your children use the computer without having to worry about who they might meet or talk with. You're in complete control.

You can use Screen Names for other things too – and delete them when you don't need them. You might, for example, want to plan the village fete via email, so you could create a name like VillageFete2k. When the fete's happened, you can delete the name, and make another one for next year. As long as you never have more than seven names, you can delete and create new ones as much as you like.

First among equals

When you set up your AOL account and chose your first name you chose what's known as a Master Screen Name. Master names are those that can create or delete names, and control what other names are allowed to do, as well as changing your AOL billing options. The name you created when you signed up is special in one other way too – it's called your Primary Master Screen Name, and you can't delete it.

Before creating Screen Names, think what you want to use your name for – it's often a good way to find inspiration. If you drive a certain type of car, you might choose a name like Citroen Driver, for example. Your names can be up to 16 letters long, including any spaces in the middle.

Remember that AOL has some rules about what your names can be. You can't put anything deliberately offensive in a name, or try to impersonate someone famous, or promote your business. And remember that someone might be able to find out more about you than you want if your Screen Name is the same as your full name.

To start creating new Screen Names for your AOL account, go to the **Customise** button at the top of the screen and click the little downward-pointing arrow to display the menu. Choose **Screen Names** and this screen will appear.

Fig. 5.1
Screen Names

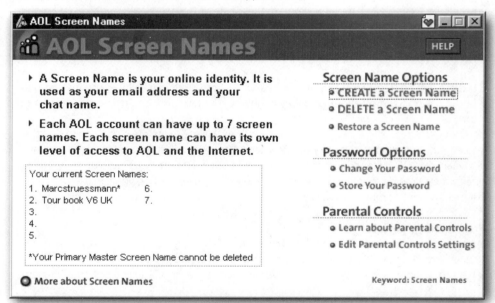

Creating a new name

Let's start by creating a name for one of your children. At the top right of the Screen Names window, you'll see the text **CREATE a Screen Name**. Click it, and the next screen to appear will explain about extra names on your AOL account, and give you another opportunity to read the note for parents. When you've read the screen, click the **Create Screen Name** button at the bottom.

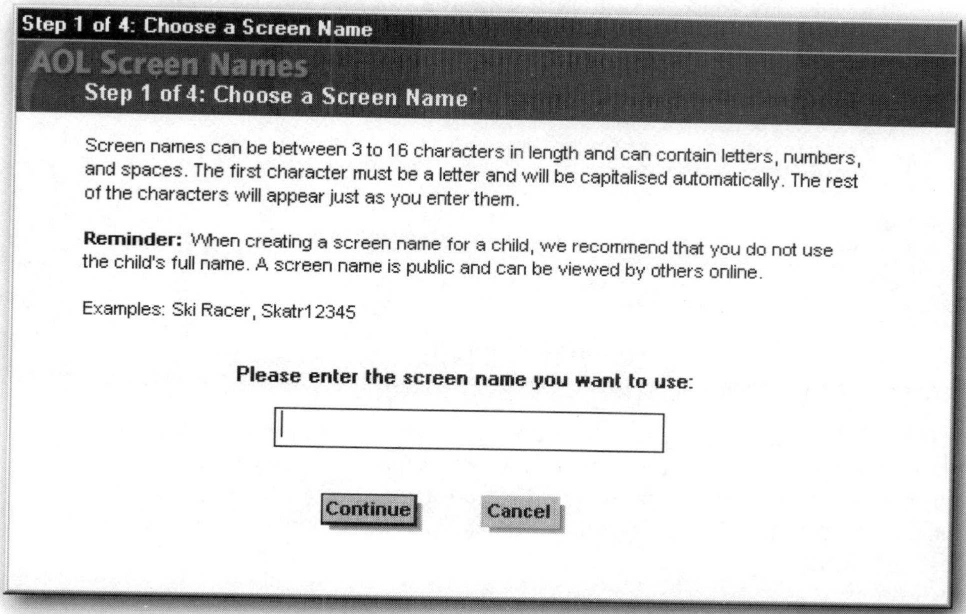

Screen Names

Step 1 of 4: Choose a Screen Name

AOL Screen Names

Step 1 of 4: Choose a Screen Name

Screen names can be between 3 to 16 characters in length and can contain letters, numbers, and spaces. The first character must be a letter and will be capitalised automatically. The rest of the characters will appear just as you enter them.

Reminder: When creating a screen name for a child, we recommend that you do not use the child's full name. A screen name is public and can be viewed by others online.

Examples: Ski Racer, Skatr12345

Please enter the screen name you want to use:

[Continue]   [Cancel]

Fig. 5.2
Screen Name entry page

On this screen, you can type in the name you want to use. AOL will automatically make the first letter a capital. Type the name you've chosen, then click the **Continue** button. If the name you want is already being used, a message will appear asking you to choose another. Click **OK** to make the message go away, and then try again.

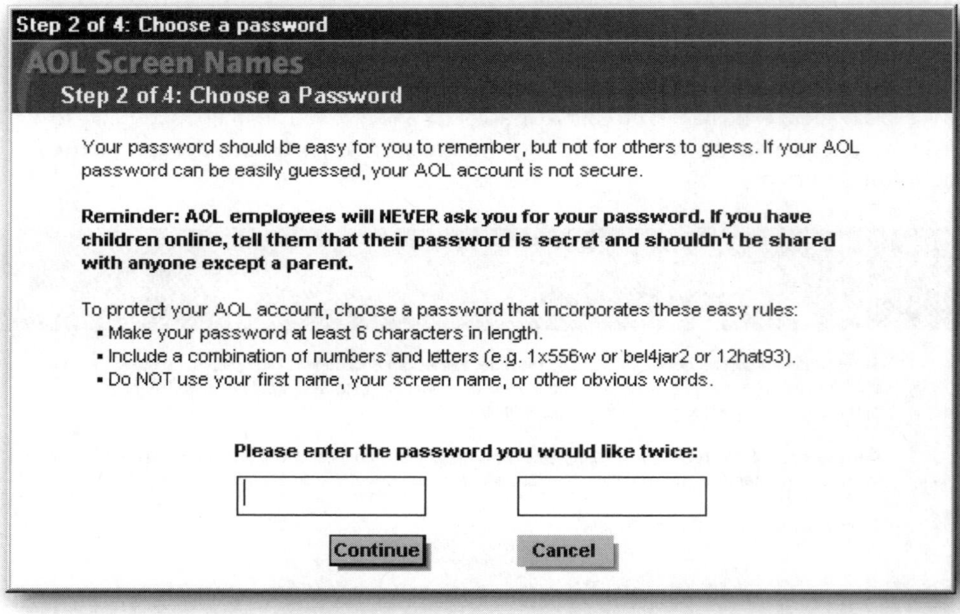

Fig. 5.3
**Password entry
page**

> **Step 2 of 4: Choose a password**
>
> AOL Screen Names
>
> **Step 2 of 4: Choose a Password**
>
> Your password should be easy for you to remember, but not for others to guess. If your AOL password can be easily guessed, your AOL account is not secure.
>
> **Reminder: AOL employees will NEVER ask you for your password. If you have children online, tell them that their password is secret and shouldn't be shared with anyone except a parent.**
>
> To protect your AOL account, choose a password that incorporates these easy rules:
> - Make your password at least 6 characters in length.
> - Include a combination of numbers and letters (e.g. 1x556w or bel4jar2 or 12hat93).
> - Do NOT use your first name, your screen name, or other obvious words.
>
> **Please enter the password you would like twice:**
>
> [Continue]   [Cancel]

If your name was created successfully, you'll see this screen next, which lets you enter a password. The password won't be displayed on the screen as you type it, so you'll have to type it twice, once in the box on the left and once on the right. That way, AOL can be sure you did type what you meant to. Read the tips about choosing a good password before you pick one.

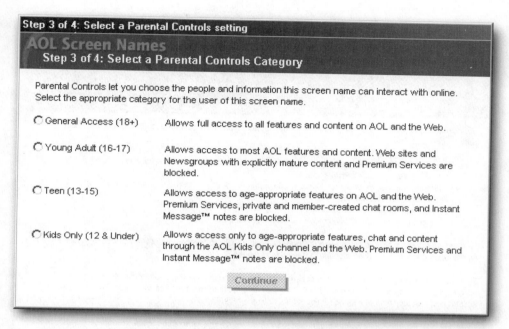

Step 3 of 4: Select a Parental Controls setting

Fig. 5.4
Parental Controls category

Now you can choose what sort of access to AOL you want this name to have. AOL has four pre-set levels that you can choose from, to make it faster to set up controls. We'll choose 'Teen' for this account, which is suitable for people aged between 13 and 15. We will go into more detail about Parental Controls later on in this chapter.

After making your choice, you'll see this screen, which allows you to fine-tune the settings if you like.

Fig. 5.5
**Confirmation
screen**

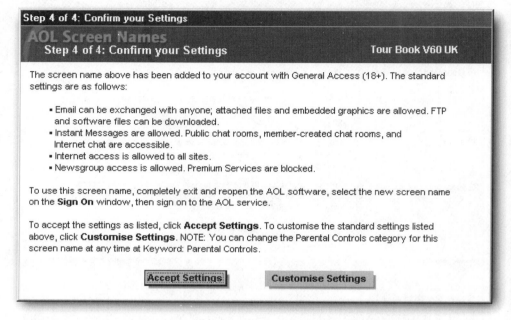

If you want to alter detailed settings, click the **Customise Settings** button and you'll be able to change the parental controls, using the instructions later in this chapter. If you're happy with AOL's settings for the time being, click **Accept Settings** and you'll be taken back to the Screen Names page. You can create another name right away if you want to get your whole family set up. AOL will automatically send you an email to confirm the creation of each new Screen Name, and the new names will receive a welcome email too.

Using your new Screen Names

The next time you start AOL, you'll see that the Member Name box on the first screen has an arrow at the right of it – click the arrow, and you can choose from a list of all the names that you've created.

The envelope to the left of each name will turn from white to yellow if there is new email waiting for that name – so you don't even have to sign on with a name if you just want to see whether or not a message has arrived for you. To switch to a name, just double-click it with the mouse. You'll see a message appear telling you how long you've been using the name you signed on with first, and asking you to click **OK** to change names. Click the button, and then type in the password for the name you want to use – if you don't want to type the password each time, you can tell AOL to remember it for you, via the **Customise** menu.

Deleting a Screen Name

If you don't want to use a name – perhaps you put your age in it, and you're a year older now – you can delete it. Since you can only have seven names at a time, you might find that you have to delete an old name so that you can create a new one.

To delete a Screen Name, choose **Screen Names** from the **Customise** menu, and click the text **DELETE a Screen Name**. You'll see a warning which you should read before you continue.

> *When you delete a Screen Name, it ceases to exist. If you saved email in your Personal Filing Cabinet, you will no longer be able to read it. And anyone who tries to send email to that Screen Name will receive a message telling them it no longer exists. Before you delete a Screen Name, make sure that you have copies of any messages from the Personal Filing Cabinet that you want to keep. Although you can recover a name you deleted by mistake, you may not be able to retrieve old messages.*

The next screen lets you choose which of the Screen Names you want to delete – and once again, read the warnings and click the **Cancel** button unless you're absolutely sure that you do want to delete the name. Remember that you can't delete your Primary Master Screen Name. You can also only delete a Screen Name if you signed on using one of your Master names.

Fig. 5.6
**Screen Name
deletion**

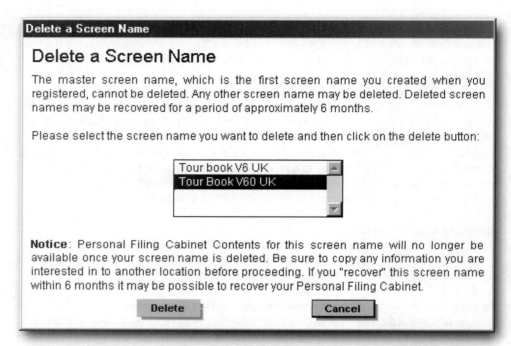

Find the name that you want to delete in the list on the screen, and highlight it with the mouse, then click the **Delete** button. You won't be asked again to confirm that you really do want to delete the name, so make sure you pick the right one! A message will appear, confirming that it's been deleted, and then you'll be back at the Screen Names page.

Help! I made a mistake

Although we said that you should always be sure what you're doing before you delete a Screen Name, sometimes people do make mistakes. To help make sure that you can undo any accidental deletions, you can often recover a Screen Name that you deleted, as long as you act quickly.

AOL will let you recover a Screen Name up to around six months after you deleted it – so if you suddenly remember that you gave the name to a friend in Australia, all is not lost.

From the Screen Names page, click the text marked **Restore a Screen Name**, and a screen like this will appear.

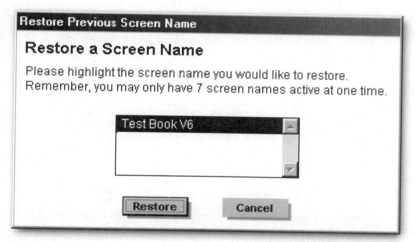

Fig. 5.7
Restore name

Just highlight the name that you want to bring back, and click the **Restore** button. Remember that you can only have seven names at any time, so if you already have that many, you'll have to delete another name before you can restore any older ones.

Other options on the Screen Names page

While we're at the Screen Names page, there are a couple of other useful options that are worth looking at.

Below the Screen Name options that you've just been using are two Password options. The first one, **Change your password**, can be used to change the password you have to type each time you connect to AOL. You should do this if you think that anyone has discovered your password, as it will allow them access to your email and other information you may have stored in your AOL Personal Filing Cabinet.

If someone has access to the password for your AOL Master Screen Names, they can access your billing information or alter the Parental Controls you've set. You should always make sure that you keep your passwords secure. Don't choose something obvious, or that could be guessed or discovered easily. It's a good idea to change your password regularly.

When you click **Change your password**, you'll see a reminder about how to choose a password. Click **Continue** to go to the new password screen.

Fig. 5.8
Change password

Change Your Password

Change Your Password

Please enter the password that you would like twice. The password must be at least 6 characters long and should contain both letters and numbers.

Old password:

Enter new password twice:

Change Password   **Cancel**

Password

On this screen you need to type in your existing password, which should go in the box labelled **Old password** and then type the new password twice, first in the bottom left and then the bottom right. None of the passwords will be shown on screen when you type them. Next, click the **Change Password** button to make the change, or **Cancel** if you decide you don't want to change your password right now. You can only change the password for the Screen Name that you've signed on as. To change the password for another name, sign on using that name first. You can also change the password by choosing **Passwords** from the **Customise** menu.

Sometimes, you know that no one else will be able to get near your computer – perhaps you're the only person in your home. Although passwords are there to protect your information, everyone knows that it can be a chore typing them each time you want to do anything.

AOL provides the ability to store your password, so that you don't have to type it each time you want to sign on. You'll find the **Store your password** option right under **Change your password** on the Screen Names page. Click this option and you can save a password for signing on and accessing the contents of your Personal Filing Cabinet.

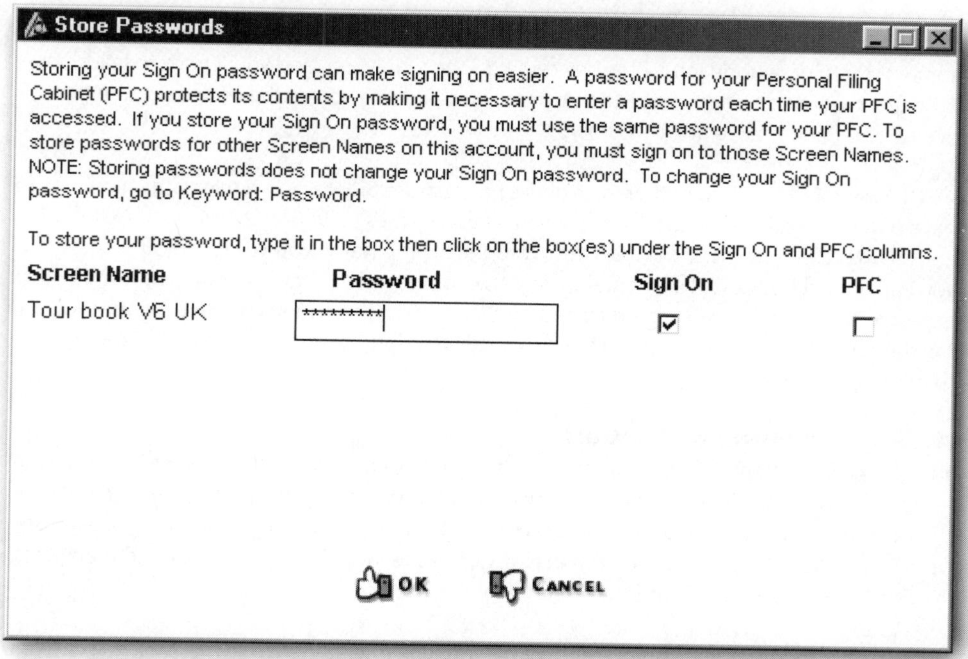

Fig. 5.9
Store Passwords

You just need to type your password once on this screen. Next to the box where you type the password you can choose whether to save it for signing on to AOL, for accessing your Personal Filing Cabinet, or both. Just click with the mouse to tick the box for each option, and then click the **OK** button.

Storing passwords saves time, but if you store the password for one of your Master Screen Names anyone with access to your computer can start AOL and access your billing information, or bypass any Parental Control options that you have set. Only store the password for Master Screen Names if you are sure that only people you trust will have access to your computer.

Parental Controls

Screen Names are one of AOL's most useful features, but if you're a parent, then there's one other tool that helps to make sure your kids are safe when they're online – Parental Controls.

Of course, you can buy programs that will filter out what you can access on the Internet, and some of them do a good job – but they don't do the whole job, and you'll have to learn how different programs work together. Often, you'll just have to accept the options you're given, even if you think they're not right for you.

AOL's Parental Controls are different. There's no separate program to fiddle with, and you can have different settings for each of the seven Screen Names on your AOL account. AOL will adjust what can be seen or done according to the Screen Name you've signed on with. And you can either choose AOL's Parental Control categories, which have been set up to give quick access to the most common settings, and then customise the options yourself, so that you and the members of your family can each have exactly the right balance between safety and access to information on AOL and the Internet.

Accessing the Parental Controls

Parental Controls

To access AOL's Parental Controls, you need to sign on using one of your Master Screen Names – such as the one you created when you first signed up with AOL. From the main screen, click the downward-pointing arrow on the **Customise** button, and choose **Parental Controls** from the menu. You can also type **Parental Controls** into the Keyword box and then press the Enter key on your keyboard.

When you first go to the Parental Controls section, you'll see a welcome message, explaining the different categories in detail. As you'll have seen when you created additional Screen Names on your account, you can use pre-defined categories for deciding what can be seen on AOL and the Internet.

Fig. 5.10
**Main Parental
Control screen**

This is the main screen for the parental controls, and if you've not already set up Screen Names for your children you can access the appropriate part of AOL from here, as well as from the **Customise** menu.

On the right, you'll find buttons that will lead you to more information about how Parental Controls work, and general guidance about online safety, which you should make the time to read.

You can also recommend or report Web sites – so if you know of a site that's perfect for homework, for instance, but find that your children can't access it via AOL, you can let AOL know about it.

To access the controls themselves, click the link in the middle of the bottom section of the window, labelled **Set Parental Controls**.

Setting Parental Control options

Fig. 5.11
Edit controls screen

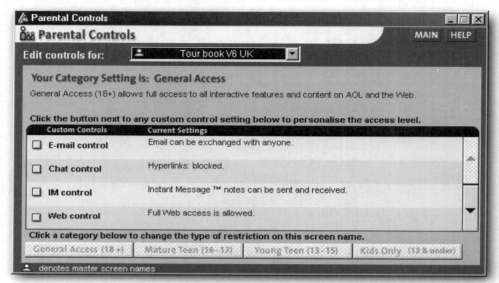

This is the screen where you can alter the options for each Screen Name on your account. Don't worry if it looks confusing – we'll work through it step by step.

Across the top, you'll see the words Edit controls for, followed by your Screen Name. Click the downward pointing arrow to the right of the name, and you'll see the list of all the Screen Names on your account. Those that are listed with a green head and shoulders next to them are Master Screen Names, which means that they can change the options of other names. Choose one of the names from the list, and the rest of the screen will update to show you what the Parental Controls settings are at the moment.

Immediately below the Screen Name is a summary of the current settings, while across the bottom of the page are four buttons – one for each of the Parental Controls categories. The button for the current setting will be dimmed, for most names. If you select a Master Screen Name, all the buttons will be dim, since you can't change the options for a Master name without changing it first to be just an ordinary name.

In the middle of the page, you'll see the detailed options which you can use to give yourself more control over which bits of AOL and the Internet are accessible to the Screen Name you've selected. To the right of this section are an up and a down arrow – you can click these to move through all the different options.

The options themselves have a name, and next to that a description of the current settings. If you change a Screen Name from one category to another using the buttons at the bottom, all the settings will update appropriately.

If all you want to do is change a Screen Name from one pre-set category to another, just choose the name you want to change, then click the category button that you want, and you're done. You can close this window and carry on with the rest of your time on AOL.

However, if you want to change some of the settings, you need to click the small green button next to the name of the setting that you want to change. Let's go through them all one at a time.

Email control
The email controls are one of the most complicated, but well worth understanding. After you've been on the Internet for a while, you'll realise that receiving unsolicited email is quite common, whether it's trying to sell you something, or for some other reason. The email controls will help you to make sure that your children aren't exposed to anything via email unless you want them to be, and that they can't contact people you'd rather they don't write to.

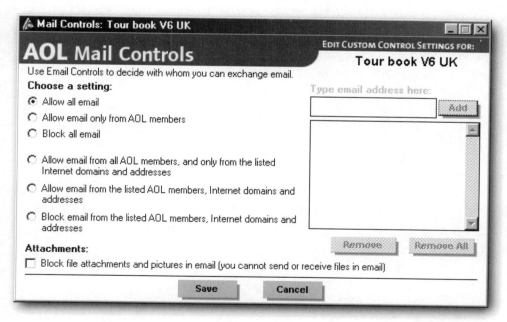

Fig. 5.12
Email control screen

The main options are listed down the left-hand side of the page. **Allow all email** is fairly self-explanatory – there are no restrictions on who email can be sent to or received from.

The next option, Allow email only from AOL members, means that your child could receive email from other people who use AOL, including AOL in other countries. But they won't be able to receive email via the Internet. While that will stop, for instance, unsolicited junk mail, it would also prevent friends who don't use AOL for their email from making contact.

Block all mail is self explanatory too. Select this option if you don't want anyone at all to be able to send email to your child.

The three final options on the email controls work with a list of addresses and domains. An address can be an AOL Screen Name, an Internet email address, or an Internet domain.

The first of the options lets you exchange email with all AOL members, and also with Internet addresses or domains that you have listed.

The next one is similar, but only AOL members you've added to the list will be able to send you email. This is probably the most secure option of all, but you'll need to remember to add all the people you want to exchange email with to the list. For your child, that could be their classmates and grandparents, for example.

The final option will allow all email, except from the people that are in the list. You could use that, for example, to stop your old colleagues sending you messages now you don't work with them.

How to list addresses
You can add an entry to the list by typing it into the box at the top of the list, and clicking the **Add** button. To remove one, highlight it, then click the **Remove** button.

To add an AOL Screen Name, just type it in and click the **Add** button.

To add an Internet address, type it in full. For example, tony@number10.gov.uk would add the whole address to the list.

To add a domain, just type it in and press the **Add** key. An example of a domain would be number10.gov.uk.

Saving your choices
When you've finished setting up the address list, and decided whom you want to allow or block from sending email to you, there's one last option to check.

Near the bottom of the screen, there's a check labelled Attachments. You can set or remove the check in the box by clicking it with your mouse. If the box is checked, then you won't be able to send or receive email messages that have attachments, or pictures embedded in them. Attachments can be pictures, or word processor files, or just about anything that you have saved on a computer disk. They can also carry computer viruses, so if you're not expecting to receive files via email, it's a good idea to check this option.

When you're sure you have chosen all the appropriate options for the Screen Name you're working with, click the **Save** button and you'll be returned to the main Parental Controls screen, where you can change the other options.

Chat control
Chat is one of the most popular features on AOL, but sometimes you might want to prevent your children from visiting some areas where they might be exposed to inappropriate comments.

Fig. 5.13
Chat control screen

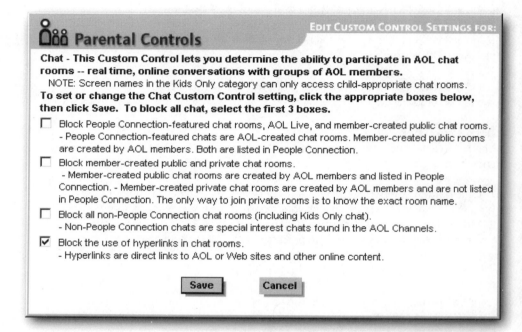

The chat controls divide AOL's chat system up into a number of different areas. In addition, if you've put a Screen Name into the Kids Only category, only chat areas suitable for children will be accessible, unless you block those too.

The option at the bottom of the screen doesn't block any chat areas. Instead, it stops hyperlinks, which are text links that you can send to a chat area so that people can click it to go directly to a site on the Internet or a part of AOL. Sometimes people use this method to give hyperlinks to inappropriate sites, so it's a good idea to block hyperlinks in chat for your children.

The top option on the Chat controls screen restricts access to chat rooms created by AOL on AOL Live, and to public chat areas created by other users in the American-based People Connection, which is accessible via the Chat Channel.

The next option blocks access to all chat rooms created by other AOL members, whether private or public.

The third option blocks access to special interest chat rooms that are found on AOL's different channels. These are created by AOL, and selecting this option will block access to the Kids Only chat area.

To block access to all chat, you should ensure that the box next to each of the options is checked. If you simply want to provide access only to chat areas suitable for children, ensure that the Screen Name you're editing is set to the Kids Only category, and that the first two options are checked, while the third is unchecked.

When you have made your changes, click the **Save** button to return to the Parental Controls screen.

IM control
Instant Messages are a very popular feature of AOL, and allow one user to send a note to another user in private. They are often sent between users who have seen each other's name in a chat room, or after looking at another user's Profile.

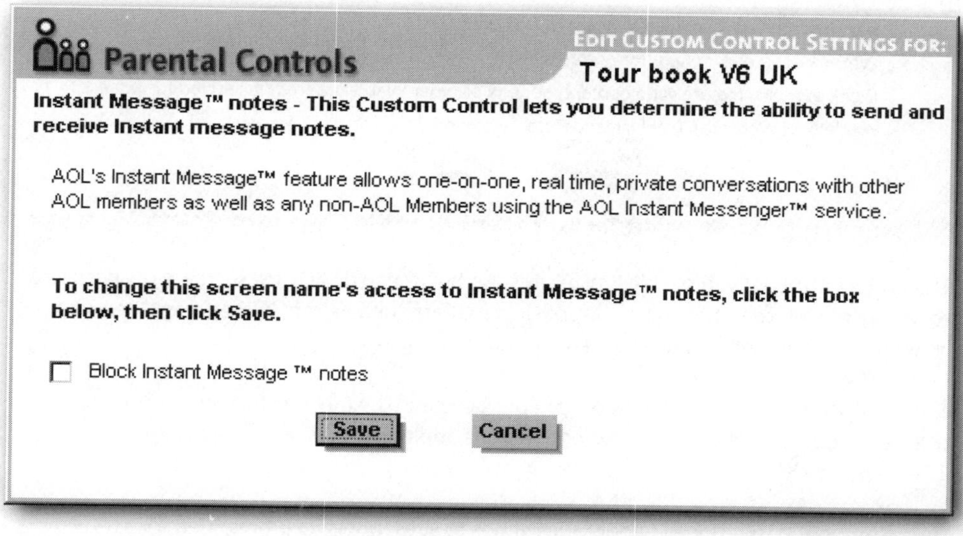

Fig. 5.14
IM control screen

Instant Messages can contain links to other parts of AOL or Internet sites, which may contain inappropriate content. You can use this page to prevent a user from being able to send and receive messages, both with other AOL members and with people on the Internet who are connected to AOL's Instant Messenger service.

Web control
As well as all the information that it provides directly, AOL gives you access to the Internet's World Wide Web – a network of sites containing just about everything you need to know.

Fig. 5.15
Web control screen

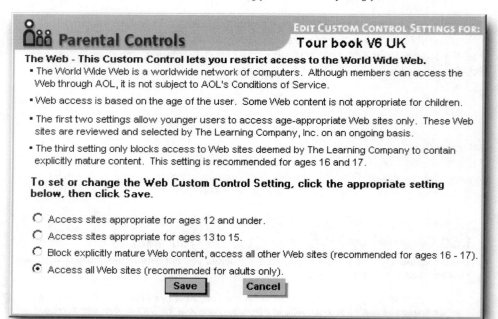

The Web controls let you decide which sites can be accessed. AOL uses a team of specialists to review the Internet, providing a list of sites that are suitable for children, together with information about which ages they are appropriate for.

This page lets you choose which sites can be accessed. The most restrictive setting is for children aged 12 or under. The next option adds additional sites, and is appropriate for 13–15-year-olds.

Next is an option that doesn't apply age ratings to sites, but is recommended for 16–17 year olds. This option allows access to all Internet sites except those that contain explicitly mature content.

The last option on the page gives complete access to all the Web sites on the Internet, which may include material that you find explicit or inappropriate in other ways.

Although AOL tries hard to make sure that only appropriate sites are accessible in each category, the sites are on the Internet, and so aren't under the direct control of AOL. They may change, and if you are concerned about the content of one of the sites, you should contact AOL. Remember that the best way to protect your children online is to supervise their use of the computer.

Additional Master

The first name you created when you signed on to AOL is your Primary Master Screen Name, which lets you alter Parental Controls as well as billing options. The Additional Master control lets you give those abilities to one of the other Screen Names on your account.

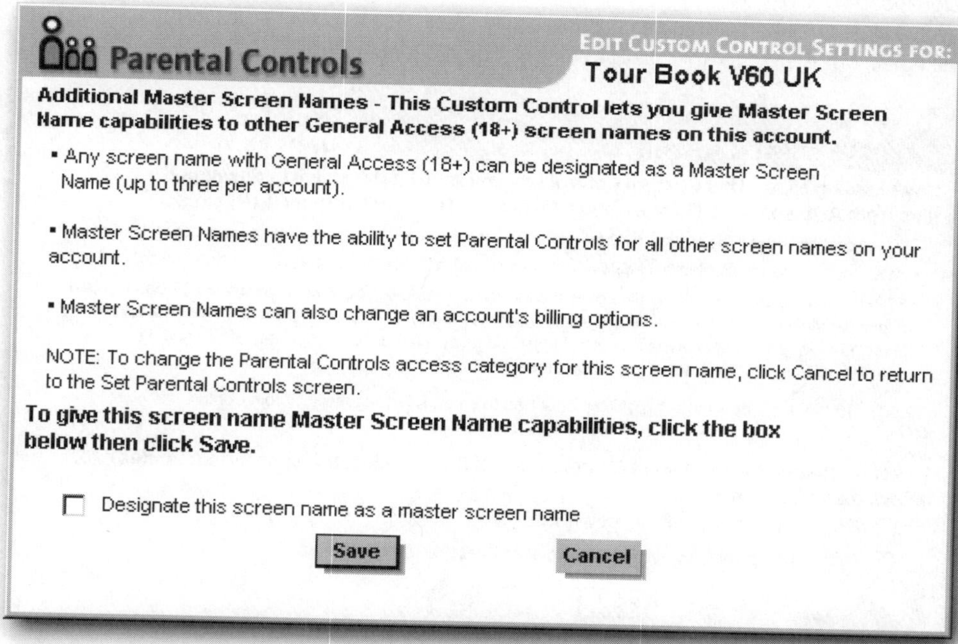

Fig. 5.16
**Additional
Master screen**

When you click the **Additional Master control**, this is what you'll see. Click to put a check in the box at the bottom of the screen if you want the Screen Name you've chosen to have Master rights. If the box can't be changed, then the name isn't in the right category – a Screen Name can only be given Additional Master rights if it's been put in the General

Access (18+) category. If the name that you want to give rights to is in another category, click **Cancel**, change the category to General Access (18+) and then return to this screen.

You can remove the Master rights from any Screen Name except the one you created when you first signed up to AOL.

Remember that Screen Names with Master rights can alter what all the other Screen Names on your account are able to access, and can view your billing information, which may include credit card details. You should be careful who you give the Additional Master rights to, and unless you are sure that your computer is in a secure place, make sure that none of the Screen Names with Master rights to your account have their password saved.

Download control
We've already looked at the email controls, which will let you prevent files from being received via email, but there are other ways to receive downloadable files.

Fig. 5.17
**Download
control screen**

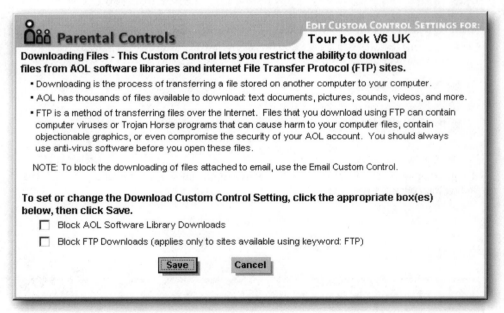

AOL provides file areas where you can download lots of useful programs, pictures and other information. You can also access files on the Internet, using a system called FTP.

Files on AOL are checked for computer viruses, but you may want to prevent your children, for example, from adding new programs to your computer without your permission. To do this, click to place a check in the box next to **Block AOL Software Library Downloads**.

Files on the Internet may not have been checked for viruses, and could cause harm to your computer, or contain material that you find objectionable. Check the box labelled **Block FTP downloads** to prevent access to these files.

When you're done, click the **Save** button to return to the Parental Controls screen.

Newsgroup control
Newsgroups are a little like an Internet version of the AOL discussion boards – but with no one in control of them. They cover thousands of topics, and some of the more technical ones are where you'll find top experts in their field. Other groups are home to what is best called robust discussion, and some contain pictures or language that you may find unpleasant. Newsgroups can also provide other files for download, and as with the rest of the Internet, those files may not have been checked for viruses.

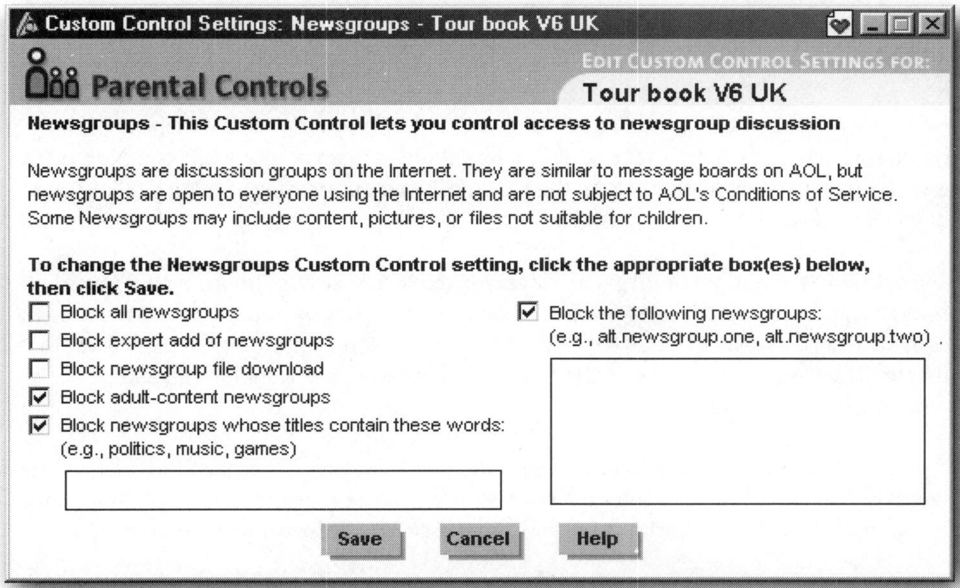

Fig. 5.18
Newsgroup control screen

This screen allows you to control what sort of access to newsgroups is available to each of the Screen Names on your account. When you access newsgroups via AOL, you can choose from a list that AOL has selected, or give the names of other groups, if you know them.

To prevent all access to newsgroups, choose the first option – **Block all newsgroups**. If you want to allow access only to those on AOL's list, click once with the mouse to place a check in the box marked **Block expert add of newsgroups**.

The next option, **Block newsgroup file downloads**, allows you to prevent any files from being downloaded from any of the newsgroups that are made available by the other options that you've chosen.

> *Remember that even if you block file downloads from newsgroups, messages in a group may contain Internet links to files or other material elsewhere, which won't necessarily be blocked. You should ensure you set Web controls as well as newsgroup controls.*

The Block adult-content newsgroups option will block all those groups that AOL believes may contain adult content. You should remember, however, that since newsgroups are not controlled centrally, it is possible that inappropriate content may occasionally be posted to other newsgroups.

The last two options allow you to specify newsgroups or types of newsgroups that you specifically wish to prevent access to.

Newsgroups are named via a series of words with a dot separating them. For instance the group soc.culture.pakistan is for discussing the culture of that country, while comp.sys.mac is where you'll find discussions about the Macintosh computer system, and talk.politics.misc is a general political forum.

The option at the bottom of the page allows you to block access to groups whose name contains particular words. You can type as many words as you like into the box, separated by a comma. Check the box to block access to those groups. You might, for example, decide to put the words sex,religion,politics,drugs in the box to prevent your children from seeing groups dealing with any of those subjects.

If you find that there are specific groups that you want blocked, rather than those with certain words in them, then you can enter their names in the box at the right of the page, separated by commas, and click to check the box marked **Block the following newsgroups**.

You could enter, for example, uk.adverts.personals if you want to prevent people looking at the British personal ads newsgroup.

After setting your newsgroup options, click the **Save** button.

Premium Services control

Premium services are areas of AOL that incur additional charges while you are accessing them. These include some online games. You will be warned when you are entering a premium area, but you may wish to restrict access to them, to ensure that you don't run up large bills.

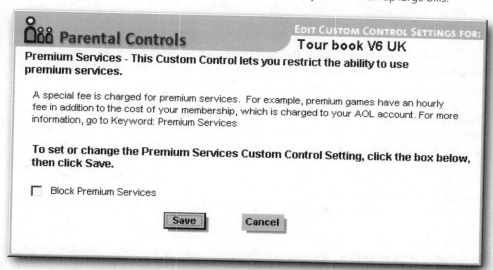

Fig. 5.19
Premium Services control screen

The Premium services control screen allows you to prevent the Screen Name you are currently changing from accessing any premium services. To stop access, click with the mouse to place a check in the box marked **Block Premium Services**, and then click the **Save** button.

That's all the controls! As you can see, it's easy to make sure that using AOL is as safe as you'd like it to be – you really can make sure that your children will only be able to access what you want, and can be protected from having strangers contact them online.

As ever, remember that while AOL gives you Parental Controls, it's up to you to use them, and nothing is ever a substitute for being involved in what your kids are doing. We'd encourage you to talk to them about what they're doing online, and make sure that they understand the basic rules of the road. To help educate your children about staying safe online take a look at keyword: **Safety Zone** with them.

5.2 People on AOL

AOL isn't just a collection of services. You might find the online shops essential for last-minute gifts, or the weather reports invaluable when you're planning a weekend away. But for many people what makes AOL so special is the people you meet online – it's not just a lot of information, but a community as well.

We've already talked about some of the parts of the AOL experience, like chat rooms and Instant Messages, that will help you to meet people and become part of the community, but there are plenty of other aspects of AOL that you'll find useful too.

You can create a Profile, so that people can find out about you, so that each conversation with someone new doesn't start with the same old questions about who you are and where you are. Or you can search through the Profiles to find other members.

Perhaps you live in a small town, and can't imagine that there's anyone else there who's interested in motorcycle maintenance – but a look at the AOL Member Directory could prove you wrong, and bring you a new friend – or at least someone to borrow a spanner from.

AOL will also remember who your friends are, and tell you which of them is connected to AOL at the same time, so you can send them an Instant Message, or invite them to a private chat area to discuss that surprise party for your partner – and you can even arrange appointments with your friends using My Calendar.

In short, AOL can help make a real difference to your social life – a sort of cross between a personal assistant and one of those friends who's always saying 'You must meet John, you have so much in common.'

Let's get on then, and see how AOL can help you make friends and keep in touch.

Creating a Profile

We've already explained in *Chapter 3, Chatting on AOL*, how you can look at someone's Profile when you see them in a chat room, or when they send you an Instant Message.

You might even have seen some people's Profiles saying that they won't respond to messages unless you have a Profile of your own. That seems rude to some people, while others think it's only fair – after all, you might not like it if someone at a party asked lots of questions about you, but refused to say anything about themselves.

So, when you're comfortable on AOL, the time is probably right to create a Profile to tell people who you are and what you're interested in.

To start creating your own Profile, go to the **Cutomise** menu and choose **My Profile**. You can also access your own Profile at keyword **My Profile**.

My Profile

When you choose the My Profile option you'll see a screen like this appear.

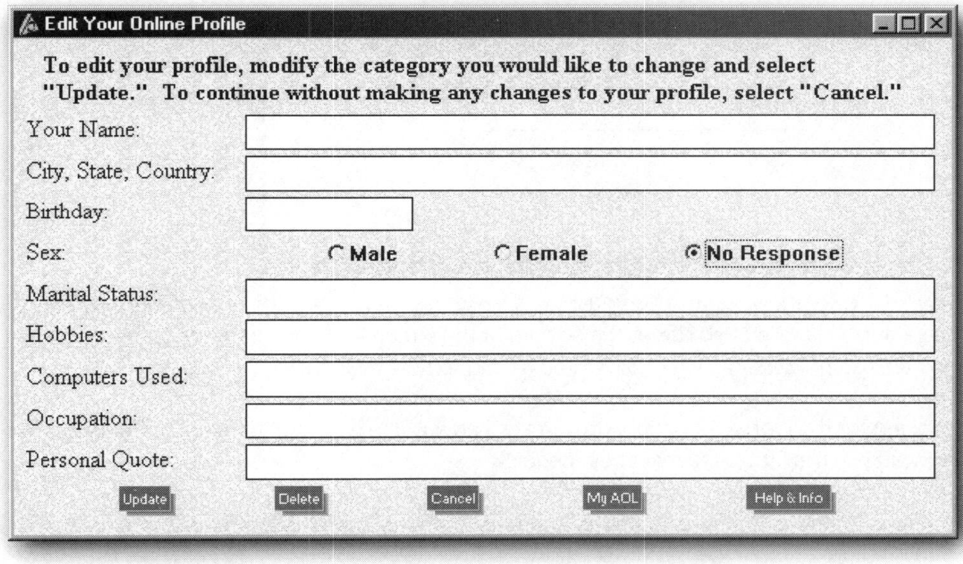

Fig. 5.20
Edit My Profile screen

This is the screen where you fill in the details you want to appear in your Profile. As you can see, each of the blank spaces has a label, which will appear next to whatever you fill in when someone asks to look at your Profile. Don't worry if you don't think they're all appropriate, though.

Although your Profile can be seen by other people as soon as you save it, that doesn't mean that they'll see you when they search the Profiles. With millions of members around the world, searching the Profiles could take a long time, so to speed it up, AOL creates an index every day. That means that it could take up to 24 hours before your own Profile will appear in the list that AOL gives people when they search.

Viewing and searching Member Profiles

If you know the name of someone – perhaps you've talked to them, or you've received an email from them – you can ask AOL to show you their Profile by choosing **Get Member's Profile** from the People menu, and typing their name into the box that appears on your screen.

Fig. 5.21
Get Profile

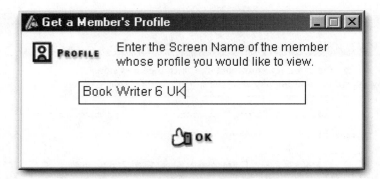

Press the **Enter** key and the user's Profile will be displayed, if they've created one. You'll also see a button labelled **Profile** at the bottom of the screen that appears when someone sends you an Instant Message, which saves you having to type their name.

Looking for the Profiles of people you already know is one way of finding out about them, but how do you use Profiles to meet new people?

It's easy! AOL lets you search through all the Profiles that people have created, looking for names, places or common interests. You can find people who are connected to AOL at the same time as you, so you can chat with them right away, or you can send them an email to look at when they next connect.

To start searching Member Profiles, click the arrow at the top of the **People** button, and choose **Search People Directory**, to bring up this screen.

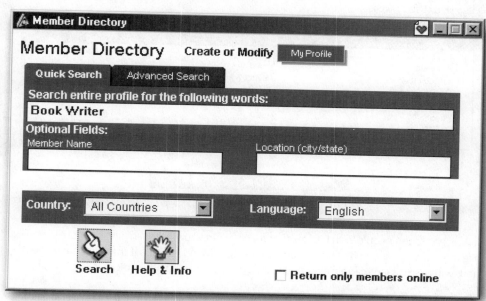

Fig. 5.22
Member search screen

As you can see, there are two tabs – Quick Search and Advanced Search. We'll look at each one of them in turn.

Quick Search

The Quick Search is the easiest way to find people on AOL. You can enter as much or as little information as you like. If you just want to find people who have the same first name as you, or perhaps people with the same surname, enter it in the space labelled Member Name.

Fig. 5.23
Results screen

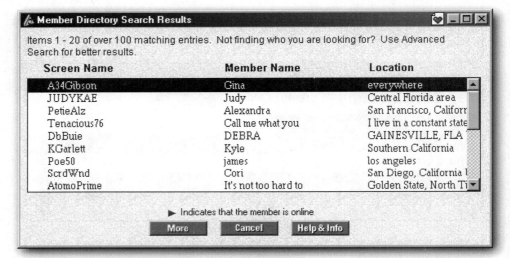

If AOL has found people with Profiles that match what you were searching for, you'll see a list like this. AOL will show the first 20 people that were found – or less if that's all that it could find, with a small red triangle next to anyone who's connected at the moment.

At the top of the list, you'll see the number of people that were found, if it's less than 100. To see more than the first 20, just click the **More** button, and another 20 names will appear below the ones already listed.

> *AOL will never display more than 100 names when you search the member directory. If there were more than 100 Profiles matching the words you entered, you'll just see the first 100. You should try adding more words to your search, to narrow it down a little.*

All you have to do if you want to see more information about any of the people listed is double-click their name with the mouse, and their Profile will be displayed.

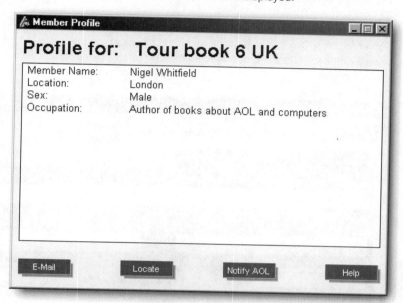

Fig. 5.24
Profile screen

From a member's Profile, you can use the buttons beneath their description of themselves to send them an email, see where on AOL they are or notify AOL if you think there's inappropriate information in their Profile.

When you click the **Locate** button, to see where someone is, you'll see a screen like this one:

Fig. 5.25
**Member
location info**

Click the **IM** button to send an Instant Message to the person you've found. If they're in a public area of AOL, rather than a private chat room, or just browsing through information, you can also click the **Go** button to join them. You might find this is a good way to find out where people talk about the things that interest you.

Advanced search
Sometimes, the Quick Search of the Member Directory won't produce the information you want – or it'll turn up so many members that it's just not practicable to look at all their Profiles in turn.

Fig. 5.26
Advanced member search screen

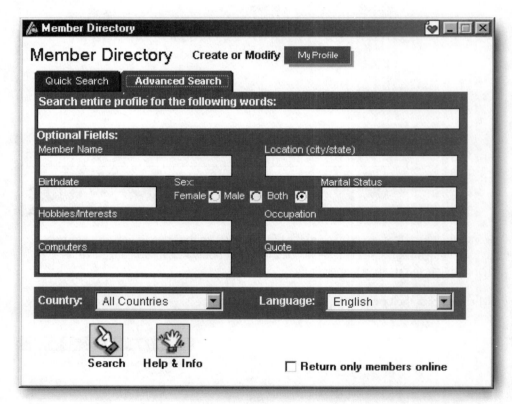

This is what you'll see if you select **Search People Directory** from the **People** menu and then click the **Advanced** tab. As you can see, the first three boxes are the same as for the Quick Search, but now there are lots more options that you can fill in.

When you've filled in the options that you want, click the **Search** button, and AOL will display a list of the people that have been found, in exactly the same was as when you used the Quick Search.

Buddy Lists

A Buddy List is a list of Screen Names that you want AOL to keep track of. When you tell AOL you want to view your Buddy List, a small window pops up on the screen, telling you who's online, and as people sign on and sign off you'll see their Screen Names appearing and disappearing from the list – so you can send them an Instant Message, or perhaps decide you should sign off if you see your boss coming online, and don't want to speak with him.

Buddy Lists

Setting up your Buddy List
So, just how do you get started with a Buddy List? It's simple. Click the down arrow on the **People** menu and choose **Buddy Lists**. Another menu will pop out to the right with two options – Setup and View. Choose **Setup**, and you'll see this appear.

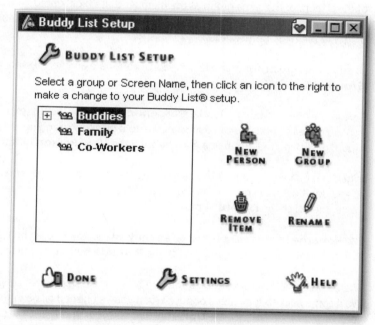

Fig. 5.27
Buddy List Setup screen

The panel at the left shows all the people whom you've added to your Buddy List. It can also show groups – you could have a list of people grouped under the heading of colleagues, for example, and another for fellow opera buffs.

To the right, you'll see the buttons that let you add and remove people and groups

The first time you visit this screen, there'll be a group created for you called Buddies. Groups have a small grey icon in the list, and next to them there's a plus or a minus symbol in a small box. Click the box and it changes from one to the other; when there's a plus showing, all you'll see is the name of the group. Click to turn it into a minus, and the list will show all the members of the group, below the group name.

So, how do you add someone to the group? Easy! All you need to do is click the **New Person** button.

Type in the Screen Name of the person that you'd like to add, and press **Enter**. You'll see their name appear in the list, if you've set it to show who's under each heading.

The person you've just added will be put in the group that's currently highlighted on the left of the screen, or the same group as the member that's highlighted. You can move someone from one group to another by clicking their name, holding down the mouse button, and dragging them to another group.

To add a new group, for example, for people you share an interest with, click the **New Group** button.

Type in the name of the group, like **Gardeners**, and press the **Enter** key. The new group will appear in the list, and you can add someone to it by either dragging their name from another group, or clicking the group title and choosing the **New Person** button.

When you no longer want to keep track of someone – perhaps your boss has left the firm, so you don't need to know when they're on AOL anymore – all you need to do is click the name, then click the **Delete** button.

The **Rename** button lets you change an entry on the list, in case you typed the wrong name. Just highlight a person or a group, click the **Rename** button, and type a new name.

There's one other useful button on the Buddy List Setup screen, which is labelled **Settings**. We'll come back to that later. For now, when you've finished filling in the names of the people you want on your list, click the **Done** button, and your Buddy List will be saved.

Viewing and using your Buddy List

Now you've created your Buddy List, you'll want to use it to see who's online when. From the **People** menu, you can choose **Buddy List** and then **View**. You can also call up your Buddy List using the keyword **Buddy view**.

Buddy view

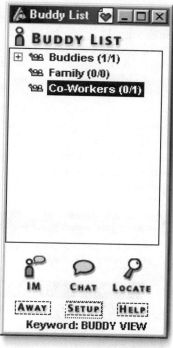

Fig. 5.28
Buddy List display

The list of Buddies here works in the same sort of way as when you set it up – you can either just see the group headings, or you can click the small square next to a heading to turn it into a list of all the people who are online.

Next to each heading, you'll see two numbers in brackets, for example (2/17). That would mean that you had 17 buddies in that group, and two of them are connected to AOL.

Sending an Instant Message to one of your Buddies when you see them online is simple. All you need to do is double-click their name, or click once, and then click the **IM** button at the bottom of the Buddy List. Whichever you do, a blank Instant Message screen will appear, with your Buddy's name already filled in for you.

You can also find out which part of AOL your friend is using, using the Locate button. Click their name first, then click **Locate**, and you'll be told where they are – you might, for example, want to use this before sending them an Instant Message. If they're not in a chat room, perhaps they're busy and don't want to be bothered with talking.

Between the IM and Locate buttons, you'll see another one, labelled Chat. You can use this button to ask your buddies to join you in a private chat room where, for instance, you could plan a surprise party for a friend, safe in the knowledge that they can't accidentally join the room and find out what you're up to. We'll explain Buddy Chat in a moment. First, let's look at the other buttons on the Buddy List display.

Sometimes, you might be a little busy to respond to Instant Messages. Perhaps someone's called you on your mobile phone, and you're engrossed in a conversation with them.

Isn't it infuriating when someone doesn't reply to an Instant Message? Well, the Away button at the bottom of your Buddy List is for just that eventuality. Click it, and you'll see a screen like this one.

Fig. 5.29
Away main screen

The first time you come here, there'll be a list of suggested responses. You can also create your own. Just click the **Create** button.

It looks a little like sending an Instant Message, doesn't it? In fact, that's more or less what you're doing, but instead of a Screen Name, the box at the top is a title, which will appear in the list on the previous screen. Click there and type a title, like 'Really busy' and then in the main box, enter the message you want to be sent to people if they try to send you an Instant Message.

After you've typed your message, click the **Save** button and you'll be returned to the previous screen. You can use the **Edit** button to change your message later if you like.

To tell people that you're away, choose one of your messages from the list, and click **OK**. Now people will receive the message when they try to contact you, until the next time you click the **Away** button on your Buddy List. You'll also be told how many people tried to send you a message, as well.

The **Setup** button lets you change, add and remove names and groups on your Buddy List, and also access the Buddy Preferences. It takes you to the screen we looked at in the previous section.

Buddy Chat
Buddy chat is just like an ordinary chat room, except only people that you invite can join in the room. When the last person leaves the room, the lights go out, and it ceases to exist. If you invite everyone to chat again, the name of the room might be something completely different.

So, how do you invite your friends for a private chat, away from the prying eyes of other users?

The **Chat** button at the bottom of your Buddy List lets you create a private chat room. You can invite up to 22 people, and only the people you've invited along will be able to join you there – so no one else can come in and find out what you've been planning for their birthday party, or report what you said back to the boss.

You can only select one thing in your Buddy List at a time, which can either be a group, or a person. If you select a group, then when you click **Chat**, all the members of that group will added to the invitation list. If you click a person, that name will be added for you. Don't worry though – like all the best parties, you can revise the invitation list.

So, pick one of the groups in your Buddy List, and click the **Chat** button. Something like this will appear on your screen.

Fig. 5.30
Chat invitation

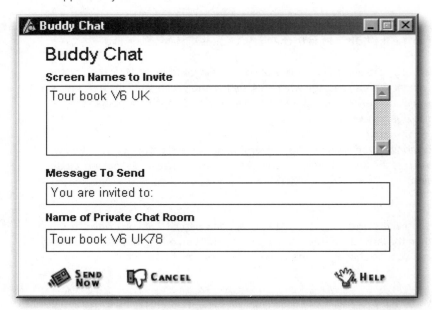

In the top box, you'll see either the name of the person you clicked on, or all the names of the members of the group you selected from your Buddy List.

By clicking in the box, you can change the names, removing some – you might want to invite all the members of a group except the one whose party you're planning, for instance – and adding others. Just put a comma after each Screen Name, and then type the next one.

The next box is for a short message, which AOL will have set to 'You are invited to'. You can change the message to something else, but AOL will always add the location to the end of the message.

The final box lets you create either a private chat room, or specify a keyword. While private chats are useful, perhaps you want your friends to join you in an AOL chat room to help back you up in an argument. If that's the case, just click **Keyword/Favourite place**, and then type the keyword into the box below. For a private chat, just leave the name of the room as AOL suggests.

Click the **Send Now** button, and all the people in the list that are signed on will receive a message on their screen.

You'll also receive the invitation yourself. To go to the chat room, just click the **Go** button. If you've received an invitation like this from someone else, and you're too busy to join then, you can tell them by clicking **Send IM** to send an Instant Message reply.

The chat room that's created looks just like an ordinary AOL room and it works in exactly the same way – but you can be sure no one else will be able to come and join you.

Customising your Buddy List
We mentioned earlier that you can set special options for your Buddy List, via the Setup screen. From the Setup screen – remember you can reach that with the **Setup** button on your Buddy List, or choose **Buddy List**, then **Setup** from the **People** menu – click **Settings**.

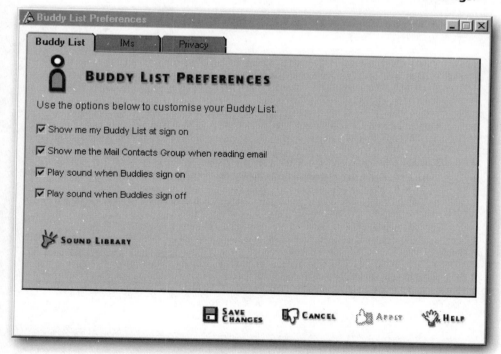

Fig. 5.31
Buddy settings

As you can see, there are three tabs on the Settings screen, labelled **Buddy List**, **IMs** and **Privacy**. You can make changes on any of the screens; just click the **Save Changes** button at the bottom when you're done.

Now you know almost everything there is to know about Buddy Lists and chatting on AOL. There's one great new feature however, which takes Buddy Lists a step further to make them even more useful. It's called Groups@AOL, and lets you share files, diaries and other information with your online Buddies. You can find out all about it later in this chapter (*5.7, Groups@AOL*).

5.3 My Calendar

My Calendar lets you keep track of your appointments and reminders, and to save you time having to look up information for popular events, you'll find that you just need to say, for example 'Add the Reading Festival' and AOL knows the dates.

What's more, you can access your calendar from any computer with an Internet connection, and even share events and appointments with other people.

Setting up My Calendar

All you need to do to get started is click the **Calendar** icon that you'll see on your toolbar – it's on the **Services** button. You can also use keyword **Calendar**.

Calendar

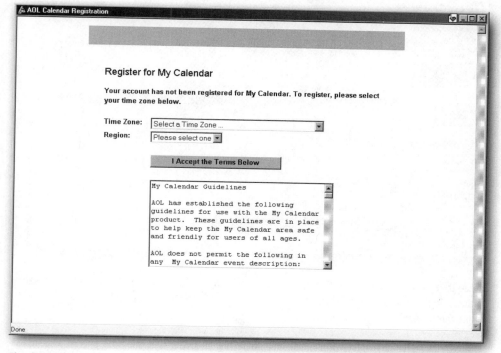

Fig. 5.32
Calendar setup screen

The first time that you use My Calendar, you'll see a screen like this one. You need to begin by telling AOL what time zone you're in, so that all your appointments show up at the correct time.

Just click the arrow at the right-hand end of the box next to Time Zone. For most of the people reading this book, you'll need to choose 'UTC +0:00 Britain, Ireland, Portugal, W. Africa'. UTC is just the new term for Greenwich Mean Time. If you happen to be using AOL from a different country, choose the time zone that you're in from the list.

When you've done that, click the **Save** button, and your calendar's main screen will appear, showing the whole of the current month.

Fig. 5.33
Calendar screen month view

Since there's so much information, you might find that you have to use the scroll bars to see the whole page. Before we go any further, we'll take a quick tour around the screen to see what the different parts of it are for.

The main area is taken up with a square for each day. The date is a link, so if you click it, you'll go to a screen where you can make an appointment for that particular day.

Along the top, you'll see three tabs. The first is for the Calendar screen that you're looking at. The next, **Event Directory**, is where you'll find information from AOL about different types of events that you might want to add to your calendar, and the last tab, **Tour** and **Help** is where you can get extra information about My Calendar service.

At the bottom, there are three more tabs, labelled **Day**, **Week** and **Month**. These control how much of your calendar you see in one go. The month view is the one that you see first, but you can switch to one of the others just by clicking the appropriate tab. When you do, the screen will update with the new view.

Finding your way round My Calendar

OK, now you know what the main tabs do, let's look at some of the other buttons and links on the Calendar main page.

At the top of the page, you'll see either the month, week or day listed, depending on which view you're looking at. For example, in the day view it might say Wednesday, while in the month view it could say August. Either side of that, there's an arrow. Click the left-hand one to move backwards – from Wednesday to Tuesday, for example, or from August to July – and the right-hand one to move forwards.

On the daily views, you'll see a small monthly calendar to the right of the main display. You can click a date here to go directly to it. Every Calendar screen also has a box below the main display with a Go button next to it. Just type a date into the box, click **Go**, and the calendar will display the page with that date on it.

The other main buttons that you'll need are the **Print** button and **Add**. The **Print** button lets you print out parts of your calendar, so you can pop your week's appointments in your pocket before leaving home, while the **Add** button lets you make a new entry – we'll explain how in detail in a moment.

At the top of the screen, you'll also see another important link. Click **Close My Calendar** to tell AOL that you've finished with My Calendar. You'll see a message asking if you want the window closed, and you should click **Yes**.

Down the left-hand side of the Calendar main page, you'll see a panel of information, which includes links to different types of information. When you click these, you could be taken to another page on AOL, or a list of events that you might want to add to your calendar. For example, there could be a link that will show you all the major sporting events this week, so that you can add them to your calendar easily.

You'll also see, when you first use the calendar, a box where you can type in your birthday to receive a horoscope, and a box you can use to tell AOL what city you're in, so that horoscopes and local weather are displayed each time you view your calendar. We'll explain more about those later, when we tell you about *Configuring My Calendar*.

Adding information to My Calendar

Now you should know how to move around My Calendar using the different tabs to select how many days you see at a time, but it's not much use unless you have things to look at, is it?

So, let's see how you can make an appointment. The simplest way is to click the **Add** button that you'll see at the top or bottom of the calendar screen. You can also click one of the dates in the month view, or the plus sign in a day or week view to add an appointment at a particular time.

When you do that, AOL will fill in the appropriate information for you on the Appointment screen, but the form itself always looks like this:

Fig. 5.34
Appointment creation form

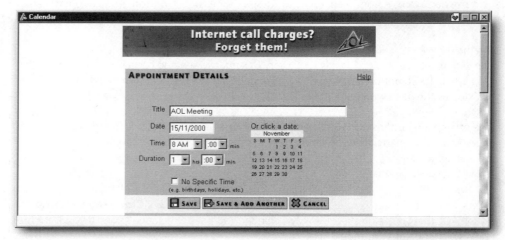

As you can see, it's a pretty large form, but don't worry – it's actually a lot simpler to use than it may look at first. There are three sections to fill in, but they're very straightforward.

The first part is the information about the appointment. In the box next to Title, type a short description, which will appear on your calendar pages. You might enter something like 'Dentist's appointment' or 'Collect kids from child-minder'.

Next, you need to enter the date. You can type in a date, or click one of the days in the small Calendar that appear to the right. It you clicked on a day in your Calendar to create the entry, rather than using the Add button, the date should have been set for you.

Below the date, you can set the time. Click first on the arrow to set the hour – just choose from the list. You'll find each hour is listed twice – once for am and once for pm – so make sure you pick the right one. You can set the number of minutes past the hour in five-minute blocks, so you can have an appointment for five past eight, or ten past eight, but not seven minutes past. Once again, if you've clicked on a time in the week or day views of the calendar, the hour will have been set for you.

Next, you can set the duration of the appointment, from five minutes upwards. If you don't change this option, AOL will assume you want a one-hour appointment.

Sometimes, of course, you just want to put something in your diary that doesn't have a specific time, like a birthday, or a day when your parents are visiting you. For those appointments, click to put a check in the box labelled **No specific time**. The appointment will be listed at the top of the day, above any appointments that have a time.

Now, we can move on to the next section – Tell a friend.

This is where you can send information about an appointment to someone else, so that they can enter it in their own calendar, or write it in their diary if they're not as technologically clued up as you are!

Just type the addresses of people that you want to tell about your appointment in the box, with a comma between each one. For other AOL members, you just need to type the Screen Name, not the whole email address.

Fig. 5.35
**Appointment
creation screen**

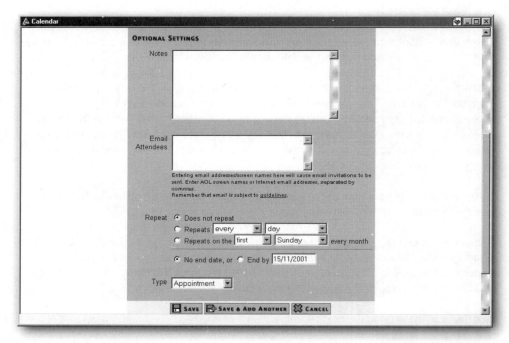

Underneath the Tell a friend box, you'll see this – though you might need to scroll down to
reach this part of the page.

In the large box, you can add extra information about your appointment. You might type,
for example, the location of a birthday party that you're going to, or details of how to get
to a business meeting.

Next, you can tell AOL that you want the event to be repeated. For example, you might have
a regular monthly meeting, or an anniversary. By using the repeat function, you can tell My
Calendar that you want the appointment to be made automatically for you. You'll just have to
fill in the details once, and it'll be there in your calendar every time.

To tell AOL that an event repeats, click one of the options. **Do not repeat**, obviously, means that the appointment you're creating will only appear once.

The next option allows you to set an event to repeat at regular intervals, every day, week, month, year and so on. Click this option, then select how often you want things to repeat from the menu. The first of the two menus lets you choose every, or every other, or every third – so you could do something every other month, or every third day. You can also choose options such as every weekday, Monday, Wednesday and Friday, or Saturday and Sunday. This is probably the option to choose for things like visiting the gym, or things like that.

The last option for repeating appointments is for things like clubs that meet on a particular day of each month, rather than a specific date. For example, you might belong to a group that meets on the third Tuesday of each month. From the first menu, choose the first, second, third and so on, then choose the day of the week for the next one.

When you've chosen all the options for how you want your appointment to repeat, the next choice lets you say whether or not you want a series of appointments to end. For example, you might be going to an evening class that's every Monday until Christmas 2001.

In that case, you'd choose every Monday from the second repeat option, and then in the bottom section, click to select **End by** and type in the date 25/12/2001. If you don't want the series of appointments to end, make sure you choose **No end date** instead.

Finally, there's one more thing you can choose. Click the arrow next to Event Type, and you can choose specific types of event, like a doctor's appointment, a work-out or a holiday.

That's all there is to it! Click the **Save** button and your appointment will be made. If you'd like to make another one right away, you can click **Save** and **Add Another** instead.

If you used the **Tell a friend** box to list email addresses for people you want to know about the appointment, you'll see another screen appear:

Fig. 5.36
**Tell a friend
message box**

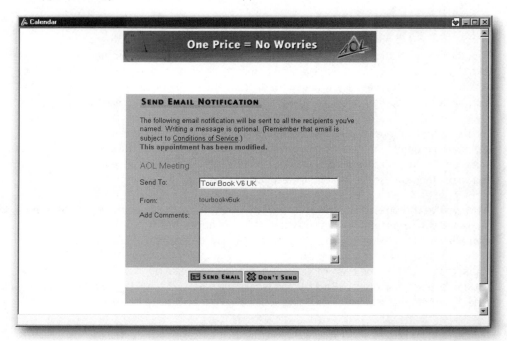

This screen shows you the message that will be sent to the people you want to tell about your appointment. AOL will use the information you typed in the Notes box as the message, but you can change it on this screen if you like.

When you're happy with the message, click the **Send** button and it'll be delivered to the people you listed.

Editing an appointment

What happens if you need to change an appointment? Perhaps a business meeting has had to be re-scheduled, or there's so much work that you can't afford to take your holiday after all.

No problem. All you need to do is go to the page in My Calendar where you can see the appointment.

Each of the appointments on the page is a link, which you can click on. When you do, you'll see the same screen that you used to create the appointment in the first place, and you can make any changes that you like. There'll be a **Delete** button at the bottom of the screen too, so you can remove the appointment from your calendar completely.

Using the Event Directory

Adding your day-to-day appointments to My Calendar is simple, as you've seen. But there are lots of things that you might want to make a note of that aren't unique to you. You might be going to a concert on a particular date, or planning to see the FA Cup Final at a friend's house. The Event Directory is a list of things from AOL that lots of people might want to put in their calendars.

By using the Event Directory, you can be sure that you have the right dates for the things that you think are important, and when you look through it you might even spot a few other things to add to your calendar. And, of course, you won't have to fill in the details yourself, since AOL has done it for you.

To start using the Event Directory, all you need to do is click the tab on the Calendar main page, and you'll see the categories of event that are available.

Fig. 5.37
**Event Directory
top page**

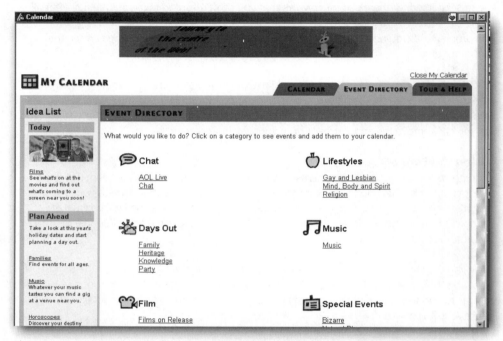

The next step is to pick one of the categories. For example, we'll look at film releases showing nearby.

Whatever category you chose, you'll see another screen, letting you choose another area – there are thousands of events in AOL's directory, so you have to narrow the choice down a little bit. We'll choose **Greater London Films**.

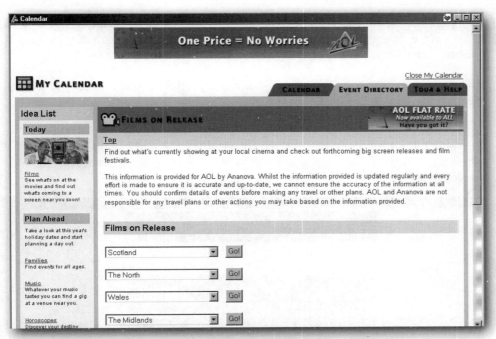

Fig. 5.38
**Film releases
page**

Here's a list of all the films in the category we chose. Next to each one, there's a check box and a date. You can add as many as you like to your calendar – just click to put a check in the box for each film you're interested in.

If you prefer, you can see the list of events by week or month, instead of a list – just click one of the tabs at the top of the page.

To find out more about a particular event, click its name, and you'll see more details.

You could click the **Add** button to add this event to your calendar, or use **Tell a friend** to let someone else know about it – useful if you come across something that you know one of your friends would be interested in. With some types of event, you'll even see a link at the bottom that will let you buy things – for example, you could buy tickets for a film. For now, though, click the **Back** button to return to the list of films, or whatever type of event you're looking at.

After you've chosen the events you're interested in from the list, click the **Add** button, which appears at the top and bottom of the list. All the events you selected will be automatically added to your calendar.

You'll be returned to the list of events after AOL has added them to your calendar – to actually see them, you need to click the **Calendar** tab.

Telling a friend
The **Tell a friend** button, which you'll see on the Events page, and when you ask for details about a specific event, tells AOL that you want to send the details of this event to someone else.

Fig. 5.39
Tell a friend screen

This is the screen that appears when you use the **Tell a friend** button. In the first box, you can type the email addresses of the people that you want to tell, with a comma between each one.

Click in the next box, and you can type a short message for your friend. AOL will automatically include the details of the event in the message for you, so you don't need to worry about typing them in yourself. When you've finished, just click the **Send Email** button.

Configuring My Calendar

Here's the main screen for your calendar again, showing the month view. Scroll down to the bottom, and next to the Print button, you'll see one that's labelled Options. That's your key to making My Calendar work the way that you want it to.

Fig. 5.40
Main screen showing Options button

Click the **Options** button and you can set a range of options, including telling AOL which city you're in so that you can see weather forecasts, and what time your day starts and ends.

Fig. 5.41
**Calendar
Options screen**

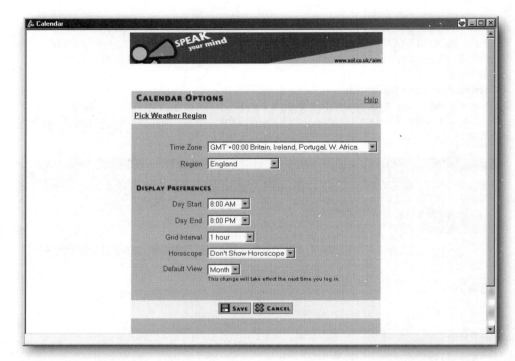

Let's go through the options starting from the top.

You might already have chosen a city – there's a link on some of the other calendar screens too. Clicking **Pick Weather Region** allows you to change to have the weather for a different city shown on your calendar. You'll see a small icon, like the ones on the TV weather forecast, telling you what the weather will be today, and for the next two days.

Just click the city you want; you'll be taken back to My Calendar options screen, and AOL will remember which city weather forecast to show you when you look at your calendar.

The next option lets you specify your time zone, just like you did when you first used the calendar.

Day start and Day end are the options to use to tell AOL when your day starts. Only times between these hours will be listed on your calendar. If all 24 hours were listed, for example, the Day and Week view screens could get pretty big. So, pick the times you want by clicking the arrows at the right of the box, and select the hour you want. You can choose times to within half an hour.

The next option, Grid interval, is used for the display in week and day views. Click the arrow at the right and you can set it to 30 minutes, one hour or two hours. This is the size of each box on the calendar, so if you make lots of short appointments then you'll probably want to set it to half an hour, instead of one hour.

If you want to know what's likely to happen in your life each time you visit the calendar, you can use the Horoscope option. You can choose Don't show horoscope, or click to show a menu of all the star signs. Select the one you want – or perhaps your partner's.

Finally, you can choose whether My Calendar starts up showing you the Month, Week or Day view, using the Default view option.

When you've made all your choices, click the **Save** button. Remember that some, like the Default view, won't actually appear to do anything until the next time you start using your calendar.

And that's it! My Calendar really is that simple to use. What's more, you can use it from anywhere you can connect to the Internet, too. Take a look at *Chapter 8, AOL Anywhere*, to find out how you can check your appointments no matter where you are.

AOL's Groups@AOL facility also allows you to create a Calendar that you can share with people, for a club, perhaps. You can find out more about groups later on in this chapter (*5.7, Groups@AOL*).

Now, though, let's take a look at some of the other ways you can make AOL work for you, by making it easier to reach the areas you like most, with Favourites, shortcuts and Preferences.

5.4 Customising AOL

As you'll have realised by now, AOL is pretty straightforward to use, but you can make it easier still.

For example, you might be interested in classic cars. You can find information about them easily in the Interests channel, but it'll take you a few clicks of the mouse, or you'll have to type the keyword **Classic Cars** into the keyword box and press the **Enter** key.

Ok, so it's not exactly an onerous task, but wouldn't it be great if you could have a button on your screen to take you right there, so you can keep up to date with the latest information each time you sign on?

Perhaps you're a little shortsighted, and you'd like AOL to use bigger letters when you're writing your email messages. Or maybe you don't want to hear about special offers that AOL has for its members sometimes.

You can change all these aspects of AOL, so that it does just what you want. Let's start by looking at how you can reach your favourite parts of AOL easily. After that, we'll take a look at the different ways in which you can customise the service.

Favourite Places
Favourite Places are one of the easiest ways to customise AOL. You'll find them on the **Places** button. A single click of the Heart icon in the **Places** button – it's the top right one on the AOL main screen – is all you need to bring up your favourites. Alternatively, you can click the arrow next to the word **Places** and choose **Favourites** from the menu.

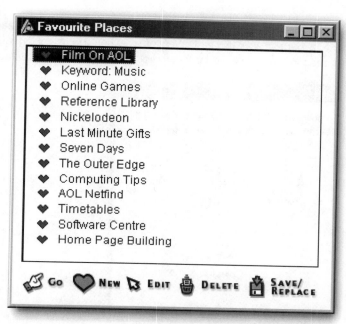

Fig. 5.42
Favourite Places

This is a list of the favourite places that AOL has added for you already. At the bottom, you'll see any other favourites that you've already added to the list. You can go directly to any of the places listed here simply by double-clicking their name.

What was that about places you've added? In case you missed it earlier, you can add items to the Favourite places very easily. Very often, when you're looking round AOL, you'll see a heart at the top right of a window. If you click the heart, a screen like this will appear:

Fig. 5.43
Add to favourite places

All you have to do to is click the **Add to Favourites** button, and a new entry will be made in your Favourite Places list.

> *There's a quick way to add the window you're currently reading to your Favourite Places. You can choose **Add top window to favourites** from the **Places** menu, or you can hold down the Ctrl key and press the plus symbol. The top window is the one whose title bar hasn't been turned to grey.*

Organising your Favourite Places
The Favourite Places screen lets you make all the changes you want very easily. Let's look at the buttons along the bottom of the screen.

Firstly, the **Go** button does just what it says. Instead of double-clicking one of the entries in the list, you can click once to highlight it, then click the **Go** button.

The **New** button lets you add somewhere to your Favourite Places by typing in it's address. It's most useful if you've been given an Internet address, and want to be able to get to it quickly. Most of the time, of course, it's much simpler to click the heart at the top of a window to add it to the list.

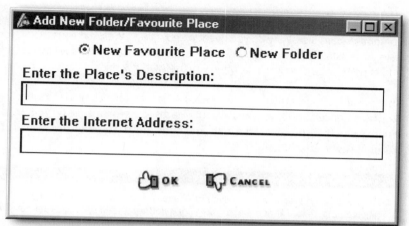

Fig.5.44
New favourite screen

This is what you'll see when you click the **New** button. At the top, you can choose whether you're adding a Favourite Place or a folder. To add a Favourite place, just type a description in the first box, and the Internet address in the second. For example, to add the British Telecom Web site, you'd type British Telecom in the top box, and below, enter http://www.bt.com.

For an Internet address, you'll usually need to put http:// at the start of the address, unless it's there already.

Folders are a handy way of organising Favourites, and they work just like the folders on your computer's hard disk. Choose the **New Folder** option at the top of the box, and you'll be asked to give a name to the new folder. Click **OK** to create it.

If you've added new folders – or you just want to change the order that things are listed in – you can move Favourites up and down the list easily. Just click once on the entry that you want to move, and while you hold the mouse button down, drag it up or down the list. To move an entry into a folder, drop it on the folder's icon.

The **Edit** button is useful if you've made a mistake typing an Internet address into your Favourites, or perhaps a Web site has moved, but you want to keep a Favourite with the same name.

The **Delete** button lets you remove an item from your Favourite Places. Just highlight the entry you want to remove and click the button. You'll be asked to confirm that you really do want to delete it. Just click the **Yes** button, or **No** if you've changed your mind.

Favourites are a useful tool, but they're not saved on AOL. Instead, they're saved on the computer's hard disk. Why do you need to know that? Well, it means that if, for instance, you have AOL installed on a computer at home and on one at work, any Favourite Places that you add at home won't be available when you use AOL at work.

That's where the last button on the Favourite Places screen comes in. It's labelled **Save/Replace** and lets you save your Favourite Places to a separate file on your hard disk, or on a floppy disk that you could take with you to the office. You could even email the Favourite Places file as an attachment.

Fig. 5.45
**Save/replace
screen**

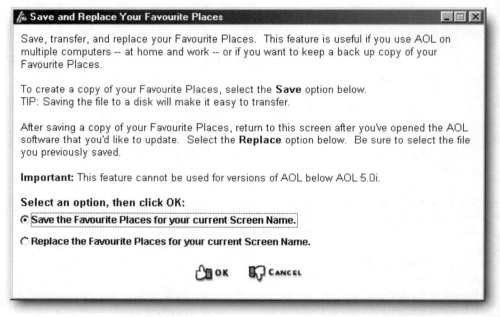

When you click the **Save/Replace** button you'll see this screen. You can choose whether you want to save the current list of Favourite Places, or replace it with another one.

Remember that when you replace your Favourites with another list, you won't be able to access any of the entries that were in it beforehand. You should consider saving your current list of Favourites, in case you want to access any of the entries on it later.

When you click **Save**, you'll see a screen similar to this. It's just the same as the box that appears when you save a file in your word processor or other programs.

Fig. 5.46
Save favourites

If you save the file to your hard disk, make sure you remember where you saved it. Although the name is usually Favourite Places, you might want to give it a different name, especially if more than one person uses your computer.

To replace a list of Favourites, choose **Replace** from the screen, and click **OK**. You'll see a similar box to the one for saving Favourites, so you can choose a file, and then click to open it. Once AOL has opened the file, it'll be installed into your Favourite Places.

My shortcuts

Favourite Places are one way of quickly reaching the parts of AOL that you like most, but they're not the only one. On the **Places** menu, you'll see an item called **My shortcuts**. When you select it, another menu will pop out to the right, with 11 entries on it.

Fig. 5.47
My shortcuts menu

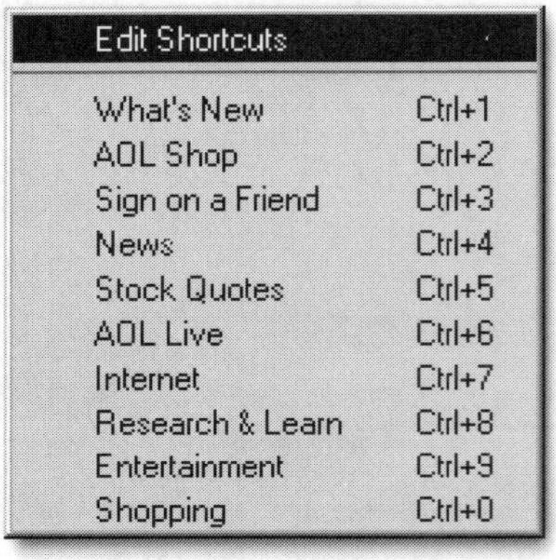

Edit Shortcuts	
What's New	Ctrl+1
AOL Shop	Ctrl+2
Sign on a Friend	Ctrl+3
News	Ctrl+4
Stock Quotes	Ctrl+5
AOL Live	Ctrl+6
Internet	Ctrl+7
Research & Learn	Ctrl+8
Entertainment	Ctrl+9
Shopping	Ctrl+0

The first entry on the menu is labelled **Edit shortcuts**, while the next ten are links to ten areas on AOL.

So what's the big deal? Isn't this just like Favourite Places?

Well, not quite. First, shortcuts can be accessed even quicker than Favourite Places. There's no need to pull up a screen with them all on, or even access a menu. You'll see that there's a shortcut listed next to each entry.

You can go directly to any of the entries in My shortcuts just by holding down the Ctrl key on your keyboard and pressing the number of the entry. So for the first one, you'd press Ctrl and 1, for instance. For the tenth entry, you use Ctrl and 0.

There's one other difference between Favourite Places and Shortcuts. You can add anything you see on AOL to your Favourite Places as long as the Heart icon appears at the top right of its window.

The only things you can add to My shortcuts are Internet addresses and AOL areas that have their own keyword. For instance, you could add the Classic Cars keyword to your shortcuts, but you couldn't add the page in that section that lists all the different marques of car featured.

Editing My shortcuts

Editing the Shortcuts list is easy. From the **Places** menu, choose **My shortcuts**, and when the menu pops out at the side, choose **Edit shortcuts**.

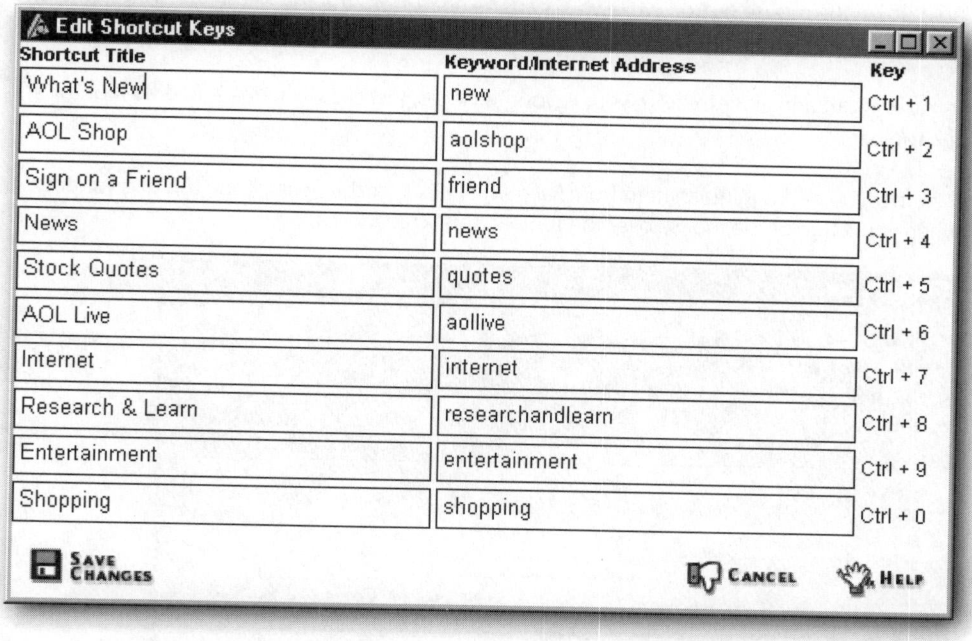

Shortcut Title	Keyword/Internet Address	Key
What's New	new	Ctrl + 1
AOL Shop	aolshop	Ctrl + 2
Sign on a Friend	friend	Ctrl + 3
News	news	Ctrl + 4
Stock Quotes	quotes	Ctrl + 5
AOL Live	aollive	Ctrl + 6
Internet	internet	Ctrl + 7
Research & Learn	researchandlearn	Ctrl + 8
Entertainment	entertainment	Ctrl + 9
Shopping	shopping	Ctrl + 0

SAVE CHANGES   CANCEL   HELP

Fig. 5.48
Edit shortcuts screen

When you've finished, click the **Save Changes** button, to update the **My shortcuts** menu.

The toolbar

Are you still having difficulty with those hard-to-reach places? Don't worry – there's yet another way that you can put information at your fingertips.

As you'll have noticed, the **Places** button at the top right of your screen is rather larger than the others. And as well as the **Heart** icon for Favourites, it already has some other entries on it.

You can add other things to it as well, which means that anything you could put in your list of Favourite Places can be turned into a button right on the AOL main screen. There'll be no need to pop up the Favourites, or remember which shortcut key takes you somewhere. Instead, you'll just need to click the icon, and you can go right there.

Adding an item to the toolbar is easy. You can add something directly, or from your list of Favourite Places. To add something directly – and remember that it could be an Internet page, or anything on AOL, as long as the Favourite Places heart is at the top of the window – just hold down the mouse button while you drag the heart from the top of the window you're reading onto the toolbar.

If you want to add an entry from your Favourite Places, just click its name and drag it onto the toolbar.

Whether you're dragging an item from Favourite Places, or the heart at the top of a window, when you let go of the mouse over the toolbar, this screen will appear:

Fig. 5.49
Add toolbar icon

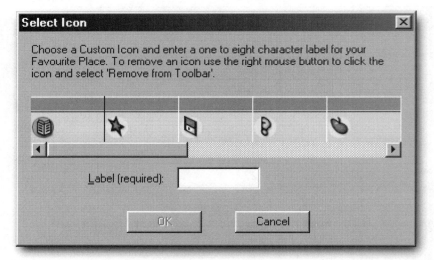

You can enter a brief label for the button in the box of up to eight letters – which will appear on the toolbar. Above the box, you'll see a scroll bar, which you can move from side to side to choose an icon. There's a small selection available, so you can choose one that's most appropriate to the place you're adding to the tool bar. For example, you could use the speech bubble if you're adding a link to a chat room, or the globe for an Internet site.

When you've chosen the icon you want, just click **OK** and your new button will appear.

What happens if you don't want the button there any more? Simple. All you have to do to remove it is point at it with the mouse, and click with the right button instead of the left. A small menu will appear with just one entry labelled Remove from toolbar. Move the mouse bar over the menu to highlight it, then click with the left button.

A small box will ask you to confirm that you want to remove the entry. Just select **Yes**, and it'll disappear, leaving more space for other entries on the toolbar.

Information direct

Now you know how to set up your AOL software so that you can go quickly to the information that you want, perhaps information that you've found already, or links that someone has sent you in an email or Instant Message.

Wouldn't it be great if you didn't have to search for information though? How about if it just came along to you, because it thought it would be useful? OK, we can't quite do that – you won't have a section of AOL popping up and saying 'Hi! I'm useful, try me!' But you can do something pretty similar, with two features called News Profiles and Member Interest Profiles.

Member Interest Profiles are a way of telling AOL what your areas of interest are. When new information is added to AOL that matches those interests, you'll automatically receive an email with links to it.

News Profiles work along the same lines. You tell AOL what sort of news stories you're interested in, and whenever a story is received from one of the news agencies – people like Reuters and the Press Association – that matches your interests, it's automatically sent to you via email.

So, News Profiles and Member Interest Profiles are great ways of making sure that you always know about the latest information, whether it's new areas on AOL, or the hottest news stories. And, just as you'd expect with AOL, they're incredibly easy to set up.

Member Interest Profiles

Member Interest Profiles are the best way to make sure that you always know when AOL has added something new that you might want to look at. Of course, if you keep an eye on the Welcome screen you'll see some new things there, but there's not the space to fit them all in.

MIP

With Member Interest Profiles you can tell AOL what areas you're interested in, and you'll receive email telling you about anything new that you should look at. And once you've looked at it, you can add it to your Favourite Places, just like anywhere else on AOL, or forward the email to a friend if you think they'll want to see it too.

Creating an Interest Profile

To get started creating your member interest Profile, type **MIP** into the Keyword box near the top of your AOL screen. You'll see a screen like this one appear:

Fig. 5.50
MIP main create screen

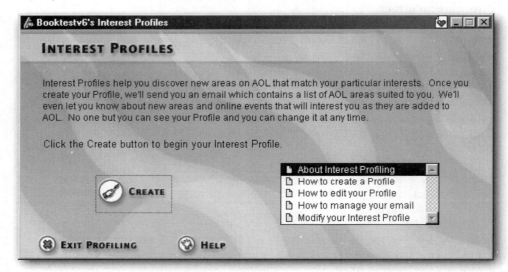

If you've created an Interest Profile before, then the button in the middle of the screen will say **Edit** instead of **Create** – but don't worry, everything will work in just the same way. You'll simply find that on the following screens, the choices you made last time will still be selected for you.

To start making your Profile, click the **Create** button. The next screen asks you what your level of computer experience is. Choose Beginners, Intermediate or Advanced, by clicking the appropriate word. The option you choose here lets AOL decide how much information you need to help you find the areas it suggests. If you've not used Member Interest Profiles before, click the **Beginners** button.

Click the **Next** button to see the list of main interest areas.

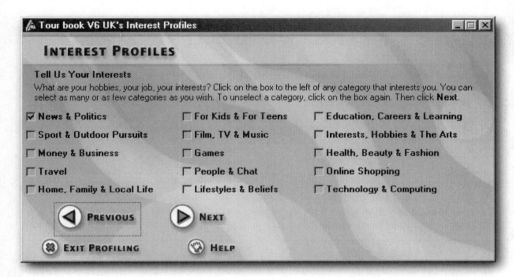

Fig. 5.51
**MIP interest
area screen**

On this screen you can select which broad categories of information you're interested in. Just click one of the titles, and a tick will appear in the box to the left of it. If you want to remove the tick, click again to clear the box.

You can select as many or as few of these areas as you like. When you've made your selections, click the **Next** button. The button marked **Previous** will take you back to the computer experience screen.

Now you'll see a series of screens. There's one for each of the categories that you chose. At the right, you'll see the category, and underneath it is a list of sub-sections for that category.

To tell AOL that you're interested in a specific sub-section, double-click it with the mouse. You'll see a blue arrow appear next to it. To change your mind, and remove the arrow, double-click the sub-section again. When you've chosen all the sub-sections you're interested in, click **Next** to move on. AOL will display a similar list for the next category you said you were interested in.

After you've selected the sub-sections for all your chosen categories, you'll see a screen like this one:

Fig. 5.52
MIP finished profile

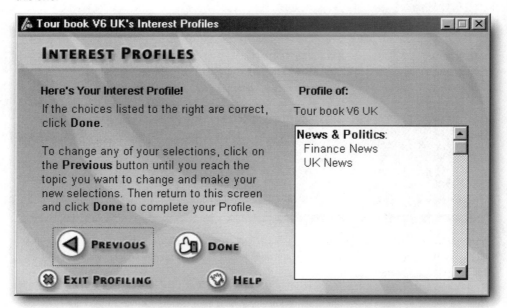

At the right hand side, you'll see a list of all the categories and sub-sections that you've selected. If you realise you've made a mistake, you can use the **Previous** button to step backwards through the screens you've just visited and make changes.

If you're happy with your choices, however, all you need to do is click the button marked **Done**. You'll see a final screen reminding you to check your email, and that's it. Click **Done**, then sit back and wait.

Receiving your Profile information
Shortly after you create your Profile for the first time, or after changing it, you'll receive a piece of new email from AOLHighlights. You can read it just like any other piece of mail. You'll find that it contains a list of areas on AOL that you might find worth visiting.

You can either make a note of the keywords in the email message and visit them later, or use the email to visit them directly.

To do that, keep the message open on your computer screen, and just click with the mouse on the words highlighted in blue in the message. AOL will go directly to the appropriate place, so you can take a look around and if you like what you see, why not add it to your Favourite Places.

As well as the email that you receive when you create or edit your Interest Profile, AOL will automatically send you another one when new areas are added, so that you always know which things might be worth visiting, as soon as they're available. How's that for service?

Controlling your Interest Profile
Sometimes, you might decide that you don't want to carry on receiving information from AOL about new services. Fortunately, it's very easy to turn Profiles off. Go to the same keyword, **MIP**, as you did when you created or edited your Profile, and in the list of options at the right of the screen, you'll see an option labelled **Modify your Interest Profile**.

Double-click that option to reach this screen:

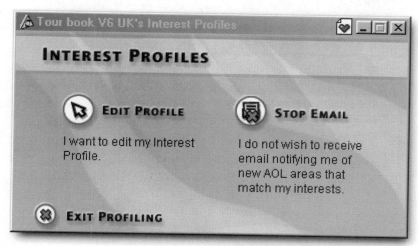

Fig. 5.53
Modify interest profile screen

You can also reach this screen directly via the keyword **Modify Interest Profile**, but that's a lot more typing! To stop receiving messages, all you need to do is click the button marked **Stop email**. Simple, isn't it?

If you want to start receiving emails with information about AOL areas again, just click the **Edit** button, and work through the screen as if you were creating your Profile again. Once you've gone through them all – you don't need to make any changes – and clicked the **Done** button at the end, you'll start to receive messages once more.

News Profiles

News Profiles

Are you a news junkie? Or perhaps you're angling for a promotion and want to make sure you keep up to date with what's happening in your industry. AOL's News Profiles at keyword **News Profiles** are like having your own personal researcher cutting out newspaper articles that will be useful for you.

A News Profile is a list of words that you want AOL to look for in news stories, and then deliver to you by email. AOL will look at news stories from sources like Reuters and the Press Association and select ones that contain the words you asked for.

Each of your Screen Names can have up to five News Profiles set up, so you could have one looking for information about a favourite celebrity, another hunting for news about the steel industry, and a third hunting for any mention of genetically modified food.

Fig. 5.54
**News Profiles
screen**

Before looking at how to create News Profiles, let's explain how they work. Each Profile has key words, required words, and excluded words. Together these describe how AOL will search for new stories.

Key words are words or phrases that may appear in a new story. Each Profile has to have at least one key word, but if there are more than one, then you'll see stories that contain one or more of the words.

For instance, if you said the words Ford and Nissan were key words, then stories about either of the car makers would be found – and so would anything about the actor, Harrison Ford.

Required words are words or phrases that must appear in the stories for them to be chosen. You can enter as many words as you like, but AOL will choose only stories that contain all of them. If you made the word car a required word, you'd probably cut out most of the stories about actors – but if there was one that mentioned Harrison Ford's car, AOL would select it for you.

The final category lets you say what you don't want in a story. So, if you said Harrison Ford was something to be excluded, then any story about cars wouldn't be chosen, if it mentioned the actor.

Creating a News Profile
OK, so now you know how the Profiles work, let's see how to create your first one. From the News Profiles screen, click **Create a Profile**.

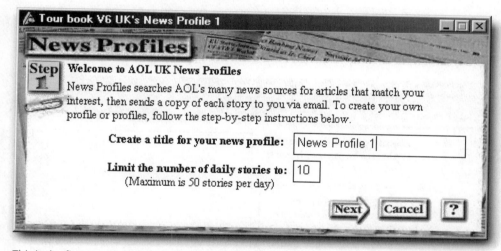

Fig. 5.55
News Profile step 1

This is the first step in creating your Profile. Fill in the top box to give it a name, like Cars. The box underneath lets you say how many stories you want AOL to send you. Normally it's set to 10, but you can change that and have up to 50 a day.

Although you can have 50 stories a day sent to you, remember that you'll have to read them all when you connect to AOL. Also, AOL only allows you to have 500 messages in your mailbox. The 551st to arrive will be sent back to the sender, with a note that your mailbox is full. If you don't sign on to AOL regularly, News Profiles could fill up your mailbox and stop you receiving other email.

When you've chosen the number of messages, click the **Next** button to go on to the next stage.

This is where you enter the key words for your Profile. For our example, you'd enter Ford, Nissan. Just type the words you'd expect to find in the stories that interest you, with a comma between each one.

If you want to look for a particular phrase, put single quotation marks round it, for example 'Ford Motor Company'.

The Wildcards button will explain how you can save typing by using wildcards. A wildcard is a special symbol that you can type instead of a letter. The * symbol means 'anything or nothing.' For example, if you type euro* then AOL would select stories containing information about the euro, or mentioning the words europe, european, europa and so on. The ? symbol means 'any letter,' so gr?y would find stories with the words grey or gray, but not greedy.

When you've typed your key words, press the **Next** button to go on to Step 3

Fig. 5.56
**News Profile
step 3**

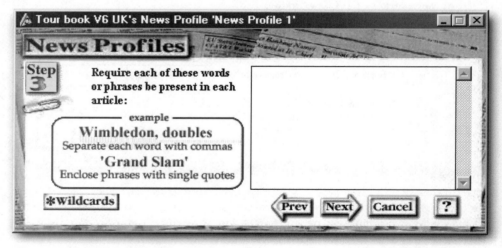

This is where you can enter the words that must be in news stories. For instance, in our example, we want the word car. We might also want to add euro* to find stories relating to how the car companies are reacting to events in Europe, or the single currency – but remember that only stories that match both would be found by AOL. When you've entered the words that must be in your news stories, click **Next**. You can use the **Prev** button to go back a step too, if you want to change anything.

Now you can enter words or phrases that you don't want to appear in news stories. To continue our example, enter 'Harrison Ford' with the quotation marks, to ensure that you don't receive any stories about the film star – even if he's driving his car in Europe. Click **Next** to choose where you want to receive news from.

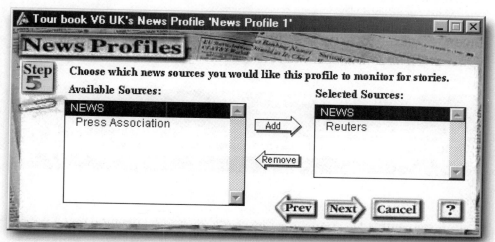

Fig. 5.57
News Profile step 5

Finally, you can decide what sources of news you want. As you can see from this picture, there are two lists on the screen. On the left are Available sources, and on the right you'll see one headed Selected sources. From time to time, AOL may add more sources of news for you to choose from.

To select news from a particular source, click it in the left-hand list, then click the button marked **Add** to move it to the Selected sources list. Similarly, if you decide that you don't want news from a particular source, find it in the right-hand list, click it, then click the **Remove** button, and it'll move over to the left.

When you've chosen your sources, click the **Next** button, and you'll see a screen summarising the information you gave AOL for your News Profile. You can use the button marked **Prev** to go backwards through the steps we've just outlined, or click **Done** to tell AOL to start searching for news.

Managing your News Profiles

Creating your News Profiles is simple, as we've seen. But what happens if you find that a particular Profile is producing the wrong sort of information for you? Maybe you don't want stories about your favourite football team any more, or you're simply going on holiday and don't want your mailbox filled up with celebrity trivia.

Whatever the reason, it's very easy to change your News Profile information. From the News Profiles screen, click the button labelled **Manage your Profiles**, and you'll see a list like this appear:

Fig. 5.58
Manage Profiles screen

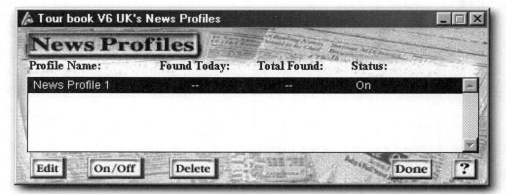

The list shows all the Profiles that you've set up for this Screen Name, with the number of news stories that have been found for you today, and the total. The next column is labelled Status, and will say either Off, or On.

If you're going away, or won't be able to check your email for a while, you don't have to delete a Profile to stop AOL sending you messages. Instead, you just need to click the name of the Profile, and then click the **On/Off** button at the bottom of the screen.

When you want to start receiving messages that match a Profile, just click it again, and use the **On/Off** button to switch it back on. You can delete a Profile completely by clicking to select it, and then clicking the **Delete** button. Remember that each of your Screen Names can only have five Profiles at a time.

To change the details of a Profile, click it, and then click the **Edit** button.

This screen is really a condensed version of the screens that you worked through to set up a Profile originally.

When you've finished making your changes, just click the **Done** button, and they'll be saved. If you decide that you don't want to keep the changes you've made, click **Cancel** and your News Profile will remain as it was.

More about wildcards in News Profiles
The Wildcards button when you're creating or editing a News Profile gives you more information about the wildcards that you can use. As well as the * and ? symbols, you can also use the ! to specify combinations of words that you don't want to see in your story. For our car example, you might say car ! car tyre ! car phone ! cable car which would tell AOL that you do want stories with the word car in them, but not if it contains car tyre, car phone or cable car.

If you want to use one of the wildcard symbols in a phrase, without AOL treating it specially, then you need to put it in double quotes. For example, if you wanted to know about any mentions of Hello! magazine, you would have to type Hello"!"

Similarly, to look for mentions of the Consumers Association magazine, Which?, you'd have to type Which"?"

Finally, if you wanted to look for something that included double quotes, use them twice, so to look for "so-called" you'd need to type ""so-called""

That's all there is to it. Now you know all there is to know about News Profiles, you're one step closer to turning AOL into the editor of your own personal newspaper.

> *When you're setting up your News Profiles, remember that AOL limits the amount of email you can store in your online mailbox. Using Automatic AOL to collect your messages for you can help stop your mailbox filling up with information from News Profiles. You can read more about Automatic AOL in Chapter 5 (5.6, Automatic AOL).*

Customisation
The things we've shown you so far are all about getting quickly to the information that you want, whether it's an area on AOL or a page on the Internet. There's much more to customising AOL than just that, however.

You can change the way that many different areas of AOL work. If you've been working through this book, you'll already have seen how you can alter some Preferences for things like chat rooms and how to set up Parental Controls (*5.1, Screen names and controls*).

In this section, we'll show you the rest of the ways you can control how AOL behaves. If your main concern is how to prevent your children from seeing things online that you'd rather they didn't then you should take a look at *Chapter 5 (5.1, Screen names and controls)*.

The key to making AOL work the way you want to is the **Customise** button, which you'll find near the middle of the AOL screen, at the top. The button has an icon on it labelled **My AOL**, which is also the first entry on the menu that you'll see if you click the arrow next to Customise, so let's start there.

Fig. 5.59
My AOL screen

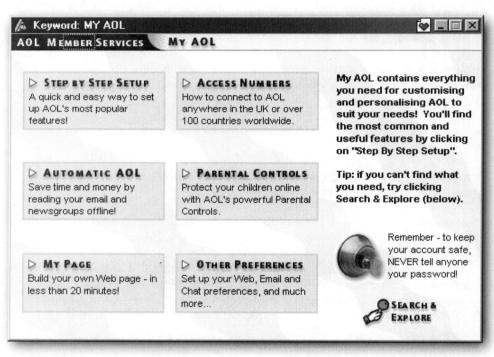

My AOL

*If you click the **My AOL** button and don't see this screen, don't worry! AOL is constantly working to make things better, and you may find that some of the features that we've described under My AOL have been moved to the **Setup** keyword, which is described a little later on, and there may be more features on the My AOL screen to customise AOL even further.*

Anyway, this screen is the best way to get started with making AOL work better for you. There are six buttons on the screen, five of which take you to common areas for customising AOL, while the last one, Other Preferences, lets you delve even deeper into how AOL works. We'll come back to that one later, but for now, let's concentrate on the other options.

If you're a new member, or you just want a little extra help, the **Step-by-Step Setup** button is the best place to start. It'll help you to configure the most common options quickly and easily.

The second button on the page is labelled **Access Numbers**. With this button, you can tell your AOL software to dial different numbers to access AOL, both within the UK and the rest of the world. Most of the time, you won't need to use this option, as long as you stay within the UK. You might, though, need to add a new phone number if you can't connect to AOL using one, or if you change to a different pricing plan.

If you click the **Access Numbers** button, you can look up numbers for the countries in which AOL operates, and read instructions on how to select a different number. You can find out more about using your computer to access AOL from different places in *Chapter 7, Advanced AOL (7.2, Locations and access numbers)*.

Automatic AOL is where you can set up your AOL software to connect to AOL, send any emails you've written, and collect all the ones that are waiting for you. Automatic AOL will even download files you want, and collect messages from message boards, all without you having to do anything. It's such a useful feature that we've given it a section all of its own (*5.5, Automatic AOL*).

Parental Controls offer you a way to restrict what your children and other users of your AOL account can do. You can prevent them exchanging email with strangers, block access to unsuitable Internet sites, and restrict them to certain areas of AOL. The Parental Controls are one of AOL's most powerful features, and a must for all parents. They're covered in detail earlier in this chapter, and we recommend that you make sure you know how to use them before letting your children use AOL unsupervised (*5.1, Parental controls*).

My Page takes you to an area of AOL where you can find out all about building Web pages, including information on the language used to construct the pages, discussion forums where you can ask questions, and competitions.

When you're a little more confident about creating Web pages, then you'll find plenty of information to help you in here, as well as in *Chapter 7, Advanced AOL*. For the time being, however, we recommend that you start building your Web pages using AOL's 1-2-3 Publish system. That's so simple that you can have a page created for the whole world to see in around only ten minutes (*5.3, 1-2-3 Publish*).

Now that you know what all the buttons are for, let's take a look at the first one, Step-by-step Setup, which is your first step towards making AOL work the way you want. You can also reach it directly using the keyword **Setup**.

Step-by-Step Setup

Fig. 5.60
Step by Step screen

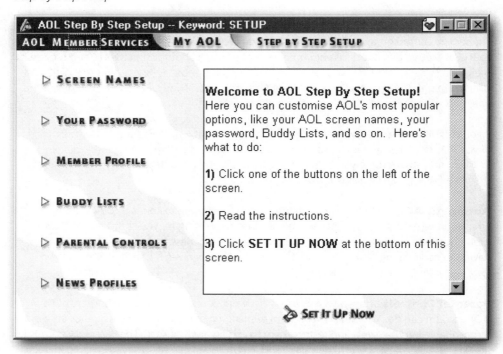

Setup

The step-by-step Setup screen lists six key areas of AOL that you might want to set up, and a short description. To find out what each option does, just click it, and the text at the right will change to give you more information about it.

To change an option after you've read about it, just click the button at the bottom labelled Set it up now.

Screen Names
Screen Names are extra names that you can use to sign on to AOL. You can have up to seven different names, and each one can have different settings. That means that you can have Screen Names for your children which are prevented from receiving email from strangers, or

seeing unsuitable Web sites. Screen Names are covered in more detail earlier in this chapter (*5.1, Screen names and controls*).

Your password

It's a good idea to change your password regularly to ensure that your AOL account remains secure. Selecting this option will take you to the Change password screen, so that you can change the password for the Screen Name that you're using at the moment.

Member Profile

A Profile is a short description of yourself, where you can tell other AOL members as much or as little as you like about you, your hobbies and your job. Choosing this option will bring up a screen where you can fill in your own Member Profile.

You can fill in all the information that you want. Don't worry about sticking to the categories listed. Some people even write a small essay using all the boxes! Click the **Update** button to save your Profile. You can find more information about Profiles earlier in this chapter (*5.4, Member Profile*).

Buddy Lists

A Buddy List lets you know when other people are online, displaying their Screen Names in a small window as soon as they connect to AOL. By clicking someone's name in the Buddy List, you can send them an Instant Message, or see what area of AOL they're using. You can also have a private chat with your buddies too. There's more about buddies in *Chapter 3 (3.2, Buddies)*.

Parental Controls

As we've already mentioned, Parental Controls are one of the most important tools that AOL offers, and it's really important that you learn about them if you have children who'll be using AOL.

Together with Screen Names, AOL's Parental Controls can help to make sure your kids are much safer online. You can find out all about Parental Controls earlier in this chapter.

News Profiles

News Profiles are a way of receiving the latest news via email. Instead of having to look through AOL's News Channel, you can have the information you want waiting in your mailbox for you. With a News Profile, you can tell AOL exactly what you're interested in, and only stories that fit your criteria will be selected. If you skipped that section, you'll find it earlier on in this chapter (*5.4, Customising AOL*).

Other Preferences
There are lots of areas on AOL that you can customise, besides the ones we've mentioned. The Other Preferences button will display a screen where you can fine-tune a lot of the ways that AOL works for you.

Preferences

This is the main AOL Preferences screen. You can reach it choosing **Preferences** from the **Customise** menu.

Preferences

Fig. 5.61
Preferences screen

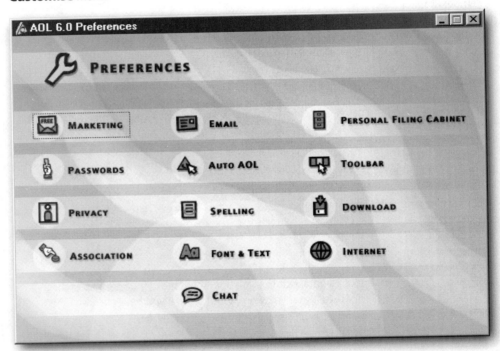

As you can see, there are lots of options on this screen that will let you control virtually every aspect of AOL. We'll work through each of the buttons in alphabetical order.

Association
When you have more than one type of Internet connection on your computer, it's sometimes not easy to know which one to use with which program. As well as providing you with its built-in access to the Internet, AOL can be used with other Internet programs, such as chat programs, or other Web browsers. If you have another Internet connection on your system but want to switch to using AOL for all your Net access, use this option.

Auto AOL
The Auto AOL button brings up a screen of Preferences for Automatic AOL. You can find more details about how to configure AOL in the next section of the book (*5.6, Automatic AOL*).

Chat
This section of the Preferences lets you control how chat rooms look when you enter them. You can also change these Preferences using the button on the chat room page itself.

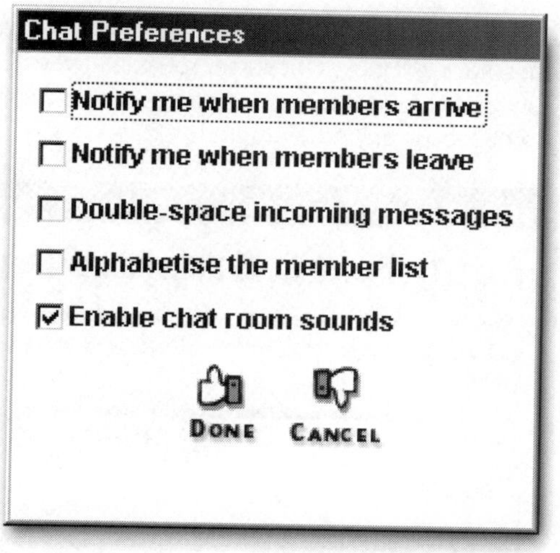

Fig. 5.62
Chat Preferences

To change any of the options, just click the box next to them. Click to put a check mark in the box to turn the option on, and again to clear the box and turn the option off.

Download
The download Preferences control how AOL deals with files that you decide to transfer to your computer, including files from AOL's libraries and files that have been attached to email messages that you receive.

You can find more information about downloading files and the download manager in the next section (*5.5, Personal Filing Cabinet*).

Download directory. The last option on the screen lets you choose where AOL will save files that you download. You can click the **Edit** button and choose a folder on your computer where you want to save files. When you've opened the folder, click the **Save** button to choose it.

Email
This screen lets you change how email messages look when you read them, and options for sending and writing email, such as spell checking and using the Address Book.

You can find out more about email Preferences in *Chapter 3, The AOL Experience (3.6, Advanced email)*.

Font and text
This control panel lets you choose how your emails, chat room comments and Instant Messages will look. Of course, you can always change the settings for each one, using the font and colour buttons, but on this screen you can set how things will appear when you don't choose anything different.

Fig. 5.63
Font and text settings

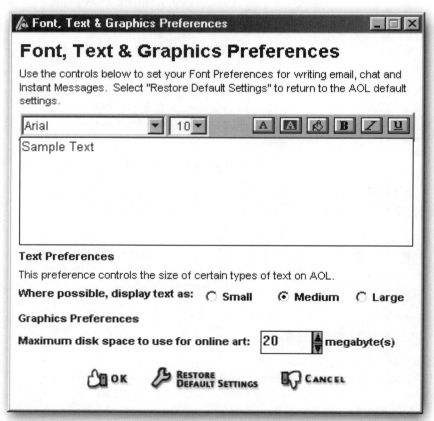

Internet
This option lets you set options related to accessing information on the Internet, rather than AOL.

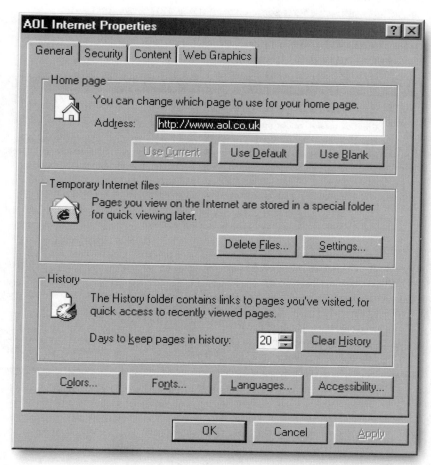

Fig. 5.64
Internet options screen

The other tabs fine-tune your Internet options, but AOL has set the best ones for you, so you won't normally need to change them.

Marketing

One of the great things about AOL is that because it's so large, it can very often do special deals with other companies to offer products or services to members. While many people find these offers useful, of course some might not want to receive them.

To make sure that you aren't bothered by offers and other marketing information that you don't want to see, use the Marketing Preferences.

Fig. 5.65
**Marketing
Preferences
screen**

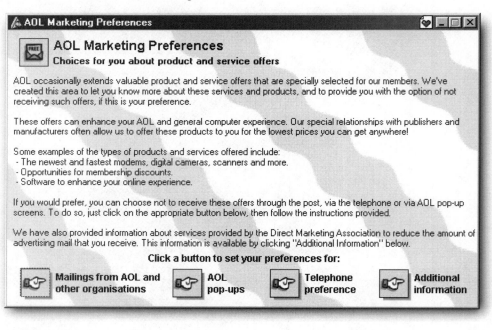

Passwords

The Passwords screen lets you save time by not having to type in a password to access AOL.

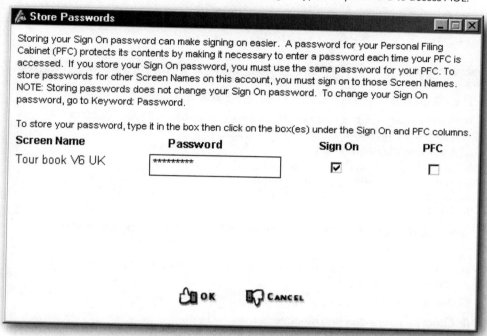

Fig. 5.66
Password preferences

Personal Filing Cabinet
Your Personal Filing Cabinet is where AOL saves messages you've read or sent, as well as message board comments and other information collected during Automatic AOL sessions. This screen lets you set some of the options for your own Personal Filing Cabinet. Remember that there's one for each of the Screen Names on your account.

Fig. 5.67
**PFC options
screen**

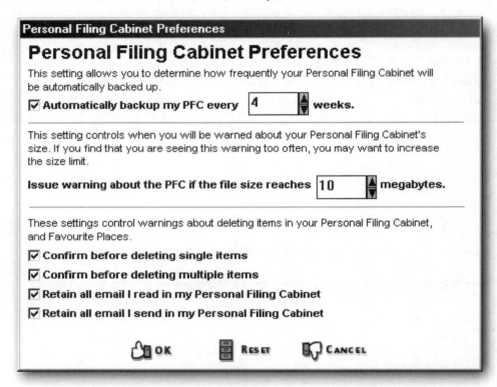

Spelling
One of the ways that AOL can help you to create the right impression when you're sending messages to other people is by checking your spelling for you. The Spelling Preferences allow you to control what sort of checks are made.

Toolbar

The Toolbar Preferences screen lets you adjust how the buttons at the top of the AOL screen work, and also change some sound settings.

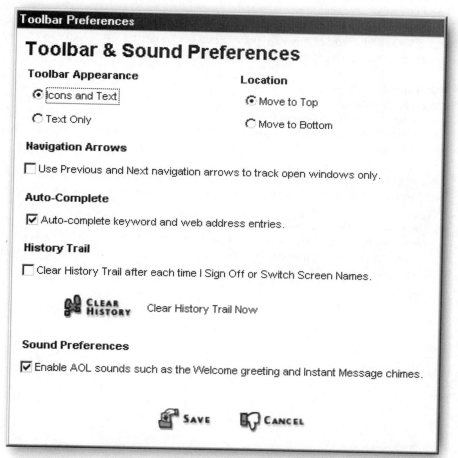

Fig. 5.68
Toolbar preferences

More customisations

The **Customise** menu is the place to find all the different ways you can change the behaviour of AOL. We've looked at My AOL and Preferences. The next four options are just shortcuts that will take you to some of the areas we've already looked at.

Parental Controls, My Profile, Screen Names and Passwords are covered in detail earlier in this chapter (*5.1, Screen names and controls; 5.2, People on AOL; 5.4, Customising AOL*).

The next option – the last real customisation one – is AOL Billing. The final two options on the **Customise** menu, **Personal Filing Cabinet** and **Sent to Personal Filing Cabinet**, are covered in the next section, which tells you all you need to know about organising your information (*5.5, Personal Filing Cabinet*).

So, now you know most of the ways in which you can control how AOL looks and behaves, let's go on to take a look at the AOL Billing option.

AOL Billing

Billing

The Billing area (which you can also reach via the keyword **Account**) is where you can keep track of how much money you're spending on AOL, view your current bill, or change to a different tariff. You can update your AOL account with a new postal address, or details of a new credit card that you want to use to pay.

Only people who have a Master Screen Name on your account, which always includes the name you first created, will be able to access your billing information.

Remember that you shouldn't tell AOL to store the password for your Master Screen Name. Although the Billing screens will ask for a password before you can change some information, you should never allow anyone you don't trust completely to sign on with one of your Master Screen Names.

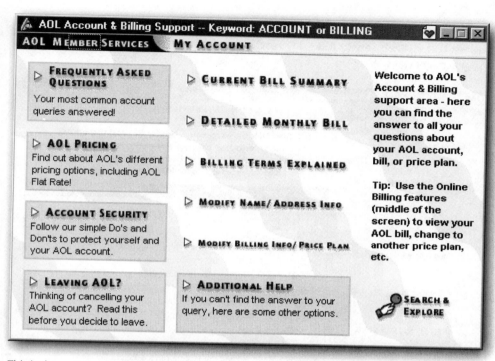

Fig. 5.69
Billing screen

This is the main screen for AOL's billing area. Down the left-hand side, you'll see a series of large buttons, which give you direct access to some of the most useful bits of information.

AOL's billing buttons

The first button, **Frequently Asked Questions**, is the way to find out most of the answers that you might want. When you click it, you'll see a screen a little like this one:

Fig. 5.70
FAQ screen

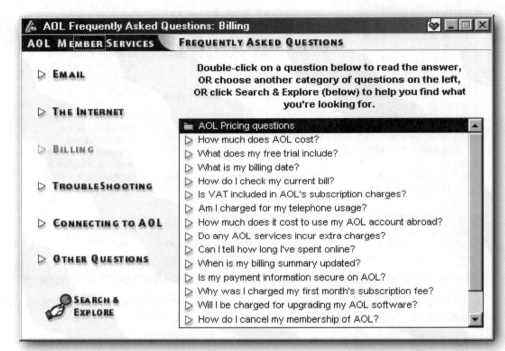

As you can see, it's not just restricted to questions about billing – though that's probably why you came here. Down the left you can see categories of questions, while the main part of the screen shows the questions themselves. Just browse through the list, and if you see the question you want answered, double-click it.

The next button on the Billing screen, **AOL Pricing**, lets you find out about the different billing options that are available. It will bring up a screen a little like this one, where you can click the options available to see how they compare.

Fig. 5.71
Pricing screen

You can also reach this screen via the keyword **Pricing**. When you've read through the options, you can click the on-screen buttons to change to the pricing plan that is most appropriate.

The screen that you see when you ask AOL for pricing information may look different, and may contain different pricing options that were introduced after this book was written. The information about pricing that's made available online is always the most current, and for that reason, no detailed pricing information has been included in the book.

The **Account Security** button gives you information and guidance on different aspects of security, including tips on how to protect your passwords and other information.

We strongly recommend that you read through the information on the Account security screen. And remember that AOL Staff will never ask you for your billing information or password online. No matter how convincing someone sounds, do not give details like passwords or credit card numbers to anyone who sends you an email or Instant Message asking for them.

Next, there's a button with information for anyone who's thinking of **Leaving AOL**. You'll find information here that might help you solve any problems that you have – but we hope you'll never need to use it. And to the right of that button, the **Additional Help** button will explain how you can find more help and assistance, if none of the other buttons have solved your problem or answered your question.

The main billing options
OK, now we've looked at the buttons on the Billing screen, let's take a closer look at the main billing features themselves.

Current bill summary
Click this to see when your next bill will be sent, and how much it will be so far. If your price plan includes a certain number of free minutes, you'll also see how many you have remaining this month.

Fig. 5.72
Bill summary screen

As you can see, you'll also see how much money you spent last month. Remember that the current account balance could change before your next billing date, especially if you access any premium areas on AOL or use up any remaining free minutes you might have.

Click the **Cancel** button to close the summary screen.

Detailed monthly bill
If you want to see more details about your bill, click this screen. You'll be asked if you want to look at the current bill, or the previous one.

You'll see a line for each time that one of the Screen Names on your account signed on to AOL. The time and date is listed, together with the number of minutes spent in free areas and paid ones, and the cost.

For a description of each column, click its label for more information. If you'd like to print out the information, click the **Print** button at the bottom of the screen.

Billing terms explained
Click this item and you'll see a small screen giving a summary of what's included in your AOL membership according to your current pricing plan.

Fig. 5.73
Billing terms explained

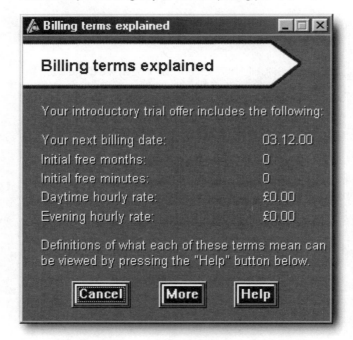

If you'd like more detailed information about what each of the items means, click the **Help** button. Click **Cancel** to close the screen and return to the main Billing page.

Modify name/address info

If you've moved house, or changed your phone number, this is the screen to use to tell AOL your new details.

Fig. 5.74
**Modify name/
address screen**

As you can see, the screen is blank, so you'll need to fill in all the details. That's a security precaution, so that even if someone does gain access to one of your AOL Master Screen Names, they can't find out where you live.

The information about where you live, and your billing details, such as credit card numbers, cannot be accessed via AOL. The only time you may be asked to confirm this information to a member of AOL Staff is on the telephone. You will never be asked to supply this information via email or an Instant Message. If you believe that AOL has an incorrect address for you, you should use this screen to update it.

When you have updated your information, click the **Save Changes** button to send it to AOL securely. If you don't want to make the changes, click **Cancel**.

Modify billing info/price plan
To change the credit card that your AOL charges are billed to, or the pricing plan that you are using, use this option.

The first thing that you'll see is a box asking you to confirm your password. This helps to make sure that even if someone has access to your computer, they won't be able to update your billing details. Type in your password and press the enter key.

Now, you need to select the type of debit or credit card that you want to use to pay your AOL bills. Choose the appropriate type of card by double-clicking it with the mouse.

This is the information for a Switch debit card. For credit cards, you may see a slightly different version of the screen. For example, other cards don't have an issue number, but have a Valid From date as well as an expiry date.

Fill in the details of the card you wish to use, then click the **Save changes** button. If you decide that you don't want to change the card details, click **Cancel**.

5.5 The Personal Filing Cabinet

Your Personal Filing Cabinet is one of AOL's most useful features. It's where you can save copies of messages that you've read or written, and keep track of files that you've downloaded to your computer.

You can also select files to download later, and organise all your messages according to who sent them, or what they're about. The Personal Filing Cabinet is where AOL stores messages that you've written when you're not connected to AOL, so that they can be sent in one go when you connect. And you can tell the AOL software to collect all your new messages at the same time, storing them in your Filing Cabinet to read at your leisure.

In short, using your Personal Filing Cabinet is the key to keeping on top of all your email and message board comments, and it can be used to help you cut down the amount of time that you spend connected to AOL. The system that does that is called Automatic AOL; it collects new messages and puts them in your Filing Cabinet, and sends any that you've written, all in one go. That way, you'll spend as little time connected as possible, cutting down on any charges you pay for accessing AOL (depending on your pricing plan) and freeing up your phone line for other things.

We'll explain how to set up and use Automatic AOL later. First, let's take a look at the Personal Filing Cabinet.

Accessing your Personal Filing Cabinet

You can reach your Personal Filing Cabinet from a number of places on AOL. For instance, you can open it by choosing **Personal Filing Cabinet** from the **File** menu, or click the arrow on the **Customise** button to display the menu, and choose it from there.

You can access it from keyword **PFC**. When you choose the **Read Offline mail** option on the **Email** menu, the screens that appear are folders within your Personal Filing Cabinet. For now, we'll concentrate on the whole of the PFC. Open it from either the **File** or the **Customise** menu, and this is what you'll see:

Fig. 5.75
PFC main screen (1)

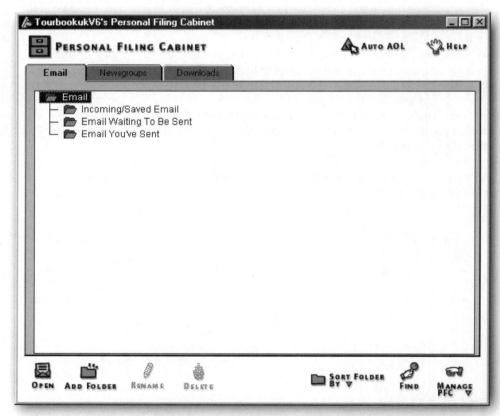

As you can see, your Personal Filing Cabinet has three tabs, labelled **Email**, **Newsgroups** and **Downloads**. These are the three types of information that you can use it to organise. The Newsgroups tab actually refers to both messages from AOL's Message boards and from Internet newsgroups.

You can read more about Internet newsgroups in *Chapter 6, The Internet*. For now, all you need to know is that they're similar to AOL message boards, but anyone in the world can access them. The messages from both will appear on your Newsgroups tab in the Personal Filing Cabinet, if you want to read them when you're not connected to AOL (*6.4, Newsgroups*).

The most important thing that most people will do with their Personal Filing Cabinet is use it to keep track of all their email messages, so let's start there. Even if you want to know about the other things your PFC can do, read this bit first, since a lot of what applies to email also applies to the other information you've saved.

Email in your Personal Filing Cabinet
When you select the Email tab on your Personal Filing Cabinet, the main part of the screen is the list of email messages that you have stored. Each message has an icon of an envelope. Messages that have a file attached to them will have a little floppy disk peering out from behind the envelope, and ones that have been read will have a tick on top of it.

You'll also see Folder icons, which are used to organise your messages. If a folder is double-clicked, its icon changes to an open folder, and you'll see a list of the messages that it contains. Double-click again, and the folder closes, hiding the list of messages.

The main email folder contains three important folders, which are used by AOL. The first one, **Incoming/Saved Email** is where all the messages sent to you will appear. If you chose to keep a copy of messages that you read, using the Personal Filing Cabinet Preferences, then this folder will have a copy of every email message you read while you were at your computer.

> *Messages that you read while you're accessing your AOL email on someone else's computer, using either the AOL software, or AOL mail, can't be saved to your Personal Filing Cabinet automatically. You need to read them on your own computer if you want them saved here (5.4, Personal Filing Cabinet Preferences).*

The folder labelled **Email Waiting To Be Sent** is where you'll see all the messages that you've written, if you clicked on the Send later button instead of Send now. You can read the messages in here, and change them or decide not to edit them, up until the time when you tell AOL to send them for you.

The last folder, **Email You've Sent**, is where AOL stores copies of email messages that you have already sent to people. You can look in here to remind yourself what time you said you'd meet someone, for example. You can use the Personal Filing Cabinet Preferences to tell AOL that you'd like a copy of all the messages you send kept here automatically.

As with messages that you read, AOL can't make a copy of a message in your Personal Filing Cabinet when you send it, unless you send it from your own computer, using the AOL software. If you're sending a message using someone else's computer, or via AOL mail on aol.co.uk, it's a good idea to add your own Screen Name to the list of people who will receive a copy of the message.

Along the bottom of the screen, you'll see seven buttons, which are there to help you manage your Filing Cabinet – don't worry if some of them are dimmed at the moment. The buttons will become active when you've selected a folder or a message that you can use them on.

The PFC buttons
The **Open** button works just like double-clicking any of the items in your Filing Cabinet. In other words, to view a message, you can either double-click it, or click once, and then click the **Open** button.

Add folder lets you add a new folder to your Personal Filing Cabinet. You might, for example, decide to add a folder to keep all the messages relating to work in one place, or another for your penfriend.

When you click the **Add Folder** button, you'll see this:

Fig. 5.76
Add folder to PFC

Just type the name that you want for the folder, and then press the Enter key. A new folder will be added to your PFC. If you clicked on a message before using the **Add Folder** button, the new folder will be in the same folder as that message. If you click a folder, it will be added inside that folder.

The **Rename** button lets you change the name of a folder that you created. You can't change the name of the three special AOL folders.

Next, the **Delete** button can be used to delete a message or a folder. You can also use the Delete key on your computer's keyboard too. Depending on the Preferences you set for your Personal Filing Cabinet, you may be asked whether you really want to delete anything.

You can't delete the special AOL folders. Remember that if you delete one of your own folders, all the messages that it contains will also be deleted. There is not an Undelete function in your Personal Filing Cabinet.

The **Sort Folder By** button works when you have selected a folder that you created. It displays a small menu that allows you to choose whether you want the messages in the folder sorted by Date, Subject, Type of message, or Email address.

The **Find** button lets you search your Filing Cabinet for messages, while the **Manage PFC** button allows you to make a backup copy of it. We'll return to both of them later.

Reading, deleting and moving the messages in your PFC
The first time you open your Personal Filing Cabinet, you'll probably see lots of email messages that you thought you'd deleted, or didn't remember sending. That's because, to start with, AOL automatically keeps copies of messages you send and receive.

You can turn that off using the Personal Filing Cabinet Preferences, described in *Chapter 5-4, Customising AOL.*

The best way to organise your email is to start by creating a new folder to put messages into. Just click the **Add Folder** button at the bottom of the screen, and type a name. You might choose Personal, for personal messages, or something to do with work instead. You can have as many folders as you like, and you can put one folder inside another. So, for example, you could have a folder called Personal, with folders inside for Aunt Sally, Homework, Football and so on.

When you're reading a message, if you click the **Save to PFC** button, you'll see that the menu is updated to include the list of all the folders that you've created, so you can save a message directly to the appropriate place.

Using folders

Of course, if you have a lot of email, it can be a little distracting and awkward trying to find everything in the long list of messages you'll see when you go to your Personal Filing Cabinet.

Fortunately, there's a way you can look at just one folder, a bit like choosing the **Email waiting to be sent** option on the **Email** menu, for example.

Just point with the mouse at any of the folders in your Filing Cabinet, and click the **Folder** icon, using the right mouse button. You'll see a small menu appear offering you the choices **Rename**, **Delete**, **New window**, **Save folder as** and **Open saved folder**.

The first two choices are just the same as the buttons at the bottom of the PFC screen. The next one, **New window**, will make the folder appear on screen looking like this:

Fig. 5.77
Folder in new window

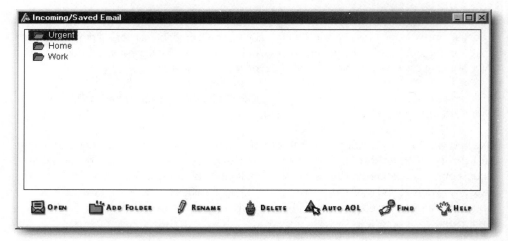

As you can see, now the only messages that are listed are those that are stored in the folder you've opened. The buttons along the bottom of the screen do the same as those in the main PFC screen, and you'll see that one's been added labelled Auto AOL. That takes you to screens where you can set up the Automatic AOL facility, which allows you to collect messages automatically. You can find out about Automatic AOL later in this chapter (*5.5, Automatic AOL*).

The **Save folder as** option lets you make a copy of a folder, and all its contents, in a file on your computer's disk. Why would you want to do that? Well, if you save the folder in that way, you could copy it to a floppy disk and take it into the office, to use on your computer there, for example. Or you could keep a copy of the messages on a disk somewhere safe, in case there's a problem with your computer.

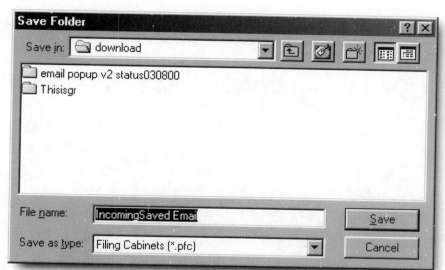

Fig. 5.78
Save folder as screen

Since all the messages in the folder are now saved as a single file, you can also send that file as an attachment to an email message, if you like. Whether you send it somewhere else via email, copy it to a floppy disk, or just leave it until you need it later, it's simple to load the messages back into your Personal Filing Cabinet.

All you have to do is right click a folder's icon, then choose **Open saved folder**. When this screen appears, find the folder you want to open, just as you'd find a file to open in your word processor or another program. AOL will read in the messages from your disk. Or, if you decide that your Personal Filing Cabinet is rather large, but you don't want to delete messages completely, you might save a folder of old messages and keep it somewhere else, so you can still access them if you need them later.

Searching the email messages in your Personal Filing Cabinet
You can search your Personal Filing Cabinet for email. You might, perhaps, want to find a message that contains the name of the company you're going to have an interview with, but you can't remember who sent it. Or you know that there's a message somewhere in your Filing Cabinet about a party next weekend.

To search for messages, click the **Find** button, which is at the bottom of the PFC screen. You should make sure that you select the Email tab first, so that you can see the results of your search.

Fig. 5.79
PFC search screen

This is the Find screen. In the box at the top, fill in what it is that you're searching for. You might, for example, type the word party.

Below, there's a check box labelled Match case. If you select this option, then you'll only see messages that are typed exactly as you say. For example, if you type Party, and say that you want to match case, you won't see messages with the word typed as PARTY or party or paRty.

When you've made your choices, click the **Find** button, and the first message that fits your criteria will be highlighted in the Personal Filing Cabinet. If there aren't any messages, you'll see a message telling you so.

To find another message, click the **Find** button again, and the next message that fits your criteria will be highlighted.

Newsgroups in your Personal Filing Cabinet
When you click the Newsgroups tab, you'll see a display similar to the one shown here. The Newsgroups tab is where you'll find messages that AOL has saved from message boards as well as Internet newsgroups.

Fig. 5.80
Newsgroups tab in PFC

You can use it to allow you to take part in discussions without having to remain connected to AOL. Automatic AOL will collect all the new messages in discussion areas you want to read offline, and post new messages that you have written for you.

Reading Message boards this way means you'll spend much less time connected to AOL than when you read them online. To tell AOL that you want to read a Message board via your Personal Filing Cabinet and Automatic AOL, you'll first need to add it to **My Boards**, and then set it for offline reading. You can find out all about My Boards in *Chapter 3, The AOL Experience* (*3.7, Message boards*).

As you can see, everything looks very similar to the **Email** tab, with folders for Incoming/ Saved postings, Postings you've sent and Postings waiting to be sent. These correspond exactly to the same folders for email. The icon for each message is a little globe, with a tick on top of it if the message has been read.

If you've used My Boards to tell AOL that there's a discussion area that you want to read offline, you'll quickly notice that there's one big difference between the Newsgroups tab and the Email tab.

With email, all the new messages are put in the Incoming folder. With discussions, new folders are automatically created, within the Incoming/Saved postings folder.

There's one folder for each discussion area, which will have the name of that area – either the AOL Message board name, or the Internet newsgroup name. Although you access each slightly differently when you're connected to AOL, when you read them offline, they look exactly the same.

If you've marked a discussion area to read offline, take a closer look at it's folder, and you'll see that each one has more folders within it, and an item marked Create new posting. To see all the parts of an individual folder more clearly, let's open one in a new window. Start by right clicking the folder name with your mouse, and select **New Window**. Now you'll see something like this:

Fig. 5.81
Discussion in new window

The first entry in any Newsgroup folder from your Personal Filing Cabinet is labelled Create new posting. You can click this to write a new message that will be sent to that discussion area when you tell AOL to send postings you've written.

So, to post a new message in a particular discussion area, you need to open your Personal Filing Cabinet, click the **Newsgroup** tab, and then find the folder for the message board or newsgroup that you want to send it to.

Then, double-click **Create New Posting**, which should be the first item in that folder. A screen like this one will appear:

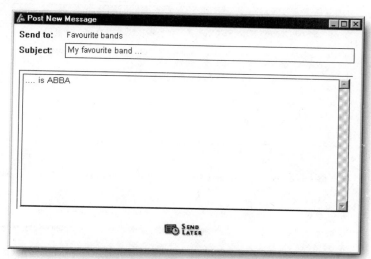

Fig. 5.82
Create new posting screen

Type a subject for your message in the box at the top, and then type the message itself in the main area below. When you've finished, click the **Send Later** button, and your message will be saved, ready for Automatic AOL to send it.

The rest of the folder for a discussion area will contain messages and more folders. A folder is created automatically when there's more than one message on a particular subject.

If, for instance, there are lots of messages with the subject 'Gawd bless the Queen', then instead of seeing all the messages in the folder, you'll see a folder with that name, containing all the messages with the same subject. That way, you can easily see, or delete, all the messages that are grouped together.

You can, of course, create your own folders too. That way you could save all the messages about a particular topic in a folder of their own, regardless of which discussion area they came from originally. When you're looking at messages on the newsgroups tab of your Personal Filing Cabinet, you can create folders and organise messages in exactly the same way as you do on the Email tab.

Reading discussions in your Personal Filing Cabinet
To read a message in one of the newsgroup folders in your Personal Filing Cabinet, all you have to do is double-click it.

Fig. 5.83
**Open
newsgroup
message**

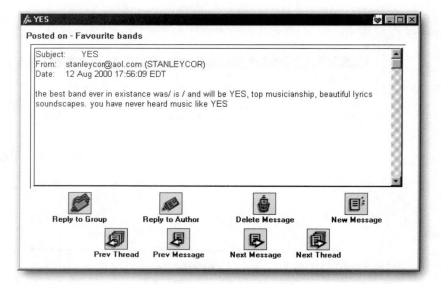

As you can see, when you read a message offline, it looks pretty similar to reading an email message. The big difference is that there are some extra buttons at the bottom of the screen, which are there to help you make your way through the threads of discussions.

Threads are just a way of describing the chain of messages in any discussion, following the comments from one person to another. Using the buttons for Previous message and Next message will move you through the current thread – usually messages with the same subject. Click **Next Thread** if you don't want to carry on reading the current one, and you'll start at the beginning of the next thread.

*Clicking the **Next Message** button when you're at the end of a thread will take you to the first one in the next thread – so you can just keep clicking **Next Message** if you want to read through all the messages.*

You'll also see buttons for **Next Group**, **Previous Group** and **Previous Thread**. Some of these buttons appear and disappear. For example, when you're reading a message in the first group in your Personal Filing Cabinet, then the Previous group button won't be there. Similarly, if there's no previous thread in the group you're reading, then that button won't appear.

Above the buttons to help you move through the messages, there are four others. The first, Reply to group, brings up the same screen you'll see if you ask to create a new posting, but with the subject already filled in for you.

Use this button if you want to share your response to a group with all the other people who read it. If, however, you just want to send your response to the person who wrote the message, in private, click **Reply to Author**.

The **Reply to Author** button creates a new email message for you, with the subject set to the same as the message you're reading, and the address of the author filled in for you. Just type your message to them, and click the **Send Later** button when you're done.

Delete Message does just that – and it will display the next message, ready for you to read. The final button, **New Message**, does exactly the same as clicking **Create New Posting** when you're looking at the list of messages in the group – fill in a subject, and write your message, then click the **Send Later** button.

That's the Newsgroups tab of your Personal Filing Cabinet. There's one more thing to remember about it, however.

When you're looking at Email waiting to be sent, if you're connected to AOL you can open the Waiting email folder, and choose to send all your messages, without learning how to use Automatic AOL.

You can't do that with newsgroup messages that you've written offline. The only way of sending them is via the Automatic AOL facility. So, if you want to learn how to configure that, skip the next section, where we're talking about the Downloads section of your Personal Filing Cabinet, and go straight on to Automatic AOL.

Of course, if you do that, you won't learn how to manage your file downloads, so why not sit back and learn about them first?

Downloads in your Personal Filing Cabinet
As you visit different parts of AOL, you'll find that there are plenty of files that you can download. There are file libraries, packed with utilities to make your computer work just the way you want them, or files that people have sent you with email messages, and plenty more.

When you want one of these files, you'll usually have two choices – a **Download Now** button and one labelled **Download Later**. When you click **Download Later**, files are added to the list in your Personal Filing Cabinet. You can see the list by clicking the Downloads tab.

Fig. 5.84
PFC downloads

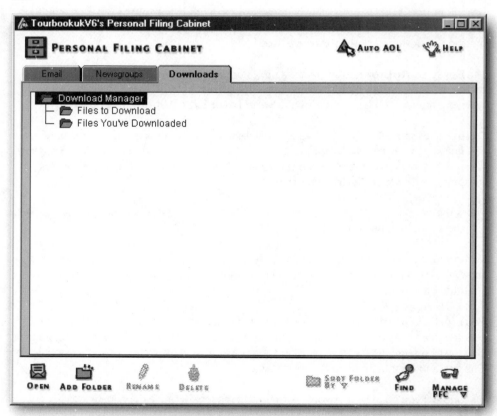

There are two folders on this tab – Files you've downloaded and Files to download. They correspond to the two screens of the Download Manager, which we looked at in *Chapter 3, The AOL Experience* (*3.5, The Download Manager*).

You'll see files appear in the list of downloaded files after they've been transferred to your computer, whether you chose to download them immediately, or later.

When you choose the **Download Later** button, files will be shown in the Files to download list. If you point at a file and click with the right-hand mouse button, you'll see a small menu appear, giving you the choice of deleting it, or downloading it.

When you choose **Delete**, the file will be removed from the list. Choose **Download**, and AOL will ask where you want to save it on your computer's disk.

Fig. 5.85
File save

If you just click the **Personal Filing Cabinet** button, AOL will save the file in the place you chose in the Personal Filing Cabinet Preferences (*5.4, Customising AOL*).

If you just double-click a file, AOL will try to take you to the place where you chose to download the file. You will need to be connected to AOL to access the place where you downloaded the file.

When a file has been downloaded, right clicking it with the mouse gives you three options – Decompress, Show status and Delete.

You can use the Decompress option when you have downloaded a ZIP file, which is a special type of file that contains one or more other files. Decompressing the ZIP file will extract all the files that it contains.

Show status pops up a small screen like this, telling you where the file was downloaded from, and where it's been stored on your computer.

Fig. 5.86
**Download
status screen**

If you click **Locate**, AOL will open the folder on your computer that contains the file.

The Delete option, just as you'd expect, tells AOL to remove the file from your computer.

Managing your Personal Filing Cabinet
Your Personal Filing Cabinet can soon start to fill up with information, especially if you use AOL features like News Profiles to send you the latest headlines via email, or if you take part in lots of online discussions using message boards and newsgroups.

In AOL's Preferences, there's a special section dedicated to your Personal Filing Cabinet, where you can set the maximum size that it will take up on your hard disk. You'll find a detailed description of the options you can set for your Filing Cabinet in *Chapter 5.4, Customising AOL (5.5, PFC Preferences)*.

One of the most important Preferences lets you say how often you want AOL to backup your Filing Cabinet. By keeping a backup copy, you may be able to retrieve information that you've accidentally deleted from your Personal Filing Cabinet.

Of course, if you set the Preferences for your PFC to backup, say, every four weeks, then if you delete information that you only received this week, you might find that it's not in the backup copy.

That's where the **Manage PFC** button, which you'll see at the bottom right of the Personal Filing Cabinet screens comes in.

Fig. 5.87
PFC main screen, menu showing

Backing up your Personal Filing Cabinet
If you click this button, you'll see a small menu appear, with three options – **Backup PFC**, **Restore PFC** and **Compact PFC**.

Fig. 5.88
Backup PFC screen

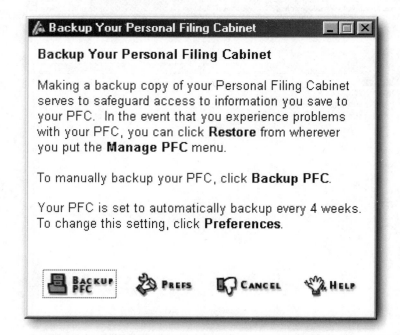

If you click the **Backup PFC** button, AOL will make a copy of the PFC on your hard disk right away. If you'd like to change how often a backup is made automatically, click the **Prefs** button to see the Preferences screen for your Filing Cabinet.

You might decide to use the **Backup PFC** option if, for example, you've just received some important news via email, and want to make sure there's a safe copy.

Restoring your Personal Filing Cabinet
The Restore PFC option replaces the entire contents of your Personal Filing Cabinet with the last backup.

Fig. 5.89
Restore PFC screen

Read the note on this screen very carefully before clicking the **Yes** button. If you are not sure you want to do it, click **No**.

Restoring your Personal Filing Cabinet from a backup replaces the entire contents, including email messages, newsgroup messages and the list of files you have downloaded.

*After restoring your PFC, you will not be able to access any items that were not in the last backup. For example, if your Personal Filing Cabinet was last backed up two weeks ago, when you choose the **Restore PFC** option, all the messages that you have received in the last two weeks will disappear from your PFC and you will not be able to access them.*

If you would like to keep newer messages, you could use the **Save Folder** as function in your PFC to save them, before using the **Restore PFC** option. After you have restored a backup copy of your Personal Filing Cabinet, you can then load messages that you have saved into other files.

Compacting your Personal Filing Cabinet

The final option for managing your PFC is **Compact PFC**. This option is used to help make sure that all the information in your Filing Cabinet is stored as efficiently as possible on your computer's disk. If your PFC isn't using space efficiently, then AOL will take longer to start, and more disk space may be used than is necessary.

When your PFC needs to be compacted, AOL will warn you automatically, by displaying a screen like this:

Fig. 5.90
PFC compact warning

You can also choose to compact the Personal Filing Cabinet at any time using the Manage PFC button, by selecting **Compact PFC**.

Click the **Compact Now** button if you would like AOL to reorganise your Filing Cabinet, or **Don't Compact** if you'd like to do it later. You'll see a message on the screen while your Filing Cabinet is being processed, with a progress bar so that you can see how much more needs to be done.

Privacy and your Personal Filing Cabinet

When AOL is installed, anyone who uses your computer can access your Personal Filing Cabinet. All they need to do is choose your Screen Name from the Sign-on screen, and then select **Personal Filing Cabinet**.

Obviously, you might have things in your Filing Cabinet that you don't want people to see – especially if you're using AOL at work, or planning a surprise for a partner or child.

Fortunately, you can add a password to protect your PFC very easily, so that even if someone does have access to your computer, they can't read email messages stored on its disk, or see the list for files that you've downloaded.

Adding a password to your PFC

Setting a password for your Personal Filing Cabinet is very simple. You'll need to sign on to AOL first, and then from the **Customise** menu choose **Preferences**, then click the button labelled **Passwords**.

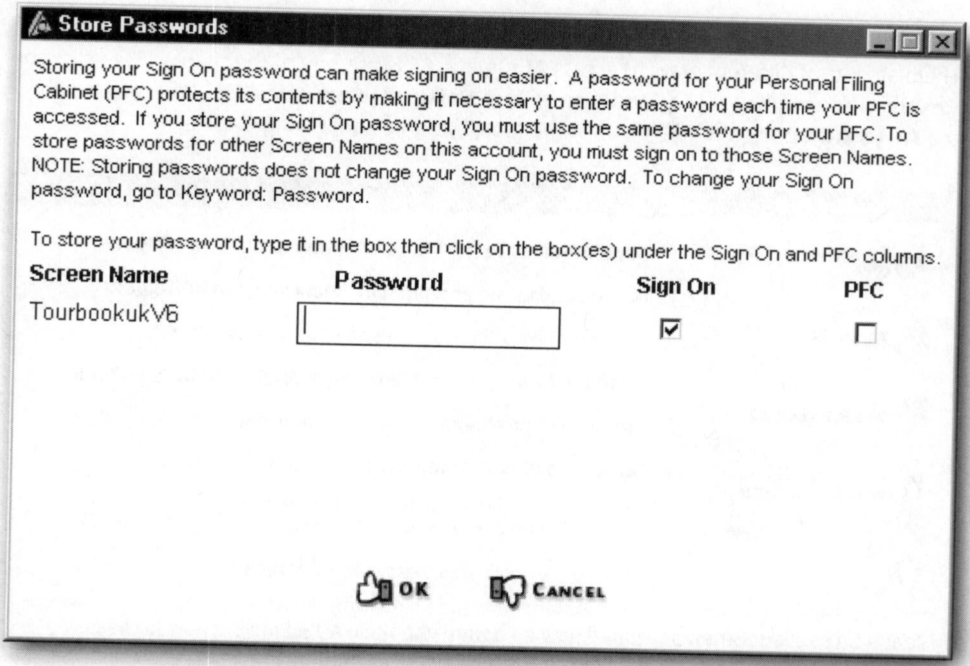

Fig. 5.91
Store Passwords screen

5.6 Automatic AOL

Automatic AOL is a feature of AOL that lets you sit back and relax (or go and make a cup of tea) while AOL fetches messages for you, sends messages you've written, and downloads files that you want.

You can even schedule Automatic AOL, which means that you can tell it to sign on at a preset time when you're away from the computer. You could come downstairs fresh from your shower every morning, and find all your new email already waiting for you on your PC, for example. Or maybe you'd like to write a birthday reminder that will be sent to someone on the day, even though you're away on holiday.

With Automatic AOL you can do all this – and since AOL won't be waiting around for you to click buttons or press keys, it'll do it all at top speed, which means less time spent connected, freeing up your phone line, and saving money if you're on a pricing plan where you're charged according to the number of minutes you spend connected to AOL.

Using Automatic AOL
There are lots of different ways to access Automatic AOL, but one of the simplest is to click the **Email** button on the tool bar, and then choose **Setup Automatic AOL**. You can also click the **Auto AOL** button that appears at the top of your Personal Filing Cabinet.

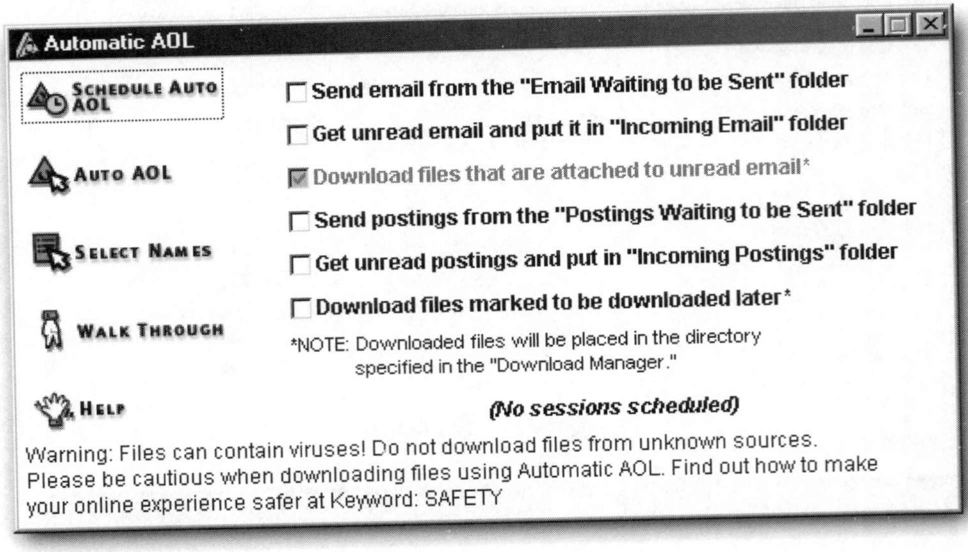

Fig. 5.92
Automatic AOL setup screen

From this screen you can choose what you'd like AOL to do for you when it runs automatically. You'll see six options, each with a box next to them that may contain a check mark, and four main buttons down the left-hand side of the screen.

Automatic AOL made easy
We'll come back to each of the options shortly, but the best way to get started with Automatic AOL is to click the button marked **Walkthrough**, and you'll be helped with all the settings.

Fig. 5.93
Walkthrough welcome

WELCOME TO AUTOMATIC AOL

Automatic AOL allows you to go online, immediately or at times you designate, to:

- read and respond to email offline;
- read and respond to newsgroup or message board postings offline;
- download files you have collected in your Download Manager.

Using Automatic AOL will save you time - because you can walk away from your computer while Automatic AOL does all the work.

This walk-through will help you set up Automatic AOL for the first time. If you are already familiar with Automatic AOL (or Flash Sessions), click "Expert Setup," and make just the changes you want to your Automatic AOL setup.

Click Continue to start setting up Automatic AOL.

EXPERT SETUP   CANCEL   CONTINUE

Running Automatic AOL
If you choose not to have Automatic AOL run according to a schedule, then it's still very easy to run it. All you need to do is select **Run Automatic AOL** from the **Email** menu.

Fig. 5.94
Automatic AOL screen

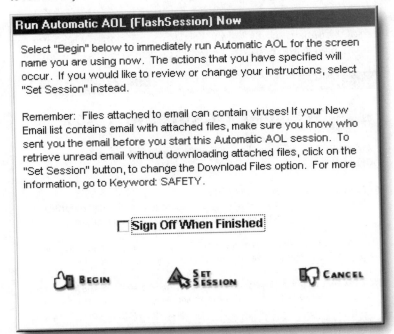

You can also run Automatic AOL from the Setup screen, by clicking the **Auto AOL** button. This is useful, for example, when you're checking the settings that you've made. If you've selected more than one Screen Name, Automatic AOL displays a message.

The Automatic AOL session will check all the Screen Names, just as if it was running according to the schedule. However, if there's only one Screen Name selected, you'll see something slightly different. There will be an extra check box on the screen that you can use to tell AOL to stay online.

Why would you want to do that? Well, if you use this option, AOL will collect all your messages for you, and send all the ones that you've written, much more quickly and efficiently than if you read the messages while you were connected to AOL yourself.

After it's finished all that, you'll still be connected, so you can visit AOL's Channels, talk to friends in chat rooms, or look up information in an online encyclopedia – in short, anything you would do if you'd signed on to AOL in the normal way.

Expert Setup of Automatic AOL
Don't let the word expert put you off here. Automatic AOL, as you'll have seen from the walkthrough, is pretty straightforward.

Expert Setup really isn't much more complicated than using the walkthrough – there are just fewer screens to look at.

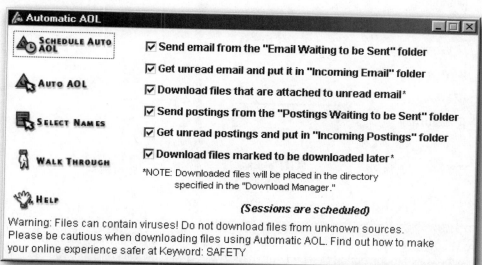

Fig. 5.95
Auto AOL setup

You've seen this screen before – it's where you can start the walkthrough to configure your Automatic AOL sessions. However, you don't need to use the walkthrough to set the options.

On this screen, there's a check box for each of Automatic AOL's functions – receiving email, sending email, downloading files, and so on. All you need to do to change the settings is click the check box to turn it on or off.

The top left-hand button, **Schedule Auto AOL**, lets you choose whether or not to have AOL run automatically at certain times.

Fig. 5.96
**Schedule Auto
AOL screen**

As you can see, this screen is really a combination of the two screens that you see if you use the walkthrough option to set up Automatic AOL. As with the walkthrough, you can set the days you want Automatic AOL to run, choose how often, and the first time to connect each day.

The check box at the top, labelled **Enable Scheduler**, lets you turn the schedule off and on. Just click to put a check mark in the box if you want AOL to run at the times you've specified, or clear it if you don't want automatic sessions.

Remember that your computer has to be turned on with the AOL software running so that schedules can happen at preset times.

We've already seen how you can use the Auto AOL button to start an Automatic AOL session whenever you want. The next button, Select names, will display the same screen you saw during the walkthrough. You can choose which of the Screen names on your account you want to run an Automatic AOL session for, and type in the passwords needed for them to connect.

Don't forget that if you set up Automatic AOL it only collects mail messages that are in your New mail list. If you read messages on another computer while you're away, or using AOL mail, then Automatic AOL won't download them, unless you click to keep them as new.

And that's all there is to it! As you can see, with the combination of Automatic AOL and your Personal Filing Cabinet, it's easy to keep on top of all your messages and file downloads – even when you're away from your computer.

5.7 Making a basic home page

One of the things that everyone says is greatest about the Internet is that it's democratic – anyone can publish information on it. You don't have to be a giant company or someone famous to be able to have your say. With a Web page of your own, you can tell people what you think about anything, whether it's the government, the joy of collecting thimbles, or the latest series of Star Trek.

But don't you need to be a technical wiz to make a Web page? Thankfully, the answer is no. With AOL, your subscription includes a space to publish your Web pages. What about creating pages? Don't worry! AOL also includes an option that will let you create your own home page without having to learn anything about what makes the Web work.

1-2-3 Publish

1 2 3 Publish

1-2-3 Publish is AOL's way of helping you to build a basic home page. You might have heard that Web pages are built using a special language called HTML, but with 1-2-3 Publish you don't need to worry about anything like that. Instead, you can just answer a series of simple questions, and AOL will do all the hard work for you.

Obviously, that means you can't create the sort of fancy site that would do a multi-national company proud, but you can tell the world about yourself with hardly any effort. It you want to learn more about creating home pages, and how you can use any Web page programs to update your pages on AOL, take a look at *Chapter 7, Advanced AOL (7.1, Advanced home page building)*.

For now, let's concentrate on 1-2-3 Publish. You'll find it by going to the **Internet** button in AOL, and clicking the arrow to view the menu. Just choose **1-2-3 Publish** and you're away.

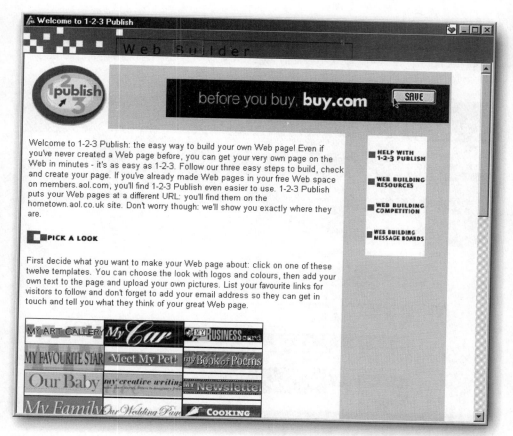

Fig. 5.97
**1-2-3 Publish
main screen**

This is the main screen for 1-2-3 Publish. It's worth reading right the way through, since it contains some handy hints and information for anyone who wants to make a home page – like remembering to check the spelling! After all, your page could, potentially, be read by thousands of people. Don't be careless and give them the wrong impression by mistake.

To start actually creating your page couldn't be simpler. Near the top of the 1-2-3 Publish page, you'll see 12 different icons on a grid, with names like Cooking, Meet my pet, My business and Our baby. These are some of the most popular things that people make home pages about, and with 1-2-3 Publish, all you have to do is choose the one that you want to use.

You can make more than one page using 1-2-3 Publish – just come back another time and pick one of the other options.

When you know what you want to make your page about, click the icon you've chosen to go to the next stage. Here, we're going to show you how to make a page using the My car template, but all the others work in exactly the same way – it's just the pictures and some of the words that are slightly different.

Fig. 5.98
My Car top of form

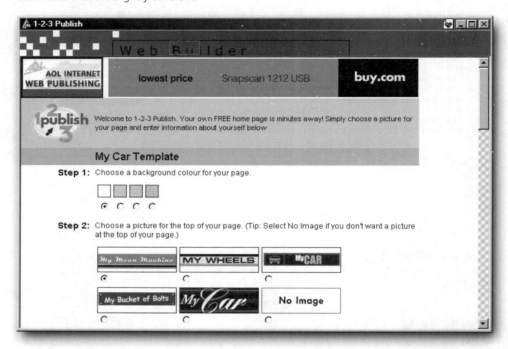

There's quite a lot on this page, but don't be put off – it's all very simple and straightforward. The first thing you need to do is choose the colour of the page – a bit like deciding what colour paper you want to print something on. Remember that if you add a picture to the page, this is the colour that will surround it, so be careful you don't end up clashing colours!

Just click a colour to select the one that you want. A small dot will appear in the circle below it.

The next step is to choose a banner – the picture that appears at the top of your page. This is a little like the headline in a newspaper, so click the ones you like most, or select the last option, **No Image**, if you don't like any of them.

Don't worry if you want to change your mind – with 1-2-3 Publish, you'll have a chance to see what the results look like, and you can also come back and change your page later.

Now, scroll down the page, to the next section, starting with Step 3, entering the title for the page.

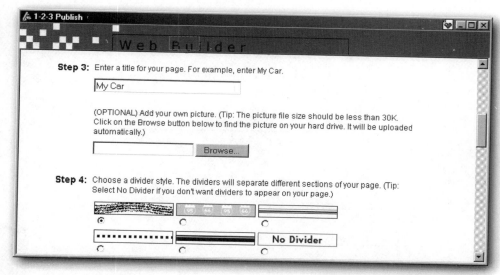

Fig. 5.99
**My Car starting
step 3**

The title for your page will appear in two places, first in the title bar of a Web browser, and secondly below the banner that you chose in Step 2. You might want to enter a more descriptive name here, like 'Ernie, my Reliant Robin'.

Next, you can add a picture of your own to the page. You don't have to, but using a picture of your own helps make your page a little more unique. Your picture can come from anywhere, for example you might have a snapshot of your car that you've scanned into your computer, or a picture taken with a digital camera. You can use any picture file you like. Just click the **Browse** button to choose it.

When you click **Browse**, you'll see the same box that appears when you want to open a file in other programs, like your word processor. Just browse through the files and folders on your computer until you find the picture that you want, and click the **Open** button.

The fourth step of creating your page is choosing a divider. You can have several different bits of information on your page, and you might want to split them up with a divider to make the page more lively, rather than just lots of words.

Just like with the picture for the top of the page, click to select one of the dividers, or No divider if you don't want one, then scroll down the page so that you can see more of Step 5.

Fig. 5.100
My Car starting step 5

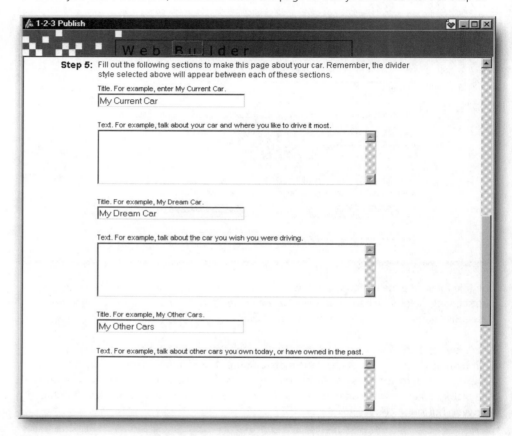

The first few steps have been setting up the general look of your page. This is where you really get to have your say. You'll see a series of six boxes, alternating between a small one for a title, and a large one for more details. That gives you a total of three sections on your page, with a title for each one.

To give you ideas, AOL will have filled in the titles for you, but you can change them if you like. Just click in one of the boxes and type, or delete information that's already there. For instance, if you're creating a page about your car, the first section will have a title My current car, and the next one will say My dream car. You might want to change these round, or make them something completely different – it's entirely up to you.

In the large box underneath each title, enter the words that you want to appear on your Web page. Unlike using email, you can't add special effects like bold or italic print. Just type the words you want people to see.

When you've filled in all your information, scroll down the page to Step 6, where you can link your Web site to other places on the Internet.

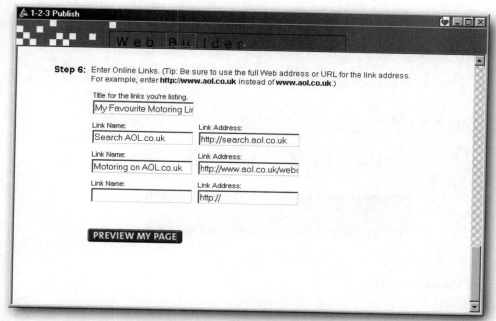

Fig. 5.101
My Car starting step 6

There are seven boxes in this part of the 1-2-3 Publish page. The first one is the title that will appear at the top of the list of links. You might change it, for example, to 'Some great car Web sites' or 'More places to read about babies'.

The next boxes let you add up to three links to other pages. In the left-hand column you can enter a description of the page you're making a link to. This is the text that people will have to click to visit the page. In the corresponding box on the right, type the Internet address of the page.

If the address that you want to link to doesn't already start with http://, you must remember to add it. For instance, to link to AOL's home page in the UK, don't type www.aol.co.uk. You must type http://www.aol.co.uk instead.

There will be a couple of links suggested already, but you can change or delete them if you like – and don't worry if you can't think of three places to link to. You can always leave the boxes empty for now, and change your page later.

Once you've filled in the links, you're ready to see what your page will look like. All you need to do now is click the button marked **Preview My Page**. If you're adding a picture of your own, you may have to wait a few moments while it's uploaded to the AOL computer. After a short pause, you'll see what your page looks like with the options you've chosen.

Fig. 5.102
Page preview

Take a look through the preview, and see what you think of your page. This is almost exactly how people will see it when they visit your new home page on the World Wide Web.

Previewing your page

Perhaps you're not satisfied with how things look, or you noticed a spelling mistake. Never mind – to make changes, click the **Modify** button. You'll be taken back to the form that you just filled in. You can go through all the words you typed and the choices of picture that you made, and change them.

If you added a picture of your own, you'll see that the form now reminds you which one you chose. You can click the **Browse** button in Step 3 to choose a different picture. To remove your own picture from the page, click to put a check in the box marked **If you do not wish to display your own picture on this page**.

Saving your page

If you're happy with how your page looks, congratulations! You're just one more click away from having your own home page on the World Wide Web.

From the preview screen, click **Save**, and in just a few seconds, you'll have joined the Net set.

Fig. 5.103
Address confirmation

You'll see a screen like this appear, telling you the Internet address of your new page. Make a note of the address – you could use it, for instance, in the links section of another page you make with 1-2-3 Publish, so that people can move between information about your car and your pet.

AOL will also send you an email message with a reminder of your page's address. If you like, you could forward the email to your friends, and they'll be able to go straight to your new page just by clicking the address in the message.

Changing your pages with 1-2-3 Publish

After a while, you might decide you want to change your page. Perhaps all the friends who visited it thought the background colour was horrible, or maybe you've taken a new photograph that you want to include.

Whatever the reason, changing a page that you built with 1-2-3 Publish is easy. All you need to do is visit the page when you're connected to AOL. You can type the address of the page into the Keyword bar at the top of the screen, or perhaps you've added it to your Favourites.

However you get to the page, you change it in the same way. Scroll down to the bottom, and beneath the links that you added, you'll see the message page created with 1-2-3 Publish. Just click that message, and you'll be taken to the same Preview screen you saw when you were making your page.

Fig. 5.104
Preview screen

Just like when you were creating the page, you can choose to modify it, or save it. To make your changes, click the **Modify** button, and you'll be taken back to the form where you filled in all the information beforehand.

Just click the items that you want to change – adding more words, perhaps, or changing the type of divider that's used between the sections. When you've made your changes, use the **Preview** button again, and then click **Save** if you're happy with what you've done. It couldn't be simpler.

What if you want to do something more complicated, that's not catered for by 1-2-3 Publish? Well, AOL doesn't stop you from doing anything that you want with your Web space, as long as it fits within the Conditions of Service. You can have up to 2Mb of Web pages and graphics for each of your Screen Names – that's a whopping 14Mb in total.

Since creating home pages is one of the most popular things that people do when they're connected to AOL, there are plenty of areas online that will help you to do it well. In fact, there's a whole Web Building area, with competitions, graphics that you can add, and message boards where you can ask for help.

If you want to know some more about Web pages, you'll find some more information in *Chapter 7, Advanced AOL*. People who are really serious should probably invest in a good book on the subject – it's really far too detailed for us to give more than an overview here (*7.1, Advanced Web page building*).

In the meantime, 1-2-3 Publish is a great way to get started. Think about what you want to say, and you really could have a page of your own ready in around five minutes!

5.8 Groups@AOL

Wouldn't it be great if you could organise your social club quickly and easily? You might want a calendar that everyone can check, so that it's easy to see at a glance when everyone's available to meet up. And a way of having private discussions would be great too, wouldn't it? What about a Web page so that people can share pictures with each other easily, too?

If you're trying to co-ordinate a group of people, whether it's friends who want to meet up from time to time, the local Neighbourhood Watch committee, or the team for a new project at work, we've got good news. That's what Groups@AOL is all about.

Groups

You can access groups by typing keyword: **Groups**. The first time you try it, this is what you'll see:

Fig. 5.105
Groups opening screen

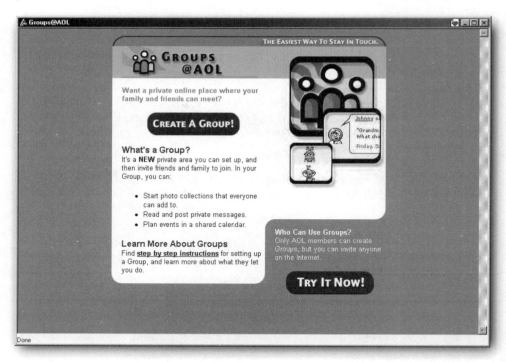

Creating a Group

Let's start by creating a group. Just click the **Create a Group** button and a page will appear where you can fill in some of the basic details of the group.

Fig. 5.106
Group setup screen 1

The first thing that you need to do to create a group is give it a name. The name can't have any spaces in it, and should be between four and 16 letters long. For example, you could call a group MyGang or 97.7FM but 2LO or Charlie's Angels wouldn't be allowed. If you use punctuation or other symbols, don't worry – AOL will let you know if you typed something that can't be used, and give you another chance to select a name.

After choosing the name of your Group – which will also be part of its Web address – you can type a short description, which will appear on the group's page. It should really describe what the group is for, so that anyone who looks at the Web page will know what it's about.

Next, you need to select the timezone that you're in, just like you did when you used My Calendar. For most people reading this book, the correct choice is probably GMT +00:00 Britain, Ireland, Portugal, W. Africa.

Finally, the last thing on this screen is confirming that you agree to the Groups@AOL Guidelines. To read the Guidelines, click the highlighted words. If you agree to them, click to put a check in the box next to **I agree**, and then click the button labelled **Submit Information**.

Now, you can choose a theme for your group. A theme is a rough outline, and just selects which order the different parts of your group pages will be listed in. You can also enter a title for the group pages. Type it in the first box on this screen – it will appear on every page in your group. You might type something like Robinson Family Group, for example.

There are three theme options – Family, Friends and Activity. Take a look at each one, and click to select the most appropriate, then use the Submit information button at the bottom of the screen.

On this screen, you can choose a style for your group. The style determines colour schemes and icons that will be used on your group's pages. You'll see several examples on the page – just click the one that you want to use, and then use the Submit Information button again.

You're almost done. Now it's time to create a Profile to let other members of your group know a little bit about you. You need to enter your first and last name, in the two boxes at the top of the screen, but the rest of the information isn't compulsory.

You can enter your birthday if you like, by clicking to select the day and then the month that you were born, and then choose an icon to represent you in the group. Just click the one that you like most to select it.

When you've finished filling in the form, with the necessary information, click **Submit Information** again.

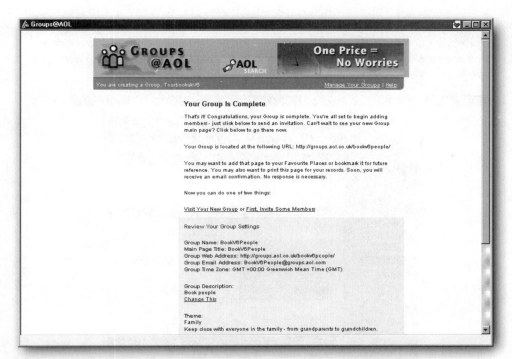

Fig. 5.107
Group setup complete screen

This is the screen that will appear to let you know that your Group has been created successfully. You should read through the information here carefully. You'll see that it has lots of important information, including the Web address of your group, which will enable other people to find it on the Internet.

There are three important links that you'll see on this page – Visit your new Group and Invite some members are listed just above the box with all your group details. Inside the box, after the description of the Group is a link that says Change this. You can click it to alter the description of your Group if you like.

AOL will send you an email with your Group details in it, and other useful information about groups. You should save the email and make sure you read it carefully – as the creator of a Group, you are responsible for the information on its pages.

Let's take a quick look at each of the links. We'll save the Invite members link till last. It's the most important one, and should be the next step you take.

Visit your new Group
Click this link and you'll see your Group page. If you entered your birthday on your Profile page, then it will be listed as one of the events – but most of the rest of the page won't have any useful information on it.

Fig. 5.108
New Group page

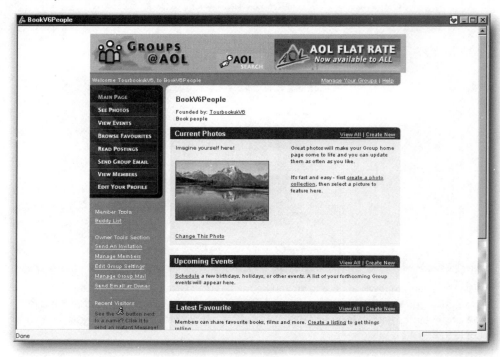

This is what people will see if they visit your Group.

Invite some members

A Group, like a club, isn't much use if you're the only member, is it? This link then is essential to getting your Group off the ground. Click it, and this screen will appear.

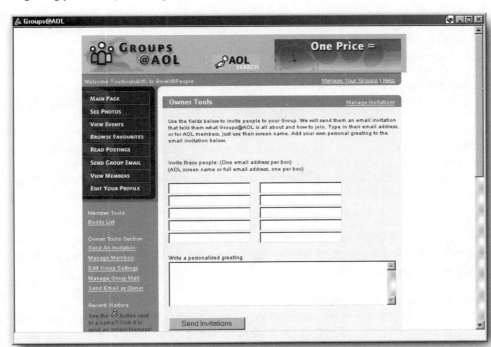

Fig. 5.109
Group invitation screen

The ten boxes in columns are for you to type the email addresses or Screen Names of people that you'd like to invite to join your Group. Remember that you can invite anyone on the Internet, as long as you have an email address for them. The people you invite will have 60 days to join the Group – after that, you'll have to invite them again.

Type one address in each box, and then use the large box at the bottom of the screen to type a personal message which will be sent to all the people you're inviting. AOL will also include some standard text in the message, explaining to everyone what Groups are. You can read the standard message by scrolling down the screen.

When you're happy with your message, click the **Send** button. After a pause, AOL will display your Group page for you.

Congratulations! You're ready to start using your new Group.

What about the people I've invited?

You might get a few questions from the people you've invited to join. How exactly do they join in?

Each one of them will receive an email message containing a link, which they should click to join your Group. If their email program doesn't allow them to click the link, then they'll need to copy it – exactly as it appears – into their Web browser's Open box.

They'll have to create a Screen Name – just like you did when you first signed on to AOL – before they can join your Group. That doesn't mean that they need to open an AOL account. Internet users can create a Screen Name free of charge.

In fact, they may already have one, if they're a user of other AOL services, like AOL Instant Messenger. If not, your friends will be able to create one when they follow the link that you send them. All the instructions they need are on the Web page – they just need to follow them and then sign in with their Screen Name and its password to join your group.

After signing in with their Screen Name and password, your friends will have to fill out a Member Profile form, just like the one that you created when you set up the Group. They need to give their first and last name, choose an icon and confirm that they agree to the guidelines for Groups@AOL, just as you did.

What can you do with your Group?

Now you have your Group, there are lots of things that you can do with it. Take a look at the Group page, and you'll see that there are sections for listing forthcoming events, which could be work deadlines, parties or anything you care to add to the Group's calendar.

There's also a postings area, which is where you can write messages that other people can read when they visit the page – and of course you can also chat with other members of your Group via Instant Messages or in a private chat room.

The Favourites area is where you can list favourite books or films – and you could use it for other things too, like suggestions for the best way to tackle a task at work, for instance. Favourites can be links to Web sites, too, so you could use this area to allow people to set up links to their home pages, or resources the Group might find useful.

How about a picture? They're worth a thousand words, or more. And you can add photographs to the Group pages, so that everyone can see them when they sign in.

Finally, there's Group email – you can send a message to all the members of the Group, perhaps reminding them of a meeting, or telling them about a new member. By using Group email, you can be sure that even if someone hasn't managed to look at the Group page, they'll still know what you're up to.

Accessing your Group

Let's take a look at how you can use your groups now. Just type keyword: **Groups**.

If you're a member of more than one Group, you'll see them all listed. To visit the page for a group, just click its name and the Group page will appear.

You can edit the list of Groups too, by clicking the text that says **Edit My Groups**.

Fig. 5.110
Edit My Groups

Here, you can click a link to remove yourself from any Groups that you don't want to belong to any more.

If you're a parent, and one of your children, with Parental Controls set to Teens or Kids Only, is also a member of a Group, they will be removed from the Group when you leave it.

If you've created a Group, you'll see that you're listed as the Founder. If you're shown as the Founder or Owner of a Group (and Owner is someone that the Group's Founder has given extra rights to), then you can also delete the Group completely.

You can't retrieve a Group when it's been deleted. All the information associated with the group will be deleted.

If you've clicked to look at this page, click the text that says **Return to My Groups**, and then click the name of your Group to visit its page.

You can go directly to your Group by putting its name on the end of the keyword that you tell AOL. For example, if your Group is called tg6-people, then you could tell AOL to go to the keyword **groups.aol.co.uk/tg6-people**.

Finding your way around your Group pages

When you join a Group, AOL remembers that you're its Founder, which gives you special rights, such as inviting new members, or deleting the group. The people you invite will be ordinary members to start with, but if you'd like some of them to help you keep things running smoothly, you can make them Owners, then they'll be able to do all the same things you can.

Fig. 5.111
Groups page

We'll explain a little more about Owners later, but we've mentioned it now because when you visit your Group's page for the first time, you'll notice there are a set of links at the left-hand side under the heading Owner tools. Those links only appear when you, or someone that you've made an Owner is looking at the page. Don't worry – other people who come to the page won't be able to use the links to invite members, or do anything else, unless you've decided that they can. Ordinary users will just see a blank space on the page.

Scroll through the page and from top to bottom you'll see the name of the Group, followed by the Founder, and a short description. Below that is a list of Forthcoming events, then Recent postings, Latest favourite and finally Current photos. Of course, the first time you visit the page, there won't be anything in these sections.

At the top left of the page, there's a series of buttons, which are what you use to move around the group pages. The top one, **Main Page**, will always take you back to the Group main page, which is a sort of summary of all the information that's in the Group.

We'll look at these buttons and the screens that they lead to first – you'll need to know how to use them whether you've created a group of your own or been invited to join someone else's. When we've looked at those, we'll explain the tools for Group owners later. Don't worry if the buttons aren't in the same order on your group page – the order depends on which theme you selected when the group was set up.

Main Page
We've already looked at the main page briefly. You'll see that the title bar for each section has two links on it, at the right-hand side. The first, **View All**, will take you to the same page as clicking the appropriate button at the top left. Next to it, you'll see a **Create New** button, which you can use to make a new entry in that section of the group. Let's look at each of those in turn.

Creating and viewing events

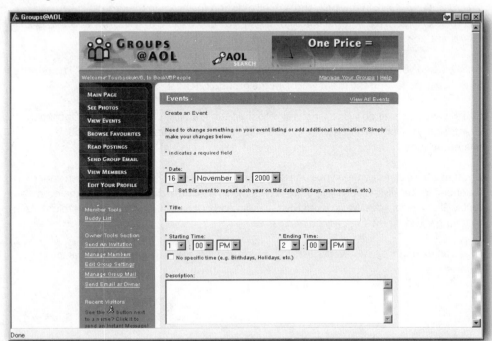

This is the form that you have to fill in to add a new event to the group's diary. You must fill in the date and time of the event, and give it a title, but a more detailed description is optional.

Choose the date by clicking the arrow at the right of the boxes for day, month and year. If you'd like the event to recur on the same date each year, click to put a check in the box underneath.

When you've given the event a title, choose the starting and ending time, once again by clicking the arrow at the right of each box to select the appropriate hour, minute and am or pm.

Some events, like an anniversary, don't need a particular time of course. For those, you can click to put a check in the box labelled **No specific time**.

Below the description box, you'll see another check box that says *Send this event to the group via email*. Put a check in this box, and as well as listing the event in the group's calendar, members will receive a note via email. That way, you can be sure they'll know about it, even if they don't sign in to the Group page for a while.

Finally, when you're sure you have all the details right, click **Create Event**. You'll be returned to the main page, and the event will be in the group's calendar.

If the event you entered was a long way into the future, it won't be listed in the Upcoming events section. Don't worry – it's still in the diary, and it will appear on the main page nearer the time.

If you use My Calendar, then you can make a copy of any event on a group page in your own Calendar very easily. All you have to do is click the small **Calendar** icon next to the event, and AOL will add it for you. We covered My Calendar earlier on in this section, so you might want to refer back to it now (*5.3, My Calendar*).

To see all the details of an event, just click it, and you'll see the full description that was entered.

Creating and editing postings

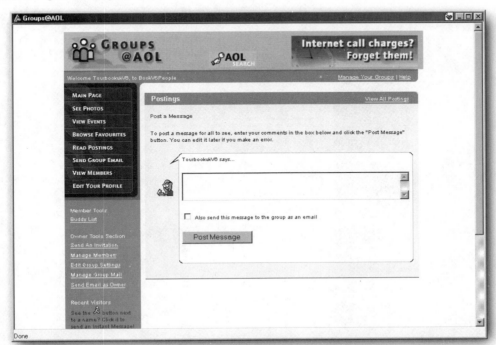

Fig. 5.113
**Create new
posting screen**

Postings are a little like a sticky note stuck on the Group page. You could use them to carry on a discussion, or just to remind people of something important each time they visit the group page.

When you click to create a new posting, you'll see a screen like the one we've shown here. All you need to do is type your message into the box, and click the **Post Message** button. If you'd like it to be sent to everyone by email, click to put a check in the box below the message area.

When the message appears on the main screen, you'll see that there are two links at the bottom right corner of it. If you click the **Edit** button, you'll be taken back to the same form you used to create the message, and you can change it if you like. Use the Delete link to remove your message from the page.

Creating and viewing favourites

Fig. 5.114
**Create new
favourite screen**

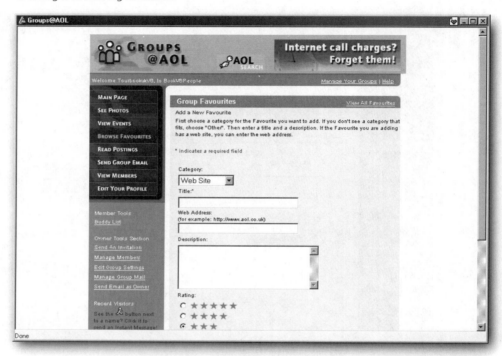

You can use the Favourites section of your group for anything – you might be recommending Web sites, or books to read, or whatever you like. Click the arrow at the right of the Category box, and you can choose from several pre-defined categories, like **Books**, **Web Sites**, **Recipes** and so on. There's an 'other' option too, in case none of them is right.

Next, you need to give a title, which is what will appear on the group page. In the box below the title, you can give a Web address.

The Web address you enter must begin with http:// so remember to add that if it's not there already. For example, to add the Web page for AOL Instant Messenger, you'd type http://www.aol.co.uk/aim and not just www.aol.co.uk/aim.

Enter a description of the entry you're making. It could be the synopsis of a book, or perhaps a reason why a particular Web site is worth visiting, or telling people that the recipe is suitable for vegans.

When you've typed the description, you need to rate how highly you think of this favourite by clicking the box next to one of the sets of stars. When you're done, click **Submit my Favourite** to add it to the list.

It's a good idea to think about the rating carefully. If the first things you add all merit five stars, what are you going to give anything better that you find later?

After adding a Favourite, you can click to **Edit** or **Delete** it, just like you did with postings.

Creating photos and albums

When you first create your Group page, you'll see that there's a photograph shown on the front page. That's one from a photo album that AOL has created for you. Before we look at how you add photos to the Group page, let's explain how they're organised.

Rather than just picking a photograph and uploading it to the Group, your photos are organised into albums. You might have an album for a holiday trip, or one showing pictures of the prototype that you're designing at work.

To view pictures, you first choose the album that you want to use, and then the picture within that album.

So, obviously, that means that the first stage in adding a picture to your group is creating an album. Click the **Create New Link** in the Photos section of the page, and you're on your way.

Fig. 5.115
**Create new
album**

This is the first stage in creating your album. Type the name for your collection of photographs, and then click **Save This Name**.

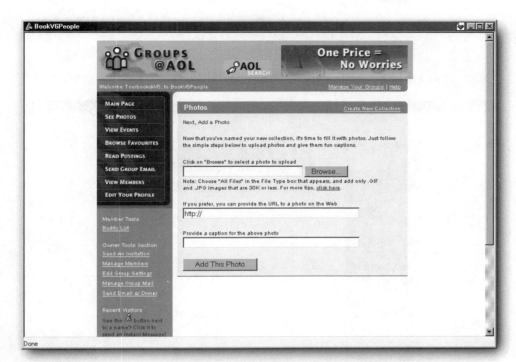

Fig. 5.116
Add first photo

Now, you need to start adding pictures to your album. There are two ways that you can add a picture. You can find a picture on your computer's hard drive by clicking the **Browse** button and choosing one or, if you have a picture on a Web site already, you can give the full address of it instead, which saves having to upload it again.

So, either click the **Browse** button, or fill in the complete URL of your picture.

You must give the complete address, which includes the name of the picture. For example, if you have a Web page at homepages.aol.co.uk/sampleuser with a picture on it called mypicture.jpg, then the full address of your picture would be something like http://homepages.aol.co.uk/sampleuser/mypicture.jpg.

When you've entered the URL of your picture, or found it on your hard disk, fill in a description in the bottom box, and then click **Add This Photo**. If you chose a photo on your computer's disk, there'll be a short pause while it's uploaded to AOL's computers.

When the first photograph has been added to your album, a screen will appear with a top section similar to the page you just filled in, and you can add more pictures if you like.

Below the form, you'll see a list of the photos you've already added to the album. You can click the name of a photo to see it, or use the **Delete** link to remove it from the album.

Click the **I've Finished** button if you don't want to add any more photos to your album.

Fig. 5.117
Complete collection

Now you have the chance of featuring one of your pictures on the main group page. If you'd like to, click the arrow at the right of the menu box, and choose the picture you'd like. Click the **Finish** button when you're done, and you'll be returned to the group's main page. You'll see your new photo collection listed at the bottom.

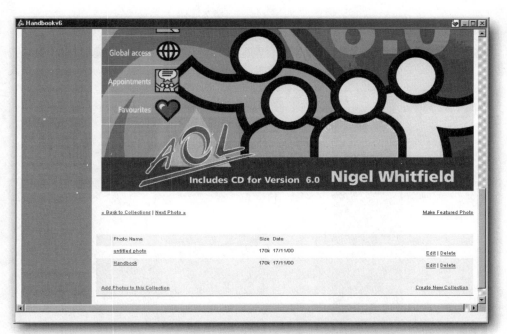

Fig. 5.118
Photo index

This is what you'll see if you click the name of one of the photo collections. You can use the links above and below each photo, on the right, to move through the collection, or go directly to one of them by clicking its description in the list at the bottom.

When you've found the photo you like best, just click the **Make Featured Photo** link at the right of the screen, and it'll appear on the main page.

So, now you know what all the links on the main page do, let's take a look at some of the other parts of your Group pages.

See photos

Fig. 5.119
**See photos
screen**

This is the screen that you'll see when you click the **See Photos** button. It lists the different albums that have been created, the number of pictures in each one, and who created it.

Keep an eye on the top line of the screen, next to the word Photos. In slightly smaller letters, you'll see a notice telling you how much of the space allocated to your Group is currently being used up.

To the right, you'll see a link that says Create new collection, which will take you through the same screens we explained earlier. To view the pictures in a collection, click its name. You can also edit the collection, if you created it, or delete it.

When you're viewing the photos, you'll see exactly the same screen as when you click the name of a collection from the main page, allowing you to move through the collection one at a time, and select a picture to be the featured photo.

View events

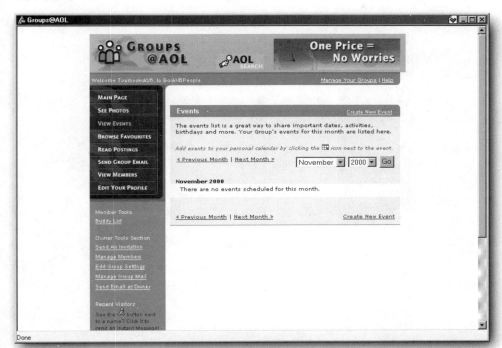

Fig. 5.120
**View events
screen**

When you visit this screen, you'll see the list of events for the current month. You can click the link at the right of the screen to create a new event, just like you did from the main page earlier.

The **Previous Month** and **Next Month** links, which appear above and below the list of events, will update the screen with all the items that have been entered into the Group diary for that month. Just like the main screen, if you use AOL's Calendar facility, you can click the Calendar icon next to an event to add it to your own calendar (*5.3, My Calendar*).

If you'd like to see the events for a month that's some time away, there's a quicker way of reaching them than clicking the Previous or Next month links. You'll see two menus, which will be set to the current month and year. Just click the arrow at the right of each one, and you can choose another month and year to view. When you've made your choice, click the **Go** button to see the events listed for that month.

Clicking on an event will display the details of it. The Edit link to the right of each event will let you change the details, using the same form you filled in originally to create it.

Browse Favourites

Fig. 5.121
**Browse
Favourites
screen**

Here's the list of all the Favourites that have been entered by members of the Group. You can see the descriptions that were given when each one was created, and the ratings. If a Web address was given when the Favourite was created, then its title will be highlighted, and you can click to visit the Web site.

Since the list of favourites could get pretty big, AOL automatically sorts it for you, depending on the categories that were chosen when each one was created. Just below the introduction, you'll see each of the categories used highlighted. Just click one of them, and the page will scroll down to the point where that category starts.

And, just like on the other pages, you can edit or delete any of the entries. If you'd like to create a new Favourite, click the link at the top right or top bottom of the page, and fill in the form – it's the same one we looked at earlier when we worked through the main page.

Read postings

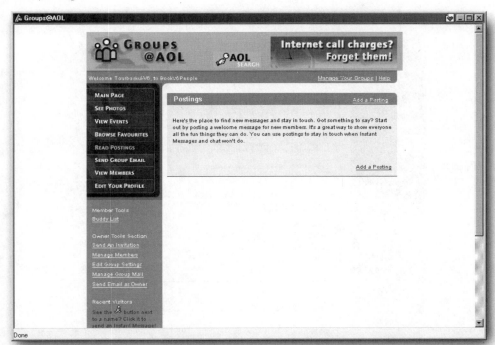

Fig. 5.122
**Read postings
screen**

When you click on this button, you'll see all the postings that have been made to the Group page. You can edit your own postings by clicking the **Edit** button inside each one. You'll see that the icon each member chose when they joined the group is next to the comment they made.

To create a new posting, just click the text that says **Add a Posting**, and fill in the form.

Send Group email

Fig. 5.123
Group Email screen

Sometimes, you might want to make sure that everyone in your Group knows about something. Maybe you've just got that promotion you wanted, or the film star that your Group is about will be visiting your town this evening. Whatever the reason, sending an email to the Group means that they'll get your news in their mailbox, whether or not they have the time to check the Group pages for the latest updates.

Groups@AOL provides two ways that you can send a Group email. You can either fill in the form on this screen, or you can click one of the highlighted addresses, and you'll see the usual Write email box appear, with the address filled in for you.

When you connect to your groups page via the Internet instead, clicking on one of the addresses may not create a blank email for you to fill in, or it may start a different email program, depending on how the computer you're using has been set up.

Why are there three addresses? That's so that you can email one of three Groups of people. You might want to share some important message with everyone in the group, in which case you'd use the All members address. Or perhaps you want to ask the Owners of the group if they can invite one of your friends to join. To do that, use the Group Owners email address.

Finally, maybe you have something sensitive to say – you've had an argument with one of the group Owners, for example – so you only want to tell the group's Founder. There's a link for that too.

If you decide to send your message by filling in the form on this page, you can choose whom you want to receive your message by clicking the arrow at the right of the first box.

Enter your subject in the next box, and then type your message in the large box, and click the **Send** button when you're done.

Remember that you can only send a text message using this form. If you'd like to email a file to the members of your Group, then you'll need to click the links, or type the appropriate address into the Send to box when you write an email using AOL.

View members

Fig. 5.124
**View members
screen**

This screen lists all the members of your Group. You can see the icon that they chose, their Screen Name, real name and their email address. Next to your own entry, you'll see a link that says Edit, which you can use to edit your own Profile.

Clicking on the email address for a member will create a blank email message for you, with their address already filled in. To find out more about a member, click on their name, and you'll see their user Profile appear.

On the Profile screen, you can read whatever information the member filled in about themselves, and once again, you can click on their email address to send them a message.

There are also two other useful links – **Add to your Buddy List** and **Remove from your Buddy List**. As you'd expect, you can click on either of these, and AOL will automatically update your Buddy List for you.

While we're looking at the View members page, you'll also notice the text NOTIFY AOL appears at the right hand side. When you click it, a form will appear that you can use to notify AOL of any inappropriate behaviour within the group.

Make sure you read the information on the Notify AOL form carefully. You should only report problems to AOL if they involve a breach of the Conditions of Service. Disputes between members in a Group should be resolved by the Founder or Owners, who are responsible for ensuring that the Group runs smoothly.

Edit your Profile
This is the last of the main pages for your Group. Click on it and you'll see a page similar to the one that you filled in when you created your group, or joined it after receiving an invitation.

You can update your first and last names, and your email address. You can't change the Screen Name that you use to access the Group. When you've made any changes that you want, click **Save my changes**, and you'll return to the main page.

If you'd like to choose a different icon to appear on your postings, click the link below your Screen Name.

Here you can choose another icon if you want, by clicking on the circle beneath the one that you'd like to use. When you've made your choice, click the **Save** button.

Finally, there's one other useful thing you'll see on the Edit your Profile page. Below the main form, there are two links – **Subscribe** and **Unsubscribe**. These control whether or not you receive the Groups@AOL Newsletter, which will keep you up to date with any changes to the way Groups work, or new features that are added.

If you click on one of these links, you'll see a new screen confirming your choice. Just click **Continue**, and you'll come back to the Edit Profile screen.

So, now you know what all the main buttons on the group page do, let's take a quick look at some of the other things you'll find on the group pages.

Member tools

Below the main buttons on your group pages, you'll see a section headed **Member Tools**. Underneath that, there's a link that says **Buddy List**.

Buddy Lists and Groups

Fig. 5.125
Buddy List screen

You can use the two buttons to automatically add all the members to your AOL Buddy List, as a complete group, or remove it. Using this option saves you having to add all the members to the group yourself, and makes sure that you'll always see when someone in your group has signed on to either AOL or AIM.

> *Although any Group member can create an entry in their Buddy List for the Group manually, the links on this screen will only work for AOL subscribers who are using the latest version of the AOL software. Group members who are using earlier versions of AOL, or using AOL Instant Messenger, won't be able to take advantage of these buttons to update their Buddy List automatically, or use other special features linking Buddy Lists and Groups@AOL.*

If you choose to add the Group to your Buddy List, this screen will appear.

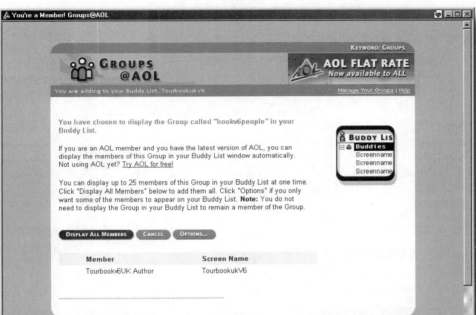

Fig. 5.126
Add Group to buddy screen

You can add all the members to your Buddy List, or just some of them. For example, you might just want to add the Owners of the Group, or new members, so that you can make them feel welcome.

You can only add up to 25 members of a Group to your Buddy List. If you want to add more members when there are already 25 on the list, then you'll need to remove some.

If you only want to add some of the Group members to your Buddy List, click the **Options** button, and this screen will be displayed.

Fig. 5.127
Add to Buddy List options

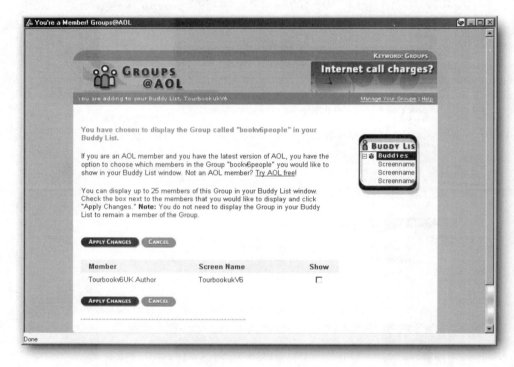

You can see the list of members, with their real names and Screen Names. At the right-hand side of each line, there's a check box that you can use to decide whether or not you want them to be in your list. Click to put a check in the box for people you want listed, or to remove it for those that you don't.

After making your changes, click **Apply Changes**.

Whether you add everyone, or just some of the members, a page will appear letting you know it's been done. Click **View Group page** to get back to the main page for your group.

> *If you can't see your Buddy List on screen, you can call it up using the keyword*
> **Buddy View**. *Chapter 5, AOL and You, explains more about using your Buddy List*
> *(5.2, Buddy Lists).*

When you've added your new group to your Buddy List, you'll be able to take advantage of a few other useful tricks, too.

You can right click the name of your group in the Buddy List, and choose **Go to Group page**. AOL will automatically go straight to the page for that Group. If you're a member of lots of Groups, it's a great way to go straight to the one that you want, without having to choose it from the groups.aol.co.uk front page.

When you right click, you'll also see a chat option, just like when you click on ordinary entries in the Buddy List. When you choose this, you'll be taken to a private chat room on AOL, and the AOL members who are in your Group and signed on will be invited to join you.

> *Selecting Chat from the Buddy List only allows you to chat with Group members who*
> *are AOL members, not members who are elsewhere on the Internet. To chat with*
> *them, you need to use the chat link that's on the Group page.*

Recent visitors

Below the **Member Tools** section on your group pages, there's another section labelled **Recent Visitors**.

If you're the Founder of a Group, or an Owner, you'll see a section between Member tools and Recent visitors, labelled Owner tools. We'll explain those later.

This is where AOL lets you know which of the members of the group have visited the page recently. If one of the Group members is still signed on to AOL or to AOL Instant Messenger, you'll see the Instant Messenger icon next to their name – it looks like a little yellow man taking a walk.

Just click on the icon to send a message to them. If you've connected to your Group page via the Internet and you'd like to know more about using AIM to send Instant Messages, you can find out all about it in *Chapter 8, AOL Anywhere* (*8.2, AOL Instant Messenger*).

Underneath the list of people who've recently visited your page, you'll see the text View all group members. Clicking it is exactly the same as using the View members button further up the page.

Finally, the last item you'll see says Join Group chat, and the name of your group is highlighted underneath.

If you click on the name, you'll be taken to a chat room exclusively for members of your group, so you can plan your outings together, or discuss the current progress of a project at work, or whatever you like.

There are some restrictions on the Group chat facility – you can't join in a group chat if the Parental Controls for the AOL Screen Name that you're using are set to Kids only or Teens.

To use Group chat, you must have AOL Instant Messenger installed on your computer, even if you are an AOL member. By using AIM for the chat rather than AOL itself, all the members of your Group can join in, whether they use AOL for their Internet access or not.

Group chat works just like any other chat room that you create with AOL Instant Messenger – or in other words, it's pretty similar to the private chats that you can have with your Buddies on AOL.

If you'd like to know more about the Chat facilities in AOL Instant Messenger, you can find all the details in *Chapter 8, AOL Anywhere (8.2, Private chat rooms with AIM)*.

Now you know about all the main features of AOL's Groups pages, there's only one thing left to learn about – the Owner tools.

Owner tools

Owner tools are what you use to manage your Group pages – you can invite new members, remove members and change other options affecting your Group.

As the Founder of a Group, you have specific obligations, including responsibility for all the messages that are posted on the Group pages. Anyone you make an Owner also has that responsibility. So, you must make sure you understand the agreement you accepted when you created your Group, and learn how to use the Owner tools, so that you can do anything necessary to keep within the Guidelines.

There are five tools for Owners: **Send an invitation**; **Manage members**; **Edit Group settings**; **Manage Group mail** and **Send email as Owner**. We'll look at each of them in turn.

Send an invitation
If you'd like to invite someone else to join your group once you've set it up, this is the option to use.

Fig. 5.128
Invitation screen

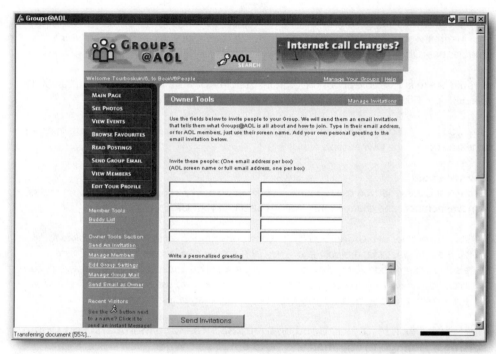

As you can see, the form here looks just like the one that you filled in when you first invited people to join you – in fact, it's the same one.

Manage members

As well as inviting new people to join your Group, there are other things you might want to do. Perhaps one of the people in a group for your local village council has moved away, so you want to remove them, or maybe someone has been upsetting all the other members, so you think it's best if they left.

And, perhaps you don't want to do all the work yourself – you'd like someone else to take a hand with adding new members, or checking on the postings to the message area. The Manage members screen lets you solve all these problems.

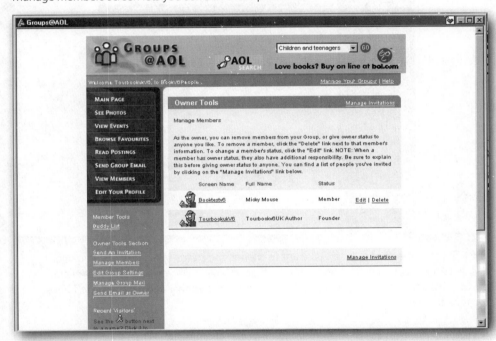

Fig. 5.129
Manage members screen

This is the main Manage members screen. It lists all the members of your group, and tells you whether they're an ordinary member, an Owner or the Founder.

If you click the Screen Name for any of the members, you'll see their Profile. At the right of each line are two links, **Edit** and **Delete**. To remove a member from your group, click the **Delete** button.

Fig. 5.130
Delete member screen

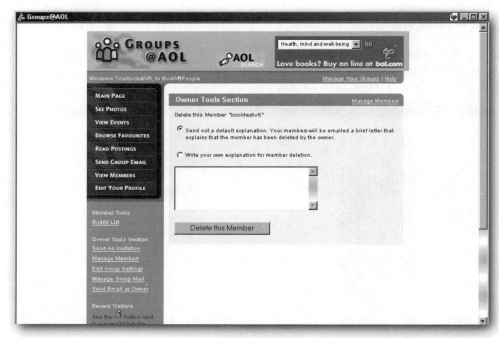

The Edit link is the one to use if you want to change the status of a member – you might decide to make someone else an Owner, so that they can help you with the administration of your Group, for example, or make them an ordinary member again if they don't have the time to help you.

Normally, people have 60 days to respond to an invitation to join. When you view this screen, you can see who has been sent an invitation, and if you decide that you don't want them to be a member after all – perhaps they've changed job, or moved, or are no longer eligible in some way – you can click the **Delete** button.

Edit Group settings

Using this section of the Owner tools, you can change the description of your group, or delete it completely.

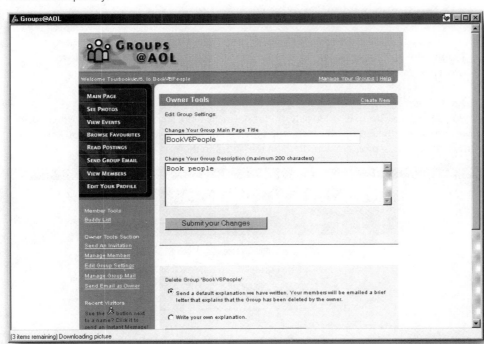

Fig. 5.131
Group settings screen

The first box on this page lets you change the title of your Group. Remember that this isn't the same as the name – it's just the phrase that appears right at the top of each page within the Group.

The next box allows you to alter the description, which appears at the top of the main page. The current title and description will be filled in for you already, and you can just click in either box to change them.

When you've made your changes, click the **Submit your changes** button.

The bottom section of the screen allows you to delete your group. You might, for example, have created a Group for a specific project that's now finished, like planning a silver wedding party.

You can tell AOL to send a standard message to everyone in the Group, or you can type an explanation of your own. Choose which option you'd like to use by clicking one of the circles next to it. If you're writing your own message, click the large box and type it, then click the **Delete this Group** button when you've finished.

*When you click the **Delete** button, your group will be removed right away. You won't see a screen asking you to confirm your choice, and it won't be possible to recover your group.*

Manage Group Email
When you use the Group Email facility, things normally work smoothly. However, you might have someone in the Group who's changed their email address without letting you know, or perhaps there was a problem with sending messages to them.

Fig. 5.132
**Group email
screen**

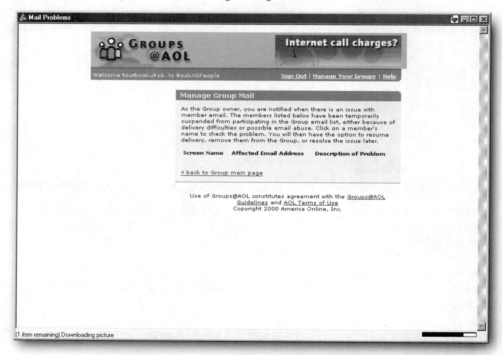

As the Owner of a Group, AOL will let you know when there's a problem with sending messages to someone using the group Email facility. When you choose this option, you'll see a list of all the email addresses that are having problems, and a summary of what the problem is.

AOL will have automatically stopped sending messages to each of the people in the list. Click one of the names to see more details about the problem affecting them.

From this screen, you have a number of options. You can remove someone from the group, using the Delete button, or choose to resume sending email to them.

Before you tell AOL to resume sending messages to a Group member, it's a good idea to send a private message yourself, so that you can be certain the email address you have for the member is correct. If the address listed in their Profile is wrong, you may need to ask them to visit the Group pages and change the address, before you can resume sending messages to them.

If you're not sure what the problem is, don't worry. You can always come back to this screen later, and make changes then.

Send email as Owner
Normally when you send an email message to the group, it will have your normal email address on it. Sometimes, though, you might want to remind people that you're in charge.

Using this option lets you send an email message to the whole Group, marked as coming from the Owner. That way, people will be able to tell easily whether you're writing in your personal capacity as a member, or expressing a view with some authority.

You might, for example, choose to send messages with your own email address on them most of the time, and only use this option if you want to remind people that they have to abide by the Groups@AOL Guidelines, or raise other important issues.

Fig. 5.133
**Send as Owner
screen**

The screen here is similar to the one you see when you click the **Send Group Email** button. Just fill in the subject and type your message in the box provided, and then click the **Send** button.

That's all there is to know about Groups@AOL. As you can see, they're pretty straightforward, and a great way to keep in touch with your friends, family or colleagues, no matter where they are.

To really make the most of Groups, you should download a copy of AOL's Instant Messenger program, AIM. You can find out how to download it, and instructions for using it, in *Chapter 8, AOL Anywhere (8.2, AIM)*.

Now, though, let's carry on by looking at how AOL lets you access the information on the Internet.

The Internet

As you'll have seen from the preceding chapters of this book, AOL's editors have put a lot of work into finding the best information for you and making it easy to reach. You could probably find just about everything you need somewhere on AOL's Channels.

But AOL also gives you access to everything that's available on the Internet too – the World Wide Web, massive libraries of files that you can download, chat systems that span the world, and discussions in newsgroups. And if there's anything that's not covered by that, don't worry!

AOL provides you with a connection to the Internet, which means that you can download and run any of the thousands of Internet programs written for your computer, without any problems at all.

So, if you want to find out about the Internet, how AOL makes it accessible, and how to track down the information that you want, this chapter will tell you how.

6.1 The World Wide Web

The Web – or the World Wide Web to give it it's proper name – is one of the most remarkable things to have been invented, and even people who have never used it will probably be familiar with the addresses like www.aol.com that appear in newspaper adverts, on the TV, down the side of buses and even on pairs of glasses.

Accessing the Web on AOL is easy. All you have to do is type a Web address into the box at the top of your screen, where it says *Enter keywords or Web addresses here*. Press the **Enter** key, and a window will appear on your computer screen showing the Web page. You can also access a Web page by pressing Ctrl-K and typing the address into the box that appears.

Fig. 6.1
Web home page

If you've not looked at the Internet yet, a good place to start is AOL's home page on the Internet, which is at www.aol.co.uk. You don't even need to type that address in – just click the **Web** icon on the **Internet** button at the top of the screen, and it should appear automatically. You can also use the keywords Web or **aol co uk** to reach the page.

If you've changed your Internet Preferences to point to a different start page, then you'll see that page instead. You can access www.aol.co.uk by typing the address into the box at the top of the screen.

As we've explained already, moving round Web pages is very simple, and pretty much like moving around AOL. Click on a link – the mouse pointer will change when you move it over one – and AOL will fetch the new page for you.

Before you get stuck into the Web, remember that it's largely unregulated, and might contain material that you think is inappropriate. If you're concerned about what you or your family might see on Web pages, you should use AOL's Parental Controls to restrict access. You can set different levels of access for different members of your family, and even block access to the Web altogether (5.1, Parental controls).

Navigating the Web

Just to the left of the Keyword box on the toolbar, you'll see a few buttons which are useful to help you move around the Web.

Fig. 6.2
Close-up picture of buttons

The rightmost button is for printing the information you're looking at. To the left of that, the red button means **Stop**. Sometimes, especially if a Web page has lots of information on it, or if it's coming from a computer that's not very fast, Web pages take a long time to appear on-screen.

You can click the **Stop** button to tell AOL that you don't want to wait for the rest of the page; you'll still be able to read anything that's arrived, and click to follow any links.

The next button along, a small house, is the **Home page** icon. Click on it and you'll be taken to the start page of the AOL browser, which is usually the AOL UK home page, unless you've changed the settings in the Internet Preferences. You might, for example, have your own Web page as the home page so that clicking the icon would always take you there, instead (*5.4, Internet preferences*).

To the left of the Home page icon is the **Reload** button. You can use this to tell AOL to fetch another copy of the page that you're looking at. Why would you want to do that? Well, sometimes a page might not all arrive, so clicking this icon will try to fetch it again, which might succeed. And there are some pages that might change frequently, so you can fetch an up-to-date copy. For instance, if you were looking at a newspaper's latest headlines page, you might want to click the **Reload** button after a while to see if any more news had been added to it.

Some Web pages can't be reloaded, especially ones that have been created specially for you, for example where you've had to enter a name and postcode to receive personalised information, or parts of a shopping site.

The next two buttons, the arrows pointing left and right, let you move backwards and forwards through the Web pages that you've been looking at.

For example, say you're looking at the AOL home page on the Web, and you click on a link to find out the news headlines. The page will change, and if you wanted to go back to the home page, you could click the left arrow. Clicking the right-hand one would take you forwards to the news headlines again.

You can go backwards and forwards like this for a few pages, but only following the most recent path you took. That means that if you read a news story, for example, then go back to the headlines, and click to choose another story, then go back to the headlines, using the Forward button would take you to the second story you'd chosen.

*Just like when you're using the **Reload** button, you won't always be able to move forwards again, especially through pages that have forms to fill in. AOL may ask you if you want to submit 'form data' again when you do this. Click **Yes**, and the page will behave as if you'd filled in another copy of the form.*

You should avoid using the backwards, forwards and refresh buttons when you're visiting shopping sites, as they could make it hard for the site to keep track of what's in your shopping basket.

There's one other useful thing to know about Web pages – you can add them to your favourites just like any other page on AOL. All you have to do is double-click on the **Heart** icon in the title bar of the window, exactly the same as with information on AOL.

AOL's home on the Web

Now you know the basics, let's take a close look at AOL's home on the Web, which is almost like another of AOL's Channels.

As you can see, there are the latest news headlines to keep you up to date, and links to lots of AOL's online shopping partners. Anyone on the Internet can access AOL.co.uk. There are even some members only areas.

While you can access the AOL Web page from anywhere, the members only areas can't be seen unless you have a copy of the AOL software on the computer that you're using to view the Web page.

There are lots of other great features on the AOL home page, which you can use to keep in touch with AOL wherever you are. One of the most useful is the box that lets you check your AOL email, even if you don't have AOL software on the computer you're using.

You can find out all about using the Web to check your email in *Chapter 8, AOL Anywhere (8.1, AOL Mail)*.

Below the boxes for your Screen Name and password, you'll see some more links to other useful tools, including AOL Instant Messenger, which lets you chat to your AOL Buddies, and AOL Mail for Palm, so you can collect your mail using a Palm organiser. If you want to find out more about either of these, you'll find all the details you need to set them up and use them later on in the book (*8.2, AOL Instant Messenger; 8.3, AOL for Palm*).

AOL's home page also has a Search box on it, which you can use to search the Internet, which we've explained in the next section, but there's more than just searching the Net on AOL.co.uk.

WOW

You can also look for businesses using the Business finder, and there are plenty of other useful resources too, like a list of hot Web sites, which you'll find at the keyword **WOW**.

You'll also find plenty of guides to common tasks, like planning a day out, or finding a new home, so when you've looked around AOL itself, make sure you take some time to explore all the extra information that's available on the AOL.co.uk Web site.

We'll explain how to use the Business finder in the next section, Searching the Internet. First, let's carry on with a little more information about looking at Web pages.

A word about Web pages

As well as text, pictures and links, Web pages can also contain all sorts of other information, including live video and audio clips – you can listen to the BBC World Service news, for example, or watch the latest trailer for a particular film.

Normally, the AOL browser will play clips like this automatically for you – it comes with add-ins for the most popular type of material that you'll find on the Internet. However, with so many Web sites around, all trying to make themselves look really attractive, there are lots of different ways of doing things.

For example, you might find that some Web sites use a system called QuickTime to show movie clips, while others use RealSystem, and others use something called VDO Live.

Why do you need to know about this? Well, unlike looking at information on AOL, where you can be sure that everything you see will work perfectly with the AOL software, on the Web, things are a little different.

Each of the different types of material needs a special 'helper' program so that your computer knows what to do with it. These are sometimes called 'ActiveX controls' or 'plug-ins.' You'll need the appropriate plug-in for each different material that you come across – which is why when you installed AOL, the most common ones were automatically added to your PC for you.

However, you might still come across pages on the Internet that your computer can't display, because it doesn't have the right plug-in. So, what happens then?

Most of the time, everything will happen automatically – if AOL discovers that it needs something extra to view a Web page, it will fetch it for you automatically and install it on your computer.

If the Web page doesn't display correctly, even after downloading any add-ins that are needed, you might need to click the Reload button to tell AOL to fetch the page again.

Sometimes, unfortunately, you'll just see an icon on a Web page, looking like a piece of a jigsaw puzzle with a red line through it. That means that the page is looking for a plug-in that AOL wasn't able to download automatically.

What do you do what that happens? Usually, the Web site that you're viewing will tell you what plug-in you'll need to see all the pages properly. You can either go on to a site that doesn't need you to spend time adding software to your computer, or you can download the plug-in you need.

Downloading a plug-in isn't as scary as it sounds. Most of the common plug-ins provide plenty of instructions on their Web pages, and an installer program that will add them to your computer without any difficulty. All you'll need to do is follow a link from the Web page to the site where you can download the plug-in. Once it's downloaded, follow the instructions – that usually means double-clicking on the file you've downloaded to open it, but make sure you check with the Web site for any special instructions first.

When a site doesn't actually provide a link to the plug-ins you need, don't worry! AOL can come to your rescue. If you visit the Web site multimedia.aol.com – just type that address into the Keyword box – you'll see links to all the most popular plug-ins for Web browsing. Just follow the links to download the software you'll need.

If the installer program for a plug-in asks you what Web browser you're using, the correct answer is Internet Explorer. Although it looks like AOL, when you browse the Web using AOL's service, Internet Explorer is working behind the scenes for you, so that's what you need to tell any programs that ask.

We keep talking about downloading plug-ins, so perhaps it's about time we looked at how you do download files from the Web. A plug-in, or its installer program, is just another file that you download like any other, so let's take a look at how that works on the Web.

Downloading files from the Web

As well as all the pages of information that you can read on the Net, and shops to buy things from, you can also download files from the Internet, just as you can from AOL. There are a number of different ways to download files – you can use FTP, which stands for File Transfer Protocol – or you can download files directly from a Web page.

FTP is so useful that there's a section all about it later on, but the first time you download a file from the Internet, it's more likely to come via a Web page. So, how exactly do you download one?

It's not quite the same as downloading files from AOL. When you click on a link to download something from a Web page, you don't get the choice of downloading right away or later as you would with AOL. Files that you download from the Web always have to be downloaded right away.

Let's see how it's done, by visiting AOL's home page and downloading a copy of AOL Instant Messenger.

Press Ctrl-K to bring up the Keyword box, and type in the address www.aol.co.uk/aim. You'll see a screen like this one:

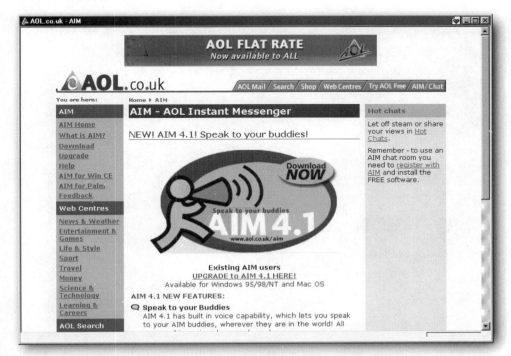

Fig. 6.3
AIM Webpage

On the left-hand side, click on the link that says **Upgrade** – you don't need to register since you already have an AOL account.

On the next screen, you'll see a list of the different versions of AIM. Click on the one that you want to download, and a message like this will appear on your computer's screen.

Fig. 6.4
Save to disk dialogue

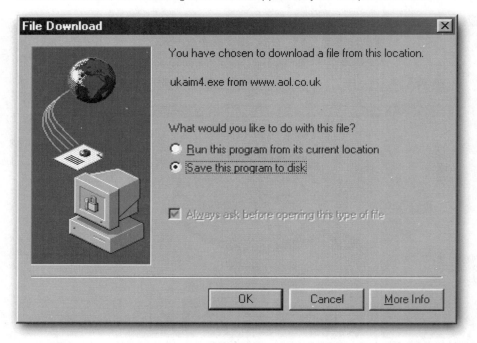

You'll see this screen when you try to download some types of file from the Web. You should choose **Save to disk**, and click on **OK**.

Fig. 6.5
Save As screen

Now you need to choose where you want to save the file on your computer's disk. Just like when you save a file in your word processor, you can choose the folder you want the file to be saved in, and click the **Save** button.

Fig. 6.6
Progress screen

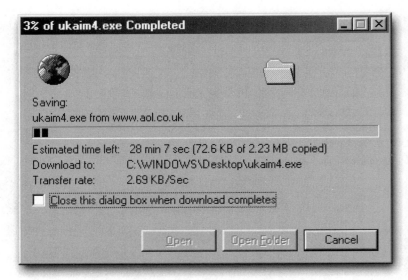

While the file is downloading, a screen like this will tell you how much of it has been downloaded. Usually, there'll be a bar displayed so that you know how much of the file has been transferred, but with some files on the Internet it's not possible to know in advance how long they are.

When the file has downloaded, the box will usually disappear. If you'd like it to stay on the screen, just click to remove the check mark in the box labelled Close this dialogue.

To cancel the file download, click the **Cancel** button. Remember that you won't be able to carry it on later, unlike downloads from AOL.

AOL has no control over the content of files that you download from the Internet. You should always check files that you download to ensure that they don't carry viruses, and make sure that your computer has up to date anti-virus software installed.

Now you know how to access a Web page and download files from it, let's take a look at one of the other useful things you can do with AOL – searching the Internet.

6.2 Searching the Internet

Everyone knows that the Internet is full of information. Whatever you want to find out about, you can be sure that someone, somewhere, has written a Web page about it, whether it's thimble collecting, how to clean stains off your leather sofa, or the continuity errors in the original Star Trek series.

Typing a few words into the toolbar on AOL and clicking the **Search** button will produce a list of both information on AOL and Web pages – and a quick glance at the total number of items found is enough to know that a simple search for a few words isn't a good way to find things on the Internet.

You can also use the Search box on the AOL.co.uk home page to search as well. Just go to the keyword Web and type what you're looking for into the box.

It might be interesting to know, for example, that AOL Search has found over 70,000 pages on the topic you're looking for, but it's not very practical is it? It would take you days just to click on all the links to those pages, let alone read what's on each one to see if it's useful.

So, the key to finding information on the Internet is really all about making sure that when you do search, the results you get are all going to be useful, and there aren't so many of them that you simply can't manage to check them all.

In this section, we're going to explain how you can use the advanced features of AOL Search to find information on the Web that you really will want to look at.

Remember that searching the Web won't always find everything that's there. For example, if you've created a home page, don't be surprised if it doesn't appear when you search. Search pages like AOL Search have to make a list of what's on the Net, and they do that by looking at where sites link to. Sites that don't have many links to them from elsewhere won't often be found by any search system on the Web.

There are, of course, other tools for searching the Web. They're often referred to as search engines, and they all work in slightly different ways, and may list different sites when you ask for the same thing. We're concentrating on AOL Search, which will find everything you need, and is just a click away in the AOL software; if you'd like to try another search engine, all you have to do is type its Web address into AOL's Keyword box.

Other searches with AOL

AOL doesn't just provide you with a way to search for Web pages. Visit the AOL home page on the Web, at keyword **Web**, and you'll see there are other tools too, including the Business Finder.

Using the Business Finder, you can track down a plumber in your area, or a glazier in Grimsby. From the front page of AOL.co.uk, click on Business finder, and you'll see a screen like this one.

Fig. 6.7
Business Finder screen

It's simple to find the businesses you want. There are just three boxes to fill in, and you only have to put something in two of them.

The first box is for the name of a company, if you know whom you're looking for. Type something like HSBC, for example. The next box is where you can say what sort of business you want. Either use this box instead of the first one, if you're looking for a bank, for example, or use it as well.

You might, perhaps, be looking for a plumber called Smith. If you just entered one or the other, you could end up with a pretty long list, so filling in both boxes would make the search much more likely to produce the results you want.

Lastly, fill in the area where you're looking for a business. You can type either the name of the place where you live or the first part of your postcode. For example, you might type Hammersmith, or W4.

When you've filled in the right information, click the **Find it** button.

Sometimes, of course, you might not have typed a word that AOL recognises as the type of business, or there could be more than one type of business. In that case, you'll see another screen like this one. Here we were looking for a glazier in W4. Now we can choose what sort of service we want, like Double Glazing, or Stained Glass.

Click on the appropriate category for the business you're trying to find, and AOL will carry on searching.

Fig. 6.8
**Business Finder
results**

And here are the results! AOL will list all the information you need to get in touch with the companies listed, and you'll see there are even consumer tips for some of the business categories, which could help you avoid making costly mistakes.

Advanced Web searching with AOL

We've already seen how you can do a simple Web search on AOL, but what about doing something more selective? It's simple. The first stage is to click on the **Search** button, which will bring up the AOL Search home page.

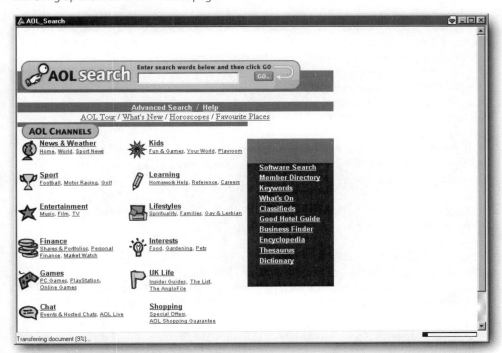

Fig. 6.9
AOL Search home page

When this screen appears, click on the text that says **Advanced Search**, and you'll see the Advanced AOL search screen that we saw earlier on in the book – however, that page is for searching the information on AOL, not on the Internet. Near the top of the page, below the search box, you'll see the text **Advanced Web Search**. Click on that, and the Web search page will appear.

Just as with the other search pages, you need to type words describing what you're looking for into the **Search** box – there's one at the top of the page and another at the bottom. Instead of clicking the **Go** button straight away, you need to choose the options you'd like for your search on the rest of the page. There are quite a few, so let's go through them one at a time.

How do you want to search?
In this section, you can tell AOL whether you want to look for all the words you type, the exact phrase you typed, or any word. For example, you might type the words classic and car into the Search box.

If you choose ALL words, then AOL will find Web pages that contain both words, but they might not necessarily be together. A page that said 'My favourite car is a Ford Mondeo, and I listen to classic rock while I'm driving' would match, for example.

Choose EXACT phrase when the words you've typed should appear exactly as you've typed them. You'd only see pages in our example with phrases like 'The Citroën DS is a true classic car' and not ones that said 'This car is a true classic'.

If you select ANY word, then AOL will find pages that contain one or more of the words you typed – which might mean they're not related. For instance a page saying 'The Fender Stratocaster is a classic guitar' would be found.

> *Choosing ALL words is a good way to narrow down a list of results, adding extra words to cut out pages that you don't want to see.*

Do you want to search the UK or the whole of the Web?
Although the Web is international, sometimes you just want local information. With this option, you can tell AOL to restrict the list of sites that's searched to just ones in the UK. Click to select **The whole Web** or **UK**, if you want to cut down the list of results.

Do you want to search for a specific domain?
With this option, you can tell AOL search that you only want to search for sites whose addresses end in a particular domain. For instance, you might be trying to find a Web page that you think is on AOL's sister service, Netscape Online. In that case, you'd click to select this option, and then in the box provided, type netscapeonline.co.uk.

AOL Search will only display results for Web sites that are within the domain you typed.

What are you searching for?
Not everything on the Web is text, of course. There are plenty of pictures, video clips and music files that you might want to look at or download to your computer. With this option, you can tell AOL to look only for one of those types of information, which will help to cut down on the number of results you see.

Just click with the mouse to select what type of information you're looking for. You can only select one of the options.

How do you want to sort the results?
In this section, you can tell AOL whether you want the results listed by domain and relevance, or relevance only. What does that mean? Well, when AOL Search finds a result, it tries to work out how closely it matches what you typed and gives it a percentage figure called the relevance. The larger the number, the more likely the page is to be useful to you.

You can have pages listed either with the most relevant ones first, or sorted by domains, with the most relevant pages in each domain listed first. That means, for example, that all the pages on aol.com would be grouped together in the list. If you know that the information you want is likely to be on a particular server, perhaps belonging to the company that makes a product, then you might find it useful to sort by domain and relevance.

How many results should the search return?
This option, doesn't limit the total number of results, but the number that you'll see on each page of results. You can choose to see five, 25, 50 or 100 results on a page. To see more, you'll need to click the **Next** link that will appear on the results screen.

What format should the results take?
Finally, you can decide whether you want the results to give a description of the sites that are found, or just their title.

If you have lots of results on one page and ask for a description as well as a title, remember that the results could take quite a long time to appear on your screen.

When you've chosen all the options for your search, and typed the words you're looking for into the search box, click the **Go** button and AOL Search will see what results it can find for you.

Fig. 6.10
**Advanced Web
search results**

This is what you'll see when AOL Search has finished looking for pages that match your query. Just like when you're using the search system to look for information on AOL, you can click **Next** to see more results.

To view one of the pages that's been found, click on the title of the site, which is highlighted in blue.

*If you'd like the page to open in a new window, so that you can carry on looking at the list of results, click on the title of a site with the right mouse button, and choose **Open in new window** from the menu that appears.*

You'll also see a short description of each site, if you told AOL to list descriptions, and underneath that, in bold type, you'll see the Web address, in case you want to make a note of it.

There's one other link that you'll find useful. Below each of the Web sites that's been found, you'll see the words Show me more like this. If you decide that a site's useful, then from the Results page, you can follow the link below the site, and AOL Search will look for more pages, using the information it has about the site you just looked at, to try and find more relevant information for you.

So, is that all there is to searching the Web? Well, not quite. Although AOL's advanced Web search screen can help you find lots of information easily, and the Show me more like this links will help you home in on what you really want, there are still more ways to search for information.

If, despite using the advanced search and adding extra words to try and slim down the number of pages the AOL Search suggests you look at, you still end up with lists pages and pages long, perhaps it's time you tried the really advanced searching – called Boolean Searching.

Boolean Searching

Don't be scared by the name! Boolean Searching just means that you're using a sort of logical language to describe what you want to find. It's a little more complicated than the type of search that you've done so far, but if you want to do the most accurate searches possible, it's well worth learning about.

A Boolean Search is simply a search that contains extra words which are commands to tell AOL Search about the results you want, rather than words that should be looked for in pages.

For example, you could search for cars AND classic, which is the same as typing classic cars into the Search box and choosing ALL words. Or you could ask for cars NOT Ford which would exclude any pages that had the word Ford on them.

You can also put brackets in your search, to group words together. *(cars AND classic) NOT Bugatti* would find pages that were about Classic Cars, except Bugattis. The brackets work a bit like they do in maths; AOL Search will check things inside the brackets first.

Another useful word is OR, which works just the way you'd expect. If you didn't want to know about Daimlers as well, you could change the last example to *say (cars AND classic) NOT (Bugatti OR Daimler)*

All you have to do to use this sort of search is type it into the box on the AOL Search screen, and then click the **Go** button. You'll see exactly the same results that you do when you use AOL Search in any other way, but hopefully they'll be even closer to what you're looking for.

More search commands

You can start using Boolean Searching with the AND, OR and NOT commands that we've already explained, and they'll improve the accuracy of your Web searches, but there are lots of other special words that you can use.

> *As well as letting you use special words to control your searching, AOL Search tries to be intelligent about the words you've typed. For example, if you type the word education, AOL will also look for words that have the same root, like educating, educational and so on. You can stop this happening by putting quotation marks round a word.*

Let's look at each of the other commands you can use to improve your searches.

ADJ

This stands for adjacent, or next to. For example, *Tony ADJ Blair* would find pages containing Tony Blair. Why would you use this instead of looking for "Tony Blair" ? Firstly, it allows you to mix different things, like *(Tony OR Cherie) ADJ Blair* to find Tony Blair or Cherie Blair, and secondly, AOL Search will be able to use intelligent word matching. For example *'education expenses'* would only match exactly that, but *education ADJ expenses* would also find *educational expenses* and so on.

NEAR

Use this command to find one word when it appears near to another, but not necessarily in any particular order. For example, if you searched for *classic NEAR car* then AOL would find pages that said 'This car is a classic' as well as 'The Citroën is my favourite classic car'.

You can restrict how close together the two words have to be by putting a / after NEAR, followed by the maximum number of words apart that the two should be. For example, *classic NEAR/3 car*.

W/

The W command means within, and you follow it with a number, like W/5. It means, look for the word to the left, followed by the word the right within a certain number of words. For example, you might look for *psychological W/7 profiling* to find information about the uses of psychological profiles in tracking down criminals.

?

A ? matches one letter, for example if you can't remember if it's a license or a licence that you're trying to find out information about, you could look for *licen?e*, and AOL Search will find pages containing either.

*

The * matches one or more letters. We've already explained how AOL Search will look for similar words, but by using * you can look for completely different words that start with the same letters. For example, *micro** would find pages containing the words Micronesia, micro-computer, microphone, microscope and so on.

!

This is one of the most powerful tools offered by AOL Search. You can use it for what's called a concept search. When you end a word with !, AOL Search works out what the word means, and looks for pages about the same concept. For example, if you typed *accident!* then you might also see pages listed that talked about wrecks, or disasters, even if they didn't use the word accident.

It may all look a bit complicated – or you may decide that you'll never need to use it – but AOL's Boolean Search can be one of the most useful tools for anyone wanting to find information on the Web.

Together with the ordinary Web search tools, and the Advanced Web Search page, you should be able to find just about anything you need to on the Web, so let's move on now and look at some more of the Internet's useful resources.

6.3 File transfers on the Internet

We've already seen how you can download files from Web pages, but there's another useful tool that AOL provides for accessing files on the Internet. It's called FTP, which stands for File Transfer Protocol.

FTP is a great way of finding information. You'll often find that files are available on FTP servers for things like updated drivers for printers and graphics cards, or utility programs, a little like the sort of thing that you can find in AOL's own file libraries. Since FTP has been around for so long, you'll find thousands of files that you can download, including some of the biggest collections of free software available.

In fact, FTP sites look very similar to AOL's file libraries, so if you've mastered downloading files from them, you should have no problems with the things we're looking at in this section.

AOL provides two different ways to access files via FTP. You can type an FTP address into the Keyword box, or you can use the **FTP** keyword, which provides more facilities, including the ability to send files via FTP. We'll look at FTP addresses first, and then explain AOL's built-in FTP system.

Before we go on, remember that FTP sites are all over the Internet and not controlled by AOL. As a result, you should treat files that you download with caution, and remember to scan them for viruses before opening them.

FTP addresses
You'll often see an FTP address written in two different ways. It could be just the name of a computer, like ftp.aol.com, or it may begin with ftp://, like ftp://ftp.aol.com. The second version is the form you'll need to use if you want to type an FTP address into AOL's Keyword box. The ftp:// at the start tells AOL that what you're typing is an FTP address rather than a Web address. You can add extra information on the end, too. For example, if someone told you that the file you wanted was in the aim/win95 folder on ftp.aol.com, you could type the whole address into the Keyword box as **ftp://ftp.aol.com/aim/win95**.

Try it now, and you'll see how easy it can be to access files using FTP. You should see a screen like this one appear:

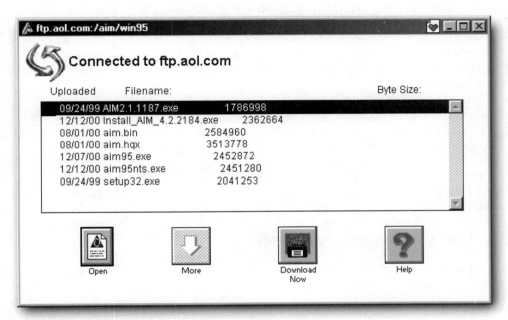

Fig. 6.11
**FTP to
aol.com/aim/
win95**

As you can see, the display shows the files in a folder, with an icon for each one. It's not really that different from what you'd see if you were browsing round your own computer's hard disk. When you see an icon for a folder, you can double-click on it to open that folder, and the screen will show you its contents.

To move back up a level, click on the folder with the name "..." – that's just two dots. If you did that in the folder we suggested as an example, you'd move from aim/win95 to aim. Simple, isn't it?

Although this is what you'll see when you connect to AOL's FTP server by typing an FTP address into the Keyword box, some sites may look slightly different. For example, the icons may change, and there may be additional information displayed above and below the list of files, depending on how that particular FTP server has been set up. But you still move open folders or download files in exactly the same way.

What about downloading a file? It's easy to do. When you've seen the file that you want to download, just click on it. You'll see exactly the same messages as when you download a file from a Web page, so you'll need to choose where to save the file on your computer's hard disk.

And that's all there is to it! If someone tells you to look on an FTP site, all you need to do is put ftp:// on the front if it's not already there, and then just point and click to download the files you want.

Although downloading files by typing an FTP address as a keyword is simple, you can't actually do anything else. On many FTP sites, that's not really a problem, since all you're allowed to do is download files, but there are lots of other things that you might want to do.

For example, your company might have an FTP server that makes all your files accessible. By connecting to the server with a name and password, you could rename files, delete them, or add new files. Of course, you can send files to someone via email, but then they need to read the email and detach the file, and so on. With FTP, you can put a file in a particular place, and then people will be able to access it right away.

FTP can be used to upload Web pages to a server too, and for all sorts of other useful things, so let's take a look at all the things you can do using AOL's **FTP** keyword.

Advanced FTP

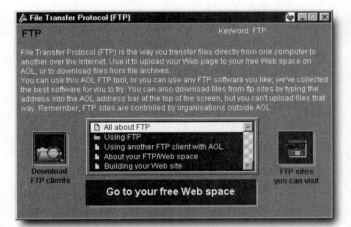

Fig. 6.12
FTP screen

This is the screen you'll see when you choose FTP from the Internet menu on AOL. You can also reach it via the keyword **ftp** too. As you can see, there are quite a few things you can do from this screen, including downloading other FTP programs which you can use with AOL.

FTP

The button on the left of the screen will let you download other FTP programs, which you might want to try when you're more familiar with FTP. In the middle of the screen, you'll see a list of documents you can read, which tell you a little more about FTP and how you can use it to help build your Web site. For now, though, we're interested in the right-hand button – FTP sites you can visit.

Fig. 6.13
FTP sites screen

This is what you'll see when you click on the list of FTP sites. The things in the list are some of the most popular sites on the Internet and you'll find a wide range of things on them, including free programs to download and updates to programs from companies like Microsoft or Corel.

Just pick any of the sites in the list, and click the **Connect** button at the bottom of the screen. The **Other Site** button is used when you want to visit a site that's not in the list; we'll look at it later.

It might take a while to connect to a site, especially since some of the FTP sites on the Internet limit the number of people who can connect to them at the same time. Other sites are 'mirrored' which means that AOL has a copy of them on its own computer, to help speed up access. You may see a message telling you this when you click on a site. If so, just click **OK** when you've read the message, and then the list of files on the site will appear.

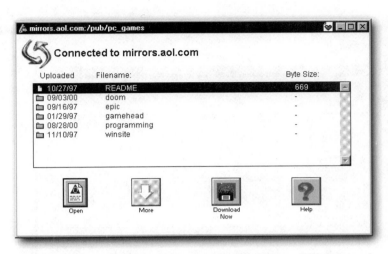

Fig. 6.14
**FTP connected
screen**

As you can see, it's not that different from the AOL file areas, is it? You can see a list of files
or folders, with the size shown for a file. Along the bottom of the screen are buttons labelled
Open, **More**, **Download Now** and **Help**.

Double-clicking on any of the items in the list is the same as clicking once on it and then
clicking on the **Open** button. If you've highlighted a folder, then a new window will appear,
showing you what's in the folder. If you choose a file, you'll see a screen like this, telling you
a little more about the file.

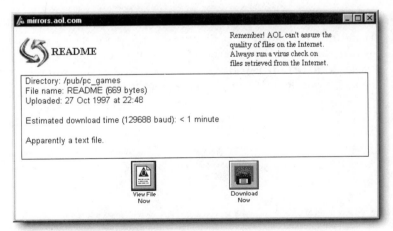

Fig. 6.15
File open info

As you can see, there's not a lot of information, is there? That's because the file is on a
system that AOL doesn't control, and so there's no extra information available. If the file is

a text file – perhaps a README document – you can click the **View File Now** button to see what it says.

Fig. 6.16
View file

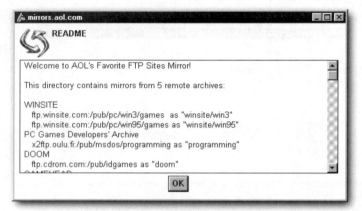

Choosing **OK** will close the window. You'll often see files called README or README.TXT when you look at FTP sites, and it's a good idea to check them to see if there are important notices in them. Many sites will also contain files with names like 00index.txt, which give more details about the different files in the folder you're looking at.

When you choose **Download Now**, either from the main list of files in a folder, or after choosing to open a file, you'll be asked where you want to save it on your computer's disk.

Just choose the folder where you want to save a file, and click the **Save** button. Next, you'll see the usual AOL progress bar, showing you how much of the file has been downloaded, and just like when you're downloading a file from AOL, you can click to put a check in the box labelled **Sign off after transfer**. When you do, AOL will disconnect from the FTP site, and then disconnect from AOL too, leaving your phone line free.

After the download is complete, if you didn't sign off AOL, you'll see this appear.

Fig. 6.17
Go to file

If you'd like to find the file on your hard disk, just click **Yes**, and AOL will open the folder where you saved the file. Files that you download via FTP will also be listed in the Download Manager, so you can use that to locate them on your computer's disk later if you like (*3.3, Download Manager*).

That's all there is to it – at least as far as downloading files goes. However, FTP is about rather more than just downloading files from the list of sites that AOL displays for you.

Connecting to other FTP sites
The FTP facility on AOL doesn't just restrict you to the list of sites that's listed when you click the **Sites to Visit** button. If you want, you can connect to any FTP site on the net, using the **Other Site** button.

When you click on it, you'll see a screen like this one, where you can type the name of an FTP site.

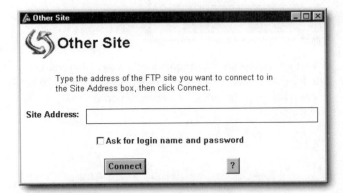

Fig. 6.18
Other site screen

You'll also see a box at the bottom labelled Ask for login name and password. If you click and put a check in the box, then AOL will ask you what name you want to use to connect to an FTP site. What's that for? Well, if you want to upload Web pages, for example, you'd tell the server who you are so that it knew where to store your personal pages. Or you might have been given a special name and password by a company that allows you to download information you've paid for from their FTP site.

Most of the sites that you download information from on the Internet, including free software, are what's called Anonymous FTP sites. That means that you don't need to give a name and password to access them, so you can safely leave the Ask for login name box blank.

There's one final thing to remember on this screen. You don't type ftp:// at the start of the name for the FTP site. For AOL's FTP server, for example, you'd just type ftp.aol.com into the box, not ftp://ftp.aol.com.

When you've typed the name of the site you want to connect to, click the **Connect** button. If you said you wanted to supply a name and password, you'll see this screen appear:

Fig. 6.19
FTP password

When you access any site anonymously, everything will look just the same as if you'd picked a site from AOL's list of Web sites to visit. However, if you supplied a user name and password, there are a few other things that you can do with FTP.

More FTP functions
As you can see from this screen, there are a few more buttons at the bottom of the list of files when you connect to an FTP site with a login name and password.

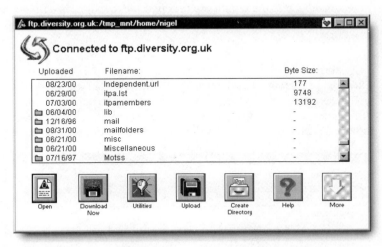

Fig. 6.20
FTP file list, logged in

In the middle of the row of buttons, you'll see three new ones that aren't there when you look at an anonymous FTP site. They're labelled **Utilities**, **Upload** and **Create Directory**.

FTP Utilities
This is the button to use if you want to rename or delete a file that's on the FTP server you're connected to. Click once to highlight a file and then click this button.

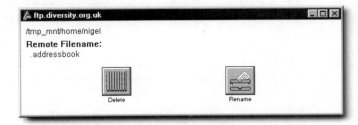

Fig. 6.21
Utilities screen

If you'd like to remove a file, click the **Delete** button. You'll see one more screen asking you if you're sure that you want to delete the file.

*If you click **OK**, the file will be deleted from the computer that you have connected to, and you will not be able to retrieve it.*

To rename a file, click the **Rename** button and a box will appear on the screen for you to type a new name for the file. Just type the name that you want, and press **Enter**.

Remember that the system you're connected to may have different rules about what letters can be included in the names of files. It's generally a good idea to avoid files with spaces, slashes or other strange characters in them.

FTP Upload

Uploading a file with FTP just means transferring it from your computer to the FTP site that you're connected to. You could use it, for example, to transfer a Web page that you've written from your computer to the Web server so that everyone else can see it. Click the **Upload** button to start sending a file. It will appear in the list of files that you're looking at.

Fig. 6.22
Upload file name

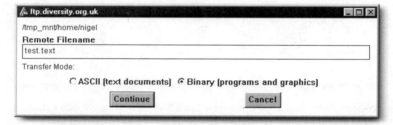

This is the first stage of uploading a file. You need to say what name the file will have on the computer you're transferring it to – it doesn't have to be the same name as it has on your computer.

Type the name into the box, and then select the type of transfer you want. An ASCII transfer is used for text files, while a Binary transfer is used for everything else, including Word Processor files.

Broadly speaking, the files for Web pages are text files, and you can upload them as ASCII. Pictures and just about everything else should be uploaded as Binary. If you're not sure, choose Binary.

After you've typed the name for the file, and chose how you want to transfer it, click the **Continue** button.

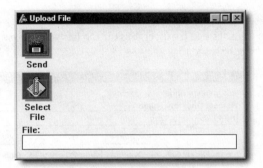

Fig. 6.23
Select file screen

When this screen appears, you need to select which file you want to send to the FTP site. Click the **Select File** button, and choose the file that you want to send, just like when you choose the file to attach to an email message.

After you've selected the file, click the **Send** button, and AOL will start to copy it from your computer to the FTP site.

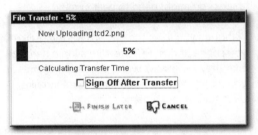

Fig. 6.24
FTP progress screen

You'll see a progress bar like this one as your file is uploaded. You can click **Cancel** to stop the transfer, or click to put a check in the box labelled Sign off after transfer if you'd like AOL to automatically disconnect when the file has been uploaded.

FTP create directory
Just as you'd expect, this button lets you make a new folder on the FTP site that you're connected to.

Fig. 6.25
FTP create directory

All you need to do is type the name of the folder that you'd like to create, and press **Enter**. After a short pause, the folder will be created for you. If you'd like to upload files into it, just double-click to open it, and then use the **Upload** button when you're looking at the new folder.

FTP problems
FTP looks pretty easy, doesn't it? And it is very straightforward. However, there are a few things you might need to bear in mind.

Although you'll see the buttons for things like **Upload** and **Create Directory** appear when you connect to an FTP site with a login name and password, that doesn't necessarily mean that they will always work. Different FTP sites are set up in different ways and, for example, you might still only be able to download files, or the FTP server might have been configured so that you can't rename certain files.

FTP sites also 'time out' as well. That means that after you've connected, if you don't do anything for a while – perhaps you've been busy making tea – you might find that when you try to download a file, or open another folder of files, you'll see a message telling you that you're no longer connected. Don't worry – just tell AOL to connect again, and everything will be fine.

Finally, as you'll have noticed, the AOL FTP tool only allows you to upload one file at a time. If you want to upload lots of files, for example all the different files that make up a new Web site, then you'll probably be best off downloading a more specialised FTP program.

You can find links to many of the best programs, and instructions about how to use them, by clicking the button on the **FTP** main screen.

Now you know all about FTP, let's take a look at another of the Internet's most popular facilities – Newsgroups.

6.4 Newsgroups

If you've been working through this book, you'll have come across the term Newsgroups already – it's the label on one of the tabs in your Personal Filing Cabinet, and we've already said that they're a little like AOL's Message boards.

So if they're like Message boards, what's all the fuss about? Well, newsgroups have been around for years – in fact, they're even older than the World Wide Web.

When a message is posted to a newsgroup, it's copied to computers all around the world. Nowadays that takes just a few hours, but 15 years ago, a message could take a couple of days to be seen everywhere – but it would still reach thousands of people all around the globe.

Just like with AOL's forums, messages in newsgroups form threads, with people contributing to them from everywhere, and the discussion in them ranges from the academic to the robust.

> *If you're a parent, you might want to restrict the newsgroups that your child has access to. You can control newsgroup access using AOL's Parental Controls (5.1, Parental Controls).*

In fact, it's the people who can help make newsgroups one of the most useful resources on the Internet. You'll find some groups that are just chatter, but there are also some very technical newsgroups and often some of the most important people in their fields can be found in them, sharing their knowledge with everyone else.

We've already said that newsgroups have been around for over 15 years, and you'll find some people who've been using them almost that long. As you'd expect, over the years rules and conventions have grown up about how to post, and what is and is not acceptable. Some people are more forgiving than others of mistakes, but it's still best to avoid making them.

> *The newsgroup called news.announce.newusers contains plenty of information for people who are new to newsgroups, and you should take the time to read the items in it before contributing to any other groups. Always observe the basic rules of good online behaviour, and read a group for a while before you make contributions to it.*

Newsgroup naming

One of the most important things to learn about newsgroups before you start reading them is how they're named. Once you understand the way the names work, then it's much easier to find groups that cover the topics you're interested in, or work out what a group is supposed to be for.

The name of a newsgroup is a little like the domain names you'll have come across for email and Web sites. It's a series of words separated by dots, which you read from left to right. Newsgroups are arranged in a hierarchy, grouping similar areas together, whether it's by subject or geographical area. For example, all the newsgroups for the UK have names that start with uk.

Let's take a look at the main collections of newsgroups, and the sort of things that you can expect to find in them.

Alt

The newsgroups with names beginning alt are 'alternative' groups and they're not quite as rigidly organised as other hierarchies. You'll find lots of fan groups with names beginning alt.fan, for example.

Comp

Newsgroups with names that begin with comp are, as you'd probably expect, to do with computers. For example, comp.sys.amiga is where you'll find discussion of the old Commodore Amiga computers.

Misc

Misc stands, of course, for miscellaneous, and you'll find all sorts of things in here that don't quite fit anywhere else, so just take a look and see what you can find.

News

Although you might think it from the name, this isn't the place to look for news headlines. The groups in this area are to do with the newsgroup system itself, including areas for discussing the pros and cons of new groups, and important announcements. One of the most important groups, news.announce.newusers is here, and you should make sure you read it before you do anything else.

Rec

Here is where you'll find recreational topics, like collecting, cars, and so on. If it's cars you want to know about, try groups with names beginning rec.autos, and how about rec.pets.cats for our feline friends?

Sci

Scientific topics take pride of place here, with some pretty heavyweight discussions in some of the groups. You could delve into how the universe works in the sci.physics groups, or read about the space shuttle in sci.space.shuttle.

Soc

Social issues can be found in groups beginning with soc, for example the group soc.culture.pakistan is where you'd find discussions about the culture of that country.

Talk

The Talk groups are home to general chatter on a range of topics – and sometimes it can all get pretty heated. People on newsgroups generally haven't had to agree to the same sort of rules as AOL's Conditions of Service, and in areas like talk.politics you could find yourself up against some experts in the art of arguing – or hurling insults!

UK

Groups specific to the UK will be found here, and within the UK groups, there are small hierarchies too. For example, uk.transport is the starting point for several groups covering road and rail, while uk.people is where the more social groups can be found, and uk.misc is a general discussion forum.

There are lots of other hierarchies of newsgroups too, some specific to a particular area, or even a company. For example, groups with names starting microsoft are where you can find detailed discussion and support of that company's products.

Now that you know how the newsgroups are named, let's take a look at how AOL lets you access them.

Accessing newsgroups with AOL

Fig. 6.26
**Newsgroups
main screen**

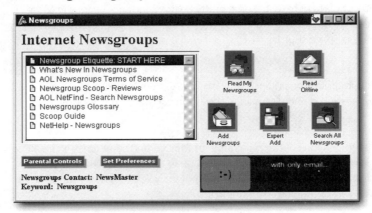

Newsgroups

The easiest way to access newsgroups on AOL is by choosing **Newsgroups** from the **Internet** menu at the top of your screen. You can also use the **Newsgroups** keyword instead.

You'll see that there are five main buttons on the screen, and also two smaller ones, for newsgroup Preferences and Parental Controls. Before we look at all those, however, a word about the other part of the screen.

At the left of the Newsgroups screen, there's a list of documents, including a guide to newsgroup etiquette, and AOL's Newsgroups Terms of Service. You can look at any of these documents by double-clicking on their title.

> *You should read, at the very least, the guide to newsgroup etiquette, before you start using newsgroups. If you don't, then it's very likely that you will make mistakes, and you'll find that people in many newsgroups will be less willing to help you solve any problems if you haven't taken the trouble to try and find out a little about how they work.*

With that warning out of the way, let's take a look at the different buttons on the Newsgroups screen.

Read My Newsgroups is the button that lets you see what's happening in the different groups, reading messages and posting comments to them.

Next to it, the **Read Offline** button lets you decide which newsgroups you'd like to have collected during Automatic AOL sessions, so that you can read the messages in your Personal Filing Cabinet.

On the next row, **Add Newsgroups** lets you browse through the list of available newsgroups – be warned, it's pretty big – and add other groups to the list that appears when you choose Read my newsgroups. The **Expert Add** button is the one to use when you know the name of the group you want to read, and finally **Search All Newsgroups** lets you find groups that have a particular word in their name.

Ok, so now you know what the buttons are for, let's explain how you start to read the messages.

There are tens of thousands of newsgroups available, so it's not really practical to provide you with a list of all the unread messages each time you want to read groups. Instead, My Newsgroups is a list of the groups that you're subscribed to – that just means the ones you want to read.

When you install AOL, a few important groups will be added to your list, so that you have something to read right away. One of the groups provides a place for you to practise sending messages to newsgroups, and there are also some, like news.announce.newusers, which have information designed to help you find your way around.

Reading newsgroup messages

To start reading newsgroup messages, all you need to do is click the **Read My Newsgroups** button.

Fig. 6.27
Read My Newsgroups screen

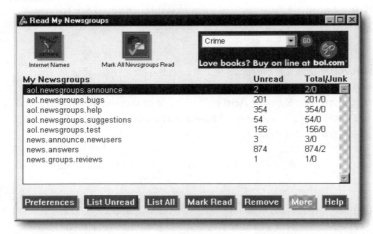

This is what you'll see the first time you access newsgroups. The main area lists all the newsgroups that you're subscribed to, with the number of unread messages in each one, and the total number of messages available, followed by the number that have been filtered out as being junk messages.

At the top, there are two buttons. The first one, **Internet Names**, is there to help you work out what each newsgroup is for, if you can't figure it out from the title. Click on it, and a screen like this will appear:

Fig. 6.28
Internet Names screen

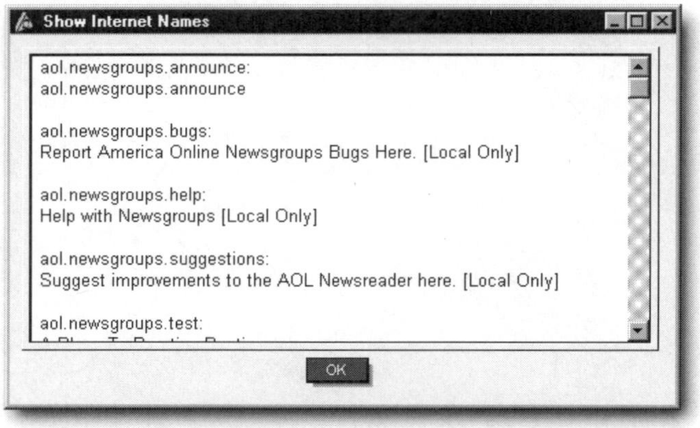

You'll see there's a short description of each of the newsgroups in your list. Take a look at it to give yourself an idea of what's going to be in each one.

Next to the Internet names button, **Mark All Newsgroups Read** tells AOL that you're not interested in any of the unread messages; you just want to skip the whole lot of them. Click this button, and AOL will behave as if you'd read all the messages. That means that the next time you access your newsgroups, you'll only see messages that have arrived since you clicked the button.

Below the list of newsgroups are more buttons. The first, **Preferences**, lets you set the Preferences for the newsgroup that's highlighted in the list. It only affects the group that's been selected. To change all the newsgroup Preferences, you need to use the button on the main Newsgroups screen.

We'll look at Preferences in a little while. For now, let's look at the other buttons.

Clicking the **List Unread** button will open the newsgroup that's selected, and show you the list of unread messages. You can also double-click on the name of a group to see unread messages.

List All shows you all the messages in a particular group, which could be useful if you marked something as read and want to read it again.

Remember that newsgroup messages are automatically deleted from AOL's computers after a while, so you may not always be able to see messages you've already read.

The **Mark Read** button tells AOL to mark all the articles in the highlighted newsgroup as read, and the Remove button deletes a newsgroup from the list. If you remove a newsgroup using this button, you'll have to add it again using either the List Newsgroups button or the Expert add button on the main Newsgroups screen.

If you're subscribed to lots of newsgroups, then AOL might not list them all in one go. When that happens, the **More** button will fetch more of your subscribed newsgroups and add them to the bottom of the list.

So, that's what all the buttons do. Let's take a look at how to read the messages in a particular group. Start by double-clicking on one of the newsgroups that takes your fancy.

Fig. 6.29
**Newsgroup
messages screen**

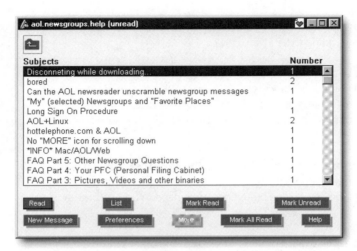

This is what appears when you read the messages in a newsgroup. You'll see a list of subjects, and the number of messages on that subject – often called a thread. The simplest way to read the messages on a particular subject is just to double-click on it, though you can also click once on a subject and then click the **Read** button at the bottom of the screen.

Next to **Read**, you'll see a button labelled **List**. You can use this button when there are lots of messages in a particular thread. Click on it, and a small screen appears showing the address of all the people who posted to the thread, the date they wrote their contribution and its size.

Fig. 6.30
Thread list

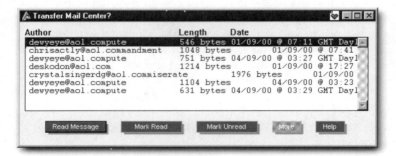

You can read any of the messages from this list by double-clicking it – so you could go directly to a message written by someone whose address you recognise, for example.

Next to the **List** button, the **Mark Read** and **Mark Unread** buttons let you choose which messages you want to read. If you want to skip a thread, then click to highlight it and click **Mark Read**. Use **Mark Unread** for the opposite effect – a little like the **Keep As New** button in AOL's email.

On the bottom row of buttons you'll see a **New Message** button. That's the one to use when you want to post a message, which we'll explain later. Next to that, the **Preferences** button lets you alter settings just for this newsgroup.

More will list more threads, if AOL didn't fit them all in the screen when you first opened the newsgroup, and Mark all read tells AOL to mark all the threads on the screen as read.

Now you know what all the buttons are for, let's start reading the messages themselves. Just double-click on one of the subjects.

The Read message screen

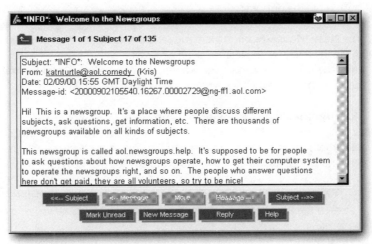

Fig. 6.31
Read Message screen

Here's the message itself. You'll see the subject of the message appears in the title of the window, and below that, AOL tells you where in the newsgroup you are – for example, Message 2 of 7, Subject 35 of 2019.

That means you're reading the second message in the current thread, and there are 2019 threads in the newsgroup – so you have just over 2000 to go before you're finished.

The main part of the screen shows the message itself; if it's a very long one, then you might see the **More** button at the bottom highlighted; click on it and AOL will fetch the next part of the message.

Either side of the **More** button, you'll see buttons labelled **Subject** and **Message**, with arrows pointing left and right. Depending on where you are in a thread, some of the buttons may be dimmed, so that you can't use them.

The **Message** buttons let you move backwards and forwards through the current thread of messages, while the **Subject** buttons move through the list of threads. So, you could start at the first message in the list, and keep clicking the right-hand **Message** button to read through the thread. At the end of the thread, click the right-hand **Subject** button to move on to the next thread -you don't need to go back to the main list of messages unless you want to.

If you decide that you'd like to come back to the message later, click the **Mark Unread** button, on the bottom row.

The **New Message** button lets you send a message to the newsgroup that you're reading, while the Reply button lets you send a message with the same subject, quoting parts of the message in your response if you want to. You can respond either to the whole group, or to the person who wrote the message you're reading.

Posting messages to newsgroups

Posting is the term that's used for sending messages to a newsgroup. It's actually fairly similar to composing an email message, but what you write can be seen by people all over the world. Anyone who's subscribed to a newsgroup will see the message that you post to it.

Before you post, you should read a newsgroup for a while to get a feel for it, and see if there's a FAQ. Make sure that you've read AOL's newsgroup Guidelines before posting.

To post a message, you first need to select which group you want to send it to. If you're not already reading a group, select Read my newsgroups from the main Newsgroups screen, and then double-click on the group you want to post a message to.

If there are no unread messages in the group, you'll see a screen appear, asking you if you want to list all the messages in the group, or post a new message. If you want to create a response to a message, choose **List All**, otherwise click to create a new posting.

When you're viewing the list of subjects in a group, you can click the **New Message** button, or use the button at the bottom of any message that you're reading. We'll explain how to reply to a message in a moment, after we've seen how to create a new message.

Creating a new message

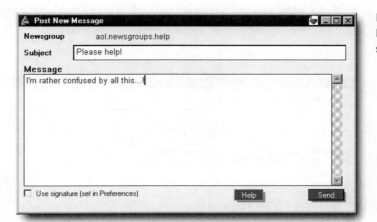

Fig. 6.32
**New Message
screen**

As you can see, posting a new message to a newsgroup isn't that different to writing an email. At the top of the screen, above the box for your subject, you'll see the name of the newsgroup for your message selected. Check to make sure you're posting to the right place, and if not, close the window.

Type a descriptive subject for your message in the box. In some groups, there might be rules about what you can put. For example, in a group discussing a TV series, there may be a rule that you should include the word 'SPOILER' in your subject, if reading the message gives away a part of the plot that people might not have seen yet.

*Always check the FAQ for a group to see if there are special rules you should abide
by before posting your message.*

Type your message in the large box, and remember to follow all the usual rules of netiquette as you write it. If you've created a signature, using the newsgroup Preferences, click to put a check in the **Use signature** box, and AOL will add it to your message automatically. You might use a signature, for example, to add a witty quote to the end of your message.

When you're satisfied with your message, all you need to do is click the **Send** button and it'll be posted to newsgroups.

Remember that when you post a newsgroup message, it will be seen by people all over the world, and thousands of copies of your message will appear automatically as it's copied around the Internet. You won't be able to unsend your message, as you can with email.

Posting a message is pretty easy, isn't it? So let's take a look now at how you can respond to someone's message.

Replying to a newsgroup posting

Fig. 6.33
**Newsgroup
followup screen**

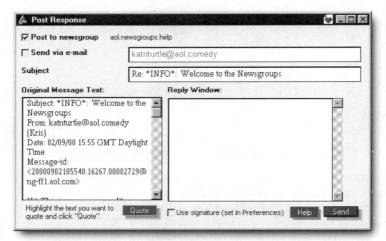

This is the screen you'll see when you click the **Reply** button at the bottom of a message. As you can see, right at the top, there are two check boxes labelled **Post to newsgroup** and **Send via email**.

In some newsgroups, there may be restrictions on where your replies can be sent. If this is the case, you'll see a brief message before this screen appears, and one of the check boxes may be disabled.

Normally, the **Post to newsgroup** box will be checked, and next to it, you'll see the group that your message will be sent to. Sometimes, that might not necessarily be the same group you read the message in. If you're not sure your message will be going to the right place, close the window.

To the right of the **Send via email** check box, you'll see a box with an email address in it. If you click to put a mark in the check box, your response will be sent via email to the address in the box.

You can send a message both to a newsgroup and via email, though many people consider it bad etiquette, since it may mean the person you're writing to has to respond twice, once in the public newsgroup and again via email.

The next box is for the subject of your message. Usually, AOL will fill in the subject and you don't need to change it. However, if you're making a public reply, but the topic of the conversation has moved on from the original subject, you could change it.

If you do change the subject, it's a good idea to keep the old one in brackets, with the word Was: in front of it. That way, other people will be able to see that your message follows on from another subject. For example, you might change a subject of *Kids TV* to *Magic Roundabout (Was: Kids TV).*

The next two boxes might look a little confusing.

At the left, you'll see the message that you're replying to. At the right, is a blank box where you can type your response. You can read the original message on the left if you want to refresh your memory, or you can quote parts of it.

Quoting means including parts of a message in your reply, and it can often make it much easier to follow the thread of a conversation. To include parts of the original message in your response, highlight the words you want to include with the mouse, and then click the **Quote** button. The text will be copied into your new message, marked as a quote.

Although quoting is useful, you shouldn't quote more text than is necessary to make your point. You should certainly try to avoid quoting more words than you have actually written yourself!

When you've finished writing your message, check through it again, and then click the **Send** button. AOL will automatically post it to the newsgroup, via email or both, depending on which options you selected at the top of the screen.

Reading newsgroups offline

As you'll discover pretty soon, newsgroups can become very absorbing, and you could end up spending a lot of time reading them and replying to messages, just like AOL's message boards.

And, just like message boards, you can save yourself a lot of time connected to AOL by reading newsgroup messages offline. If you select newsgroups for offline reading, and then tell Automatic AOL to collect them, you can read and respond to messages at your leisure, without worrying about how long you're connected to AOL.

You can find out how to set up Automatic AOL and read messages offline in *Chapter 5, AOL and You* (*5.5, Newsgroups in your Personal Filing Cabinet, 5.5, Automatic AOL*).

First, though, you'll need to say which newsgroups you want to select for offline reading. You do that by clicking the **Read Offline** button on the main Newsgroups screen.

Fig. 6.34
Read Offline screen

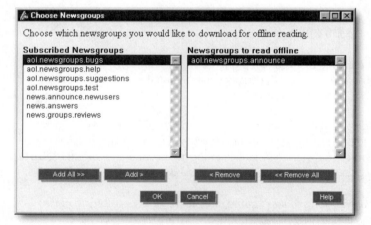

There are two lists of newsgroups on this screen. The one on the left shows all the newsgroups that you're subscribed to, while the one on the right shows the ones that you've marked to read offline – so of course it'll be empty the first time you come to this screen.

To select a group for reading offline, you just need to click on it with the mouse, then click the **Add** button, or double-click on it. Clicking **Add all** will tell AOL that you want to read all your messages offline.

You can remove a group from the list on the right by highlighting it and either double-clicking, or using the **Remove** button, and **Remove All** will move all the groups back to the list on the left, leaving you with no groups to collect with Automatic AOL.

When you've selected which groups you want to read offline, click **OK**, or choose **Cancel** to abandon any changes you made to the screen.

When you're selecting groups to read offline, remember that AOL will download all the unread messages in the groups during an Automatic AOL session. That could result in a lot of messages to look at when you open your Personal Filing Cabinet. It's a good idea to read a newsgroup online for a while before you decide to collect it using Automatic AOL, so you know how many messages to expect.

Newsgroup Preferences

Before we look at adding new groups to the list that you want to read, it's worth looking at the newsgroup Preferences. You can use them to restrict which articles you see, which will make using newsgroups much easier.

There are two types of newsgroup Preferences in AOL, global Preferences and group Preferences. The global Preferences affect all the groups, while the group Preferences just affect each one individually. You could, for example, ignore all the messages over a certain length in all groups, but have an even smaller limit set in one particular one.

Clicking the **Set Preferences** button on the main Newsgroups screen will display the global Preferences, while clicking on **Preferences** when you're looking at a particular newsgroup will display the Preferences for that group.

Let's start by looking at the global newsgroup Preferences.

Global Newsgroup Preferences

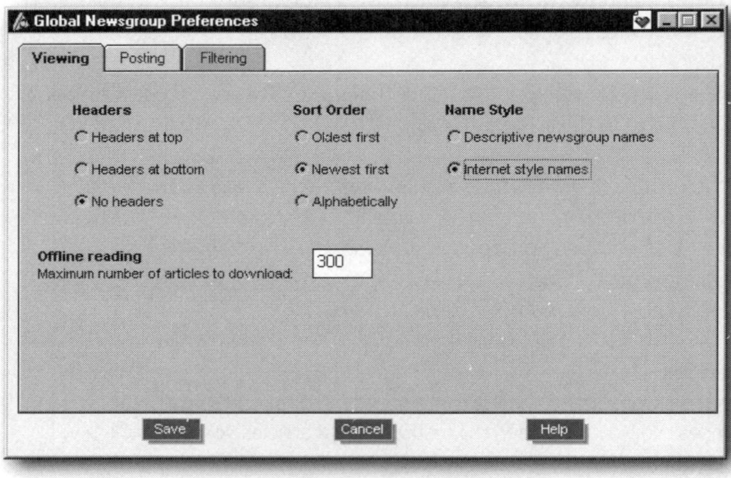

Fig. 6.35
**Global
Newsgroup
preferences**

As you can see, there are three tabs on the Preferences screen; **Viewing**, **Posting** and **Filtering**. The **Viewing** tab controls how newsgroup messages are displayed, **Posting** sets options for creating messages of your own, and **Filtering** is used to restrict which messages are shown in the list of subjects.

Viewing newsgroup messages
We'll start with the **Viewing** tab, which is the first one to appear when you enter the newsgroup Preferences. There are three sections to this tab – **Headers**, **Sort Order** and **Name Style**.

Under **Headers**, you can choose whether or not you want to see all the headers of a message. They're similar to the headers that you see on email received from the Internet, and show the path a message has taken to reach AOL, as well as other information about the poster and sometimes the Internet company they use.

You can choose to have headers displayed at the top or bottom of a message, or not displayed at all. Unless you really want to see them, it's probably best to select **No headers**.

Sort Order controls how the list of subjects appears. You can choose **Oldest first**, **Newest first**, or **Alphabetically**. Normally, AOL will display the newest messages first.

Name Style allows you to change the way the names of groups are listed. You can either see the Internet style names, like news.announce.newusers, when you click **Read My Newsgroups**, or you can see descriptive names instead. Although the descriptive names may be helpful when you're getting started, you'll soon get used to them. Remember that if you choose one type of name, you can see the others by using the button on the Read my newsgroups screen.

There's one final option on this screen, which is used when you collect newsgroups using Automatic AOL. In the box labelled Maximum number of messages to download, you can set how many will be collected. AOL will set the number to 300 when you install it, but if you read lots of newsgroups, you might want to set it to a larger figure.

Automatic AOL stops downloading newsgroup messages when it has collected the number that you specify here, but all your email will still be collected, and any messages waiting to be sent will be posted for you.

When you've changed all the settings you want to on this tab, click **Posting** to set Preferences for newsgroup messages that you write.

Posting to newsgroups

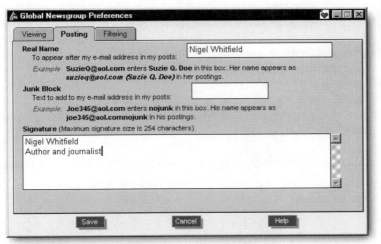

Fig. 6.36
Posting preferences

There are only three options on this panel, and they're very simple to set up. The first box is for your Real Name – or at least, the name you want to appear on your newsgroup postings.

Postings you make will have your email address on them already. You just need to type a name in here, so that instead of appearing from *SampleUser@aol.com*, your message will appear as *SampleUser@aol.com (Joe Bloggs)*.

> *Of course, you can use a false name, but if you want people to take your comments in newsgroups seriously, you should really use your real name, or your first name at least.*

The next box is labelled **Junk Block**. What's that about? Well, some people look through newsgroup postings, and 'harvest' all the email addresses, then send junk email to them. If you post to a newsgroup, it's likely you'll receive junk email, unless you use the Junk block feature.

When you type something into this box, usually a short word like nojunk or nospam, AOL will add it to the end of your email address. For example, if you type nospam, and your Screen Name is SampleUser@aol.com then the address will appear in newsgroup postings as SampleUser@aol.comnospam.

> *If you use the junk block, it's a good idea to make sure you include a signature on your postings, so that people can see your real address easily.*

The final box, **Signature**, is where you can type a short message that will appear on any newsgroup posting where you checked the Signature box before clicking Send. You can type up to 254 letters or numbers, and people typically include their real name, and things like a job title, or a witty phrase.

You shouldn't use your signature for overly commercial messages, like 'Bodgit Limited – the best builders in Bognor', and it's generally considered inappropriate to have a signature that's more than four lines long.

When you've written your signature, you can go on to look at the **Filtering** preferences.

Filtering newsgroup messages

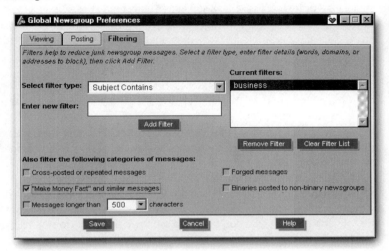

Fig. 6.37
**Filtering
preferences**

This tab controls which messages AOL shows you and which it doesn't. Why would you want to do that? Well, filtering means you can cut out messages from particular people, or ones that are very long, and so on.

By using filters well, you can make it much easier to handle newsgroup messages. After a while reading a newsgroup, you might decide, for example, that one contributor is just trying to start arguments all the time, so you could choose not to see messages from them anymore. Or in a group talking about cars, perhaps you'd like to filter out all the messages about Ford, because you drive a Vauxhall.

The Filter screen is very easy to use. The top section is where you can set up filters based on a number of criteria. The key thing to remember is that filters exclude messages. You can't, for example, set a filter that says 'only show me messages with the word platypus in the subject'.

There are four types of filter that you can select from the **Filter type** menu – **Subject is**; **Subject matches**; **Author is** and **Domain is**. When you've selected the type of filter, you need to type the text you want to use as a filter into the box **Enter new filter**.

Filtering messages by subject can be done in two ways: searching for a specific subject – Subject is – or for words within a subject – Subject matches. The first looks for an exact match, so you'll need to type the whole of the subject that you want to exclude, exactly as it appears on messages. For example, to block messages with the subject 'Why the Capri was a great car' you'd have to type exactly that into the box that says Enter new filter.

If you chose to filter by Subject matches, however, you could just type the word 'capri' and AOL would filter out both that subject, and any other that contained the word Capri.

To filter by author, type the email address of the person whose messages you don't want to see, for example bill.clinton@whitehouse.gov would filter out messages from people pretending to be Bill Clinton.

You might decide that you don't want to see any messages at all from a particular place, rather than an specific person. Maybe you've seen lots of adverts from different people at we-sell-junk.com and you don't want to see them anymore. To stop all their messages, you need to choose Domain is as the type of filter, and them just enter we-sell-junk.com as the filter text.

When you've entered the text for your filter, click the button labelled **Add Filter**, and you'll see the new filter appear in the box at the right.

> *Remember that filters you set up here will apply to all the newsgroups that you read. If you just want to filter out messages in a single newsgroup, use the Preferences for that newsgroup.*

If you decide that you don't want to filter out certain messages later, just highlight the filter in the box on the right of the screen, and then click the **Remove Filter** button. You can also remove all the filters in one go by clicking the **Clear Filter List** button.

The bottom section of the filters tab allows you to filter out messages based on other criteria. Just put a check in the box to tell AOL that you don't want to see certain types of posting.

Cross-posted messages are ones that have been sent to more than one newsgroup at the same time. Although messages are sometimes cross-posted for legitimate reasons, junk messages are also posted this way, so that the sender only has to post them once and they appear in lots of groups.

Make Money Fast was a message urging people to join a pyramid scheme, and it's still being sent round, trying to encourage gullible people to send money to strangers. Checking the box next to this option will filter out both the original and many similar scams.

> *AOL updates its message filters regularly, but sometimes it's not possible to filter out every single message, especially if it's a new one. You may still see some messages offering you ways to get rich quick, even if you select this option. You should never respond to such offers.*

Forged messages are messages that someone has posted using a different person's email address, so that they appear to be from, for example, the President of the USA. AOL will hide these messages from you if you check the **Forged messages** box.

Binaries posted to non-binary newsgroups controls whether or not you see newsgroup postings that have files attached to them. Posting files to newsgroups is very inefficient, and wasteful of computer resources. So that people don't have to see them unless they want to, files are supposed to be posted to groups specifically for that purpose – after all, you don't want to run AOL and find that it's taking hours to download messages, because someone's posted a large picture of themselves. Choose this option, and AOL will filter out any messages with files that have been posted to a group that's not designated as suitable for them.

The final option on the screen, **Messages longer than**, allows you to tell AOL that you're not interested in messages that are bigger than a certain size. After checking the option, click the arrow on the box to the right, and select one of the sizes from the list.

Remember that this setting applies to all the newsgroups that you read, so if you set it very low, you may not see many messages at all.

When you've made all your choices, click the **Save** button and AOL will remember your newsgroup Preferences. Click **Cancel** if you don't want to save any changes that you've made.

Individual newsgroup Preferences

As well as Preferences that affect all the newsgroups you read, AOL lets you set Preferences for each newsgroup individually. You can change the Preferences for a particular group by clicking on it in the **Read My Newsgroups** screen and then clicking the **Preferences** button, or using the **Preferences** button that you'll see at the bottom of the list of subjects when you're reading a group.

Fig. 6.38
**Newsgroup
preferences**

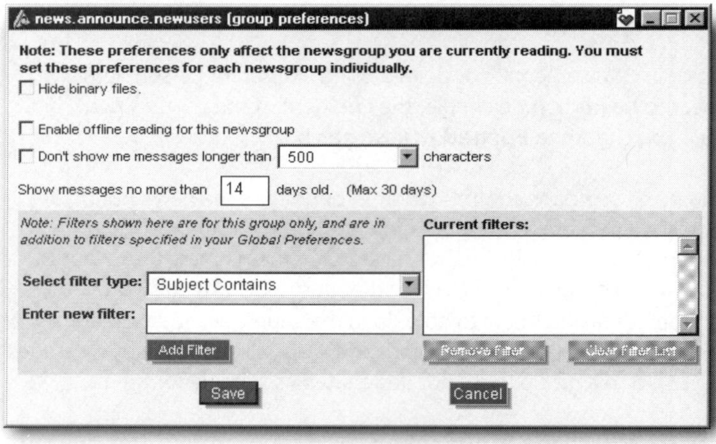

This is the Preferences screen for an individual group; you'll see the name of the group in the title bar so that you can be sure you're setting Preferences for the right one.

The first item on the Preferences screen, **Hide binary files**, allows you to tell AOL that you don't want to see any messages in this newsgroup that have files attached to them. Remember that you can also set a global preference to hide files in all the newsgroups that aren't specifically meant to contain them.

Next, **Enable offline reading for this newsgroup** is another way to tell AOL that you want this group to be available when you collect newsgroup messages using Automatic AOL. Changing this option will update the list of offline newsgroups that's displayed when you click **Read offline** on the main newsgroups screen.

The next option lets you set the maximum size of messages that you want to see in this particular group. To enable this option, click to put a check in the box, and then choose the maximum size from the list, by clicking the arrow at the right of the box.

You can tell AOL the maximum age of the messages you want to see in a group using the next option. Click in the box and type the number of days. Even if you haven't read them, you won't see any messages older than this when you visit a newsgroup. If you've been away from a busy newsgroup for a while, it's often a good idea to change this setting, so that you don't have so many messages to read through.

Finally, the bottom section of this screen allows you to set up filters, just like on the **Global Newsgroup Preferences** screen. You can choose from the same four types of filter, but this time they'll only apply to the messages in one group.

When you're changed the settings, click **Save**, or **Cancel** if you don't want to keep any changes you've made.

Adding newsgroups

Now that you know how to read and post to newsgroups, and set the Preferences, let's look at how you can add new newsgroups to your list.

There are three ways of adding a newsgroup. You can browse through all the groups, add a group directly, if you know its name, or search the list to find a group with a particular word in its title.

If you're just starting out with newsgroups, the simplest way to find them is probably to browse through the list, using the **Add Newsgroups** button – but be warned, there are tens of thousands of groups.

Using the Add newsgroups button
To start with, you're probably best off looking at the groups in the main hierarchies that
we mentioned at the start of this section. Click on **Add Newsgroups** and you'll see a
screen like this.

Fig. 6.39
**Add
Newsgroups
screen**

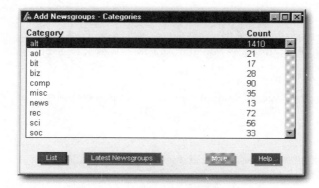

As you can see, there's a list of the hierarchies of newsgroups, and the number of groups
within each one. Click the **List** button at the bottom of the screen to see the groups in a
particular area, or choose **Latest Newsgroups** to see if there have been any new groups
added since your last visit.

When you choose one of the hierarchies of newsgroups, you'll see a list like this one, which is
for groups beginning with rec – recreational topics.

Fig. 6.40
Rec categories

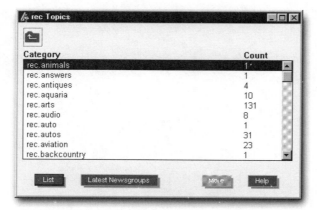

As you can see, this screen is similar to the last. You can click the **Folder** icon in the top left to go back up to the previous screen, or look through the list until you find a category that looks interesting. Just double-click on it and you can see the list of groups.

Depending on what set of groups you're looking at, you might not see the previous screen – if there aren't lots of categories within a hierarchy, AOL will show you the list of groups right away instead.

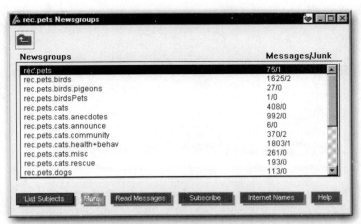

Fig. 6.41
**Group list
rec.pets**

Here we've chosen groups starting with rec.pets, and as you can see there are quite a few of them. The list shows how many messages are in each of the groups, and how many of them are junk.

If you'd like to add one of the groups to the list that appears when you click on **Read My Newsgroups**, highlight it and click the **Subscribe** button.

Of course, sometimes you might not be sure whether or not you want to subscribe to a newsgroup, so instead of using the **Subscribe** button, you can click on a group and then click the **List subjects** button. The screen that appears next looks just like when you're reading a group you've already subscribed to – you can click on a subject to read the messages in that thread, and move through it in the normal way. The only difference is that there's a **Subscribe** button, so you can add the group to your list easily.

You can also read the messages in a group without looking at the list of subjects, by choosing the **Read messages** button. AOL will display the first message in the first thread of the group, and you can move around the messages just as if you were subscribed.

Finally, if you need a little guidance on what the names of all the newsgroups mean, click the **Internet names** button to see their descriptions.

After you click the **Subscribe** button, the Preferences screen for the newsgroup you're adding will appear, so that you can set any options you'd like for it. After you've made the changes you want, just click the **Save** button.

Using the Expert add button
If you already know the name of the group that you want to subscribe to, this is the button to use.

Fig. 6.42
Expert Add screen

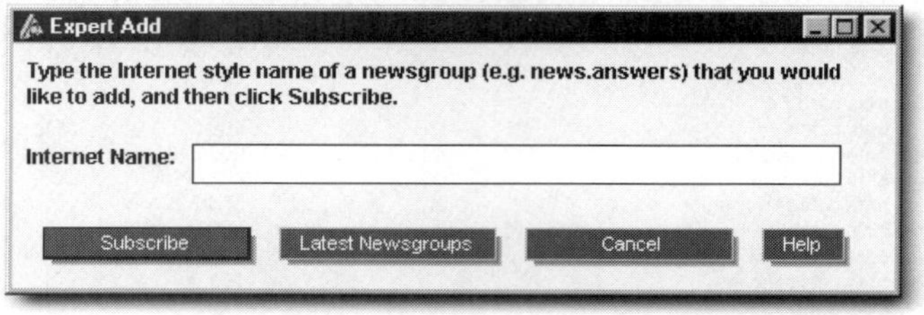

This is the box that appears when you click the **Expert add** button. As you can see, there's also a button here that you can use to list the latest newsgroups if you like. It works just the same as the one on the Add newsgroups screen.

Normally though, you'll just type the name of the group you want, and press the Enter key, or click **Subscribe**.

When you do, the Preferences screen for that group will appear, and you can set any options you'd like for reading it, then click on **Save**.

Searching newsgroups
As you've already realised, browsing through the list of newsgroups to find ones that you want to read could take hours – or more likely days. So if you don't know the name of the group you want, and you don't want to wade through the list, then you'll probably need to use the Search facility.

All you have to do is click the **Search All Newsgroups** button on the main Newsgroups screen.

Fig. 6.43
**Search
Newsgroup
Titles**

This box will appear, and you can type a word into it, which AOL will look for in the title of the newsgroup. AOL will display up to 150 newsgroup titles that contain the letters that you were looking for.

It's a very simple search – for example, if you type in mac, then you'll receive information about groups like comp.sys.mac, or alt.clothes.macintosh, if it existed.

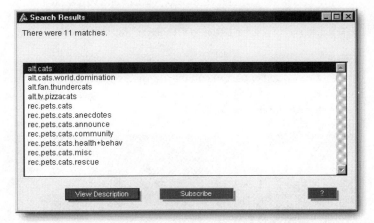

Fig. 6.44
Search Results

When the list of results appears, you can double-click on a group that looks like it might be interesting to see the description, if there's one available. If you like the look of it, just click the **Subscribe** button. Once again, the Preferences for that group will be displayed, so you can create any filters you like, then click the **Save** button.

Whichever way you add groups, they'll all appear in your newsgroups list, when you click **Read My Newsgroups**. Don't forget that if you want to find out how to read newsgroup messages after you've disconnected from AOL, you'll find all the details in *Chapter 5, AOL and You* (*5.5, Personal Filing Cabinet*).

6.5 AOL and other Internet tools

The Internet, of course, is much more than just Web pages, file downloads and newsgroups. There are chat areas, a little like the AOL chat rooms, Instant Messages, using AOL's Instant Messenger service, and services designed to let you listen to radio broadcasts via the Internet, so you'll never miss your local station again.

And did you know you can access all of this via AOL? When you dial into AOL's service, you can run any program that would normally connect to the Internet, and it will connect via AOL's network.

What programs are there?

There are programs you can download from the Internet that will do just about anything you'd like, from accurately setting your clock, to allowing you to share music files on your computer with other people, or even having a phone conversation via the computer. There are so many that we really can't even begin to list them here.

IRC

Another very popular pastime on the Internet is chatting, just as it is on IRC. There are Web sites where you can use chat rooms that look very similar to AOL's, but the most popular chat system is IRC – Internet Relay Chat.

Fig. 6.45
IRC keyword screen

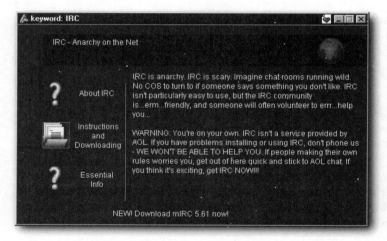

IRC is divided into channels, which are a little like AOL's chat rooms, except that there's no central control, and no Guides to keep everything in order. As well as chatting, you can send files to people via IRC, and carry on talking to them while the files are being transmitted, which makes it very popular with people who want to make new friends.

> *Because there's no central control of IRC, there is a greater danger of viruses and other unsuitable files being transmitted. If you decide to use IRC, you should never accept a file from a stranger without asking what it is, and you must make sure your computer has up-to-date anti-virus software installed.*

Just like with FTP, there are lots of programs that you can use to connect to IRC. You'll find some of them, along with instructions for how to get started, on AOL at the keyword **IRC**.

Email
Email is, of course, one of the most popular things on the Internet. You can find free email addresses on a number of Web sites – but remember that rather than use one of those, you can access your AOL email via the Web too. That means you can check your messages wherever you can access the Internet via aol.co.uk.

One question that's often asked is whether or not you can use other Internet email programs with AOL.

The answer depends what you really mean by the question. If you want to install an Internet email program to collect messages from, for example, the computer where you work, then it will work happily via your AOL connection.

However, you cannot use a standard email program to collect messages from your AOL mailbox or to send messages via AOL's servers. If you want to read your AOL messages, you need to use either AOL, or AOL on aol.co.uk.

You can read more about accessing your AOL messages via the Web in *Chapter 8, AOL Anywhere (*8.1, AOLmail*)*.

Making sure Internet programs work with AOL
Although most Internet programs should work with AOL right away, if you have another Internet connection installed on your computer, you may find that when you start one of your Internet programs, it says that it can't connect.

If that happens, you should check the Preferences of the program to make sure that it's not asking your computer to connect using a specific connection. Usually, it's best to start AOL and sign on before you start any other programs that want to use an Internet connection.

If you still have problems, then you should use the **Association** button in AOL's Preferences to tell your computer that all your Internet connections should use AOL.

Using the **Association** button may prevent other Internet connections that you have installed from working correctly afterwards.

You can find out more about the Preferences in *Chapter 5, AOL and You* (*5.4, Preferences*).

And that's all we have to say about the Internet. By connecting to AOL, you've become a part of one of the biggest communities ever created, and you can find programs both on AOL and the rest of the Internet to help you do things that you never imagined. So sit back and browse around. Just remember – the Internet is a big place. Be careful out there.

7

Advanced AOL

ADVANCED
HOME PAGES

USING AOL FROM
ANOTHER COMPUTER

So far, we've covered the main features of AOL, including some pretty tricky stuff, but nevertheless, it's all things that you'll find useful from day to day.

In this chapter, we're looking at some aspects of AOL that aren't quite such everyday tools, so if you're new to the service, or just not feeling quite up to it yet, don't worry. You can always come back to this chapter later, or you could even skip it altogether.

So what's in here? Well, in this chapter you'll find out how you can use any program that you like to create a truly fabulous home page on AOL, and for the travellers amongst you, we'll show you how to use AOL when you're away from home.

What more could you want?

7.1 Advanced home page building

Everyone dreams about having a home of their own, the Internet is no exception to that rule. If you don't have a home page, you'll probably be in the minority. As we've seen, home pages can be used for all sorts of reasons, and with AOL you have plenty of space to create your own Web site that everyone can look at.

Earlier on in this book, we looked at AOL's 1-2-3 Publish system, which makes it easy to create Web pages, even if you've never done it before (*5.6, 1-2-3 Publish*).

Of course, while 1-2-3 Publish is great if you just want to take your first steps on the Net, for some people it just isn't powerful enough. With 1-2-3 Publish, you're really just filling in the blanks on a Web page that AOL has already designed, and if you want to do something that doesn't fit, then you'll have to use a different approach.

That's no problem – you can use any tool you like to create Web pages on AOL, not just 1-2-3 Publish. There are hundreds of different programs to create Web pages, and you might already have one on your computer. Programs like Adobe's PageMill and Microsoft FrontPage Express are good for people who are starting out with Web pages, while there are also much more powerful programs, such as Macromedia DreamWeaver or NetObjects Fusion. You can even create simple Web pages with some word processor programs!

Whatever program you want to use, in this chapter we'll show you how you can upload your pages to AOL's Web servers so that they can be seen by anyone who wants to visit your site.

What we won't be doing in this chapter is giving you a tutorial in creating the pages themselves. There are so many programs, and so many different things you can do with Web pages, that we'd need a whole separate book to do that.

Resources for Web builders on AOL

AOL has plenty of information for people who want to create their own Web pages. You can find it all by choosing **My Web page** from the Internet menu, or visiting the keyword **Web Building**.

Fig. 7.1
Web Building screen

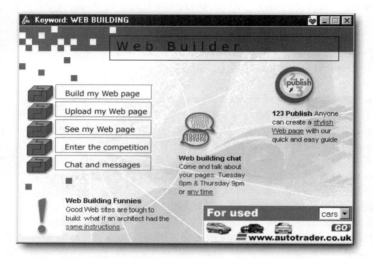

This is the Web Building screen, where you can find out all the information that you need for creating your Web pages, including tips on building the page, how to upload it and forums where you can ask for help if you're stuck.

Before we look a bit closer, let's explain exactly what you get from AOL in terms of Web space.

There's plenty of space for you to publish your pages. It might not sound like a lot if you're used to a computer that has a disk measured in Gigabytes, but in fact, Web pages don't take up much space at all. You could fit hundreds of pages into your space – but remember that the space has to include all the pictures and sounds you put on your pages too.

Your own space is divided up by AOL into chunks, for each of seven Screen Names. Of course, that doesn't mean that the largest site you can create is 5Mb; you could always upload files using one Screen Name and refer to them on the Web site of another.

You can also use your space for FTP too, so you could have files in it for people to download, like reports that you want to share with colleagues, or perhaps a piece of music you've written that people might want to fetch.

AOL also provides a program to help you design your Web pages, called AOL Press. You can download a copy of it from the keyword **AOL Press**, where you'll also find help and advice about using it.

> *Although you can download AOL Press, it's not officially supported by AOL anymore, since there are so many other programs that people can use to create their pages. We recommend that you use one of the programs we mentioned earlier, but if you can't find one, you can use AOL Press free of charge.*

OK, now you know what space you have to play with for your Web pages, let's take a look at what you'll find in the Web building area of AOL.

Down the left-hand side of the screen, you'll see the main function of AOL's Web building area. The top button, **Build my Web page**, will take you to an area where you can find tips and information about the techniques you can use on your Web site, whether you're a complete beginner, or an expert wanting to find more information about Java and ActiveX.

The next button, **Upload my Web page**, is the one to use when you want to copy the files that make up your Web site from your computer to AOL's servers.

Click on **See my Web page**, and AOL will open your Web page in a new window, with extra buttons to take you to helpful areas in the Web building section.

Finally, you'll see there's a competition for members' Web pages, and a **Chat and Messages** button, where you can talk with other AOL members for help, advice and inspiration.

Building your Web page

The Build my Web page section on AOL is packed with information, including details of some of the most powerful tools and techniques for creating your Web pages.

Fig. 7.2
Build my Web page

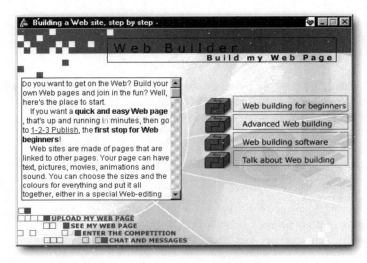

You can choose from information for beginners or advanced users. In the Beginners' section, for example, you'll find tools like 1-2-3 Publish, and a basic introduction to HTML, the Web writing language, while the Advanced section covers the latest Web technologies.

If you know what you want to do with your Web site, one of the main questions you'll probably have is 'What can I do with AOL?'

The good news is that, as long as you don't break the Conditions of Service, you can do anything you like with your AOL Web space. You can use Java, ActiveX and even add Virtual Reality to your Web pages.

There are some things that you can't do with your pages, since to allow them could potentially cause problems for other AOL members. You can't, for example, write your own Web programs (called CGI scripts) to run on AOL's servers.

Instead, AOL provides a selection of scripts for you, which allows you to include features such as email forms, counters and guestbooks on your pages. You can find out the details of how to use these on the Web page at **hometown.aol.com/wwwadmin**.

AOL doesn't support the Microsoft FrontPage Extensions, so if you're using FrontPage to create your Web site, you'll have to remember not to use the Microsoft-only facilities, otherwise parts of your Web site may not work when it's uploaded.

Uploading your Web site

However you choose to build your Web site, you'll have to upload it to AOL before anyone else will be able to see it.

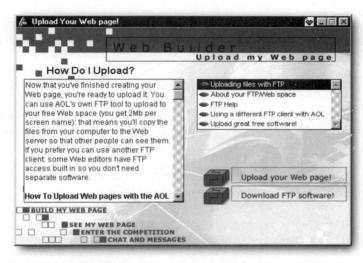

Fig. 7.3
Upload your Web page

When you click the **Upload your Web page** button on the Web building screen, this is what you'll see. To upload your page using the AOL FTP tool, click **Upload your Web page**.

You can also reach this screen by clicking **Go to your free Web space** on the **FTP** screen. As you can see, uploading your Web page is done just like uploading any other file. If you skipped it earlier, now's the time to read about using FTP in *Chapter 6, The Internet* (*6.3, Uploading files with FTP*).

While using the AOL FTP tool may be ok for a small Web site, if you've created a complicated one with lots of files, you'll probably find that it's not very convenient to upload if that way.

Some Web design programs include an FTP uploader, and you might find that's more useful to use – especially since it may allow you to automatically transfer just the pages of your site that have changed since the last time you uploaded it.

You can use any FTP program you like to upload your Web pages to AOL. You need to be connected to AOL and your FTP program should be using your AOL connection, not any other connection to the Internet that you may have on your computer.

If you're not signed on to AOL with the appropriate Screen Name and password, you won't be able to upload files to your Web site. You cannot upload files to your Web site by connecting to the AOL FTP server using a different Internet connection.

FTP programs typically ask for several pieces of information – a site name, a login name, a password, and a directory that you want to access. If the Web design program you're using includes an FTP facility, it too will want the same information.

The site that you need to tell your FTP program to upload to is members.aol.com.

For the login name, don't use your Screen Name. You should use the name ftp, and give your full Internet email address as the password. For example, if your Screen Name is JoeBloggs, then the password you should use is JoeBloggs@aol.com.

Leave the directory, if your program asks for one, blank. When you connect, you'll automatically be in the appropriate place to upload your files.

After they've been uploaded, you can visit your site using the address http:// members.aol.com/screenname, for example http://members.aol.com/JoeBloggs.

That's all there is to it! Now you know how to upload files to your Web space using the program of your choice, it's up to you to design a Web site that stands out from the rest on the Net.

7.2 Using your AOL account from another computer

Sometimes you might want to access your AOL account when you're away from home, perhaps visiting a friend. If they also use AOL, then you're in luck – you can access your own AOL account as a guest, and read your email, using their computer.

AOL has made it easy for anyone to connect from a computer with the AOL software on it. When you start the AOL program, you'll see the usual sign-on box, listing all the Screen Names installed on that computer.

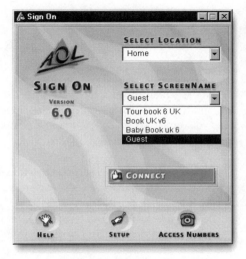

Fig. 7.4
Guest selection

Click on the arrow to the right of the names to see the whole list, and right at the bottom you'll see the name Guest.

That's a special name that you can use to connect to AOL with your own Screen Name and password. Select it from the list, and just like when you've saved your own password, the Password box will disappear.

Now you just need to click the **Connect** button and the computer you're using will dial into the AOL service. When the connection has been made, the Guest sign-on screen will appear.

Fig. 7.5
Guest Sign-On

Guest Sign-On:

Enter Screen Name:

Enter Password:

Use The Tab key to move between input fields.

OK   Cancel

When this screen appears, type your own Screen Name in the top box, then press the tab key and type in your password. You'll be signed on to AOL in the normal way, so you can read your email, access chat rooms and do just about everything else you could when you're using your own computer.

There are some things that you can't do when you're signed on as Guest. For example, since your Personal Filing Cabinet is stored on your own computer's hard disk, it's not available when you connect in this way. If you want to be sure that messages will still be available for you to read when you return home, you should use the Keep as new button to ensure that they're not deleted from the Read mail list.

Don't worry if the computer you're sitting in front of doesn't have AOL software on it. Although you can't access any AOL content, you can still read your email, without having to install any more software on the computer. You need to use AOL's AOLMail service on aol.co.uk, which lets you read your messages from any computer that has a connection to the Internet and a Web browser. You can read more about this, and other ways of accessing AOL when you're away from home in *Chapter 8, AOL Anywhere (8.1, AOLMail)*.

Travelling with your computer
Although AOL in the UK provides a single phone number that you can use for the same cost from everywhere, if you have a portable computer, you might end up further afield.

While travelling in the UK is a simple matter of plugging your computer into the nearest phone socket, it's a little more complicated – but not much. So let's see how you can set up your computer to connect to AOL without any trouble, no matter where you are.

You might even need to do this if you never go abroad. For example, in some offices, you have to dial 9 to access an outside telephone line, while at home it's not necessary.

AOL takes care of simple changes like that, or completely different phone numbers, by using something called Locations. When you created your AOL account, a default location will have been set up for you, called Home. You'll see this on the Sign-on screen, above the list of Screen Names. You can click the arrow to the right of the location name to see the list of locations that have been set up – usually there won't be any more to start with.

A location is just a handy way of referring to settings like the phone number AOL has to dial, whether or not a special number is needed to get access to an outside phone line, and any commands that your modem needs to dial from that location. Once you've set them up, you don't need to change anything more. All you do is select the location you're in from the list, and then AOL will connect without asking you any awkward questions.

Creating a new location

So, let's assume that you want to use your computer in the office as well as at home, and in your office you need to dial a 9 before any outside numbers. From the **Sign-on** screen, which you see each time you sign on, just click the button marked **Setup**, which is at the bottom, below the large Connect button.

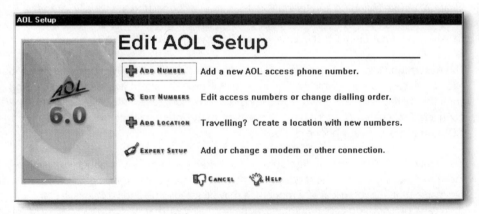

Fig. 7.6
Setup screen

The first stage is to click the button labelled **Add location**. The other buttons allow you to add a new number, or manually change them. You can use those later to change the options for a particular location. For now, we'll move on and show you how to create a new one from scratch, so click the **Add location** button.

Fig. 7.7
Add location

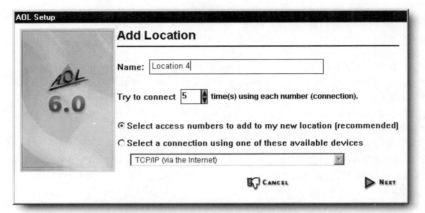

This is the first screen you see when you add a new location. The first box is where you can give the location a name, which will appear in the list on the Sign-on screen. Try to make sure it's meaningful – there's no point having 'location 1', 'location 2' and so on if you can't remember which one is which. For your office, type Office. You might have entries for, for example, Paris or Brussels Hotel if you travel a lot.

Next you can choose how many times AOL will try to dial each of the numbers for this location, before giving up and telling you it can't get a connection. It's usually set to five, which will work most of the time. In fact, usually AOL will get through first time, but it's as well to ask for a few attempts, just in case you get a busy signal somewhere.

The next option lets you choose how to connect. You should normally choose the first option, to select access numbers which your computer will dial. The alternative is to connect using something other than a modem. You'd choose that option, for example, if your computer is connected to a network which has a connection to the Internet. That way, you could link to AOL without paying any phone charges.

If you have more than one modem on your computer, you can use this option to create a location that uses a particular modem. For instance, if you have a mobile phone with software or a cable that lets you use it as a modem, it may be listed here, and you can select it, then carry on choosing access numbers in the normal way. That way, you can have a special location that will use your mobile phone instead of your normal modem.

Connecting to AOL via the Internet will depend on how the network your computer is plugged in to works, and what security software the network has on it. Unless you're an advanced user, you don't need to worry about this option. Choose to select access numbers instead.

Now, click the **Next** button to carry on setting up your location. AOL will ask you which country you want to search for access numbers in. You can click on the list to choose one of the countries around the world where AOL can be accessed.

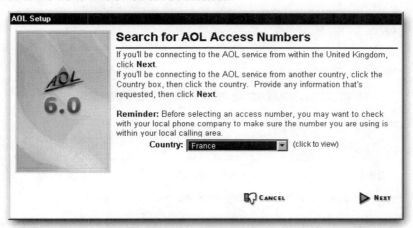

Fig. 7.8
Select country

Although the numbers that will be found should be a local call, you should check to make sure. In particular, some hotels might charge extra fees, even for calling numbers that are supposed to be free, and if you're connecting via a mobile phone linked to your computer, you may incur other charges too.

When you've chosen the country, click the **Next** button to continue, and AOL will display a list of phone numbers for that country, so that you can choose which ones you want to use.

Fig. 7.9
Select numbers

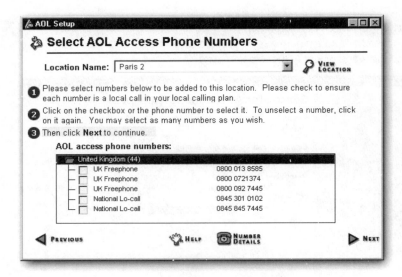

You can choose as many of the numbers as you like, and AOL will try to connect using all the ones that you've chosen. Just click on a number and a red tick will appear next to it. Click again if you decide that you don't want to use it.

Depending on the numbers you've chosen, you may be charged by AOL as well as by the phone company for the call that your computer makes. To find out details about a particular number, click on it with the mouse and then click the button marked **Number Details**, which is at the bottom of the page.

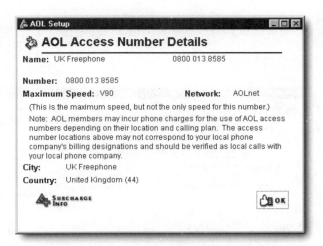

Fig. 7.10
Number details

The Number details screen tells you what speed the number will let you connect at. Most of the numbers for AOL will let you use the V90 speed, which is the top speed of most modern modems. In some countries, however, the maximum speed might be lower, and this screen will tell you. If you're expecting to receive lots of large messages, or you want to spend a long time online, it's probably a good idea to avoid any numbers that aren't capable of supporting the fastest speeds.

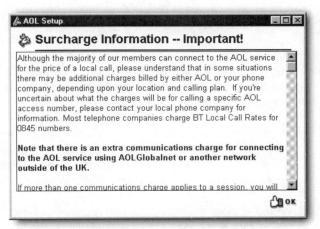

Fig. 7.11
Surcharge information screen

Some numbers, especially when you're using AOL from overseas, will attract a surcharge, which will appear on your AOL bill. That's because although you may be dialling a local number in, for example, France, the information to and from your computer still has to reach AOL UK. You can find out about surcharges by clicking the **Surcharge Info** button.

When you've finished choosing the numbers that you want, and you're sure that you understand how much it will cost you to call each one, click the button marked **Next**, to move on to the next screen.

Fig. 7.12
Confirm numbers

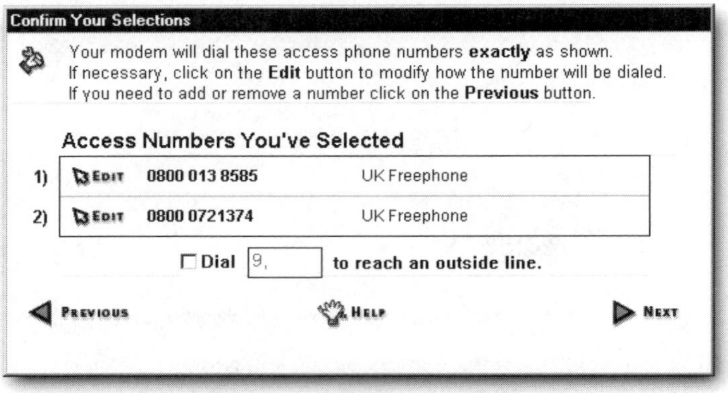

The screen shows the numbers that you've chosen, and a brief description of them. At the bottom of the list, you'll see a check box next to the word Dial, and a box with a number 9.

If the location that you're creating requires a specific code to access an outside telephone line, click to put a check next to Dial, and enter the code in the box if it's not 9.

You can also change some of the numbers if you like, by clicking the **Edit** button.

Although most people in the UK won't need this screen, it might come in handy. You can use the two options to make sure that the number that's listed at the top, which is exactly what your modem will dial, is correct.

You might, for example, want to use the first option if you have a smart dialler box that saves you money on long distance calls. Depending on the phone company, it might be cheaper to send your AOL calls via BT instead. If your smart dialler had a code, like 121, to tell it to use BT instead of another phone company, you could enter it here.

When you've made any changes to the number, click **Next** to continue. If you've been editing a number, click **Next** again from the list of numbers to move on to the next screen.

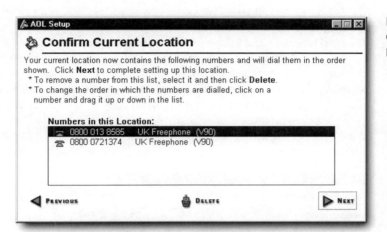

Fig. 7.13
Confirm Current Location

Here you can see all the numbers that AOL will try to use when you connect, listed in no particular order. You might decide that you want to change the order, for example to try numbers that cost less to dial first, or perhaps if you're not paying the phone bill, it's more important to you that numbers with no surcharge are tried first.

To move a number up and down the list, just click on it with the mouse, and hold the mouse button down as you drag the number up or down. When you have the numbers in the right order, click the **Next** button.

You're done! You should be back at the main AOL Sign-on screen now, and you can choose your new location from the menu before connecting.

Adding and editing numbers

The **Add Number** and **Edit Number** buttons on the Setup screen let you change the current location. If you simply want to add another number to the current location, perhaps because you keep getting an engaged signal from one you're using, just click on **Add Number** and you'll be shown the same list as you were when you created your location, so you can follow the instructions on the previous pages.

When you click the **Edit** button you'll see a screen like this one. It's similar to one of the screens that you saw when you were creating your location, but with a few more options.

Fig. 7.14
Edit numbers

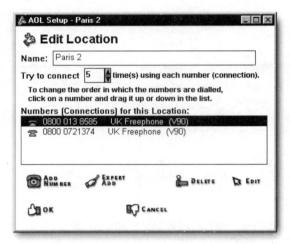

Just like when you were creating a location, you can click on the numbers here and drag them up and down to change the order in which they're dialled. You can also change the name of the location if you like, by clicking in the box at the top of the page.

Below the location name you can change the number of times each number will be dialled, and underneath the list of numbers you'll see buttons for Add number, Expert add, Edit and Delete.

The **Delete** button removes a number from the list for this location, and the **Add** numbers button works the same as the one on the main Setup screen.

If you click either **Expert Add** or **Edit**, you'll see the same screen. The only difference is that when you use **Add**, there'll be no number filled in for you. This screen is part of the Expert settings, so we'll cover it along with the Expert Setup function.

Most users won't need to use this screen, or the Expert Setup button on the main Setup screen. You can safely skip this section.

The Expert settings

The Expert settings are just that – meant for experts. If you don't feel confident with them, then you should leave them alone. The **Add Location** button will usually do everything that you need.

If you do want to look at your settings in detail, click the **Expert Setup** button and you'll see a screen that looks something like this:

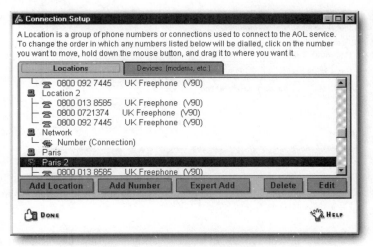

Fig. 7.15
Expert setup – locations

At the top of the page, there are two tabs, labelled **Locations** and **Devices**. When you have **Locations** selected, you'll see a list of all the locations that have been created, showing the phone numbers for each one.

Expert location Setup

If you want to remove a phone number from a location, just click on it, and then click the **Delete** button. If you highlight a location instead, you can delete it, along with all the phone numbers for it.

To add a phone number to a location, click either on the name of the location, or on one of the numbers that's already been added to it, and then click the **Add** button at the bottom of the page. The screen that you saw earlier will appear, so that you can select a country, and then choose the numbers to add, just like using the **Add Numbers** button on the main **Setup** screen.

Choosing the **Add Location** button works in the same way as the button on the Setup screen.

Ok, so far, none of it looks too expert, does it? The next two buttons bring up a rather more complicated screen. Both **Expert Add** and **Edit** take you to a page that looks like this:

Fig. 7.16
Expert add screen

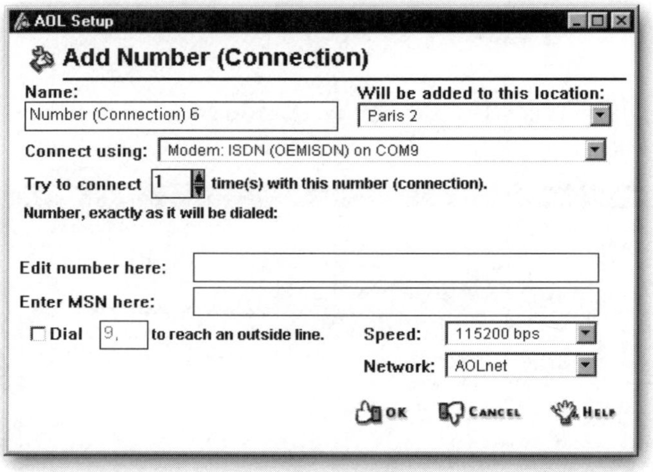

The first box lets you give a name or description to the number. If you're editing a number, some of the information will be filled in for you already. If you're adding a new one, most of the boxes will be blank.

Next to the description is a list of the locations that have been created. If you want to add a new number to a new location, just choose **New location** from the list, otherwise check that the location is set correctly.

Below is a list of all the devices – that's computer jargon for things like modems, mobile phone connections, and so on – that can be used to connect to AOL. Most people will just have the one modem, but if you have more, then make sure that you've chosen the right one from the list.

Underneath, you can say how many times you want the AOL program to try connecting to this number. It's normally set to 1, but if you don't have many numbers in the location you're editing, you might want to increase it.

Now, it's time to enter the phone number. You should enter it exactly as you want it to be dialled, including any special prefixes for accessing a particular phone company, for example.

The check box next to Dial is where you can select whether or not you need to dial a code to access an outside line, from an office, for example. If you do, click to put a check and make sure the right code is entered in the box.

The speed should be set to the fastest possible, usually 115200. Below the speed is a setting labelled Network. You shouldn't change this setting, or the speed, unless you're told to do so by AOL's Technical Support team.

Expert Devices Setup
On the Expert Setup screen, clicking the **Devices** tab produces a display like this, which shows the different ways that the AOL software can connect to AOL using your computer.

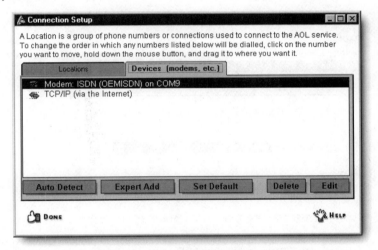

Fig. 7.17
Expert devices

Usually, all the devices that can be used will have been automatically detected by AOL when you installed the software, but if you add an extra modem, or want to fine-tune the settings, you might need to use this screen.

The best way to use this screen is by clicking the **Auto Detect** button. That will make AOL search your computer for ways to connect, and if you've added a new modem, for example, it'll be found and installed for you.

If there's more than one way that you can connect, you'll be given a list, and you can choose the one that's most appropriate, for example, you may want to use your normal modem most of the time, even though AOL may have detected you have a special card for connecting via your mobile phone.

The **Set Default** button lets you choose which of the devices will be used unless you choose a different one for a particular location. Choose your normal modem, and click the **Default** button. You'll be asked if you want all your connections to use that modem. Click **Yes**, and all the locations that were using the old modem will be updated to use the new one.

The **Delete** button, as you'd expect, removes a device from the list, so that you can't use it to connect to AOL anymore. AOL will automatically update other numbers to use a difference device to connect, if it can.

Be careful when you delete a device – it may have unexpected effects on some of your connections, especially if you don't have another way of connecting to AOL.

When you click the **Expert Add** button, you'll be asked what type of device you want to add.

Fig. 7.18
Expert add device

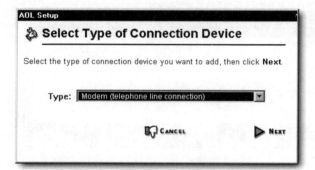

You can choose to add a modem, or an Internet connection. Unless your computer is connected to a network, for example in an office, that already has a link to the Internet, you'll need to choose to add a modem.

Connecting via the Internet may save you call charges, but it's up to you to make sure that the network connection on your computer is configured correctly. AOL's Technical Support people can only help you with the connection to AOL itself, not with making your network work.

After choosing to add a modem, click the **Next** button and this screen will be displayed. Scroll through the list to find your modem – it may take a while, since AOL works with a lot of modems – and click to select it.

Underneath the list of modems, you can select the port that it's connected to. If it's an external modem, the connectors on the back of your computer will be labelled, while for an internal one, you probably had to set it up when you installed it. Choose the right option, and then choose whether or not you want the modem's speaker on, and the connection speed.

The connection speed is not the speed of your connection to AOL. It's the speed that your modem talks to the rest of your computer, and you should set it as high as possible – usually 115200 bps. Modems use clever tricks to move data quickly, and if you set the speed lower than this, you may not get the most from your modem. However, if you do experience problems, you might try decreasing the speed, which may improve reliability on bad phone lines.

When you've selected your modem, just click **OK** to save your choices.

If you really are an expert, you can use the Edit commands button to control the commands that are sent to the modem by AOL to make it do things like hang up the phone or reset it.

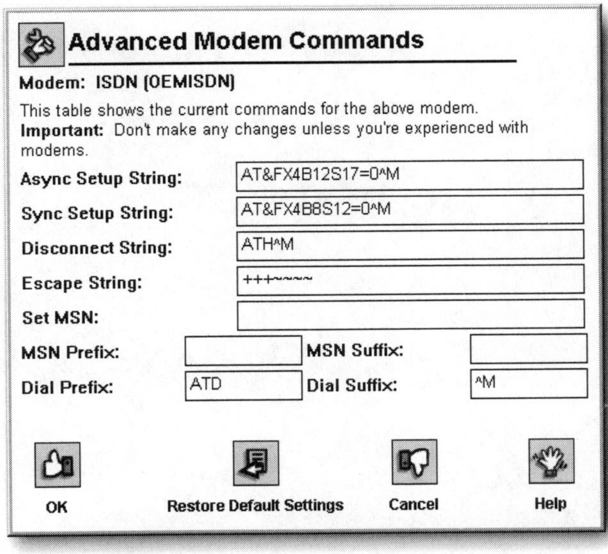

Fig. 7.19
Edit commands screen

You can fill in the information you need on this screen, but you'll probably also need to refer to the handbook that came with your modem. If you accidentally make changes, you can use the **Restore Default Settings** button to reset the commands to the ones that AOL thinks are right for the modem.

Don't adjust the commands unless you know what you're doing, or you're following the instructions of AOL Technical Support. Making incorrect changes could stop your computer from being able to access the AOL service.

The **Edit** button on the devices panel takes you to the same screen, where you can edit the information for a modem, or use the Edit commands button to change the commands that are sent to it.

A word about AOL Anywhere

Now you know how to set up your computer to access AOL from wherever you are – but sometimes you'll be elsewhere, away from your own computer or from one that has the AOL programs installed on it.

AOL Anywhere is the name for a whole range of services that help to make sure you can access key AOL sevices from wherever you are, even if you're not near a PC.

You can read more about AOL Anywhere in *Chapter 8*.

8

AOL Anywhere

AOLMAIL

AIM

AOL FOR PALM

AOL MOBILE

AOL Anywhere is AOL's name for a whole range of services that help to make sure you can make the most of your account, even if you are not near a PC.

Once again, if you're a new user, you might want to come back to this later, but please don't skip this chapter completely. If you do, you'll miss out on information about how you can access your email messages from cybercafés around the world, or keep up to date with your Buddies via Instant Messages and chat from any computer on the Internet.

And, like we said, you don't even need access to an ordinary computer. We'll show you how you can still keep up with things using just a handheld organiser like the 3Com Palm III or a mobile phone.

AOL Anywhere really does mean just that. If you never want to lose touch, this chapter will make sure you stay in the picture. Watch out for new services from AOL Anywhere, too, which may allow you to access AOL via a television set and in all sorts of other exciting ways in future.

8.1 AOLMail

When you've been using AOL for a while, you'll probably realise that email is one of the indispensable tools of modern life. In fact, you might even start to worry when you've not checked it, especially if you're been using your email for business.

We've already shown you how you can use someone else's computer to access your AOL account using the Guest sign-on, but sometimes you just won't be near a computer with AOL on it (*7.2, Guest sign-on*).

With AOLMail, you can access your AOL email messages from anywhere you like. All you need to do is find a computer that's connected to the Internet and is running a Web browser.

If you're not familiar with what we mean by that, don't worry. A Web browser is not that different from the AOL software, except that it just allows you access to Web pages. Like with AOL, there's a box at the top of the screen where you can type in a Web address, and that's just about all you need to know.

When you're travelling round, you'll find cybercafés in cities everywhere – even in countries where you might not expect. And of course, if you stay in an hotel that has an Internet terminal, or with a friend who's on the Net, they'll have a Web browser too. And that means that you can keep up to date with your AOLMail messages.

Getting started

To start using AOLMail, you need to visit the home page for AOL UK. Just find a Web browser, and type in the address www.aol.co.uk.

If you can't see a box to type the address into, then you can usually press the Ctrl key and either L or O at the same time, and type www.aol.co.uk into the box that appears. Press Enter and in a few moments the AOL UK page will appear on the screen.

Fig. 8.1
AOL UK homepage

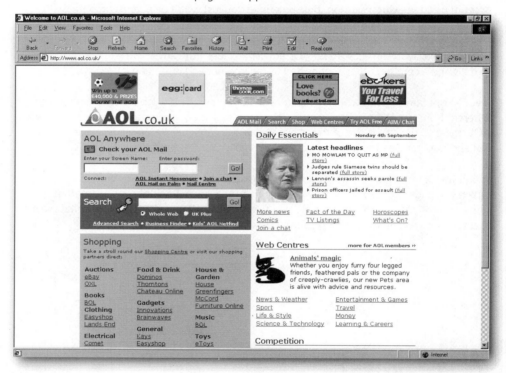

In the top left-hand corner of the page, you'll see a section called AOL Anywhere. The quickest way to get started from here is to enter your Screen Name and password into the boxes and click on **Go!**

AOL uses a secure connection on the Internet to help keep your mail private, so you don't need to worry about other people being able to intercept any of your messages.

When your password has been verified, you'll see this screen, which confirms that the connection to AOL's computers is secure. Click on the large button to carry on.

Fig. 8.3
Complete sign-on screen

Once you've clicked on the button to continue to the AOLMail main screen, you'll feel right at home. It's been designed to look very similar to the mailbox that you see when you sign on using the AOL software.

The AOLMail screen

Let's start by taking a quick look at what's what on the main AOLMail screen. Just like when you're reading messages on AOL, there are three tabs across the top of your mailbox, labelled **New mail**, **Old mail** and **Sent mail**. These work in exactly the same way as they do when you're using the AOL software, selecting which messages you see.

The list of messages itself works slightly differently, however. You'll see that the subject for each message is highlighted, and the mouse pointer changes when you move over it.

To read a message, all you need to do is point at the subject, and click once with the mouse.

The check box at the left of each message is used to select a message, just like clicking once on it with the mouse in the AOL program. You can select as many messages as you like, and then use either the **Keep as new** or **Delete** buttons to delete all the selected message or mark them as new.

Below the list of messages you'll see another check box. If you click with the mouse to check this box, AOLMail will select all the messages in the list, so it's easy to delete them all in one go.

At the top of the screen, the button labelled **Write** is for creating a new email, while the one labelled **Exit** will finish your AOLMail session.

Before we look in more detail at reading messages, a word about the **Keep as new** button, which is more important than usual for AOLMail.

Normally, when you read messages using the AOL software, they're transferred to your computer's hard disk. AOLMail doesn't do that, since it's designed to be used from lots of different computers. That means that if you leave a message on the Old mail list, when it's removed after 3 days, it's gone for good.

If you're using AOLMail on a long trip, you should mark messages as New if you want to be able to access them on your own computer when you return home, or change the email Preferences to keep messages in the Old mail and Sent mail lists for longer. You'll need to change the email Preferences before you leave home, since you can't change them using AOLMail (*3.6, Advanced Email*).

Reading a message with AOLMail

All you have to do to read a message is click on the subject, and you'll see a screen like this appear. This screen shows a message that has a file attached to it. If there aren't any files with the message, then you won't see the Download now button.

Although you can receive messages using AOLMail that have files attached to them, you can't receive ones with pictures embedded in them. Instead, you'll see the text '[unable to display image]'. If you keep the message as new, you'll be able to see it properly when you next sign on using the AOL software. Some effects, like coloured text, might not always work well when you read a message using AOLMail.

The **Close** button takes you back to the list of messages, while **Keep as new** and **Delete** work just like the same buttons when you're reading your messages via the AOL software. Next to them are two buttons that you can use to move backwards and forwards through the message list, rather than closing the message and then choosing another one.

Down the right-hand side of the message you'll see the buttons for **Reply**, **Reply all** and **Forward**. Once again, these work like the buttons on AOL itself. There's one small difference, however – if you want to include the text of the message that you're reading in a reply, you need to click on the small box marked **Include original text in reply**, before clicking on the **Reply** or **Reply all** button.

Downloading a file from AOLMail
If the message that you're reading has a file attached to it, you can click on the name of the file, which will be highlighted and underlined, or click the **Download now** button.

AOLMail will remind you of the dangers of downloading files from email. Click the **Cancel** button to stop the download, or click **OK** to continue.

Depending on the type of file that you've been sent, it may be displayed in the Web browser, or you may be asked to save it to a location on the computer's disk. If the file opens in the Web browser, you can usually call up a menu giving you the option of saving it by clicking with the left mouse button on the picture, or holding down the button while you point at the picture, if there's only one button on the mouse.

Sending a message with AOLMail

To write a message, just click the **Write** button and a screen like this one will appear. The list of messages that you were looking at will still be on the screen in its own window.

Fig. 8.4
AOLMail write mail

Fill in the address that you want to send your message to in the **Send To** box, and if you want to send copies to other people, enter those in the **Copy To** box – just like writing an email using AOL.

When you're sending messages via AOLMail, you can't use special features like AOL Stationery, coloured text, or different sized letters. Just type your message in the blank box, and give it a subject.

When you're done, you can click the **Send Now** button to deliver it. If you want to know when AOL members have received their messages, you can use the **Request return receipt** box. Just click on it, and you'll be told when people have received and read your message.

Unlike when you're using the AOL software, AOLMail doesn't have the option to look at the status of a message to see if it's been read. Instead, you'll need to ask for a receipt if you want to check whether or not your message has been received.

When you reply to a message, you'll see the same screen, with one small exception. Below the **Send Now** button there's an additional one labelled **Review Original Message**. When you click on that, the screen containing the original message will appear, so you can check anything that you need to. Just click again on the window that appeared when you chose the **Reply** button, and you can get back to writing your response.

Sending files using AOLMail
AOLMail lets you attach a file to your message, so even if you're away from your computer, you can still upload a file, and send it off to people. If you have a digital camera that saves pictures on a floppy disk, for example, you could take the disk along to a cyber café and send your holiday snaps to people back home.

You can only attach one file to each message.

To attach a file, click the **Browse** button at the bottom of the Write message screen, and you'll see a small window open, letting you find the file on the computer. When you've located the file, double-click on it, and you'll see its name appear in the box to the left of the **Browse** button.

If you browse again, you can change the file to a different one. To remove the file from the message, click the **Detach** button.

*When you're sending a picture from a floppy disk, don't remove the disk until after you've finished the message, clicked **Send**, and received the message telling you that your message has been sent.*

Exiting AOLMail
When you're finished with AOLMail, all you have to do is click the **Exit AOLMail** button, which you'll find at the top of the screen. You may see a message asking you to close the Web browser for extra security. If that appears, then we recommend you follow the instructions, to make sure that your AOL account remains as secure as possible.

8.2 AOL Instant Messenger

Sending Instant Messages is one of the AOL facilities that many people find most useful, but did you know that you don't have to be connected to AOL to do it?

AOL Instant Messenger, or AIM, is a program that lets you exchange Instant Messages with people on AOL when you're using a different Internet connection. For example, you could install it in the office, and talk with your AOL friends, without having to install the main AOL program.

Even better, anyone on the Internet can sign up with AIM. They just need to create a Screen Name, a little like you did when you signed up to AOL, and then they'll be able to swap messages with other AIM and AOL users, completely free of charge.

So, if your friends use someone other than AOL to connect to the Internet, as long as you get them using AIM, you'll be able to send them Instant Messages, and they'll appear in your Buddy List too. They'll be able to take advantage of other AOL services as well, such as the AOL Calendar.

If you'd like to get them all signed up, just tell them to visit www.aol.co.uk/aim and follow the instructions – or, if they get stuck, lend them your book and turn down the corner of this page so that they can find it easily.

Screen Names

The first thing that you need to do when you want to use AOL Instant Messenger is create a Screen Name – and you'll also need one to access AOL Calendar, or AOL Groups. Of course, if you have an AOL account already, you can just use the same Screen Name and password to access any AOL services via the Internet, but your friends will need to sign up for a new one, so let's see how it's done.

Creating a Screen Name on the Internet is completely free – because an Internet Screen Name doesn't give you access to all the exclusive information on AOL itself, just to AOL services like AIM and Groups@AOL. Your friends won't be asked for any billing information, nor will they be charged to create Screen Names.

Don't just 'lend' one of your own Screen Names to a friend so that they can use AIM or other AOL Internet services. Your Screen Names will give access to your AOL account, and if they're used to access AOLMail or the AOL service itself, then you could incur charges as a result. And, of course, you should never tell anyone, even a friend, your AOL passwords.

If your friends have already registered for some services on the Internet, like Netscape's NetCenter, or AOL's My News, then they'll already have a Screen Name. If not, then the place to start is AOL's home page, www.aol.co.uk/aim

Fig. 8.5
AIM UK homepage

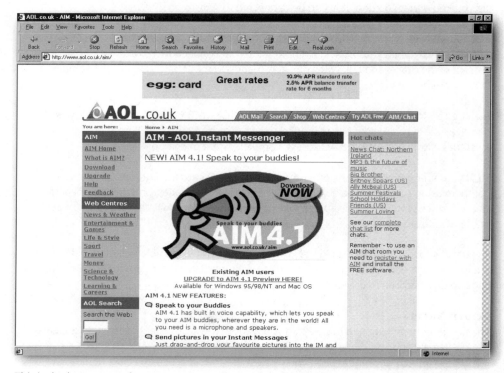

This is the home page for AIM, and you can read about all the features it offers – which now include the ability to speak to people, if your computer has a microphone attached to it.

To start, before downloading, your friends will need to register, which will give them a Screen Name they can use. Click the **Download** link in the left-hand column of the page.

If you'd like to download AIM for yourself, or if your friends already have a Screen Name, click the Upgrade link, which will take you directly to the page where you can download AIM.

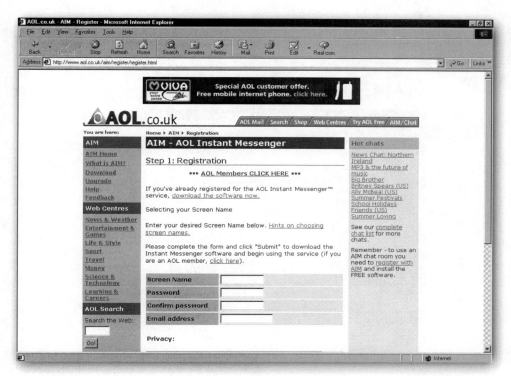

Fig. 8.6
AIM register page

Here's the registration page for AIM. All you need to do to get a Screen Name is fill in the form with your choice of Screen Name, which can be from three to ten characters long, including spaces.

Remember that since there are millions of people using AIM and AOL, common Screen Names, like John Smith, will almost certainly have been used already, so try to pick something that's likely to be unique. If the name you choose has already been taken, you'll be asked to pick another one when you click the **Submit** button at the bottom of the page.

As well as the Screen Name itself, you'll need to pick a password, which you need to type in twice. As you type the password, a row of dots will appear in the box. By typing the password twice, AOL can be sure you didn't make a mistake as you entered it.

Finally, you need to enter an email address. When you've filled in all those details, you can move on to the next part of the form, which is where you can set your privacy options. These control whether or not people will be able to find you if you're an Instant Messenger user. Choose the most appropriate of the three options, and then click the **Submit** button.

Fig. 8.7
**Congratulations
screen**

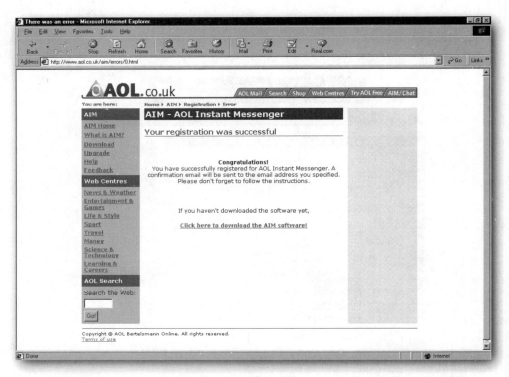

If all went well, this is the screen you'll see, confirming that you've created a new Screen Name to use with AIM. Now, just click on the link to download the AIM software.

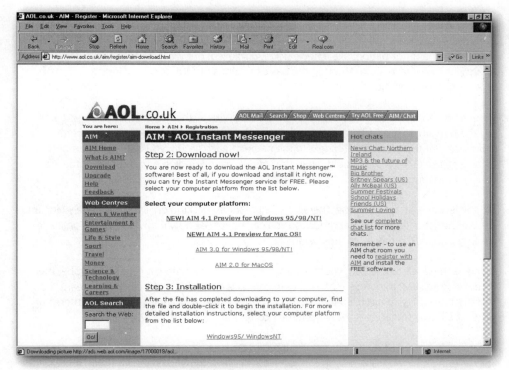

Fig. 8.8
**Download
screen**

This is the Download screen. As you can see, there are a number of different versions of the AIM software. You need to choose the appropriate one, depending on what sort of computer you're using. You'll see there are versions for PC and Macintosh, and there may be more than one version for each.

Usually, it's best to download the most recent version. Here we'll be talking about AIM 4.1, which was the most up to date one when this book was written.

When you click one of the links on the download screen, your computer will start to transfer the AIM install program to your disk. Depending on what sort of computer you're using, you might see a progress bar, or be asked where you want to save the file.

After the file has been transferred, you need to find it and double-click on it to start the AIM installer.

Using AIM

This is the main window you'll see on your screen when you're running AIM. There may also be some other information, like a news ticker, displayed, but we'll come to those later. To start with, we'll take a tour through the basic functions of AIM, and then look at some of the more advanced facilities later.

The main part of the screen shows your Buddy List, with all the groups that you've created. At the bottom, in the Offline section, you'll see the names of all the people who aren't connected at the moment, and next to the name of each group, you'll see two numbers in brackets, like (3/7), which would mean that of the seven Buddies in that group, three are online at the moment.

To the left of each group name, there's a small triangle. Clicking on it will alternately hide and reveal the list of names in that group, so you can either see how many people are online in each group, or the names of those who are.

When someone's connected, you'll see an icon next to their name. It it's a small globe, then they're using AIM; a triangle means they're connected to AOL, and a clock dial means that they're idle – they've not used their computer for a while. A Notepad icon means there's a message to say someone is away from their computer.

There are two tabs at the top of the list, labelled **Online** and **List Setup**. Click the **Online** tab to bring it to the front, so you can see who is connected and chat with them, and use the List Setup tab to make changes to your Buddy List.

We'll explain that later; for now, let's concentrate on sending messages; the buttons at the bottom of the AIM window are what you use to communicate with other people. From left to right, you'll see IM, Chat and Talk buttons.

To send your first message to someone, wait until you see one of your Buddies online, and double-click on their name, or click once on it and then click the **IM** button.

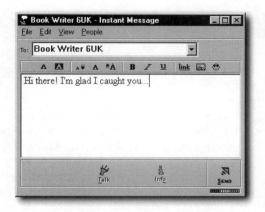

Fig. 8.9
IM screen

This is the screen you use to send a message to someone. Along the top, there are buttons that you can use to select the colour and size of your text – experiment with them later. For now, just type a simple message, like Hello, and click the **Send** button, or press the **Enter** key.

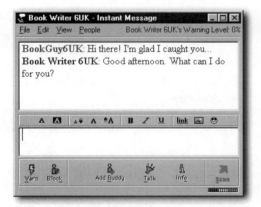

Fig. 8.10
IM with reply

Once you've started chatting with someone, the screen will change to look like this. In the top section, you can see the conversation you've having, while the bottom is where you type your new comments.

Isn't that simple? Just a few clicks of the mouse, and you're having a conversation already. There's much more that AIM can do, however. Let's start by looking at the buttons along the bottom of the Instant Message window.

The first button is labelled **Warn**. When you click this, it's a bit like someone getting points on their driving licence. At the top of the screen, you'll see the current warning level of the person who's sending you messages. If you're being pestered by someone, you can click the **Warn** button, and their level will increase. When someone has received too many warnings, AIM will restrict what they can do.

Don't use warnings maliciously. They should only be used when someone is behaving inappropriately. You must not use warnings as a way of trying to have someone else's access to AIM restricted without reason.

Next to the Warn button is one labelled **Block**. When you click on this, the person you're talking with will be automatically added to your Block list, and they won't be able to contact you using AOL Instant Messenger unless you choose to remove them from the list.

In the middle section of the window, you'll see three buttons. The first, **Add Buddy**, will add the person you're speaking with to your Buddy List – it's handy if someone you don't know has started speaking with you and you'd like to keep in touch with them in future.

The **Talk** button lets you use AIM as a sort of telephone system. When you click on it, AIM will make a connection directly to the other user and you'll be able to talk to them via your computer's sound card and microphone.

Talking via AIM is only possible if both people have the latest version of AOL Instant Messenger.

When you click on the **Talk** button, the person you want to talk with will see a screen like this, asking them if they'd like to access your invitation to talk.

Fig. 8.11
Talk accept

If they do accept, then you'll see a Talk screen a little like this one – though it may be slightly different, depending on what sort of sound card you have.

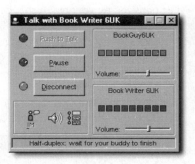

Fig. 8.12
Talk screen

You'll see a **Disconnect** button, and a Push to talk button. Click on it to talk with your Buddy, and then click again when you've finished, so that you can hear them. The **Speaker** icon will bring up the controls for your soundcard.

Next to the **Talk** button on the Instant Message screen, clicking **Info** will bring up a small screen with the details that the user entered about themselves, like this:

Fig. 8.13
User info screen

You can also use the **Add Buddy** button at the bottom of this screen to make an entry in your Buddy List.

Now you know the basics of sending an Instant Message, let's look at chatting using AIM.

Chatting with Buddies

What's the difference between chatting and Instant Messages? Well, an Instant Message is just between two people. A chat can have lots of people, all sharing a chat room.

Messages that are typed in a chat room appear on the screens of everyone simultaneously. You could use a chat room to plan a meeting, for example, or discuss a project you're working on.

To invite people to a chat room, click on their names in your Buddy List, and then click the **Chat** button at the bottom of the screen.

Fig. 8.14
Chat setup box

You can type a message into the box on this screen to give people a reason why you're inviting them to chat. Click the **Send** button to send the invitation. People you've invited to the chat room will see a screen like this one – and you'd see exactly the same if someone invited you to chat with them.

Fig. 8.15
Chat invite box

You can also access chat rooms from links on some Web pages, too. For example, if you use the Groups@AOL facility, there'll be a link on the page for your group that will take you to a special room just for members of that group. You can find out more about groups in *Chapter 5, AOL and You* (*5.8, Groups@AOL*).

Fig. 8.16
Chat Room screen

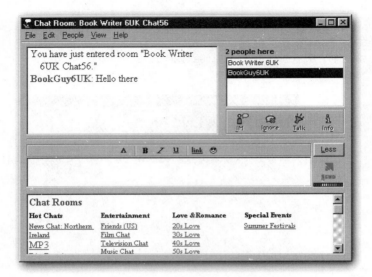

As you can see, the chat room looks very much like an Instant Message, with an area at the top of the screen showing the comments everyone is making, and a space for you to type your own messages below.

To the right, there are two lists of members, one showing who is in the room, and one showing who has been invited. Below the lists of members are four buttons. The **IM**, **Talk** and **Info** buttons let you send an Instant Message, Talk or look up information about people in the room. Just click on their name, then click the appropriate button. You can also double-click on one of the names in the list to send an Instant Message to that person.

The **Ignore** button lets you ignore the comments from someone in the room. When you click it, an X will appear next to the name of the person you're ignoring. Highlight the same person, and click the **Ignore** button again to stop ignoring them.

All you need to do to start chatting is type in the box at the bottom, and press **Enter**. Your comments will appear on the screen of everyone else in the chat room. Simple, isn't it? Now, let's take a look at how you can manage your Buddy List.

Managing your Buddy List
One of the other important things you'll need to do is keep track of your Buddy List. You might want to remove people if they're not working with you any more, or perhaps you want to add a new group to the list for the people planning a party you're going to.

To manage the Buddy List, click the **List Setup** tab on the main AIM screen.

Fig. 8.17
List setup

As you'll see, this screen looks very similar to the Online tab, but there are different buttons at the bottom.

There's a **Folder** icon for each of the groups in your Buddy List, which you can double-click on to open, and show all the members of that group, or double-click again to hide the members.

If you'd like to move someone from one group to another, just click on their name, hold the mouse button down, and drag it to another part of the list. It'll appear wherever you let go of the mouse button.

To add someone to the list, click where you'd like them, then click the **Add** button – it's the one with a + symbol and one person on it. An entry called NewBuddy will appear, highlighted. Just type the name of your Buddy to add them to the list.

You can add a new group to the list in the same way, using the next button along. The text New Group will appear, and you just need to type to replace it with the name you'd like. Click **Buddies** and drag their names to move them into the new group.

To delete an entry from the list, click on it once, and then click the button with the – symbol to the right of it.

If you delete a group from your Buddy List, you'll also delete all the Buddies that are in that group. You may want to move the Buddies to another group first, if you want to keep in touch with them.

Finally, the magnifying glass lets you search. When you click on it, you'll see three options. The first two are Web searches, but the last one lets you find people to add to your Buddy List easily. When you choose it, you'll see the same screens we explained earlier, allowing you to search for a Buddy by email address, location or interests.

Sending pictures and files with AIM
We've looked at the basics of chatting with people, using either Instant Messages or chat rooms, but AIM can do much more than that. You can also send files to other users, so you could swap a picture with someone else, for example, to see what they look like. Or you could send a copy of a report to someone in the office when you're working at home, and stay connected to AIM to give them comments while they read it.

You can even share a folder on your computer's disk, which is a great way to let a group of people work together.

> *Whenever you exchange files with people on the Internet, including using AIM's file transfer and file sharing facilities, you should remember that you may receive material that you consider inappropriate, and you expose yourself to the risk of computer viruses. Never allow people you don't know to have access to your computer via shared file areas, and check files for viruses before opening them. You should install an up-to-date virus checking program on your computer.*

Let's start by seeing how you can exchange pictures via AIM.

Sending pictures in your Instant Messages
When you're chatting to someone, it's only natural to want to know what they look like, isn't it? With AIM, it's easier than ever to see what someone looks like. You can add a picture to your messages, in the middle of the text that you're typing. They'll appear almost instantly

when you send your message, and of course the picture could be of anything, like the new car you're thinking of buying.

To send pictures to someone, you first have to make what's called a direct connection. That means that instead of the message you send going via the AIM computers, it will go directly from your computer to your Buddy's, making it much quicker.

Fig. 8.18
Instant Message window

As you can see, on the toolbar when you're composing your messages, between the word link and the Smiley face, there's a small icon, which represents images. You need to click on this to add a picture to your message.

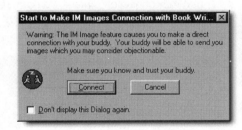

Fig. 8.19
Image connection warning

The first time you click the button when you're talking with someone, you'll see this warning screen. Click the **Connect** button to carry on, and the person you're talking with will see a screen like this one.

Fig. 8.20
Incoming image connection

You'll see the same thing if someone decides to send you a picture and you've not already started a direct connection with them. You can click **Accept** to allow the connection, **Reject** to refuse it, and **Ignore** to ignore any more messages from that person.

If the person you're trying to connect with isn't using a compatible version of AIM, then you'll see a message telling you that you can't open a connection with them.

When you click **Accept**, or when the person you're trying to reach has clicked **Accept**, a message will appear to say that you have established a direct connection.

Now that the connection is made, you can both send and receive images. All you need to do is type your message in the normal way, and when you want to add a picture, click the **Image** button again. This time, instead of the Warning screen, you'll see this window appear.

Fig. 8.21
File open window

All you need to do is find the file that you want to send, click on it with the mouse, and then click the **Open** button. You'll see the picture appear in the box at the bottom of the IM screen, and when you click the **Send** button, it'll be transferred to the other person's computer. As it's sent, you'll see a progress bar appear at the bottom of the window, so you know how much of the file there is to send.

Although we've talked about sending pictures, you could actually send a sound clip too, if you like. Just choose the file in the same way as you would for a picture.

Exchanging files
Pictures and sounds are great things to exchange with someone while you're chatting, and they'll help you see what someone looks like, but there are other types of files that you might want to swap.

AIM lets you send and receive any type of file that's on your computer. You can carry on chatting while the file is copied from your computer to your Buddy's, and you'll know for certain when it's been received.

Sending a file is simple. You can click on a Buddy's name in the Buddy List with the right mouse button, and choose **Send file**, or if you're already talking with them, you'll find the Send File option on the People menu at the top of the Instant Message window.

Fig. 8.22
**Send file
dialogue**

To select the file that you want to send, click the **Browse** button, and find the file on your computer's disk. Fill in a description in the large box, and make sure you read the security warning underneath it, then click the **Send** button.

The person you're sending a file to will see this screen, and you'll see a similar one when someone tries to send a file to you.

Fig. 8.23
**Receive file
warning**

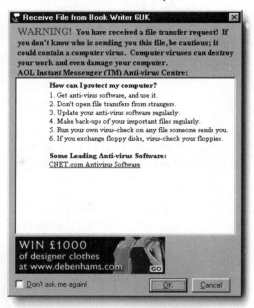

If you'd like to accept the file, click the **OK** button, and you'll see the description appear on a screen like this one:

Fig. 8.24
**Receive file
dialogue**

To save the file in a specific place, use the **Browse** button to choose a folder on your computer's disk. If you don't select anywhere special, like the folder where you have the files for a particular project, AOL will save all the files you receive into the same place.

Below the description you'll see two check boxes. The first, **Check file for viruses after transfer**, will only be activated if you've told AIM about any anti-virus software you have on your computer. When there's a check in the box for this option, files will be automatically scanned as soon as they're received.

The next box, **Open file after transfer**, tells AIM to open the file. If it's a word processor file, for example, then your word processor would start up when the file arrives.

You should be very careful about opening files you receive, especially if you don't have anti-virus software on your computer. Before accepting files from strangers, install an anti-virus program, and make sure that it's regularly updated.

Finally, at the bottom of the screen, you'll see buttons allowing you to accept the file, cancel the transfer, or issue a warning to the person attempting to send it to you.

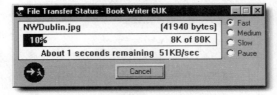

Fig. 8.25
File transfer progress

While a file is being transferred, you'll see a progress bar on your screen, showing you how much of the file still has to be sent. You can use the options at the right of the progress bar to slow down the speed of the transfer – you might find, for example, that if the file is being sent very fast, then emails you're trying to send are taking longer.

Sharing files
While sending and receiving files to people is a great way to distribute information, sometimes it might not be convenient. For example you might be working on a Web site for a group you're involved in, and you've invited everyone in the group to join you in a chat room.

They'll probably all want to see some of the pictures you've designed for the site, and maybe read the text. But sending the same file to everyone is a little tedious. You'll have to select each person in turn, then send them the files, and so on. You could easily lose track of who's been sent what.

AIM allows you to share a folder of files on your computer, so that you can tell your Buddies, and then they can access any of the files that they want, as long as you're connected.

Although sharing files can be useful, remember that if you don't set it up correctly, you could be giving everyone who uses AIM access to files on your computer's disk, which could include confidential information. Follow the instructions carefully; it's best to create a folder specially for files that you want to share.

Fetching shared files from another users
Before we look at how you can share your own files, let's see first how you can access the files that someone else is sharing.

To start, right click on a name in your Buddy List and choose **Get file**, or if you're already chatting with someone, choose **Get file** from the **People** menu.

Fig. 8.26
Get file warning

You'll see this Warning screen appear. Read it carefully, and then click the **OK** button. Now, AIM has to get a list of all the files that are available from the person you're connecting with. Depending on how many files they have available, it might take a while. After a pause, you'll see the list of files appear.

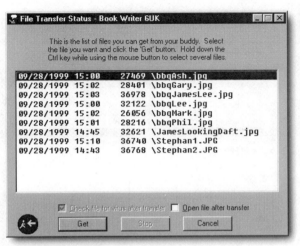

Fig. 8.27
Get file list

You can see the date and time the file was changed, in the first two columns, followed by its size, and then the name. To get a file, just click with the mouse to highlight it. If you hold down the Ctrl key and click again, you can choose more than one file to fetch at the same time.

At the bottom of the screen, you'll see the same check boxes that appeared for receiving files – one to check for viruses, and one to open the file after it's been received.

Although some people may allow anyone to connect to them via AIM and retrieve files, you should only use the Get files facility to fetch files from people you know and trust. Always check files with anti-virus software before opening them.

When you've picked the files, you want, click the **Get** button.

Fig. 8.28
**Files being
received**

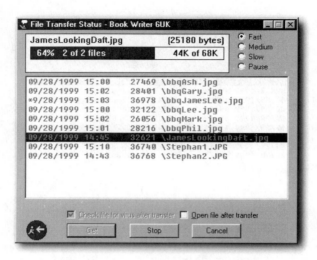

You'll see the top of the window has now changed, showing a progress bar, and allowing you to slow down the file transfer if you like. Slowing it down might, for example, give more time to your computer to transfer a Web page that you're looking at.

You can click the **Stop** button while files are being transferred, and use **Cancel** to close the list of files when you've fetched the ones that you want.

So, fetching a file that someone else is sharing is pretty simple, isn't it? Now let's take a look at how you can set up your computer to share files with other AIM users.

Sharing your own files with other AIM users
Sharing files is fairly simple to do using AIM, but you should take the time to set it up properly, otherwise you could inadvertently give someone access to files on your computer that you'd rather they didn't see. You don't really want your boss to see all those job application letters you've written, do you?

When you share files, you have to choose a folder on your computer's disk that you'd like to share. AIM will allow people to fetch all the files in that folder, and any files in folders that are contained within the one you're sharing.

That means, for example, that if you have a folder called Work, which has folders in it called WebProjects and JobApplications, then sharing the Work folder would allow people to see files in both your WebProjects and JobApplications folder. If you just want someone to see the WebProjects folder, you should share that one.

To make sure people can only see files you want them to, it's a good idea to make a new folder specially for sharing, and copy the files you want people to access into that folder.

With those warnings out of the way, let's see how to set up file sharing. From the main AIM window, you need to choose **Edit Options** from the **My AIM** menu, and another menu will pop out from the side. Select **Edit Preferences** from that menu, and the AIM Preferences screen will appear.

Look along the tabs at the top of the screen, and click the one labelled **File Transfer**, which should display this page:

Fig. 8.29
File transfer preferences

As you can see, there are a lot of options on this screen, for all the different ways that you can swap files with other AIM users. Before looking at the options for sharing, we'll just mention the other things here briefly.

Firstly, the options under **Allow receive file access** let you choose to block everyone from sending you files, to allow only people in your Buddy List to send you files, to accept files from everyone, or to be asked if you want to accept each file. That last one is probably the best option to select for the time being.

To the right, you can set the speed for sending and receiving files. When a file is being transferred, you can still change the speed, but these options control the speed the file starts being sent at.

The largest area of the screen is the settings for **Allow get file access**. This is where you decide whom you want to share your files with.

The safest option is probably the first, to allow only people in a particular group on your Buddy List to access files. You might have a group for a project you're working on, or a group called Trusted People, perhaps.

To select this option, click to put a check in the box, and then choose the group that you want to give access to your computer.

If you'd prefer to give more widespread access, click the box to clear the check mark for that option, and use the two lines of options underneath.

The first of the two lines controls access for people on your Buddy List, no matter what group they're in, while the second controls access for everyone else.

For each group of users, you can select to allow them access to your shared files, to display a screen asking if you want them to access files when they try to connect, or not to allow them.

Click on the circle to the left of an option to select it. You'll notice that the second row, for users not in your Buddy List, may change when you alter options in the first. That's because AIM won't let everyone have more privileges than people in your Buddy List. You can't, for example, be asked whether someone in your Buddy List should be able to get files, but allow everyone else to do it without you being asked.

> *Although it's possible to allow everyone to access files on your computer without you being asked, we don't recommend that you use this option. For maximum security, you should only allow people in a specific group on your Buddy List to access files that you are sharing via AIM.*

Underneath the options that control who can access your files, there are two more check boxes. Click the first one to tell AOL that you don't want to see information about the status of files that are being transferred, and the second if you'd like AOL to keep a log of all the requests for files that are made.

The final stage in setting up your computer to share files is selecting which folder you want to share. The option that controls this is labelled Directory from where others can get my files. When you installed AIM, a special folder will have been created, and we recommend that you copy files you want to share into that folder. If you'd like to choose a different one, click the **Browser** button.

Fig. 8.30
Browse directory screen

Find the folder that you'd like to use, and click the **Select** button.

Remember that any folders contained within the folder you're sharing will also be available to people who connect to your computer.

The last option on this screen allows you to select the folder where files you receive from other people will be stored.

When you've made all your changes, click the **OK** button, and other AIM users will be able to connect to your computer and access files. Files will be shared until you change the settings on this screen, as long as you are signed on to AIM.

Keeping track of your Buddies with AIM
Now you've seen how AOL Instant Messenger can be used for chatting, talking, and exchanging files, as well as Instant Messages. Would you believe there's more?

Although you might make a habit of running AIM each time you start your computer, that doesn't mean that you'll always be willing to respond to messages that people send you. You could be away from your computer, making a cup of tea, or you might have to speak to someone on the phone.

If you don't respond to people when they send you a message, they might think you're being rude – but AIM can take care of that for you. You can create messages which will be sent to people while you're away, and if you're wanting to get hold of someone who is away, you can tell AIM to let you know when they're no longer idle.

First, let's look at how you can send an automatic response when someone sends you an Instant Message.

Creating and using Away messages
The messages that AIM sends on your behalf are called Away messages, since the main reason for using them is to tell people that you're away from the computer.

Although there's a standard Away message that you can use, you'll probably want to create a personalised one instead. From the **My AIM** menu, choose **Away message**, and another menu will appear. Choose **New message**, and this screen will appear:

Fig. 8.31
**Create away
message**

In the box at the top, you can type a short name, which you can use to refer to this message later. In the main box, type the message that you want to send to people who try to contact you.

Underneath the space for you to type your own message, you'll see that there are some 'special characters' listed. You can use these to customise the message. For example, you'll see that %n means Screen Name of Buddy.

That means that if you type the message 'Thanks for your IM, %n. I'll get back to you later' and then someone with the Screen Name JoeBloggs sends you a message, they'll receive a response that says 'Thanks for your IM, JoeBloggs. I'll get back to you later'.

When you've typed your message, you need to decide if you want to save it for later; click to put a check mark in the box, and the message you've just created will appear on the Away message menu, so you can select it easily in future.

Finally, to tell people that you're away, click the **I'm Away** button.

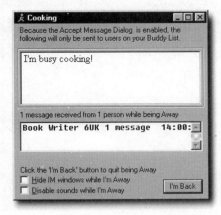

Fig. 8.32
Away box

This is what's displayed on your screen when you're away. You can see a list of all the people who've sent you messages, together with the date and time. The first of the two check boxes at the bottom of the screen allows you to hide the messages themselves, so that you don't come back to a cluttered screen full of messages. Instead, you can double-click on the name of a Buddy in the list to see what they said to you while you were away.

The second box turns off the sounds – useful if you're having a nap, perhaps, or in a meeting and don't want your computer making noises all the time.

When you want to switch off the Away message, just click the **I'm Back** button.

Creating and using alerts
Away messages are handy if you can't respond to someone else, but what happens if you're the person trying to get in touch with a Buddy who's away? You might have an urgent message for them, and if all you receive is their Away message, how can you be sure they've seen it?

AIM can automatically alert you when a particular Buddy is available, by playing a sound, or displaying a new window on your screen.

To set up an alert, right click on the name of a Buddy in your Buddy List, and choose **Alert me when *Buddyname* is available**. You can also create an alert from the People menu. For example, if you've highlighted JoeBloggs, the option will say Alert me when JoeBloggs is available.

Fig. 8.33
Alert screen

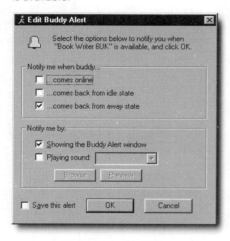

At the top, you can choose three different things that you might want to be alerted about. The first is when someone signs on, in case you don't notice them appear in your Buddy List.

Below that, you can choose to be alerted when a Buddy is no longer idle, so you'll know that they've started using their computer, and finally, you can be alerted when they're no longer away.

Just click to put a check in the box next to the things you want to be alerted about. In the next section of the screen, you can choose whether you want to be alerted with a special window on your screen, or a sound being played, or both.

If you check the Playing sound box, you can hear the sound by clicking the **Preview** button. Choose from one of the built-in sounds on the list, or click **Browse** to find a sound file on your computer's disk.

Finally, at the bottom of the window, there's a box labelled **Save this alert**. If you click to put a check in this box, then AOL will remember it, and you'll always be alerted, for example, if someone signs on, or when they stop being idle. If you don't put a check in the box, then you'll only be alerted once.

Click **OK** to activate the alert. Now AIM will keep an eye on your Buddy for you. When the alert is triggered, you'll see this on your screen:

Fig. 8.34
Alert box

Use the **Send IM** button to send that important message to your Buddy, or click **OK** to carry on with what you were doing.

If you'd like to change an alert, just select the Buddy in your list, and click with the right mouse button to display the menu, then choose **Change alert**. You can stop the alert repeating, or delete it by simply choosing not to be alerted about anything.

8.3 AOL for Palm

So far, everything we've looked at has been to do with connecting to AOL or AOL services, like Instant Messaging, using a computer. But AOL Anywhere is about a lot more than just using an ordinary computer.

You can access AOL using a personal organiser, a mobile phone, and there are plenty of other options coming up in the future, including AOL via your television set and on dedicated AOL gadgets. You'll be able to access AOL anywhere you want, whenever you want.

Right now you can access AOL via any WAP enabled device, or via the Palm-based organisers from 3Com, Handspring and other manufacturers. If you have one of these – and they're the most popular electronic organisers in the world – then you can access your email and Instant Messages wherever you are. All you need is a phone link for your Palm – and if you have a mobile phone that links to it, you could even access your messages while you're sitting on a double-decker bus!

AOL for Palm

PalmMail

AOL for Palm! Are they kidding? No – you really can access AOL from something as compact and easy to carry as a Palm organiser. With AOL for Palm, you can access your email messages, compose messages offline to send later and keep in touch with your Buddies via Instant Messages.

At the moment, you can't access AOL's Message boards or other content, like the AOL Channels, but if just you need to be able to keep in touch when you're on the move, AOL for Palm could quickly become an essential tool.

What do you need?
To use AOL on your Palm device, you'll need a modem connection, which can be via a plug-in modem, like 3Com's palm modem, a cable link to a mobile phone, or an infra-red connection to a phone.

> *Remember that if you want to use your mobile phone to connect to AOL, you'll need to ask your mobile phone network to enable your phone for data. Some mobile phones may not be compatible with your Palm organiser. Also, remember that AOL does not offer support on connections via mobile phone. If you have difficulties, you will need to contact your phone's supplier or the phone network.*

AOL needs about 400k of memory on your organiser, and additional memory for the messages that you download and store in your Filing Cabinet. Your organiser must be running

Palm OS 3.0 or above, and AOL will work in colour if you have a Palm IIIc or Handspring Visor Prism.

There are a few limitations to AOL for Palm, of course. You can only download messages up to 32,000 characters long, and you can't download files that have been attached to messages. The Address Book used when you're composing email messages is the one stored on your Palm, not your AOL Address Book.

You need an AOL account to use AOL for Palm, but you don't have to open a new one – you can sign on with your existing Screen Name and password, and you'll be charged for your use in the normal way.

Remember that even if you are connecting to AOL using a phone number that is normally free of charge, your mobile phone network may make additional charges. You should check with them if you are unsure how much they will charge you to connect to AOL.

To download AOL for Palm, go to the keyword **PalmMail**. If you're can't reach a computer with the AOL software on it, you can download AOL for Palm from the Internet too, at the Web address www.aol.co.uk/anywhere/. Wherever you download the file from, you'll need to install it on your organiser via the HotSync cradle, just like any other application. There's just one file that you need to install, and then you're ready to get started.

PalmMail

Setting up AOL for Palm
After you've installed AOL on your Palm, you'll see the **AOL** icon when you tap the **Applications** button. Click on it and you're ready to run AOL for the first time. As part of the initial Setup, you'll need to tell AOL what country you're in and select the numbers to use.

To start, tap the option to confirm that you already have an AOL account, and that you want to add a local access phone number.

You'll now be asked to create a location, much like you can when you're using AOL on your desktop computer. Enter a name for the location, and then tap the **Next** button when you're sure that the other options, on the screen are correct.

On the next screen, tap **Search for AOL access numbers**, then tap **Next** again. Now you need to say which country you want to add numbers for. You can pick any country, and you'll see a list of possible numbers to use. Tap the screen to put a check in the box next to a number that you want to use.

Remember that mobile phone networks may charge differently for calls to numbers, including numbers that are free from a fixed phone line. If you are using your Palm organiser with a mobile phone, check with your phone company for details of call costs, which are separate from any fees that AOL may charge you for accessing your account.

After picking the numbers you want to use, tap **Done**.

Now that you've created a location, you'll see the AOL sign-on screen.

Fig. 8.35
Palm sign-on screen

The first time you connect, you'll have to select **Existing member**, and then fill in your Screen Name and password after tapping the **Sign On** button to connect to AOL. AOL will display the password as you enter it, so that you can see if you made any mistakes writing it. However, even if you choose to store your password, don't worry – no one will be able to find it out by picking up your organiser later.

During the initial sign on, AOL will download a list of all the Screen Names on your account, so that the next time you run AOL on your Palm, you can choose any of your seven names from the Sign-on menu.

Once you're connected, the main AOL screen will appear.

Fig. 8.36
AOL Palm main screen

As you can see, there's a series of icons around the screen, with a **Sign-off** icon in the centre. If you click that, then you'll be disconnected, and the icon will change to **Sign On**.

Starting from the top and going clockwise round the screen, the **Mailbox** icon takes you to your online mailbox. **Filing Cabinet** is where you can save copies of messages you've received, or view messages that are waiting to be sent.

Instant Message lets you send an Instant Message to a Buddy, or read one that you've been sent, while **Buddy List** is where you can check to see which of your friends are online.

Tap on **Write to compose an email message**, and use **Auto AOL** to send and collect all your messages in one go. We'll look at each of those in turn.

Using AOL on your Palm

Using AOL on your Palm is simple. If you're not already connected, tap the **Sign-on** icon in the middle of the screen.

Fig. 8.37
Pick screen name

You'll see this screen, where you can choose which Screen Name you want to use, which location you're calling from, and enter your password, if you haven't saved it yet.

If you'd like to create another location, for example if you're abroad and want to find a local phone number to use, tap on the **Setup** button. Now, click **Sign On**, and AOL will try to connect. When the connection has been made, you'll be back at the main screen.

Accessing your mailbox

Tap the **Mail** icon, which is at the top of the screen, below the AOL logo, and you'll see a screen like this, with the same three tabs you have when you use AOL on your desktop computer.

Fig. 8.38
Mailbox screen

To read a message, just highlight it and tap the **Read** button. Just like when you're using AOL on the computer, there are buttons to keep a message as new – labelled **Keep** – to **Delete** a message, and to **Write** a new one. Tapping on the arrow at the bottom left of the screen takes you back to the main AOL screen.

Using the Filing Cabinet
The Filing Cabinet on the Palm version of AOL isn't quite as flexible as on your computer –
there aren't different folders, for example.

Fig. 8.39
Filing Cabinet

Once again, there are three tabs. On the **Saved** tab you'll see messages that have been
saved from your AOL mailbox, while on the one labelled **Sent**, you can see messages you've
written. Tap the **Waiting** tab and you can check the messages that are waiting to be sent.

If you highlight a message on the **Waiting** tab, you can tap one of the buttons at the bottom
of the screen to edit it or send it right away.

Sending Instant Messages
To send an Instant Message, tap the **Instant Message** icon, in the bottom right of the main
screen. You'll see a small area window pop up for you to write your message.

Fig. 8.40
Send IM

On the top line, enter the Screen Name of the person that you want to send an IM to. If you're
responding to someone who's sent you an IM, you'll be able to pick their Screen Name from a

menu by tapping on a small triangle at the right of the line. Now, tap on the next line and start writing your message. When you've finished, tap on **Send**.

To save writing the name of Buddies, why not use the Buddy List? There, you can send Instant Messages by tapping to choose whom you want to contact.

If the person you're trying to reach isn't available, you'll see a message telling you so, but if it was sent then the screen will change, to look something like this.

Fig. 8.41
IM conversation

It's not that different from using Instant Messages on AOL, is it? If you're talking with more than one person, you can switch between the Instant Messages from each of them by tapping the Screen Name at the top of the screen and picking another from the menu.

To send more comments, just tap on the blank lines at the bottom of the screen and then write your message then tap on **Send**.

If you'd like to include a Smiley face, don't worry about not remembering the Graffiti you need to make one. Just tap the button with the face on it, and you can choose from a list. The next button calls up the shortcuts that you've defined on your Palm.

Finally, the **End** button closes the IM session that you're having. If you want to carry on this conversation, use the arrow at the left of the screen. When you next receive an IM from the person you're talking with, your conversation will still be there. If you click **End**, the conversation will be lost.

Receiving Instant Messages
When you're sent an Instant Message, you'll hear a sound, and then the icon in the top right of your Palm's screen will flash. Tap the icon to receive the message, and you'll be taken to the screen we've just seen, where you can carry on your conversation.

Using the Buddy List
The Buddy List is the easiest way to exchange Instant Messages with people that you know.

Fig. 8.42
Buddy List screen

Once again, it looks very like the list that you see when you use your Buddy List, or AOL Instant Messenger. To send a message, just tap on a name and then on **Instant Message**, or double-tap on the name.

To add or remove people on your Buddy List, tap on the **Setup** tab. You can add, delete and rename entries, just like when you're using your computer.

Remember that changes you make to your Buddy List when you're using AOL on your Palm will affect the Buddy List you see when you're signed on to AOL.

Fig. 8.43
Buddy List with IM active

If you're having a conversation with someone on your Buddy List, you'll see a slightly different version of the main screen, like the one above. The top section, Active Instant Messages, makes it much easier to get back to a conversation with someone. Just double-tap the name of the Buddy you want to talk with, and you'll be taken back to their IMs.

Writing email

Tap on the **Write** icon and you'll see a blank email message, ready for you to fill in the address, subject and the message itself.

Fig. 8.44
Blank email

Entering long email addresses can be tedious, but don't worry – you don't have to. If you tap on the **To** or **Cc** buttons on the screen, you'll be taken to your Palm Address Book, showing all the email addresses.

Fig. 8.45
Email address list

All you need to do is tap to select the person you're writing to, then tap the **Add** button. After adding one address, you can tap either of the buttons again to add more addresses to your message.

When you've written the message, tap on **Send Now** to send it right away, or **Send Later** if you'd like to put it in your Filing Cabinet to send with Auto AOL, or after reviewing it later. You can also edit messages in your Filing Cabinet before sending them, if you like.

Auto AOL

Auto AOL on the Palm lets you send and receive waiting messages. Tap the icon, and you'll see a few options appear.

Fig. 8.46
**Auto AOL
options**

As you can see, you can choose to send mail, collect new mail, or both. If you tap Put unread email into saved, which tells AOL for Palm that you want to pick up new messages, you'll see another option appear – Keep all email received as new.

If you tap to select that option, then when your messages have been transferred to your Palm, they'll be marked as New on AOL. That means that when you return home and connect to AOL using your computer, the messages will still be there, ready for you to download.

AOL for Palm Preferences

As you can see, AOL for Palm is a pretty straightforward program, and if you're used to using AOL on your computer, you'll find that you can get to grips with it in hardly any time at all. There are a few Preferences that you can set, however, to help make it work better for you.

To access the Preferences, tap the **Menu** button on your Palm, then choose **Preferences**.

Fig. 8.47
Preferences screen

The first two options allow you to automatically save copies of messages that are sent or received. Just tap to select, and messages will be automatically copied to the appropriate tab in your Filing Cabinet.

Under **Confirmations**, you can tap to choose whether or not you want to be asked before you delete any messages.,

Choose **Enable Instant Message sounds** if you'd like your Palm to beep when you receive an Instant Message. If you don't select this option, then you'll have to watch for the flashing icon in the top right corner of the screen to know when you've been sent an IM, or look for active Instant Messages in your Buddy List.

The last option allows you to choose how you'd like messages sorted in your Filing Cabinet. You can choose from **Date**, **Sender** and **Subject**.

There's one other screen of Preferences that you can access when you're online, which controls your privacy.

Fig. 8.48
Privacy preferences

To reach this screen, tap the **Menu** icon when you're connected to AOL and viewing your Buddy List, or reading an Instant Message. By using this screen, you can restrict who is able to send you messages when you're using AOL for Palm.

The bottom part of the screen is a list of Screen Names. You can use the **Add** button to make a new entry in it, or tap on a name then tap **Delete** to remove the name.

The list is used if you select either **Allow only the users listed below** or **Block the users listed below** from the Privacy Preferences screen.

You can also choose to allow everyone to send you messages, to block everyone, or to allow only people on your Buddy List to send you Instant Messages.

Preferences you set here do not affect Instant Messages when you're using AOL on your normal computer.

When you've made your selection, tap on **Done** to return to the previous screen.

And there you have it. If you have a Palm organiser with a modem, or a compatible mobile phone, there's no reason you need ever be out of touch with AOL again. Best of all, AOL for Palm is completely free to download, so why not try it out?

If you don't have a Palm yet, what better excuse do you need to treat yourself to one?

8.4 AOL Mobile

AOL Mobile

If you don't have a Palm organiser, but you do have a mobile phone or any device with a WAP browser, you can still access AOL, using the AOL Mobile service. You'll need a WAP phone, which is one that has a small browser built in, a little like a Web browser.

*If you're not sure whether or not you have a WAP phone, there are picture of some of the most common ones at keyword **AOL Mobile**, or you can contact your mobile phone company for advice. You can't access AOL Mobile without WAP.*

When you connect to AOL Mobile with your phone, you can access your email messages, find out the latest news headlines, or look up the details of the nearest cinema to you. There are TV listings, weather, and all sorts of other information available too. Best of all, you can use AOL Mobile as much as you like – once you have an AOL account, the mobile service is free.

Although AOL doesn't charge anything for you to access AOL Mobile, you have to make a call on your mobile phone to access any WAP service, such as AOL Mobile. You will have to pay your mobile phone company for these calls, which are not included in any AOL price plans. You should check with your mobile phone supplier to find out how much you will be charged for WAP calls.

Getting started with AOL Mobile

Starting to use AOL Mobile is easy. Just go to keyword **AOL Mobile** and you'll see a screen like this one.

Fig. 8.49
**AOL Mobile
main screen**

Before you can access your AOL account from a WAP phone, you need to register. You can either register on AOL, at the keyword **AOL Mobile**, or you can register via your mobile phone. Since entering information on the keypad of a mobile phone can be quite fiddly, it's probably easiest to register online first. If you do decide to register via your mobile phone, read this section first – you'll have to fill in similar details, however you do it.

When you first see the AOL Mobile screen, read the Welcome information, and then click on the first step in the **Signing up** section, which will show you some of the phones that are compatible with AOL Mobile. The next section, **Enabling my phone**, gives you the numbers you'll need if you have a WAP phone, but haven't had it enabled for use on your mobile network.

If you have a new phone, it's probably enabled already, but if you do experience problems, use this page to find out how to have your phone connected to the network. Remember that AOL's technical support team can only help you with AOL itself, not with all the different combinations of mobile phones and networks.

If you know that your phone is already ready for WAP, you can go straight to step three, **Registering for AOL Mobile**.

Fig. 8.50
Registration screen

When you register, you need to fill in this screen, giving your AOL password, and a PIN that you can use to access the service from your mobile; using a PIN can be easier than a password, on a mobile's keypad.

You are then presented with Sign In options. You can choose to log onto AOL Mobile in one of three different ways, depending on the level of security that you are most comfortable with.

Whichever option you choose, AOL will generate a unique personal URL for you – that's a special address that you can enter into your phone's list of bookmarks and save, so that you can log on to AOL Mobile without having to input your AOL Screen Name every time.

The first option, **Auto Login**, means that you won't need to enter any information to log on to the service – you'll just have to select the bookmark on your phone and you'll go straight to the main menu.

The second option, **Pin Login**, means that when you select your bookmark you will be asked for the 4-digit pin in order to log on to AOL Mobile.

The third option, **Password**, means that when you select your bookmark you will be asked for your AOL Password.

> *Although it's far easier to access AOL Mobile using the Auto Login option, remember that if you have the bookmark saved in your phone, anyone with access to your phone could connect to AOL Mobile and read your email, or send messages from your address, without having to enter any password or PIN. You should only use the Auto Login option if you're confident that your phone will be safe.*

After choosing your Sign In options, you then need to fill in details about your mobile phone – the number, model and the network you're connected to – as well as your postcode. AOL Mobile uses your postcode to personalise information for you area, such as cinema listings.

When you've entered all this information, click the **OK** button right at the bottom of the page to complete your registration.

The next screen will display your unique personal URL so that you can go ahead and add it to your phone's list of bookmarks. Write it down or add it to your phone right away. You'll also receive an email confirming the address and the PIN that you chose.

> *You'll need to refer to the instructions for your particular phone to find out how to add the bookmark to your phone, and how to select it when you want to use AOL Mobile.*

If you pick up someone else's mobile phone, or don't put a bookmark in your own phone, you can sign in to AOL Mobile by going to **http://mobile.aol.co.uk/** and choosing the **Sign In** option. When you do that, you'll have to enter your Screen Name, and if you chose PIN or Auto Login, you'll need to enter the PIN you chose. If you chose Password Login, you'll have to enter your normal AOL password.

Fig. 8.51
**Personalisation
screen**

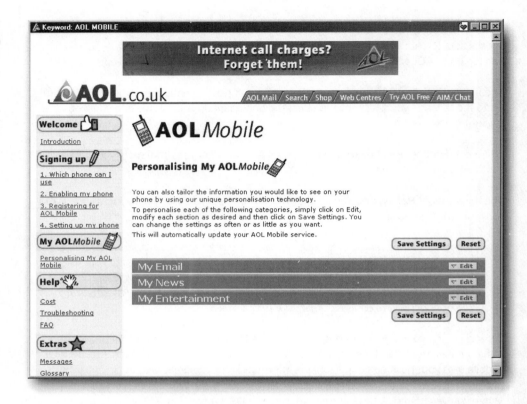

Now you can go on to the next stage, **Personalising My AOL Mobile**. On this screen, you can change the settings for AOL Mobile to make sure that the information you want is easy to reach whenever you access the service.

As you can see, there are three sections, **Email**, **News** and **Entertainment** – though as AOL Mobile grows, you'll see more added.

Personalising Email
Click on the word **Edit** at the right of the blue bar labelled **My Email**, and you'll be see
something like this:

Fig. 8.52
**Email address
edit for mobile**

You can use this option to build an Address Book for AOL Mobile, separate from your main
AOL Address Book. To add an entry, just click on **New Contact** in the list of contacts, and
fill in a nickname, email address and real name in the boxes provided. Now, when you want
to send an email to that address, you'll be able to select if from a list on your mobile phone,
instead of having to key it all in by hand.

You can delete an entry from the list by highlighting it and clicking on the **Delete** button
below the list.

Personalising News
Click the **Edit** button on the **My News** bar, and you can select three areas of news that
you're particularly interested in, so that you can reach them easily on your mobile phone.

Personalising Entertainment

Fig. 8.53
**My AOL Mobile
personalising
entertainment**

The **My Entertainment** section allows you to customise the information you'll see on AOL Mobile's Entertainment channel.

When you first visit this section, you'll see the three cinemas nearest to the postcode you entered originally. You can type another postcode into the box and click **Search** to find cinemas in other areas – you might want to add some near your office, for example, as well as near home.

After searching, you'll be given a list of cinemas with a check box next to each one – click the box to select any cinemas that you add to your list.

The next section, **TV**, lets you add types of TV channel to your AOL Mobile entertainment listings. You'll always be able to see what's on the five terrestrial channels; choosing options here will add listings for appropriate satellite and cable channels.

Finally, at the bottom of the page, you can select your star sign, so that your daily horoscope will be available each time you connect to AOL Mobile.

When you've made the choices you want in each section of the page, click the **Save Settings** button at the bottom. Now you're ready to use AOL Mobile from your phone.

Registering via your mobile phone
If you sign on to AOL Mobile for the first time via your mobile phone, at http://mobile.aol.co.uk, you'll have to enter your Screen Name, PIN of your choice, AOL password, and your postcode, but you won't have access to all the other personalisation options.

You can change the options at any time, by signing on to AOL and visiting keyword **AOL Mobile**, then choosing **Personalise My AOL Mobile** from the menu at the left of the screen.

Using AOL Mobile
Once you've set up AOL Mobile using the AOL software on your computer, it's easy to access the information you want on your mobile phone, wherever you are.

Access to AOL Mobile depends on being able to access WAP services from your mobile phone, which may not be possible if you're travelling abroad, or if you have not had WAP enabled on your phone. For information about using WAP on your particular phone and mobile network, you should contact your mobile phone network. AOL technical support cannot provide assistance with problems related to your phone or your mobile telephone network.

If you added a bookmark to your mobile phone containing your unique URL when you registered for AOL Mobile, all you need to do is select it, and you will go to your own personal AOL Mobile home page.

If you didn't bookmark the special address you were given during registration, or if you're using someone else's mobile phone, then you should tell the phone to connect to **http://mobile.aol.co.uk/**.

When you connect, you'll see the AOL logo, followed by a screen of options, of which the first is Members Sign In. Select that, and on the next screen you'll be asked to enter your Screen Name. Fill in the box, and then choose **Next**.

Different mobile phones let you select options from WAP screens and fill in boxes on screen in different ways. You should refer to the instructions for your phone if you are not sure how to use its controls. Your mobile phone network may be able to offer you assistance.

On the next screen, you need to enter either your password or your PIN, depending on the options you chose when you registered for AOL Mobile.

However you enter the service you'll get through to your own personal home page. This lists all the different categories of information that are available. If there's new email waiting for you, there'll be an entry right at the top of the list to say how many you have and to take you directly to the newest messages.

At the moment, the categories available are **Email**, **News**, **Sport**, **Weather**, **Entertainment**, **Travel**, **Finance** and **Logout**. When you've finished using AOL Mobile, you should choose the **Logout** option.

Fig. 8.54
**AOL Mobile
Channels**

From any of the other screens in AOL Mobile, choosing AOL Mobile will bring you back to the front screen.

Email
When you select AOL Mobile's **Email** option, you'll see a list of three types of email, just like your AOL mailbox on your PC – **New Mail**, **Old Mail** and **Sent Mail**. The fourth option, **Write Email**, lets you compose a new message.

Fig. 8.55
My Email

When you choose any of the first three options, you'll see a list of the messages in that section of your main AOL mailbox – people don't need to use a different Screen Name to reach you when you're reading mail via AOL Mobile.

Just select the message you want to read, and it'll appear on the screen of your phone.

Below the text of the message, you'll see options for dealing with the message – **Reply**, **Reply To All**, **Forward**, **Keep As New**, **Delete** and **Show Recipients**.

The first five options are identical to the buttons that you'll see when you read your email on AOL, so if you can use AOL's ordinary email, you'll have no trouble with AOL Mobile. The last option, **Show Recipients**, will list all the people that the message was sent to. Choose **Back to Folder** to return to the list of messages, or **My Email** to go back to the list of your mail folders.

Writing email
Reading your email using AOL Mobile is simple – just select a message, and scroll through it. Writing messages is slightly different, however.

To make writing messages as simple as possible, it's a good idea to use the AOL Mobile Address Book, which you must set up using your computer. You can read how to add addresses to it in the section Getting Started with AOL Mobile.

When you write an email, you can either fill in an email address, which could be quite fiddly using your phone's keypad, or select **Use Address Book**, which will let you select one or more of the nicknames that you added to your AOL Mobile address list.

Fig. 8.56
Write Email

After adding addresses to the Send To box, you can choose **Copy To**, to add **CC addresses** if you like, or carry on to write the message itself, by selecting **Enter Subject & Body**.

On the Subject & Body screen, there are two boxes. Select the first one and enter the subject of your email, then select the second and enter the message you want to send.

Fig. 8.57
Enter Subject and Body

You can choose to alter the **Send To** and **Copy To** addresses if you like, or just select **Send** when you've finished writing your message, and it'll be delivered. It really is very simple – you just need to work through the screens, filling in the address, subject and then your message.

Replying to a message works in the same way, except that AOL Mobile will have filled in the address and subject information for you already.

AOL Mobile's other channels
On the other channels of AOL Mobile, you'll find plenty of information, some of it from AOL's
main service, and some specially created for mobile users. For example, in the Entertainment
section, details of what's on at the cinemas that you selected when you personalised will
be automatically relisted and you can change to other areas too. You can even read a short
summary of each of the films.

Fig. 8.58
My Cinema

The travel section is packed with useful information like city guides, so you can find out where
to eat, or what to do, no matter where you are. Just like with AOL, the best way to find out
what AOL Mobile can offer you is to browse through it – you'll be surprised what you can find.
And don't forget – all you need is a WAP-enabled mobile phone; you don't need to pay any
extra subscription, and AOL doesn't charge you anything for accessing AOL Mobile.

Sending text messages from AOL to mobile phones

Have you ever used the text message service – its full name is Short Message Service, or
SMS – on a mobile phone?

SMS

It's a little like Instant Messages: you can send and receive short text messages, up to 160
characters long, between mobile phones. It's really handy, for example, if you know someone's
in a meeting and can't take a call. With an SMS, they can quietly read a note telling them that
their dinner date has been moved, or that you've just got a new job.

What use is this to AOL members? Well, these days, even if you don't have a mobile phone,
you're sure to know people who do, and so AOL has provided a way to send SMS messages
from your computer. There's no more fiddling around entering messages on the phone
keypad. Just type, and send. And the best thing about it is that it won't cost you a penny
extra as it's all part of the AOL service.

To start, you need to go to the keyword **SMS**.

Fig. 8.59
SMS screen

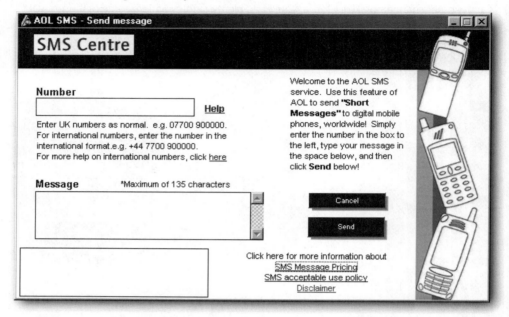

As you can see, this is a pretty simple screen. There are just two boxes to fill in. You need to type in the mobile phone number that you're sending the message to in the top box, and then type your message in the bottom one.

> *Remember that you can only send a message of up to 135 letters, and the message will appear to be from a special phone number. The person who receives it won't be able to use the reply function on their phone to send a message back to you. It's strictly one way.*

If you're sending a message to someone in the UK, they you can just fill in their phone number, just as you'd dial it from an ordinary phone. To send to an international number, enter the plus symbol + followed by the country code, and then the phone number, with the initial 0 missing. For example, a UK number 07000 900000 would become +4470009000000 in international format.

After you've filled in the information, all you need to do is click the **Send** button and that's it! If your friend's mobile phone is turned on, then they'll receive the message in a few seconds. If not, it'll arrive when they next turn it on.

AOL in the future

AOL on mobile phones and on Palm devices are here already, but in the future, it's likely you'll be able to access AOL in lots of different ways – via your television, on other pocket sized computers, or dedicated AOL devices. Of course, AOL on your computer won't be standing still either. It's always being improved, and one of the things you can look forward to is high-speed broadband access using the new high-speed phone lines.

Many phone lines can be upgraded to use a facility called ADSL (it stands for Asymmetric Digital Subscriber Line, but don't worry about that). What's the point? Well, with ADSL you will be able to access information on AOL or the Internet at speeds roughly ten times those you achieve with your modem.

That means that you'll be able to see better quality video clips, or listen to live music via the Internet much more easily than you can at the moment. It'll even be practical to buy computer programs over the net and download them directly – something that you certainly can't do with a modem for anything but the smallest programs.

So what's the catch? Unfortunately, at the time of writing, ADSL is only available to a small proportion of the UK population, and services that have already launched are quite expensive. It's also still quite tricky to install and set up – in fact, you need a BT engineer to do that.

But AOL's Broadband service – AOL Plus – is ready for the challenge. It's already available in the US, and as high speed connections become widely available elsewhere, including in the UK, it'll be offered to more subscribers. When you connect to AOL Plus, you'll have access to extra information designed to take advantage of your faster connection.

So, whether you want to connect via a mobile phone, your organiser, or experience the latest high speed connections, you'll be able to get it all with AOL.

1

Keywords
for AOL UK

As well as using the menus and buttons on screen, there are lots of areas on AOL that you can reach by using a keyword. You can type the keyword into the box at the top of the screen, or hold down the Ctrl key and press K, then type the keyword into the box that appears.

The letters in brackets next to each keyword tell you whether it's a UK specific keyword, or not. UK keywords can only be accessed by people with a UK AOL account. That means that you can't give a keyword to your friends who have accounts with AOL in other countries – if it's a UK keyword, they won't be able to use it. They will just be told it doesn't exist, or they may see information specially for their country.

Remember that the **Kids Contents** keyword in the Kids Channel will give a list of all the keywords specially for children. And don't forget that as new areas of AOL are introduced, they'll have their own keywords too. You can always find the most up-to-date list of at keyword **Keywords**.

A

AAA   All about AOL (UK)

ABOUT EMAIL   Everything you need to know about electronic mail (UK)

ACCESS NUMBERS   Accessing AOL worldwide (UK)

ACCOUNT   Account billing and support area (UK)

AIM   AOL Instant Messenger (UK)

ALL ABOUT AOL   (UK)

ANGLING   Everything to do with fishing (UK)

ANGLOFILE   Guide to what makes Britain great (UK)

ANNE DETTMER   Food and drink column (UK)

AOL LIVE   Online interview channel (UK)

AOL PRICING   Guide to our price plans (UK)

AOL SHOP   Buy goods online (UK)

AOL TODAY   What's happening in AOL (UK)

ARTS   Stage, books, visual arts and events (UK)

ASK CONNIE   Make the most of your online time (UK)

B

BANKING CENTRE   Everything to do with banking (UK)

BARGAIN HUNTER   Bargain holidays and travel (UK)

BARGAIN FLIGHTS   (UK)

BARGAIN HOLIDAYS   (UK)

BARGAINS   Travel and holidays savings (UK)

BEAUTY   Advice from the professionals (UK)

BELIEFS   Spirituality and religion (UK)

BIKE   Complete Bike magazine (UK)

BILLING   Account and billing support (UK)

BLACK BRITAIN   Black culture in the UK (UK)

BLOOMBERG   Business news (UK)

BOL   Buy books online (UK)

BOOK CLUB   Discuss your favourite books (UK)

BOOKS   The latest books released (UK)

BUDDY HELP   See when your friends are online (UK)

BUILD YOUR WEBPAGE   All you need to know (UK)

BUILDING   Build your own Web page (UK)

BUSINESS FORUM   Small business centre (UK)

BUSINESS CENTRE   Small business info (UK)

C

CANCEL   How to cancel your AOL account (UK)

CAPTION   Caption competition (UK)
CAR   News and events for car enthusiasts (UK)
CARD   Classic card games online (UK)
CAREERS   Advice on all things job related (UK)
CAR SHOWROOM   (UK)
CHARITY   All about charities in the UK (UK)
CHARTS   The UK Hit Parade (UK)
CHAT   Chat Channel (UK)
CHAT ROOMS   Chat rooms available worldwide (UK)
CHATEAU ONLINE   Buy wine online (UK)
CHAT HELP   All about using Chat rooms (UK)
CHATTERBOX   The latest on the Chat Channel (UK)
CHESS   Play online (UK)
CHIT CHAT   Chat for kids (UK)
CHRISTIANITY   Our Christian community (UK)
CINEMA GUIDES   What's showing near you (UK)
CLASSICAL   Latest from the classical music scene (UK)
CLASSIFIEDS   Buying, selling and personal ads (UK)
CLIMBING   Climbing on the Sport Channel (UK)
CLIP CLOP CLUB   Kids Pony Club (UK)
CLUBS CORNER   English Premiership (UK)
COLLECTORS   Get all your collectables here (UK)
COMICS   Online cult comic capers (UK)
COMMUNICATIONS CENTRE   Keep in touch (UK)
COMPANY RESEARCH   Latest business news (UK)
COMPETITIONS   (UK)
COMPLETE BIKE   All about motorbikes (UK)
COMPUTER BUYER   Consumer magazine (UK)
COMPUTER ADS   Buy and sell computers online (UK)
COMPUTER CHAT   Hosted chats (UK)
COMPUTER CLASSROOM   Classes, courses and training (UK)
COMPUTING   Computing Channel (UK)
COMPUTING EVENTS   What's on, where (UK)
COMPUTING SHOP   Buy online (UK)
COMPUTING COMPETITIONS   (UK)
COMPUTING HELP   From beginners to emergencies (UK)
COMPUTING NEWS   Latest headlines (UK)
COMPUTING TIPS   Hints and advice for PCs and Macs (UK)
CONFETTI   Interactive wedding guide (UK)
CONNIE   Service guide around AOL (UK)

CONSUMER CID   Our buying police force (UK)
COOKING   Food, drink and recipe ideas (UK)
COUNTRY PROFILES   World guide (UK)
CRAFT CORNER   Learn new hobbies and get tips (UK)
CROSSWORD   (UK)
CULT   Film and TV out of the mainstream (UK)
CULTURES   Lifestyles from around the world (UK)
CURRENCY   Money around the world (UK)
CURRENCY CONVERTER   How much the pound is worth (UK)
CV   Careers advice and jobs online (UK)
CYCLING   Latest news and resources (UK)

D
D&B   Dun and Bradsheet business news and advice (UK)
DANCE MUSIC   All the latest from the UK Dance scene (UK)
DAY TRIP   What's on and where to go in the UK (UK)
DEALS   Special offers when you buy online (UK)
DEAR JOANIE   Agony aunt for kids (UK)
DESKTOP THEMES   Windows wallpaper (UK)
DICTIONARY   Check your spelling online (UK)
DILBERT   Corporate cartoon capers (UK)
DOMINIC   Editor's letter (UK)
DOWNLOAD   Software centre (UK)
DOWNLOAD HELP   Software help (UK)
DOWNLOADS   Game downloads (UK)
DREAMCAST   Sega's next generation machine (UK)
DRINK   All about wine, spirits and beer (UK)
DRIVE   The latest on cars and motorbikes (UK)

E
EBAY   Online trading community (UK)
EBOOKERS   Book holidays and travel online (UK)
ECONOMIST   Weekly news journal online (UK)
EMAIL   How to use your AOL email (UK)
EMAIL EXTRAS   How to get the best out of your email (UK)
EMAIL HELP   All about the AOL email service (UK)
ENGLISH   Study resources for English as a subject (UK)
ENTERTAINMENT   The latest from the world of showbiz (UK)
ETHNIC   Global cultures (UK)
ETOYS   The Internet's biggest toy store (UK)

ETRADE   Online share trading, research and prices (UK)
EVENT GUIDE   What's on, where (UK)
EXAMS   Revision resource (UK)
EXHIBITIONS   Guide to the UK's museums and galleries (UK)
EXPEDIA   Book holidays online (UK)

F
FACE OFF   Ice Hockey (UK)
FAMILY SHOPPING   Buy gifts for relatives (UK)
FASHION   Latest from the catwalk (UK)
FAULT   Report AOL UK Software faults (UK)
FAVOURITE PLACES   Bookmark our best areas! (UK)
FEATURE   In-depth guide to film (UK)
FEEDBACK   Tell us what you think (UK)
FERRIES   Book a ferry on AOL (UK)
FESTIVALS   Guide to music's summer gatherings (UK)
FILES   Free software downloads (UK)
FILM   Film news and reviews (UK)
FINANCE   Finance Channel main screen (UK)
FINANCE NEWS   What's going on in the money world (UK)
FITNESS   Guide to getting and staying fit (UK)
FLIGHTBOOKERS   Book flights online (UK)
FLIGHTS   View timetables and book online (UK)
FONTS   Fancy texts a-plenty! (UK)
FOOD   UK food and drink area (UK)
FOOD SHOP   Guide to food and drink online (UK)
FOOTBALL   AOL guide to the beautiful game (UK)
FOOLUK   The Motley Fool UK (UK)
FOREIGN EXCHANGE   International money info (UK)
FORTNUM AND MASON   Hampers, wine and more (UK)
FT   FT Your Money with AOL (UK)
FTP   File Transfer Protocol info (UK)
FTSE   FTSE updates (UK)

G
GAME ON   Games reviews and contests (ALL)
GAMES   Games Channel main screen (UK)
GAMESDOWNLOADS   UK download area for games (ALL)
GAMES CHAT   (UK)
GAMESPOT   Games content provider (UK)

GAMES SURVEY   Give us your views (UK)
GAMES WEB   Our guide to games on the Web (UK)
GARDENING   Advice and guide to events (UK)
GAY   Resources for gays and lesbians (UK)
GENEALOGY   Trace your family history (UK)
GEOGRAPHY   Brush up knowledge on land-based matters (UK)
GETTING THERE   Getting from A to B made easy (UK)
GHG   The Good Hotel Guide (UK)
GIFTS   Choose a perfect present from our database! (UK)
GIFT REMINDER   Get us to remind you of important dates (UK)
GLOBAL   GlobalNet International Access numbers (UK)
GLOBAL NEWSSTAND   Pick of international papers (UK)
GOLF   Sporting resource (UK)
GOOD HOTEL GUIDE   Good Hotel Guide on AOL (ALL)
GOSSIP   All the latest in entertainment goss (UK)
UKGOVERNMENT   Political information (UK)
GRAPHICS FORUM   Learn about images (ALL)
GREEN TED   Online storybook for children (UK)
GSP   Language and general interest CD-ROMs for sale (UK)
GUIDE APPLY   Guide programme application (UK)
GUIDEPAGER   To report COS problems (UK)
G&W   Major companies database (UK)

H
HEALTH   Fitness forum (UK)
HEALTH INSURANCE   (UK)
HELICON   Hutchinson Encyclopedia online (UK)
HELP   Member Services area (Free, UK)
HIGH SPEED   Upgrade to a rapid access number (UK)
HOLIDAYS   Plan your vacation (UK)
HOLIDAY REPORT   Members report on their holidays (ALL)
HOME ENTERTAINMENT   Latest in hi fi and home cinema (UK)
HOMEPAGE BUILDING   Web building tips (UK)
HOME NEWS   Latest UK news (UK)
HOMEWORK HELP   Assistance with schoolwork (UK)
HORSE RACING   News, tips, results and more (UK)
HOST APPLY   Apply to be an AOL Host (UK)
HOSTED CHATS   UK Hosted Chat Schedules (UK)
HOTELS   Accommodation help (UK)
HOT SOFTWARE   Latest free software downloads (UK)

HOT SITES   Selection of favoured sites (ALL)
HOUSE   A shop for elegant living (UK)
HPUK   Hewlett-Packard UK Forum (ALL)
HTML   A beginner's guide to HTML (UK)
HUTCHINSON   Hutchinson Encyclopedia online (UK)

I
IG   UK insider guides (UK)
IG SUBMIT   Submit your insider guide (UK)
IIJ   Investor's Internet Journal (UK)
IM   Turn your Instant Messages on and off (UK)
IMAC   Guide to Apple's new computer (UK)
IMDB   Internet Movie Database (ALL)
INDIE   Indie and alternative music guide (UK)
INDUSTRY NEWS   Inside the business world (UK)
INSIDER   Insider guides (UK)
INSIDE SOAP   Inside Soap online (ALL)
INSURANCE   Online financial resource (UK)
INTERACTIVE INVESTOR   Personal finance advice (UK)
INTERESTS   Get pleasure from your leisure (UK)
INTERFLORA   Online flowers service (UK)
INTERNATIONAL   AOL across the world (UK)
INTERNATIONAL REPORT   Global news (UK)
INTERNET   Internet Channel main screen (UK)
INTERNET EXPLORER   Install Internet Explorer (UK)
INTL   AOL International (UK)
INVESTMENT   Get your money to make money (UK)
IRC   To download Internet Relay Chat software (UK)
ISA   A guide to ISAs and how to invest in them (UK)

J
JOBMAG   Employment news (UK)
JOBS   Employment resource (UK)
JOC   The Journal of Commerce (UK)

K
KEOWN   Footballing opinion from Martin Keown (ALL)
KEYWORD   Lists of AOL Keywords (UK)
KIDS   Kids Channel main screen (UK)
KIDS' AOL NETFIND   Search engine for children (UK)

KIDS' OUT THERE   News service for children (UK)
KIDS' SHOP   Online shopping for the little ones (UK)

L
LANGUAGES   Language resources (ALL)
LASTMINUTE   Entertainment, travel and gifts (UK)
LEARNING   Improve your knowledge (UK)
LIBRARY   Educational resources online (ALL)
LIFE INSURANCE   In-depth info from AOL (UK)
LIFESTYLES   Something for everyone (UK)
LINUX   Linux forum (UK)
LIST   Events guide for Glasgow and Edinburgh (UK)
LOCAL   UK Life Channel (UK)
LOGGING   Transfer text to save money (UK)
LOL   Those funny symbols explained here :-) (ALL)
LONDON   Local Life London areas & information (UK)
LONDON ART
LONDON CLUBS
LONDON COMEDY
LONDON FILM
LONDON FOOD
LONDON GAY
LONDON KIDS
LONDON LEISURE
LONDON MAYOR
LONDON MUSIC
LONDON NEWS
LONDON PEOPLE
LONDON SERVICES
LONDON SPORT
LONDON THEATRE
LONELY PLANET   Down-to-earth travel area (ALL)
LOTTERY   UK Lottery Syndicate (UK)
LOVE SHACK   UK personals (ALL)
LOVE STARS   Carole Golder predicts (UK)
LURVE   Love Shack (ALL)

M
MACGAMES   Games for the Macintosh (UK)
MACHELP   UK Mac help forum (UK)

MACOS   Mac OS 8.1 download (UK)
MAC USER   Online magazine (UK)
MAIL CONTROLS   Control the mail you receive (UK)
MAPS   Find your way around the world! (UK)
MARKETING PREFS   Mailing list controls (UK)
MAX DAVIDSON   Resident expert gardener (UK)
MEMBER SERVICES   All your queries answered (UK)
MILITARY   Army, navy and airforce news (UK)
MONARCHY   Royal resources (UK)
MOREINTERESTS   All your hobbies covered (UK)
MORTGAGES   All you need to know (UK)
MOTLEY FOOL   Financial know-how from the fool (UK)
MOTORBIKES   BSH custom bike magazine (ALL)
MOTOR INSURANCE   (UK)
MOTOR RACING   (UK)
MOVIE BABYLON   Hollywood gossip (UK)
MP3   Music area (UK)
MULTIPLAYER   Multiplayer gaming on AOL (UK)
MUSEUMS   Museums, galleries, etc. (UK)
MUSIC   AOL's music magazine (UK)
MUSIC & VIDEO   Buy from a wide selection of music sites (UK)
MUSIC NEWS   Rock and pop music news from the NME (UK)
MY ADDRESS   What's my email address? (UK)
MY AOL   Customise and personalise AOL (UK)
MYSTIC GARDENS   Mystic Gardens (ALL)

N
NAMES   Change or add names to your AOL account (ALL)
NEW   What's New area (UK)
NEW HELP   New members help (UK)
NEW PRICING   No more Internet phone bills! (UK)
NEW SCIENTIST   Online magazine (UK)
NEWS   News Channel main screen (UK)
NEWS CAPTION   News Caption (ALL)
NEWS DEBATE   News Debate (ALL)
NEWSGROUPS   Converse with others on topics of interest (ALL)
NEWS ON THE WEB   The latest on the Web (UK)
NEWS PROFILES   News you want, emailed free everyday (UK)
NEWS SURVEY   UK News Survey (UK)
NICKELODEON   Nickelodeon online (UK)

NINTENDO   Console news (UK)
NME   Music news from the famous rock weekly (UK)
NORTH OF THE BORDER   Learn more about life in Scotland (UK)
NOTIFY AOL   Report inappropriate behaviour (UK)
NOTES   London issues explored (UK)
NSPCC   Campaign to end cruelty to children (UK)

O
OBJECTS OF DESIRE   Cool gadgets and gizmos (ALL)
ONE ASIA   The British Asian perspective on life (UK)
ONLINE GAMES   Download and play games online (ALL)
OTREPORTS   News features from top global correspondents (UK)
OUTEREDGE   UK Teen area (ALL)
OUTTHERE   Out There News (UK)
OXFORD DICTIONARY   The New Oxford English Dictionary (UK)

P
PAPERSAY   See what the papers say (ALL)
PARANORMAL   The unexplained (UK)
PARENTAL CONTROL   Parental Controls setup (FREE, UK)
PASSWORD   Help and info (UK)
PC FINDER   PC dealer search and free quotes service (UK)
PC GAMES   Computer games forum (ALL)
PC PRO   Online magazine (UK)
PC SOUND   Make music on your computer (UK)
PC WEB   The best computing Web sites (UK)
PEOPLE   Lifestyles Channel (UK)
PENSIONS   All your questions answered (UK)
PETS   Care for your creatures (UK)
PET TAILS   Tell us about your pets (UK)
PHOTOGRAPHY   Resources for snappers (UK)
PICTURES   A pictorial review of the week's news (UK)
PIN   Advice on computers and software for parents (ALL)
PLACES TO STAY   New online booking service (UK)
PLAYSTATION or **PSX**   Sony console gaming area (UK)
POP   All the latest from the pop scene (UK)
PORTFOLIOS   Customisable share service (UK)
POSITIVE GENERATION   Help and advice on HIV/AIDS (ALL)
PRACTICAL PC   Online computer magazine (UK)
PRICES   AOL prices (FREE, UK)

PRIMARY SCHOOLS   Learning Channel schools (UK)
PRIVATE ROOM   Set up your own private chat room (UK)
PROFESSIONAL   Professional Forums (UK)
PROFILE   Create or edit your online Profile (ALL)
PSX   Playstation info (UK)
PSK   PC Survival Kit (UK)
PUB   Virtual pub (UK)

Q
QUESTIONS   AOL FAQs (FREE, UK)
QUICK CHAT   Rapid route to chat area (UK)
QUICK TOUR   Easy access to all areas of AOL (UK)
QXL   Online Auction House (UK)
QUOTES   International Company Quotations (UK)

R
RADIO GUIDE   What's on the wireless (UK)
REAL TIME PRICES   Up-to-the-minute share values (UK)
REFERENCE   Reference library (UK)
RELIGION   Spiritual information (UK)
REMINDER   We alert you to send gifts! (UK)
REVISION   Prepare for exams here (UK)
RNID   Area for deaf and hard of hearing (UK)
RUGBY   The Rugby Club (UK)
RULES   AOL Member Services rules (UK)
RUSSELL GRANT   Russell Grant's astrology area (ALL)

S
SAFETY ONLINE   Password and virus advice (ALL)
SAFETY ZONE   Online safety area for children (UK)
SCHOOLS   Community area (UK)
SCIENCE & TECHNOLOGY   (UK)
SCITECH   Science and technology area (UK)
SCHOOL'S OUT   What to do over the holidays (UK)
SCOTLAND   News and chat from north of the border (UK)
SEVEN DAYS   What's happening this week (UK)
SF   Science fiction (UK)
SHARES   Track your finances here (UK)
SHAREWARE   Free software (UK)
SHARPSHOPPER   No-nonsense shopping (UK)

SHOPHELP   All about shopping on AOL (UK)
SHOPMAG   Consumer reports and much more (UK)
SHOPPING   Shopping Channel main screen (UK)
SHOPPING NEWS   Read the Shopping Newsletter here (UK)
SHORTHAND   Online smileys and acronyms (UK)
SIMCITY   Insider's guide to the popular game (ALL)
SIMPLY FOOD   Culinary articles and competitions (UK)
SIGN ON A FRIEND   Get a friend online and receive £30 (UK)
SKI   Snowsports central (UK)
SLINGO   A cross between the slots and bingo! (UK)
SMALL BUSINESS CENTRE   Small business know-how (UK)
SOAF   Sign on a friend (UK)
SOFTWARECENTRE   Latest free downloads (UK)
SPAM   Say goodbye to junk mail with mail controls (UK)
SPACE   All about the final frontier (UK)
SPIRITUALITY   Area for discussion of beliefs (UK)
SPORT   Sport Channel main screen (UK)
SPORT CHAT   Discuss sports news and views (UK)
SPORT NEWS   The latest results (UK)
STAGE   Theatre news (UK)
STATELY HOMEPAGE   Page-building forum (UK)
STATUS   Current system status (UK)
STOCKS   Market reports (UK)
STORYMAKER   Story-writing device for children (ALL)
STRESSED OUT   Advice area for teenagers (ALL)
SUBJECT MATTER   Learn about a variety of subjects (UK)
SUGAR   Girls' magazine (UK)
SUGGEST   Feedback area (UK)
SUGGESTED SURFING   Where to go on the Web (UK)
SURPRISE   Click to be taken to a surprise destination (UK)
SWC   AOL Software Centre (UK)
SYSTEM RESPONSE   System response problems (Free, UK)

T
TALK TIME   UK Sport Chat Channel (UK)
TAX   Tax matters made simple (UK)
TEACHERS   UK teachers area
TECH   Technical Support (UK)
TECH CHAT   UK Tech Support (FREE, UK)
TELEVISION   Guide to programmes and their stars (UK)

TELEWORK   Telework Forum (FREE, UK)
TENNIS   The latest from AOL and the Web (UK)
TERRIS   Terris role-playing game (ALL)
THEATRE   Keep updated with the thespian world (UK)
THE FAITH   Christianity column (UK)
THE FEATURE   Planet Ealing film feature (UK)
THE LIST   Central Scotland guide to what's on (UK)
THESAURUS   Improve your vocabulary (ALL)
THESTREETUK   Latest on the markets (UK)
THIS IS LONDON   News, features and information for London (ALL)
THORNTONS   Luxury chocolates online service (UK)
TIL   This is London Evening Standard online (UK)
TIL CROSSWORD   This is London crossword (UK)
TIL FILM   This is London film (UK)
TIL THEATRE   Theatre with This is London (UK)
TIMETABLES   Road, rail, air and sea timetables (UK)
TIPBITS   Share tips from the weekend press (UK)
TIPSHEET   UK pop chart and forum (ALL)
TITAN AE   Area dedicated to the new film (UK)
TOP TEN   Sports, guests, funnies the list goes on… (UK)
TOE   The Outer Edge, UK teen area (ALL)
TOUR   Introduction to AOL Content Areas (UK)
TRADING PIT   Market trading updates (UK)
TRAVEL   Travel near or far with AOL's guide (UK)
TRAVEL BARGAINS   The best holiday deals (UK)
TRAVELFINDER   FREE holiday email service (UK)
TRAVEL SHOP   Choose and buy holidays online (UK)
TRAINS   Train times, prices and booking (UK)
TROUBLE   GuidePager screen (UK)
TUNED IN   Driving forum and Community area of Car Channel (ALL)
TVGUIDE   What's on television (UK)

U
UK CHATS   UK Hosted Chat Schedules (ALL)
UK FAMILIES   Family help and resources (UK)
UK GUIDE   Guide to areas of the UK (UK)
UK HEALTH   Health and fitness resources (UK)
UK HOTELS   Hotel Guide (ALL)
UK GOVERNMENT   Political information (UK)
UK LIFE   Front Screen regional and local news area (UK)

UKLIVE   UK Live events and special chats (ALL)
UKMEETS   Events and meeting area for AOL members (UK)
UNIVERSITY   Universities online (UK)
UPGRADE   Upgrade your AOL software (UK)
UPGRADING FORUM   PC upgrade help area (UK)
UP MY STREET   All about where you live (UK)
URBAN GARDENER   Max Davidson writes (UK)
URL   World Wide Web access (UK)
UTOPIA   UK gay/lesbian area (ALL)

V
VIRTUAL WALES   An introduction to Cymru (ALL)

W
WEATHER   Weather Channel main screen (ALL)
WEB BUILDING FORUM   Help with your Web page (UK)
WINDOWS   Everything you need to know about Windows (UK)
WHAT PC   Online computing magazine (UK)
WHATS WRONG   Check if there are any system problems (UK)
WIN95   Windows 95 files area (ALL)
WINDOWS 98   Windows 98 information area (ALL)
WINDOWS FORUM   Windows help area (UK)
WINE   Drink area (UK)
WIRE   Games Channel newsletter (UK)
WORLD GUIDE   Global guide (UK)
WORLD NEWS   Latest global updates (UK)
WOW   AOL UK's hot sites (UK)

X
XMAS SHOP   Buy gifts online (UK)

Y
YOU'RE THE BOSS   Football Manager Game (UK)

Z
ZDUK   Ziff-Davis UK Forum (ALL)

APPENDIX

2

How
Do I ...?

AOL is pretty simple to use, as we hope you'll agree, if you've read through the rest of the book. While we've tried to make it as easy as possible to find the information that you need, sometimes it might not seem obvious exactly where you need to look.

That's what this section of the book is for – to help you find the answers to some of your questions, we've listed the questions and where you'll find the information you need in this book.

The basics

How do I read my email?
It's easy, and you can find out how in *Chapter 2, First steps on AOL* (*2.4, Email basics*).

How do I send a file by email, or read a file someone's sent me in mail?
You need to learn about file attachments, in *Chapter 3, Advanced AOL* (*3.6, Advanced email.*)

How do I chat with other members?
You can use Instant message, chat rooms or message boards (*3.1, Instant Messages; 3.1, Chatting on AOL; 3.6, Message boards*).

How can I share my AOL account with other family members?
You need to create a new screen name, explained in *Chapter 5, AOL and You* (*5.1, Screen names and controls*).

How can I make sure my children don't see anything unsuitable?
Give them their own screen name and use AOL's Parental Controls to control access (*5.1, Screen names and controls*).

How do I download software from AOL for my computer?
It's very simple, and all the details are in *Chapter 3, The AOL Experience* (*3.5 The Download Manager*).

How do I access Internet pages?
Just type the address into the keyword box at the top of the screen. You can find out more about the Internet in *Chapter 6* (*6.1, The Web*).

How can I get back to a part of AOL that I like?
Why not add it to your Favourite places or shortcuts? You can find out more about these in *Chapter 5, AOL and you* (*5.4, Customising AOL*).

How do I make a Web page?
The simplest way is using AOL's 1-2.3, Publish system, which will take you just a few minutes, but there are more advanced options too (*5.6, Making a basic home page; 7.1, Advanced home page building*).

How do I find help online?
You need to use Member Services, which is where you can find all the help you need (*2.5, Member services*).

How do I report problems?

Use the **Trouble** keyword, which is part of Member services (*2.1, A Cautionary word; 2.5, Member services*).

How can I tell other people about my interests?

You need to create a profile, described in *Chapter 5, AOL and You* (*5.2, People on AOL*).

How can I find the areas of AOL that will interest me?

You can create an Interest Profile, and AOL will tell you every time there's something new that fits your interests (*5.4, Customising AOL*).

Intermediate topics

How can I write email when I'm not connected to AOL?

You'll find the details in *Chapter 3, Advanced AOL*, and more information in Chapter 5, in the Automatic AOL section (*3.6, Advanced email; 5.6, Automatic AOL*).

How can I keep a list of email addresses I use regularly?

AOL has a built-in address book, which is described in *Chapter 3, The AOL Experience* (*3.6, Address book*).

How do I keep a record of Instant Messages and chat room conversations?

The Log manager will keep a record for you (*3.5, Log manager*).

How can I listen to music files that I've downloaded, or watch video clips?

AOL's Media Player does what you want, and it's in *Chapter 3, The AOL Experience* (*3.4, Media Player*).

How do I download files from the Internet?

You need to use something called FTP, which is explained in Chapter 6 (*6.3, FTP*).

How do I ask AOL to search for news that interests me?

Use the News Profiles facility, and you'll receive news via email (*5.4, Customising AOL*).

How can I find out when friends are online, so that I can chat with them?

Create a Buddy List, so you know when they're online – you can have private chats with them too (*5.2, People on AOL*).

How can I keep track of my appointments?

You can use AOL's calendar facility, described in *Chapter 5* (*5.3, My Calendar*).

How do I organise all my email messages?

Use your Personal Filing Cabinet (*5.5, Personal Filing Cabinet*).

How do I tell AOL to collect all my new messages while I'm away from the computer?

Automatic AOL is what you need, and it's explained in *Chapter 5, AOL and You* (*5.6, Automatic AOL*).

How do I talk with friends who aren't AOL users?

Get them to download AOL Instant Messenger, then you can add them to your Buddy List. You can invite them to join you in one of AOL's online groups, too (*8.2, AOL Instant Messenger; 5.2, People on AOL; 5.8, Groups@AOL*).

How can I use my AOL account on a friend's computer?

If they have the AOL software installed, you can sign on as a Guest, which is explained in Chapter 7. If they don't, then you can read your email via the Internet using AOLMail (*7.2, Using your AOL account from another computer; 8.1, AOL Mail*).

How can I send a message to a friend's mobile phone?

Use the AOL SMS service. You'll find details in *Chapter 8, AOL Anywhere* (*8.3, AOL SMS*).

Advanced topics

How can I set up my computer to access AOL when I'm abroad?

You need to add a new 'location' to your AOL software, which is explained in *Chapter 7, Advanced AOL* (*7.2, Travelling with your computer*).

How do I read discussions on the Internet?

Internet discussions take place in Newsgroups, which are like AOL's message boards (*6.4, Newsgroups*).

How can I read my AOL mail when I'm in a cyber-café?

You need to use the AOLmail Internet service, explained in *Chapter 8, AOL Anywhere* (*8.1, AOLmail*).

How do I change my billing information or pricing plan?

You'll find all the billing information explained in Chapter 5 (*5.4, Customising AOL*).

How can I access AOL using my Palm organiser?

There's a special cut-down version of AOL just for Palm users (*8.3, AOL for Palm*).

How do I change my modem settings?

You can use the setup options described in *Chapter 7*, and the expert options if you need to fine-tune the details (*7.2, Creating a new location; 7.2, Expert settings*).

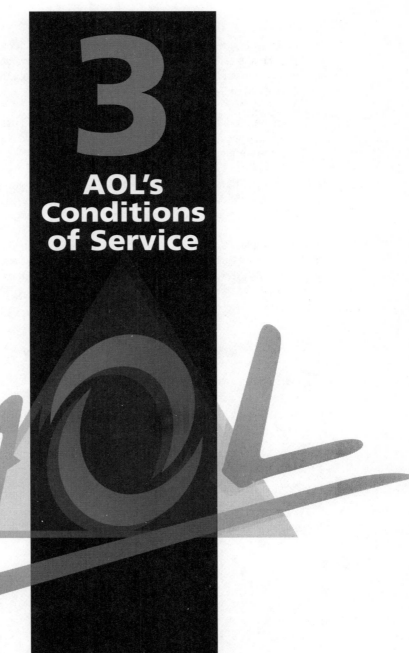

3

AOL's Conditions of Service

When you signed up to AOL, you agreed to the Conditions of Service, which explain what you can and can't do, and how you should behave towards other members and Internet users when you're online. If you see someone talking about COS on AOL, they mean the Conditions of Service.

Read the conditions carefully, but remember that if you use common sense you'll usually be fine. However, if you're ever warned by a Host or Guide about breaching them, you should take the warning very seriously indeed.

So that you have a handy reference, we've printed a complete copy of them here. However, remember that sometimes they are updated, so it's as well to check online at the keyword **COS**, where you'll be able to see the last time any changes were made.

The complete Conditions of Service are made up of the Member Agreement and the Community Guidelines, which we've listed here. We've also included the guidelines for Groups@AOL, which cover any of the groups you might create online.

Member Agreement

This AOL Member Agreement is a legal document that details your rights and responsibilities as an AOL member, and those of America Online Inc., a US company ('AOL Inc.', 'we' or 'us') as the provider of the AOL service ('AOL') to subscribers in the UK.

After you completed the AOL registration process, you became an AOL master account holder. *To be an AOL master account holder you must be at least 18 years old*. If you're not, you may still use AOL through a sub-account where you are authorised to do so by the master account holder, but only if the account was created and registered by your parent or a supervising adult.

Because protecting your privacy is especially important, we would first like you to have a clear understanding of how your personal data will be used.

1. Personal Data

By personal data we mean any data that identifies or relates to you or your individual AOL account. It includes identity and billing information which you agree to supply to us accurately, and to keep up-to-date by using keyword: **Billing**.

Personal data will be collected, processed and used by AOL Inc. for the purpose of providing and billing for AOL, and other purposes mentioned below. AOL is global, and many of the computer systems that provide it are currently based in the United States. Thus, your personal data will be transferred to, processed and held in the United States and in countries within the European Union.

AOL Inc. has national joint ventures ('AOL Group Companies'), such as AOL Bertelsmann Online, a United Kingdom limited partnership, which promote and provide local content and services and provide customer support for AOL. To carry out these limited functions, AOL Group companies may have access to your personal data.

We encourage you to tell us what your marketing preferences are for your personal data. For this purpose, please note that unless you 'opt-out' you are agreeing that your name and address may be disclosed to selected third party suppliers of goods and services and advertisers, who may use it to market to you their products and services. You can opt-out at any time after you have completed the registration process by using keyword: **Marketing Prefs**.

To provide a service which meets our members' needs, we may collect personal data relating to the popularity and usage of the various services offered through AOL. However, this data will be used or disclosed only on an anonymous, aggregated basis.

We may hold personal data relating to the transactions you enter into with us or others through AOL, such as online merchants. We will disclose this data to a party to the transaction, but only to facilitate your transaction. AOL Group companies may also use this data to let you know about products and services that may be of interest.

When you call our Customer Service department, we may monitor or record your calls and store details of the phone number(s) you use to make the call. This information is used only to track reported problems, and better address your customer service needs.

We will retain your personal data only as long as is necessary for the purposes to which you consent under this Member Agreement, and then we will delete it from our systems.

To inspect, change or correct your identity and contact information, you should use keyword: **Billing**. To find out how you can inspect or correct other personal data please contact our member services at 0800 376 5432. If you have other questions about the handling or protection of your personal data or your rights under this agreement, please contact AOL Bertelsmann Online, Attention: Data Protection Officer at 80 Hammersmith Road, London W14 8UD or via email at DataInfoUK@aol.com

We may disclose your personal data if we are either compelled to do so by law, or in response to a valid, legally-compliant request by a law enforcement or governmental authority.

2. Some Basics of Your AOL Membership
This Agreement is intended to contain your entire agreement with AOL Inc. relating to your use of AOL; we believe it to be fair and reasonable. However, additional terms and conditions may apply if you use affiliate services like our international areas, other AOL services (such as AOL Instant Messenger) or third-party software or services.

As AOL Inc's business and the online world continue to evolve, we will need to change provisions of this Member Agreement and the Community Guidelines. If AOL Inc. makes any changes to the Member Agreement, we will notify you of them at least thirty days in advance. If you don't agree to those changes, you may terminate your AOL membership.

By continuing to use AOL, you will have accepted the relevant changes.

AOL Inc., and its content providers and other third party suppliers, may from time to time modify or remove aspects of AOL, including various types of content and services. AOL Inc. will not, however, remove aspects of AOL which are fundamental to its nature without first giving notice to members in the same manner as changes to this Member Agreement.

AOL limits you to one free trial offer.

When you complete the AOL registration process and become the master account holder, AOL Inc. grants you a non-exclusive licence for the duration of your membership to use the 'screen name' selected by you (and confirmed by AOL Inc. as accepted for your use with your master account) during the registration process, as well as those screen names assigned to any sub-accounts which you establish during your membership. Your screen name is the online identity of the master account or sub-account to which it relates. You may not use a screen name that is used by someone else, and your screen name(s) cannot be vulgar, or be used in any way that does not comply with the other parts of this Member Agreement or AOL's Community Guidelines.

As the master account holder, you are responsible for all activity on your master account and all sub-accounts and any breaches of this Agreement and the Community Guidelines which may result. You will receive important notices about your membership by email from time to time which may not be sent to your sub-accounts, so it is important for you to check your master account mailbox regularly. You are responsible for all use of your master account and its sub-accounts, therefore you should supervise the use of them by others.

You are responsible for the security and proper use of your password, and must take all necessary steps to ensure that the password is kept confidential and used properly. You must notify us promptly if you have any reason to believe that your password has become known by an unauthorised person or is being used in an unauthorised manner. If AOL Inc. has reason to believe that there is likely to be a breach of security, AOL Inc. may change your password and notify you of the change which has been made.

3. Charges and Billing
The answers to many common billing questions can be found by selecting 'My Account' within Member Services or by using keyword: **Billing**.

You will be charged for using AOL in accordance with the billing plan that you selected during registration for AOL. We may change our fees or billing methods, but will provide you with at least thirty days' advance notice of any such change. If you don't like the changes we make, you can terminate your membership at any time.

As the master account holder, you are responsible for all charges incurred and purchases made by you or others using you're master account or any sub-accounts.

We offer premium content and services through AOL. If they are accessed through your master account or sub-accounts, then additional charges (known as surcharges or premiums) will be incurred. You are provided with notice of the relevant surcharges or premiums when you enter any surcharged or premium area. You are responsible for all additional charges incurred using your master account or sub-accounts; they apply even during any free trial of AOL.

AOL's Parental Controls allow you to prevent sub-accounts from entering premium or surcharged content. For more information go to keyword: **Parental Controls**.

Most members pay by credit card from a credit card account selected during the sign-up process (as that account may be changed by agreement with us from time to time). In certain circumstances, we may authorise you to pay by debit card or by electronic funds transfer from a bank account. By selecting either of these options, you authorise AOL Inc. to make electronic transfers from your nominated bank account. If we don't receive payment from your designated credit card or bank account, you remain obliged to pay us the sums in question. We will be charging your designated account every month, but some charges may be accumulated before they are charged to it. You authorise AOL Inc to charge certain purchases you make online to your account; you will be informed when this is happening.

We expect you to pay your account balances on time. If we do not receive payment within 30 days from the date on your AOL account statement, you agree to pay all outstanding charges due to AOL Inc. on demand, and AOL Inc will be entitled to charge interest of 1.5% per month on all those charges. You agree that you will immediately pay any then-outstanding charges if your membership is terminated for any reason.

You should let us know about any billing problems or discrepancies promptly after they first appear on your account statement. If you do not bring them to AOL's attention within 180 days, you will have waived your right to dispute those problems or discrepancies.

Telephone charges for connecting to AOL are your responsibility. There are a network of telephone access numbers throughout the United Kingdom; you are responsible for selecting the least costly of these numbers during registration (and afterwards using the 'Setup' button on the AOL Sign-On Screen). There are also telecommunications surcharges, which arise when you use AOL from certain locations or via certain networks; these surcharges will apply during any free trial of AOL. You are responsible for checking the amount of any telecommunications surcharges by using keyword: **Global**.

If you have any other questions about access numbers you should consult keyword: **Access**.

4. Online Conduct and Content
Content
By content, we mean the information, software, communications, images and sounds

provided online. The content available through AOL is provided by AOL Inc. and its affiliates, our members, independent content providers and other third parties. In general, AOL Inc. does not pre-screen content available through AOL, but does reserve the right to remove or filter any that does not meet its standards or comply with the Community Guidelines.

We are not responsible for content that is provided by others or for any failure or delay in removing it from AOL. Members must take responsibility for managing their own online experience, and that of others, who use their AOL master account or sub-accounts. This is especially important where children are using AOL; they are safer online – and get more out of the experience – with adult supervision. You should review the Parental Control facility (at keyword: **Parental Controls**) and AOL's Community Guidelines.

You are responsible for evaluating the accuracy, completeness and value of content, goods and services offered by third parties through AOL or the Internet; AOL Inc. will not be party to any transaction concerning such content, goods or services.

AOL Inc. is not responsible for content available on the Internet, although we reserve the right to block or filter access to areas on the Internet which may contain illegal or harmful content, or which may be used for purposes that are injurious to AOL Inc., AOL service or its members.

This medium allows individuals to create their own content and voice their opinions; AOL members are encouraged to do so. But you must abide by certain rules and standards as an AOL member.

In essence, you must ensure that your master account (and each sub-account) is used, whether by you or anyone else, only for lawful purposes and in a manner which does not in our reasonable opinion infringe the rights of any person or entity, or restrict anyone's enjoyment of AOL or the Internet. As an AOL member, you agree to adhere to these principles – which are more fully described in AOL's Community Guidelines – and you acknowledge that AOL Inc. has the right to enforce them in its sole discretion. If you, or anyone using your AOL master account or any sub-account, breach these guidelines, AOL Inc. may take action against you or your account. This action can range from a warning about the breach to the termination of each of your AOL accounts.

You may have access to services provided by AOL Inc. and its affiliates, such as AOL Instant Messenger, which are available both to AOL members and other Internet users. When using these other AOL-branded services your conduct remains subject to this Member Agreement; however, non-AOL members who use these services are not subject to this Member Agreement and may not be governed by the same rules or standards.

AOL's Community Guidelines may change from time to time. We will try to notify you in advance of significant changes to them; you can always find the most current version at keyword: **COS**.

Junk Email
Your accounts may not be used to send unsolicited bulk email (or 'junk email'). Further, you may not use the AOL member directory, or any other area of AOL to collect information, such as screen names, about AOL members, nor use this information for junk email purposes. If you have received junk email and want to report it, simply use the 'Forward' button on the email screen and send it to cosmail1 or cosmail2. AOL Inc. may, without prior notice, take such measures as it deems fit to block or limit the transmission through AOL of junk email. Information about unsolicited bulk email can be found at keyword: **Mail Controls**.

Proprietary Rights
The content on AOL is owned by AOL Inc. and others, and is protected by copyright, trade marks, and other intellectual property rights. It is very easy to copy things in cyberspace, but this does not mean it is acceptable or legal. You must not copy, modify, distribute, show in public or create any derivative work from any of the content you find on AOL, unless you have a right to do so. Doing so can lead to the termination of your AOL account – and may even breach the criminal law. Further, content owners may initiate criminal or civil action against you. In that event, you will be required to indemnify AOL Inc. and others against liabilities which may result (see Section 7 'Indemnification' below).

You agree only to make authorised, legal uploads and downloads of content through AOL, whether the content is software, music, video, graphics, text or anything else. All the content you transmit must either be your own or you must be expressly authorised to distribute it on AOL.

Some areas of AOL are generally accessible to other members (we refer to them as 'public'), like message boards, chat 'rooms', auditoriums and the AOL Member Directory. By submitting content to a public area, you are representing that you are fully entitled to do so, and that you grant to AOL Inc. the non-exclusive right to copy, modify, distribute, show in public and create derivative works from that content in any form, anywhere. You also grant AOL members the right to use such content for personal, non-commercial purposes.

5. AOL Software Licences
You use AOL proprietary software to access AOL, which you agree to use in accordance with this Member Agreement. You may not sub-license, or charge others to use or access, our software. We may occasionally provide automatic upgrades of both AOL Inc. proprietary software and third party software bundled with AOL to improve your online experience, and

we employ virus-screening technology to assist in the protection of our network and our members. We reserve the right automatically to log off accounts that are inactive for an extended period of time; if this occurs, you will need to sign on again to recommence your use of AOL. You must not use tools that defeat AOL's automatic log-off feature.

AOL Inc. grants to you a non-exclusive, limited licence to use AOL proprietary software to connect to AOL from authorised locations in accordance with this Member Agreement. This licence is subject to the restriction that, except where expressly permitted by law, you may not translate, reverse-engineer, reverse-compile, decompile, disassemble or make derivative works from, AOL software; nor may you modify AOL software or use it in any way not expressly authorised by this Agreement. You agree that the technologies introduced by AOL Inc may not be consistent across all platforms (e.g., Macintosh).

6. Warranty and Liability

You agree that AOL, AOL software, third party virus checking technology, any other bundled third party software and the Internet are supplied or made available to you as is, as available and for your personal use only, and that your use of each is at your sole risk. AOL Inc. does not make (and expressly excludes) any warranty, representation or undertaking that you will be able to access AOL at a time or from any location of your choosing, or that there will be adequate capacity for AOL as a whole or for particular products, services or content. However, AOL Inc. will use reasonable skill and care to provide and maintain the availability of AOL.

This Member Agreement is intended to contain all of the undertakings and warranties we give about the AOL Software and AOL, which we believe to be fair and reasonable. Accordingly, we propose to exclude from this Member Agreement all representations and warranties relating to its subject-matter (including any about content or the AOL Software), whether they are statutory or otherwise, as far as is possible by law.

AOL Inc. will not be liable to you or any third party for any indirect or consequential loss or damage, or for any loss of data, profit, revenue or business, howsoever caused (whether arising out of any negligence or breach of this agreement or otherwise), even if that loss or damage was foreseeable by, or the possibility of it was brought to the attention of, AOL Inc.

Without limiting the above three paragraphs (and except for any liability which may not by law be limited), the liability of AOL Inc. under this Agreement (whether arising in negligence or otherwise) will not under any circumstances exceed an amount equal to the fees owed to AOL Inc. by you during the six-month period preceding the time liability arises, regardless of the cause or form of action.

As much of the content over AOL is supplied by third parties (such as content providers), those third parties shall have the benefit of this Clause 6 (apart from its first paragraph) as if they were referred to as AOL Inc. there. However, in using content and areas provided by third parties, you may be required to agree to additional terms and conditions: AOL Inc. will not be a party to any contract which results.

7. Indemnification

Upon request by AOL Inc., you agree to indemnify AOL Inc. and its affiliates (that is, AOL Bertelsmann Online in the UK, AOL Inc. and their respective subsidiaries and affiliates), their employees, contractors, officers, directors, telecommunications providers and content providers from all liabilities, claims and expenses that arise from any breach of this Member Agreement, use of AOL or the Internet, or the transmission of any content on AOL by you or through your master account or sub-accounts. AOL Inc. reserves the right, at its own expense, to assume the exclusive defence and control of any claim which is subject to indemnification by you under this Member Agreement, in which event you will (from that time onwards) have no further obligation to provide indemnification for that claim.

8. Termination

This Member Agreement runs for successive periods of one month beginning on the date when you commence your membership and automatically renews at the end of each month unless terminated by you or us. Either AOL Inc. or you may cancel this Member Agreement at any time for any reason effective upon 30 days notice. You can cancel your membership by notifying the AOL Customer Services Department by telephone 0800 376 5432, email sent from your master account to UKBilla@aol.com or letter to Gilde House, Eastpoint Business Park, Fairview, Dublin 3, Ireland marked for the attention of UK Customer Services. Termination will be effective and your account cancelled within 72 hours of the time of delivery of notice. Where you are on a monthly payment plan, AOL Inc. will not refund any charges relating to the remaining portion of the month in which you terminate your account.

Termination by you of your account is your sole right and remedy against AOL Inc. where you are in any way dissatisfied with AOL or AOL Inc., including if you are unhappy with: any term of this Member Agreement, any policy or practice of AOL Inc. or any changes made to them in accordance with this Member Agreement; your ability to access and use AOL; or the amount and types of fees incurred by you or any of our billing methods. Where you have terminated in these circumstances you may be entitled to a refund of any unexpired portion of AOL's charges where you have paid more than a month's charges in advance. You will not be entitled to any refund for credits or other benefits applying to any of your accounts.

If you seek to reactivate AOL membership, you must resolve any delinquent or unpaid AOL accounts with AOL's COS staff before doing so.

AOL Inc. may terminate your membership immediately without notice in certain circumstances, such as where you have breached one or more of your obligations in this Member Agreement and your breach is, in AOL Inc.'s reasonable discretion, especially serious. This kind of breach generally arises where applicable laws or third-party rights have been violated in some way, or your online conduct has adversely affected someone's (including AOL Inc.'s) interests or another member's use of AOL. Non-exhaustive examples include:

(i)   online behaviour – or the distribution of content – which is likely to infringe the criminal law or someone's rights;
(ii)   the sending of unsolicited bulk email;
(iii) behaviour which affects AOL Inc.'s ability to provide AOL; or
(iv) failure to pay charges in accordance with this Member Agreement.

Alternatively AOL Inc. may decide, in its discretion, to suspend your membership or to issue a warning to you instead of terminating your membership immediately. Non-exhaustive examples of activity which AOL Inc. may decide to treat in this way include:

(i)   non-critical breaches of AOL Inc.'s Community Guidelines;
(ii)   online behaviour which causes annoyance, but which is not (in AOL Inc.'s opinion) serious or intentional.

If there is any subsequent breach, AOL Inc. will be entitled to terminate your membership immediately.

If your AOL membership is terminated as a result of a breach of this Member Agreement, you must obtain AOL Inc.'s permission (and provide such undertakings as AOL Inc requires) before you can use AOL again. You must cease to use AOL Software and AOL upon termination.

Termination of this Member Agreement shall not affect any rights accrued in favour of you or us. This Section 8 (Term and Termination) and Sections 6 ('Warranty and Liability'), 7 ('Indemnity'), 9 ('Law'), and 10 ('Miscellaneous') of this Member Agreement shall all survive such termination.

9. Law
This Agreement shall be governed by and construed in accordance with the laws of England and Wales.

10. Miscellaneous
Precedence
Where there is any conflict or discrepancy between any provision of this Agreement and the AOL Community Guidelines or any other policy issued by AOL Inc. at any time to its members, the terms of this Agreement shall take precedence, unless the policy in question states that it takes precedence.

Notice to You
Under this Agreement, we may be required to give you notice about important matters from time to time. Such notice may be given to you, amongst other methods, by email or letter. Email notice will be sent to your registered account over AOL. Postal notice will be sent to the address you provide us in your registration, and which you may modify by consulting keyword: **Member Services**.

Notice to Us
You may give notice to AOL Inc. by writing us an email at UKBilla@aol.com, by phoning our Customer Service office at 0800 376 5432 or by writing a letter to us at Gilde House, Eastpoint Park, Fairview, Dublin 3, Ireland.

Effective Dates of Notices
Emailed notice will have been given two days after the date of its delivery. Postal notice will have been given to you two working days (Mondays to Fridays, UK bank holidays excluded) after proven dispatch by first class recorded delivery post.

Assignment
AOL Inc. reserves the right to assign or subcontract any of its rights or obligations under this Agreement. You may not without the written consent of AOL Inc. assign or dispose of this Agreement.

Matters Beyond Our Reasonable Control
AOL Inc. shall not be liable for any failure or delay in performance of its obligations under this Agreement caused by matters beyond its reasonable control.

No Waiver
If you or we fail to exercise any right or remedy under this Agreement, that failure won't operate as a waiver of that right or remedy, or prevent it from being exercised subsequently.

11. Questions about this Member Agreement
If you have questions about the Member Agreement, or about your rights and responsibilities as a AOL member, please contact us by email at COSMonitor@aol.com

AOL Community Guidelines

Like any city, we take pride in – and are protective of – our community. That's why our community standards are important. Communities of all sizes rely on civic pride and the duty of all citizens to help with things like picking up litter, getting out of the way of ambulances, reporting crime, and abiding by the law. These Guidelines tell you what you can expect from AOL, as well as the kind of online behaviour we expect of you. We also include some tips for protecting yourself online. The Guidelines are intended to be read in conjunction with AOL's Member Agreement, to which you are subject (and which is available at keyword: **Rules**).

Here are the basics (read further for more detail):

- Follow basic guidelines for appropriate material.
- Don't break the law.
- Proper Online Conduct is Essential
- Business Use of AOL is Regulated: Unsolicited email is prohibited.
- Respect intellectual property.
- The Internet is different from AOL
- Respect cultural differences.
- Help control your online environment.

Follow basic guidelines for appropriate material

Content – By content, we mean the information, software, communications, images, sounds, and all the material and information you see online. It is provided by AOL, our affiliates, our members, or under license by our content partners. We do not pre-screen content generally, but we do work closely with our content partners to make sure that their content on the service reflects our community standards. We reserve the right to remove content that does not meet those standards.

Members like you also generate content in chat rooms, message boards, Web pages, etc. It is essential that this kind of content also reflects our community standards, and we may remove it if, in our judgement, it does not meet those standards. When we do, you may receive a warning about the breach of AOL's standards if your account (any of the screen names) was responsible for putting the objectionable content online. If it's a serious offence or you've violated our rules before, we may terminate your account.

AOL applies the same standards to its own and its partners' content that it applies to member content. Remember that community standards vary from community to community. Some chat rooms may use stronger language than others. Obviously, some online areas may deal with more adult-oriented topics, such as sexual dysfunction, rape, or infidelity, and we offer our members Parental Controls so that you may ensure that kids who use your account can't see that mature content (see 'Help Control Your Online Environment' below). In most places on AOL, crude language or sexually explicit conduct are no more appropriate online than they would be at a dinner-party. So while the guidelines may vary a bit depending on the online area you're in, in general, these guidelines apply:

Language – mild expletives and non-sexual anatomical references are okay, but strong crude language, crude or explicit sexual references, hateful language etc. are not. If you see it, report it at keyword: **Notify AOL**.

Nudity – Photos containing revealing attire or limited nudity in a scientific or artistic context is okay in some places (not all). Partial or full frontal nudity is not okay. If you see it, report it at keyword: **Notify AOL**.

Sex/Sensuality – There is a difference between affection and crudity. There is also a difference between a discussion of the health or emotional aspects of sex using appropriate language, and more crude conversations about sex. The former is acceptable, the latter is not. For example, in a discussion about forms of cancer, the words 'breast' or 'testicular' would be acceptable, but crude versions of those words would not be acceptable.

Violence and drug abuse – Graphic images of humans being killed, such as in news accounts, may be acceptable in some areas, but blood and gore, gratuitous violence, etc., are not acceptable. Discussions about coping with drug abuse in health areas are okay, but discussions about or depictions of illegal drug abuse that imply it is acceptable are not.

Please bear in mind that these are only guidelines; there is always a 'grey area.' Use your best judgment. Ask yourself if this is something that you would say in a room full of people you never met, or in the workplace. However, AOL makes the final determination about whether content is objectionable or not.

With all the content posted on AOL every day by our members, we can't possibly monitor all of it, and we do not attempt to do so. Therefore, you might occasionally encounter something you don't want to see. You can ignore it, but we prefer you report it using keyword: **Notify AOL**. Good judgment is important, especially when you encounter the opinions of others. AOL doesn't endorse or oppose opinions expressed by our members, but we do sometimes take issue with the manner in which the opinion is expressed.

Don't break the law

The laws that apply in the offline world must be obeyed online as well. We have zero tolerance for illegal behaviour on AOL. We terminate accounts and cooperate with the police and other law enforcement agencies on such matters.

In addition to providing you with an easy way to report illegal activity, we or our partners may in some instances monitor public areas on AOL. Our Community Leaders are there to help you and to help us maintain community standards. We do not monitor private areas, such as private chat rooms, Instant Messages, or email. Regardless of the area, AOL may be used only for lawful purposes. Simply because the grocer didn't see you take the apple doesn't mean it was okay to swipe it. Similarly, just because we may not be monitoring the area you're in at that point in time doesn't mean we don't care about our standards.

Proper online conduct is essential

Online conduct should be guided by common sense and basic etiquette. You will breach the Member Agreement if you (or others using your account) do any of the following:

- Post, transmit, promote, or distribute content that is illegal.

- Harass, threaten, embarrass, or do anything else to another member that is unwanted. So don't say bad things about them, don't keep sending them unwanted Instant Messages, don't attack their race, ethnicity, etc. If you disagree with someone, respond to the subject, not the person.

- Transmit or facilitate distribution of content that is harmful, abusive, racially or ethnically offensive, crude, sexually explicit, or in a reasonable person's view, objectionable. Community standards may vary, but there is no place on AOL where abusive or hateful speech is tolerated.

- Disrupt the flow of chat in chat rooms by using crude language, abusiveness, hitting the return key repeatedly or inputting large images so the screen goes by too fast to read, etc. This is online vandalism, and it ruins the experience for others.

- Pretend to be anyone whom you are not. You may not impersonate anyone – whether it is another member, a non-member, an AOL employee, or a Community Leader.

- Attempt to get a password or any other personal or AOL account information from or about any member. Because a member's account is that person's online persona, it is sacrosanct. Remember: AOL employees will NEVER ask for your password. Don't give your password out to anyone.

Obey the relevant rules wherever you are. These include the rules of other interactive services, guidelines applied to particular AOL areas, and laws and community standards which apply in AOL's various International services (see Respect cultural differences below).

'Netiquette' is used all over the Internet. Whether you are on AOL or using other Internet functions, it's important to be polite. Many newsgroups, Web communities, and the like have their own community guidelines or standards, and you should consult them before participating.

AOL offers Web site publishing capability to encourage you to participate in a variety of online communities on AOL. We regard those communities as part of the AOL service and we will enforce our community guidelines for member-created Web pages.

Business use of AOL is regulated

- Unsolicited bulk email (or 'junk email') is strictly prohibited.

- Chain letters and pyramid schemes are not allowed. Many such things are illegal. Even the ones that aren't illegal are annoying to most people and tie up online resources, so we don't allow them.

- You may place advertisements only in areas designated for that purpose. Unsolicited advertising is not allowed. This includes the sending of junk email.

- Use of a member Web site for business purposes is not permitted.

- You may not collect or 'harvest' the screen names of members.

Respect intellectual property

As the Member Agreement points out, the content on AOL is owned by AOL Inc. and others, and is protected by copyright, trade marks, and other intellectual property rights. Even though it is very easy to copy things in cyberspace, this does not mean it is acceptable or legal. So you must not copy, modify, distribute, show in public or create any derivative work from any of the content you find on AOL, unless you have a right to do so.

Also, you must only make authorised, legal uploads and downloads of content through AOL, whether the content is software, music, video, graphics, text or anything else. All the content you transmit must either be your own or you must be expressly authorised to distribute it on AOL.

The Internet is different from AOL

AOL provides you with access to the Internet, which is different from AOL. Email to or from non-AOL members, newsgroups, FTP, the World Wide Web, etc. is outside of the boundaries of AOL. However, as an AOL member you are required to follow our Member Agreement and Community Guidelines no matter where you are on the Internet. If another ISP or Internet organization reports you to us, we reserve the right to take appropriate action against your account in the same way as if you had committed a breach on AOL itself.

Use of the Internet is at your own risk, and AOL cannot be responsible for the content and conduct you may encounter. If the content or behaviour originates from outside AOL, we cannot remove it and are limited in the actions we can take. In addition, not every Web site you encounter will deal with your personal or private information in the same way that AOL does. Be very careful about giving out personal information.

Since the Internet contains goods and services that may not be appropriate for minors (or some adults!) you may want to use our parental controls (keyword: **Parental Controls**) to block access to certain parts of the Internet for your account or sub-accounts, especially if kids are online in your home.

Respect cultural differences

AOL also allows you to visit AOL's various international services online (such as AOL Germany, AOL Japan and America Online in the USA). These areas may have slightly different rules for conducting yourself, and different standards for acceptable content. You should refer to the local rules in those areas; in general, 'when in Rome' do as the people there do. For example, words which are harmless in the United Kingdom might take on a completely different meaning in the United States. Guides or hosts in those areas may issue a warning to you – and termination of your membership is possible – if you breach the rules that apply to that international service. Bear in mind that the law that applies to interactive media is evolving, so it's a good idea to review the rules of your favorite areas frequently.

Help control your online environment

Like the rest of the world, AOL may contain some material that is inappropriate for kids, or for some adults. Content in chat rooms is expressed immediately, so it can't be monitored in advance. Whether or not content is appropriate for children or for your tastes is up to you. We want to make sure that you are aware of your ability to control what you or your children see.

AOL provides various means of modifying the online environment, all of which can be controlled by the master account.

Parental Controls (keyword: **Parental Controls***)*
Our Parental Controls allow the AOL master account holder to block or limit access to various features available on AOL. Thus the master account holder can limit each account's ability to use or access Chat, Email, Downloading, Premium Services, AOL's Instant Message facility and Internet Newsgroups. Parents are strongly advised to review the Parental Control features, and (where appropriate) to apply them to AOL accounts which they control. But remember: No system of controls makes up for appropriate parental supervision. We recommend that you monitor your child's use of AOL and that you make sure that your children understand AOL's Online Safety Tips (available at keyword: **Parental Controls**).

Mail Controls (keyword: **Mail Controls***)*
Mail Controls allow you to:

- Block or allow all Email

- Block or allow Email from specific addresses or from the Internet

- Block domains (the sources of the mail)

- Block file attachments to Email

Marketing Preferences (keyword: **Marketing Prefs***)*
We encourage you to tell us what your marketing preferences are for your personal data. By visiting this Keyword, you can do so.

For more information about online safety and security, check out:

Member Services (keyword: **Help***)*
This area has answers to a wide range of questions about AOL's service.

How To Notify AOL of Problems Online
If there are any breaches that you see or are subject to online, you should go to keyword: **Notify AOL**.

Using keyword: **Rules** *will allow you to review these guidelines whenever you like.*

Private Groups Guidelines

The following Guidelines have been established for use with Private Groups. These Guidelines, or Terms of Use, are in place to ensure that Private Groups remains a fun and friendly place for all viewing ages. Please remember that you must be at least 18 years of age to create a Private Group.

A Group's Founder is responsible for managing all content and activity in the Group. Participation in a Group is on a volunteer basis, and if, for any reason, you do not agree with the Group or its activities, you may elect to leave that Group. If the activity you are uncomfortable with is not a violation of these Guidelines, you should talk to the Founder to try and solve the problem.

Private Groups found to be in violation of these Guidelines are subject to removal without notice. AOL reserves the right to investigate a private Group when a violation has been reported or is suspected by AOL.

Examples of activities that this product may not be used for
- Post, transmit or facilitate distribution of unsolicited bulk email, advertising or any other unauthorised solicitation including chain letters, multi-level marketing and pyramid schemes.
- Harvest or collect information of users, including screen names or email addresses.
- Post, transmit or facilitate distribution of any material containing software viruses or any other computer code, files or programs designed to interrupt, destroy or limit the functionality of any computer software or hardware or telecommunications equipment.
- Attempt to get a password, or other private information from a member. Remember: AOL employees will NEVER ask for your password.
- Post, transmit, promote, or distribute content that is illegal, or use the Software or Service to conduct illegal activities.
- Post, transmit, promote or distribute content intended to victimise, harass, degrade or intimidate an individual or group of individuals on the basis of religion, gender, race, ethnicity, age, disability, sexual orientation or other unalterable characteristics. Hate speech is unacceptable.
- Impersonate or represent, without limitation: AOL, AOL staff, AOL volunteers, other members, names of any celebrities and/or government officials.
- Soliciting for the exchange, sale or purchase of content that infringes anyone's intellectual property rights including but not limited to any copyright, trademark, rights of publicity, rights of privacy, or other proprietary rights.

- Requesting personal or other information from a minor (any person under the age of 18), including, without limitation, any of the following: full name, home address, social security number, email address, telephone number, picture or name of their school.
- Create Group names or links to, and/or reference, content not allowed under these Guidelines.
- Advertising and/or promoting the sale of products or services not allowed or deemed suitable on AOL, including, without limitation:
  - Baby Adoption (solicitation or offers)
  - Lotteries
  - Ammunition
  - Firearms
  - Fireworks, or other explosive materials
  - Tobacco
  - Alcohol
  - Adult products and services, such as phone sex or escort services
  - Illegal activities, including but not limited to illegal drugs and drug-related paraphernalia
  - Other products and services AOL deems inappropriate
  - Other uses AOL deems inappropriate

Note: AOL does not endorse content found in any given Private Group. If at any time you feel Group management (e.g. Founder participation) is inadequate, please notify us.

By using the Private Groups product you agree to comply with these Guidelines. Determination of whether there has been a violation of these Guidelines, and any resulting action taken, are at AOL's sole discretion. Violations of these Private Group product guidelines may result in actions ranging from a warning, to suspension of access to this feature, to appropriate legal action. A violation of these Guidelines by AOL members may also be a violation of the AOL Community Guidelines and the Member Agreement, and AOL may take actions consistent with those documents as well.

AOL reserves the right to make changes to these Guidelines at anytime and you agree to be bound by any such changed Guidelines. Please check these Private Group Guidelines periodically for any changes.

Safety and security
Keep your kids safe in cyberspace
Children are an integral part of our online community. One day the Internet will play as central a role in our children's lives as the television or telephone – and will be even more valuable. So being online and learning new communication skills are essential for today's children. Working

together, we can make the online environment a safe and rewarding experience for children. This page provides you with three easy steps to get started and to become 'Net Wise'!

Here's How:

1   *Take advantage of filtering tools*. Like the rest of the world, the Internet may contain some material that is inappropriate for young audiences. There are a number of ways you can control what your child can see and do online.

     If you are an AOL member, make the most of AOL's built in Parental Controls. For other internet users, filtering software like CyberPatrol, NetNanny and SurfWatch can help to keep children from inappropriate online areas.

     You can learn more about filtering options at GetNetWise | Tools for Families.

2   Teach your children about online safety. If you are an AOL member, explore our safety tips and links for kids at keyword: **Safety Zone**.

     Disney's *Safe Surfing with Doug* guide provides parents and children with a comprehensive and fun guide to using the Internet. Topics range from a Parent's Guide to Safe Surfing to Patti's CyberNetiquette Comix.

     Nickelodeon's *Byte-Size Online Safety Guide* tells kids how to stay safe, with information about viruses, personal information and downloading. The site also goes into issues such as 'flaming' and online etiquette.

     ChildLine (AOL keyword: **Childline**) includes a down to earth online safety guide in their list of factsheets: *ChildLine: Factsheets: Safe surfing*. Here, kids are reminded about several valuable safety points in easy to understand language. Similarly, NCH Action for Children provides a comprehensive list of sensible safety hints in its *Parents' Guide to the Internet*.

3   *Get to know your children's online world*. Spend time with your children when they go online. The more involved you are with your children's online activities, the easier it will be to set limits that are appropriate. Filtering tools are a great way to tailor your child's online experience, but there is no substitute for parental involvement online.

     As parents, you should get to know your children's online friends and their favourite online areas, just as you know their neighbourhood friends and what they watch on television. In the end, there's no better safeguard than parental supervision.

Email and hyperlink safety

As new products such as Groups@AOL are released and the world of the Internet grows, so do the problems of 'junk' email (unsolicited, unwelcome email). Scammers may use hyperlinks to direct you to Web sites that look like official AOL, Groups@AOL or AOL.CO.UK pages, but are not the real thing. The emails and Web pages may claim that you've won a prize or encourage you to sign up for testing of a new product or service. They may even look identical to AOL services such as Groups@AOL. NEVER click on hyperlinks in email sent to you by strangers. The official email address for all invitations to Groups@AOL is AOLGroupsUK@groups.aol.co.uk. You should only consider invitations received from this address as legitimate Group invitations.

Hyperlinks (blue, underlined words or phrases that link to AOL or on the Internet) can be used as handy shortcuts to online areas. However, beware of hyperlinks in emails from strangers. These often ask you to enter your AOL screen name and password. AOL Staff will NEVER ask you for your password or credit card information either by email or through instant messages. If you see a Groups@AOL page that asks for your AOL screen name and password, look at the Web address of the page and make sure it starts with http://groups.aol.co.uk. If it does not, the page is a scam and you should close your browser immediately.

Some Web pages may also automatically download computer viruses or Trojan Horse programs to your computer. These programs can damage your computer files or send your password back to the scammer. With your screen name and password, the scammer can sign on to your AOL account, read your email, send email in your name, and even violate AOL's Terms of Use which may result in the termination of your account.

To keep your computer and your AOL account safe, NEVER click on hyperlinks in email sent to you by strangers. And NEVER enter your screen name and password into a Web page unless it is an official AOL Web page. Official AOL Web pages can be found on AOL.CO.UK at http://www.aol.co.uk. Official Groups@AOL Web pages will start with http://groups.aol.co.uk.

If you are an AOL member, you can learn more about email safety at keyword: **Account Security**.

Privacy and your Group

Private Groups offer an excellent way to stay in touch with family, friends and colleagues. Please keep in mind the importance of being careful about who is invited into a Group, who is given 'owner' status, and how much information is shared within a Group. There are people who try to take advantage of others online and can misuse this information if you are not careful.

4

Connecting
to AOL

While AOL is working on bringing you new ways to connect as part of AOL Anywhere, most people will still be using a computer on their desk for some time to come.

You can read more about AOL Anywhere in Chapter 8, including how to access your email from cyber cafés, or via a Palm organiser, but here's what you'll need to do it all at home.

PC users

Technical specifications

- AOL 6.0 is available for Windows 95/98/Millennium/2000-12-04.
- The browser embedded into AOL 6.0 is Microsoft Internet explorer (MSIE). The version of MSIE will vary depending on the current browser used by the member. Any member who currently MSIE 5.0 will remain with that browser. Any other members will be upgraded to MSIE 5.5.
- A Macintosh version of AOL 6.0 is planned. We'll have more information on availability soon.

Minimum system requirements are as follows.

Windows 95
Pentium-class processor
16MB RAM
70MB of hard drive space for installation (NOTE up to 180MB if IE 5.01/4.0 /3.0 is installed)
14.4kbps or faster modem or other means of an Internet connection
VGA/SVGA 640×480, 256 colours minimum (optimised for 800×600 and above)

Windows 98
Pentium-class processor
16MB RAM
80MB of hard drive space for installation (NOTE up to 180MB if IE 5.01/4.0/3.0 is installed)
14.4kbps or faster modem or other means of an Internet connection
VGA/SVGA 640×480, 256 colours minimum (optimised for 800×600 and above)

Windows Millennium
Pentium-class processor
32MB RAM
80MB of hard drive space for installation
14.4kbps or faster modem or other means of an Internet connection
VGA/SVGA 640×480, 256 colours minimum (optimised for 800×600 and above)

Windows 2000
Pentium-class processor 166MHz or higher
64MB RAM
80MB of hard drive space for installation (NOTE up to 190MB if IE 5.01/4.0/3.0 is installed)
Remote Access Services (RAS) installed
14.4kbps or faster modem or other means of an Internet connection
VGA/SVGA 640×480, 256 colours minimum (optimised for 800×600 and above)

Mac users

As with PCs, all the modern Mac systems – that includes the iMac, G3 and G4 systems – will be able to run AOL. You can run it on any Mac that has the PowerPC mark on the front, as long as you meet these requirements:

MacOS 8.1 or higher
32 MB of RAM or higher
40 MB or more of free disk space
Monitor with a resolution of 800x600 and 256 colours or better
CD-ROM drive.
Modem or other Internet connection

Modems

The modem is the thing that links your computer to AOL and here it's a clear case of the faster the better. AOL can send information to your computer at the fastest speed commonly used, which is 56,000 bits per second (don't worry what that means – it's fast). You need to look for a modem that supports what's called in computer jargon v90. That's the standard that allows modems to talk to each other at the same speed.

You can use older modems (standards called v32bis and v34, for example) to talk to AOL, but they're much slower, so it'll take longer to get to the information that you need. A v34 modem runs at only two thirds the speed of v90, for example, and a v32bis one at half the speed. AOL will work with any modem that works at 14,400bps or above, but if you have an old modem, it's probably worth upgrading to a v90 model. You can pick them up for under £100 now, and many new computers come with one built-in.

A new modem can be built into your computer – an internal modem – or an add-on that plugs in with cables. External ones have pretty flashing lights, which show you when information is being sent and received, while internal ones are tidied away inside the computer's case. The choice is entirely yours – either type will work just as well with AOL.

5

AOL for Macintosh users

Although throughout most of this book we've been talking about AOL for PC users running Windows, that doesn't mean that you have to miss out if you're using a Macintosh.

Mac users are just as welcome on AOL, and if you look on the Technology Channel, for example, you'll find an online edition of Mac User. There are also plenty of Mac files to download, and even dedicated areas, like the one at the keyword **MacHelp**.

However, there are some differences between AOL for the PC and AOL for Mac users. The most important of them is that, while most of this book has been written about AOL 6.0 for the PC, at the time the book comes out, AOL for the Mac will be version 5.0. Don't panic though, as a new version of AOL for Mac is in the pipeline.

So, what's the difference? Well, in a lot of areas, you won't notice many differences. The Channels will look the same when you access them, and you'll be able to see all the great information that's on AOL. But some things will behave slightly differently. Let's take a look at the main AOL screen on the Macintosh for starters.

Fig. A5.1
**AOL for Mac
main screen**

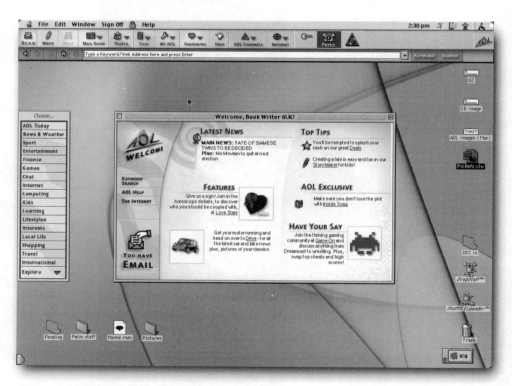

AOL Handbook 6.0

Perhaps the most immediate difference that you'll notice is that on the Mac, AOL doesn't really take over the whole screen in quite the same way as it does on a PC. You still have the toolbar at the top of the screen, but not all the same buttons are there.

What does that mean? Well, for instance, you don't have a button that takes you to My Calendar. But the good news is that you can still use the calendar service. Instead of clicking on a button, just type **Calendar** into the Keyword box at the top of the screen.

You'll also notice a few differences when you use Groups@AOL, which you can reach on the Macintosh via the keyword **Groups**. The buttons that automatically add a new entry to your Buddy List for a group don't work if you're on a Macintosh.

Buddy Lists work slightly differently too. You can't use the Ctrl key and click on Entries to invite them to chat, for example.

In case you didn't know, holding down Ctrl and clicking is the Macintosh equivalent of using the right mouse button on a PC. You'll usually find a helpful menu pops up when you Control click anywhere in AOL for Mac.

What else is different? Well, you can't play as many different types of music and video file using AOL for Mac as you can on the PC and, of course, the windows on your screen don't all work in quite the same way.

We've mentioned in the book that you can close windows by clicking on the X in the top right-hand corner, but as a seasoned Mac addict, you'll probably know that you need to click in the top left instead, to close a Mac window.

You should also bear in mind that where we've mentioned keyboard shortcuts, they're not quite the same on the Macintosh. As a rule of thumb, you need to use the Command, or Apple, key instead of Ctrl.

So, where the PC keystroke that we've mentioned in the text is Ctrl-K – which brings up a box to type in a keyword, Mac users need to press **Command-K** instead. That's not so hard to remember, is it?

Good news!
You might think all we've got to tell you is things that you can't do with AOL for Mac, but there's good news too. You can do a few things with the Mac that you can't do on the PC.

How about this for a nifty trick? **Control-Click** on the toolbar and choose **Unanchor toolbar**. Hey presto, you end up with this.

Fig. A5.2
Unanchored toolbar

Now you can move the AOL toolbar anywhere on the screen, to make it more convenient for you. To put it back, **Control-Click** again, and choose **Anchor toolbar**.

Depending on where you clicked on the toolbar – and whether or not you have all the Apple System software installed – you might have heard your computer say what one of the buttons did. Yep, that's right! AOL for Mac can speak.

Fig. A5.3
Speech preferences

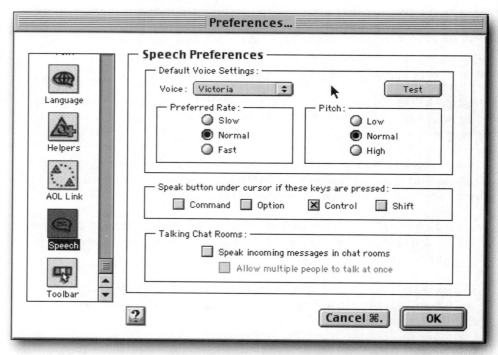

You'll find the Preferences for AOL on the My AOL button, and if you look through all the sections you'll see this panel, for Speech. You can choose which of the standard Macintosh voices is used, and choose which key will be used to make the computer say what the button you're pointing at does.

You can even have AOL read out all the messages in a chat room. When you're reading an email message, or an Instant Message that someone's sent you, click on the **Edit** menu, and you'll see an option that says **Speak text**. Choose it, and your computer will read the email message to you!

As a Mac-only shortcut, you can press **Command-H** too, and if you don't want everything read out, highlight the section you want to hear first.

Your friends with PCs might have a slightly newer version of AOL, but we bet they can't make it speak!

There's another neat multimedia trick too – if you have a Macintosh that can capture video, like one of the new iMac DV systems, just you can capture a picture, right inside AOL – just choose **Capture picture** from the **Edit** menu.

So, while you miss out on a few buttons, and some of the new features that are in AOL 6.0, don't worry – you have some special features all of your own, and most of the things that we've described in this book will work just fine for you, though they may look slightly different.

Index